THE RISE OF THE LUFTWAFFE

Herbert Molloy Mason, Jr.

THE RISE OF THE LUFTWAFFE

Forging the Secret German Air Weapon

1918–1940

THE DIAL PRESS ☐ NEW YORK

Designed by Lynn Braswell

CONTENTS

ILLUSTRATIONS

To
Martin Caidin

THE RISE OF THE LUFTWAFFE

I
HERITAGE

We officers did our duty for four long years. We risked our bodies for the Fatherland. Now we come home—and how do they treat us? They spit on us and deprive us of what we gloried in wearing. I therefore implore you to cherish hatred, a profound, abiding hatred of those animals who have outraged the German people. But the day will come when we drive them out of Germany. Prepare for that day. Arm yourselves for that day. Work for that day.

—Hermann Goering
December 1918

Ernst Udet in 1918. This flamboyant ace would later be the wrong man in the wrong place at the right time. *(Author's collection.)* □

The primary use of air power during World War I was reconnaissance. These Rumpler two-seaters are warming up for patrol across
Allied lines.   *(Martin Caidin Archives.)* □

Multi-engined Zeppelin Giants (opposite) and Gothas (below) were sent across the English Channel for strikes against London and other targets, but without significant results.

(Martin Caidin Archives.) ☐

In a rare encounter at sea, a Brandenburg floatplane fighter catches a British seaplane resting on the water and sets it aflame in a strafing run. *(Martin Caidin Archives.)* □

Left: The most feared fighter of the war was the fast-climbing, acrobatic Fokker D.VII. Although Armistice terms required all such aircraft to be surrendered, Goering had other ideas. *(Martin Caidin Archives.)* □

Right: Gentlemen flyers such as highly decorated Walter Hohendorf were popular heroes one minute and hounded victims of revolutionary zeal the next. *(Author's collection.)* □

Hermann Goering (left) as a World War I aviator.
(The Bettmann Archive.) □

1
DARK NOVEMBER

I knew that all was lost. Only fools, liars and criminals could hope for
mercy from the enemy.
—Lance Corporal Adolf Hitler,
16th Bavarian Reserve Infantry Regiment,
November 10, 1918

They fought well. Let them keep their weapons.
—Marshal Ferdinand Foch,
November 11, 1918

Late in the morning of April 21, 1918, with the early mists
burned from the valley of the Somme, combat aviation's most
glittering star and the great German national hero, *Rittmeister*
Manfred von Richthofen, prepared to lead a handful of pilots on
patrol. Richthofen, noted for his Prussian bearing and grudging
humor, was in unusually high spirits. He roughhoused with his
brindle great dane, Moritz; he playfully upset a cot, spilling
Lieutenant Wenzl onto the wet grass; he enthused over an
upcoming woodcock shoot in the Black Forest, and he again
cautioned his younger cousin, Wolfram, against taking undue
chances on this, his first offensive outing. Only the day before,
Manfred had shot down his seventy-ninth and eightieth victims,
a pair of British fighters. Nevertheless he constantly preached
respect for the enemy and the mortality rate among German
pilots lent authority to his admonitions.

Shortly before 10 A.M. Richthofen pulled on knee-length fur
flying boots, buckled a worn black leather helmet to his head,
gave Moritz a whack and climbed into the cockpit of his pure
red Fokker triplane. An hour later he lay dead beside a dirt road
inside British lines, machine-gunned through the chest, while
Australian soldiers swarmed over the crashed airplane like

hyenas tearing at a zebra carcass, stripping the wreckage of everything that could be cut, torn or pried loose. An outraged chaplain of the Eighth Field Artillery Brigade steamed into the middle of the pushing, shoving soldiery and shamed the men into returning Richthofen's personal belongings, looted from the still-warm body.

Richthofen was buried the next afternoon in the verdant cemetery at Bertangles, his coffin borne by six British and Commonwealth officers, and the service read from the Church of England manual; the firing party was composed of men from the Australian Flying Corps, and large floral wreaths decorated the grave. Richthofen was claimed both by Canadian-born Captain Arthur Royal Brown of the 208th Squadron, who had shot down eleven other German planes during the war, and by machine-gunners of the artillery brigade deployed in the area. Brown didn't really care who got the credit for bringing down the Red Baron; in almost constant pain from stomach ulcers, he was invalided home after flying only one other patrol.

Richthofen's own choice as successor to command was a pilot of long seniority, but with only one kill to his credit, Captain Wilhelm Reinhard, a steady, low-key personality who had survived ground warfare in Belgium, bombing missions over Verdun, typhus in the Balkans, and the fighter school at Warsaw. When Reinhard was killed in a flying accident less than sixty days later, he was replaced by a new commander from outside the group, who would continue to lead the group until the final shot.

He was as lean and as hard as a whip, with a square, strong face, straight black hair, and a long, thin mouth as cruel as a razor. At twenty-five, First Lieutenant Hermann Wilhelm Goering was a seasoned air warrior credited with twenty-one kills, decorated with the Blue Max, holder of the Iron Cross, the Hohenzollern Medal with Swords, the Zaehring Lion with Swords, and a member of the Order of Karl Friedrich. He had been a fighter pilot since 1916, an observer on reconnaissance craft previously, and before that an innovative and fire-eating officer of the Prinz Wilhelm Regiment.* There was no question of Goering's personal courage, but he alienated his command at the start by first praising Richthofen as a combat pilot, and then suggesting strongly that his methods of command had been entirely wrong. From now on, Goering said in a strangely insistent tone of voice, Richthofen's laissez-faire attitude toward individual initiative and free chase after enemy aircraft was out. He, Goering, would direct squadron and group attacks how, when, and where he deemed best, and woe to any pilot who disobeyed his commands. Goering's imperial manner did not go down well with the others, some of whom, like the audacious and irreverent Ernst Udet and Manfred's brother Lothar, had far higher scores, all of whom had revered Richthofen, and none of whom liked the idea of cavalry-style regimentation that is inimical to the spirit of the hunter.

Goering quickly proved his mettlesomeness on July 18 by leading the group hurtling down on a formation of French Spads and gunning down his twenty-second, and final, victim of the war. On this same day, a noncom pilot named Willi Gabriel flaunted the new commander's instructions by flying off on his own to singlehandedly attack two separate enemy formations, blowing three French fighters and a bomber out of the sky. Goering rewarded Sergeant Gabriel with a blistering public rebuke and transfer to a rear-echelon depot.

Goering's natural irascibility increased as the weeks flew by due to fatiguing pressures exerted on the thinly stretched fighter units all up and down the line. He complained of lack of proper telephone communications between squadrons and groups. He peevishly reported having to fight what he believed to be armored French reconnaissance planes, upon which his machine guns had not the slightest effect, and demanded the

---

*With the war barely a week old, Goering led six men on bicycles in a dash into French-held Mulhausen in Alsace-Lorraine, hoping to capture the commanding general there. The wild scheme failed, but Goering and the others managed to return home by pedaling back furiously across the lines under fire from the astonished French outposts.

employment of additional 77-millimeter flak batteries to help his fighters perform their defensive mission. Goering reported back to the air force commander in chief, General Ernst von Hoeppner, that his pilots were often forced to fly five patrols each day, warning that "in the long run neither the men nor the engines can stand up to such strain." But there were never any complaints by either Goering or any other German pilot about the new equipment they were flying, thick-winged Fokker D. VII biplanes with 185 horsepower BMW (Bavarian Motor Works) engines that provided dramatically increased time-to-climb capability and a service ceiling exceeding 20,000 feet. ("They climb like elevators," commented American pilot Elliott White Springs, "and just *hang* there on their props, shooting your belly full of holes.") Moreover, the new Fokkers were tough, acrobatic, easy on the controls, and forgave beginners' mistakes, an important consideration as more replacements began to show up with fewer hours in the air. Appreciated even more were the parachutes that became available during the summer of 1918; no longer would German pilots face the prospect of roasting to death when incendiary bullets slammed into the fuel tanks. No Allied pilot had them.

The three fighter groups of the German air force, Jagdgeschwaders 1, 2 and 3, became true aerial circuses, quick-erecting tents, trucks, and all, likely to move on an hour's notice, thrown into whichever sector was most threatened by superior Allied numbers. Goering's JG.1 was shuttlecocked from Berne to Busigny to Metz and then to Marville, all within six weeks. Goering was like a sheriff with a dwindling number of deputies trying to keep at bay an ever-increasing number of brigands scattered across seemingly endless amounts of territory. On October 10, ten of Goering's Fokkers were jumped by three times that number of French Spads flown by American pilots of the 94th and 147th Pursuit Squadrons. Captain Eddie Rickenbacker shot down one of the German fighters in flames as the two formations split apart in a wild melee. The pilot, Lieutenant Kohlbach, took to the silk and floated to earth under a canopy of dueling planes. The circus was reinforced by a German squadron falling out of the sun, and in the end, five Spads were destroyed, one in a midair collision with one of Goering's men.

The skies over France and, increasingly, over Germany as well buzzed with hostile aircraft coming in from all altitudes, at all hours of the day and the night, bound on every kind of offensive mission. Low-flying machines strafed and bombed German infantry lying in shallow rifle pits and along broken roads leading back to their own frontier. Precious Fokker D.VIIs and weary Gotha bombers were burnt in hangars and blown to pieces in sudden raids on airfields. The great Handley-Page bombers of the newly created British Independent Air Force ranged high overhead and deep inside the Ruhr and unloaded cargoes of high explosive on the faltering German war industry. Even as the war entered its final days, the tempo of air fighting increased. On October 30, fatigued German pilots were up at dawn, fighting until the sun went down. In the British sector alone they lost 67 planes, while bringing down only 43 of the enemy's. This raised the number of German aircraft lost in action during the preceding seven months to 2,463, and the losses could not be made up. The fuel shortage was so critical that new planes could not be flown from factories directly to air parks or front-line squadrons, but were sent as disassembled freight aboard coal-burning trains. None of the three German fighter groups could muster more than 60 per cent of assigned planes and pilots. Planes were sent up with spare parts cannibalized from others, and on dangerously thin rubber tires for which there were no replacements.

November began darkly, with low-hanging clouds shrouding the battlefields and drizzle saturating the sky. German pilots, their planes grounded, stared glumly at the weather, listening to the continuous mutter of Allied guns, some of which were close enough to throw shells on their airdromes. Communications with the rear were uncertain, and they had only vague ideas of the dramas being acted out in the homeland, and none at all of the agonizing emotional struggles going on inside Supreme Headquarters at Spa. In Kiel, German sailors were in open revolt, refusing to obey orders to prepare the long-dormant fleet for a final, suicidal sortie against the British navy. Red flags of the Bolshevik revolution were broken out and run up the halyards. The average German civilian was literally starving, forced to subsist on less than a thousand calories a day, a diet largely composed of turnips and ersatz bread. There were food riots in Berlin, and formerly loyal newspapers were calling for the Kaiser's abdication. Wilhelm II fled his capital city aboard the cream and gold imperial train and sought refuge at Spa, where neither Field Marshal Paul von Hindenburg nor General Erich Ludendorff's replacement, pragmatic General Wilhelm Groener, know what to do with him. Groener believed the best solution to the problem would be for the Emperor "to go to the Front, to some trench which was under the full blast of war. If he were killed, it would be the finest death possible. And if he were wounded," Groener mused, "the feelings of the German people would completely change toward him." The Emperor was shocked at the idea, which was quickly vetoed.

On November 3, 4 and 5, the weather along the Front cleared enough for Goering to lead his group into action. In this three-day period they claimed twenty kills, while losing two of their own planes. On the afternoon of the fifth, Goering was ordered to move the group back to Tellancourt to avoid being overrun by the advancing American infantry. They took off in blinding rain.

On November 7, a German delegation crossed the lines and reached the sodden Forest of Compiègne where it was brusquely handed terms under which an armistice would be granted. It was painfully clear that the terms were drawn so as to preclude any possible chance of Germany's renewing hostilities should the eventual peace treaty prove unacceptable. Article IV, for instance, demanded "Surrender, in good condition, by the German Army, of the following war material: 5,000 field guns, 25,000 machine guns, 3,000 trench mortars, 1,700 fighting and bombing aeroplanes—in the first place all D.VIIs and all night bombing machines." Further down, Article XXVII stipulated that the entire German air force was to be concentrated at designated points and delivered intact to Allied teams. The provinces of Alsace and Lorraine were to be returned to France, which had given them up in 1871; every German soldier was to withdraw to the north side of the Rhine, and the Allies were to be provided three bridgeheads across that river for a foothold in Germany. Marshal Ferdinand Foch told the Germans that they had seventy-two hours to think it over and sign, take it or leave it, and meanwhile, the fighting would continue.

On November 9, a republic was proclaimed in Berlin, and the German emperor abandoned all thoughts of empire. During the dark predawn hours of the following morning, he and eighteen others of the imperial retinue boarded the train, and the splendid carriages slipped away from Spa in dense and silent fog, bound for Holland, sanctuary, and oblivion.

The armistice agreement was signed by the German delegation two days later at 5:05 A.M. inside the railway car parked in the gloom of Compiègne Forest, to become effective five hours and fifty-five minutes afterward—time enough, it was hoped, for the cease-fire order to filter down to the two million men still locked in combat along 360 miles of front. General John Joseph Pershing, who had wanted to keep going straight to Berlin, pushed his divisions harder than any other commander, and the Americans reached Sedan ahead of the infuriated French, who had sworn to liberate the city themselves. Men continued to die until the final moments of the war. They died in ditches filled with water and along embankments slippery with mud from the November rains. They died in dank woods floored with sodden autumn leaves and in dark and evil-smelling cellars and on glistening streets in ugly little red-brick French and Belgian towns.

The temper of the German soldier at the final moments was revealed to troops of the South African Brigade, which was attached to the British First Army, following the capture of Mons after a see-saw battle that raged all through November 10. Reported one of the South Africans, "One German machine gun, which throughout had been maddeningly raucous, fired the longest burst anyone had ever heard, lasting two minutes, and ending dead at 11 A.M. A German soldier then stood up, removed his helmet, bowed to his audience, and walked slowly away."

At the airdrome at Tellancourt, Hermann Goering watched the eight big trucks loaded heavily with men, machine guns, spare instruments packed in cases, group records, magnetoes, cooking utensils, tools, and spark plugs move slowly up a muddy road, bound for Darmstadt, more than one hundred miles to the north. In his pocket was a crumpled order, delivered only that morning, instructing him to ferry his planes to Strasbourg and turn them over to the French. Goering, like every other pilot on the field, felt betrayed—but not defeated—and he refused to accept the humiliation of abject surrender. He would instead lead the group to Darmstadt, still a German city and a long way from Allied occupation. He climbed into the cockpit of an oil-stained, pure white Fokker, trundled across the thin gruel that overlay the field, and lofted into the air, followed by the others, who contour-chased through the heavy drizzle. Not all of them made it. Some landed at Mannheim, twenty-seven miles south of Darmstadt, where a mob of the Bolshevik so-called Soldiers' Council stripped the pilots of sidearms and decorations and ordered them on their way to Darmstadt by truck.

When Goering learned that his officer pilots had been manhandled by enlisted swine under the Red banner, he flew into a Prussian rage and ordered the group back into the air. They were over Mannheim fifteen minutes later, and Goering sent the dishonored fliers down to land with an ultimatum for the Reds: return the confiscated arms and decorations with apologies or face machine-gunning from the air.

Goering led the others in menacing low-level passes over the field with guns charged, and the mutineers had second thoughts about upholding egalitarian ideals by defying the formidable Richthofen Group; the looted symbols of class and authority were found and handed over. The pilots got into their planes again and followed Goering back to Darmstadt where, one after the other, the Fokkers were deliberately smashed up in landings that would have done credit to the rawest student.

Here and there the sun broke through the overcast sky, the weak shafts of autumn light filtering through to illuminate fields where men stood boldly upright and moved around freely, no longer concerned with death's sudden rush. The guns had fallen silent only hours before, but already platoons were forming into companies, companies into battalions, battalions into regiments and regiments into divsons for the long march back to the Rhine, across the bridges, and home. The soldiers went about the business of packing up quietly, in stolid humor, and with purpose: any man left beind in France, Belgium, Luxembourg, Alsace-Lorraine or the near side of the Rhineland after thirty days would be liable to capture by Allied patrols, and no man wanted to risk a POW stockade and hard labor when peace and return to the homeland to pick up the threads of civilian life were so tantalizingly near at hand.

There were not many who believed that the German siege engine composed of two million men and everything needed to keep it running could be extracted from more than fifteen thousand square miles of territory in only four weeks; Hindenburg announced that the operation was "technically impossible" within the allotted time, claiming that three months would be needed at the very least. But the first long gray columns were on the move early that afternoon, their halting places, billets and rest periods already planned down to the smallest detail. While they dozed, other columns stumbled past in the dark, bound for villages or rail heads further on. Day and night the unending caterpillars of men squirmed across the rolling countryside. Burdened only with light combat packs and personal weapons and blessed with unusually dry roads for that time of year, the weary columns made good time, occasionally outdistancing advancing Allied units on their own march to the Rhine. Encounters with the victors were awkward, but never hostile. The Americans, eager, big strapping fellows, were a wonder to behold.

"They are wearing new uniforms and greatcoats"; observed an astonished German noncom, "their boots are water-tight and fit well; their rifles are good and their pouches full of ammunition. They are all fresh and unused. Compared to these fellows we are a perfect band of robbers. Our uniforms are bleached with the mud of years, with the rains of the Argonne, the chalk of Champagne, the bog waters of Flanders; our great-coats ragged and torn by barbed-wire, shell splinters and shrapnel, cobbled with crude stitches, stiff with clay and in some instances even with blood; our boots broken, our rifles worn out, our ammunition almost at an end; we are all of us dirty, all alike gone to wrack, all weary. The war has passed over us like a steamroller."

The occupied lands were quickly emptied of the German army, with only scattered remnants left to clear out of the Rhineland. The clockwork precision of the withdrawal bore the hallmark of the German General Staff, and was as flawless in execution as had been the first great attack sweeping to the Marne four years earlier. Under the eyes of officers and men of the Allied Occupation Army, the thin battalions and divisions disappeared across the bridges of the Rhine in perfect order. They marched to the spirited chiming of the glockenspiels and the metronomic beat of snare drums. They were worn, tattered and impassive, yes; but no British, French, or American who saw them go believed they were watching the exit of a defeated army.

Among the last German soldiers to turn their backs to the eerie wasteland where they had lived for so long was a twenty-year-old corporal named Erich Paul Kramer.* He was one of the thirty-two men left of a battalion five hundred strong that had been shoveled into the furnace of the Western Front. As Kramer's skimpy platoon painfully started moving to the rear, he thought of the dead they were leaving behind them.

They are many indeed that lie there, though until now we have not thought of it so. Hitherto we have just all remained together, they in the graves, we in the trenches, divided only by a few handfuls of earth. They were but a little before us; daily

---

*But better known as Erich Maria Remarque, whose chosen surname is, phonetically, Kramer pronounced backwards. His realistic books on the war were banned by Adolf Hitler, and Remarque came to America to live and work. The lines quoted are from his novel *The Road Back*.

we became less and they more, and often we have not known
whether we belonged to them or not. And sometimes too the
shells would bring them back among us again—crumbling
bones tossed up, scraps of uniforms, wet, decayed hands, al-
ready earthy—to the noise of the drumfire issuing once more
from their buried dugouts and returning to the battle. It did not
seem to us terrible; we were too near to them. But now we are
going back to life and they must stay there.

Ludwig, whose cousin was killed in this sector, blows his nose
through his fingers and turns about. Slowly we follow. But we
halt yet a few times and look about us. And we stand still.
. . . We shake our heads—but whether it be the lost years that
remain there, or the comrades who lie there, or all the misery
that this earth covers—there is a grief in our bones, enough to
make us howl aloud.

And so we march out.

What Kramer felt was not the defeat of any army, but a defeat
and a bewilderment of the human spirit barely flickering with
life, unable to comprehend the purgatory that bridges the dark
limbo between war and peace.

Along the road, step upon step, in their faded, dirty uniforms
tramp the grey columns. The sunshaved faces beneath the steel
helmets are haggard, wasted with hunger and long peril,
pinched and dwindled to the lines drawn by terror and courage
and death. They trudge along in silence. . . . Old men with
beards and slim lads scarcely twenty years of age, comrades
without difference. Beside them their lieutenants, little more
than children, yet the leaders of many a night raid. And behind
them, the army of the slain. Thus they tramp onward, step by
step, sick, half-starving, without ammunition, in thin compa-
nies, with eyes that still fail to comprehend it; escaped out of
that underworld, on the road back into life.

On November 19, the remnants of the war's most famous
group of fighter pilots gathered for a final binge in a beer cellar
in the old Bavarian town of Aschaffenberg, east of Darmstadt.
The thirty-odd pilots, with Hermann Goering at their head,
almost filled the main room of the Stiftskeller; when Goering

rose to speak, the room fell silent and his strident voice penetrated throughout the restaurant, as his paean of praise for the
Richthofen Group evolved into a diatribe against the German
nation. The behavior of the people, Goering said, was "disgraceful." Members of the Soldiers' and Workers' Councils were
beneath contempt. They, as combat airmen, had given four
years of their lives to maintain honor in the face of overwhelming odds, and had seen too many cherished comrades die to
allow their honor to be stained by traitors and the faint of heart.
"The new fight for freedom, principles, morals and the Fatherland has begun. Our time will come again," he snapped.

The fight began for Goering and some of the others when the
party broke up and they stepped outside to make their way
back to the billets in town. They were jeered and jostled by a
waiting crowd of civilians and ex-soldiers wearing red arm-
bands. Somebody grabbed at Goering's medals and badges of
rank, but he shoved his way through the mob and stamped off
through the darkened streets.

2

DECISION AT VERSAILLES

This is not peace; it is an armistice for twenty years.
—Marshal Ferdinand Foch

Home was now a dismal landscape where starvation and revolution stalked the streets. More than half a million had died of cumulative malnutrition during the final eighteen months of the war; with the weekly individual ration cut to half a pound of meat, three-quarters of an ounce of butter, one and a half ounces of margarine and three ounces of pearl barley, the toll would rise steeply as the winter progressed, lives expiring inside shabby rooms as cold as crypts. The Allied blockade was not lifted with the signing of the armistice agreement; this was yet another garrote twisted around the neck of the enemy, keeping the prostrate body moribund and incapable of resistance when it came time to present the terms of the peace agreement.

To the continually erupting food riots and naval mutinies and industrial strikes the German communists could add hunger to the list of tools of exploitation of the masses, recognizing in the nation's wretchedness the climate necessary for the Red revolution to leap successfully across the Volga and spread to the North Sea. Three days before the war ended, Berlin was invaded by the *Volks Marine Division*, the so-called People's Naval Division, made up of some three thousand deserters and mutineers armed with rifles looted from warships abandoned in Kiel, Bremen and Hamburg. They occupied the Emperor's castle, Schloss Berlin, intending to stay until the revolution was secure. The loosely organized mob prowled Berlin's depots, taking what they wanted, and they roamed the streets beating up luckless officers and noncoms still wearing decorations or rank badges. They frightened the new chancellor, a forty-seven-year-old saddlemaker and tavernkeeper named Friedrich Ebert, who was a dedicated socialist—but no Bolshevik. Ebert anxiously awaited the coming of the disciplined combat troops from the battlefields of France.

They arrived in Berlin on the crisp, cold morning of December 11, swinging up the Unter den Linden in perfect order, oak leaves garlanding their helmets. But they found the people on the streets sullen and indifferent. Ebert greeted the vanguard enthusiastically, and in a speech proclaimed them "unvanquished in battle." But the effect was lost in the presence of so many groups of hostile sailors and in the lethargic atmosphere that hung over the city. The long gray columns simply melted away. The troops, as tired as men can be, worn by living with death for so many years, sick deep inside at the futility of their sacrifice, spat upon, jeered at, ignored, in many cases carelessly gave away or sold their weapons and vanished as soldiers. Others checked out of the army at the nearest barrack, turning in their rifles in order to receive their reward from a grateful government: new boots, a new greatcoat, and fifteen dollars in mustering-out pay. An army of two million men demobilized itself practically overnight, leaving only a remnant of professionals to cope with rapidly approaching crises.

On December 23, an acrimonious dispute over pay owed the riffraff of the People's Naval Division for "guarding" Schloss Berlin resulted in the seizure of Ebert's military governor of the city, Otto Wels, who was beaten severely and thrown into a coal cellar as hostage. Then the Chancellery was surrounded, the gates locked and the switchboard seized, cutting Ebert off from normal communications—but not from Supreme Command, which had since moved from Spa to Kassel. Ebert picked up a phone linking the Chancellery with Kassel via a private line and called for help. Were there still any loyal troops available to get Berlin out of the hands of the dangerous rabble? Ebert was told that there were. Rescue would soon be on its way.

At Potsdam barracks, fifteen miles away, the eight hundred troopers and officers of the Imperial Horse Guards were told to turn out and prepare for combat inside the capital. Carbines were slung, machine-gun carts were hitched up, a number of small field pieces were readied, a bugle blew, and the regiment trotted smartly out of the caserne and headed for Berlin. They were joined by a thousand infantrymen, who agreed to act as reserves in case the cavalry needed support. The Guards reached Berlin that evening and quickly deployed for battle in the great cobblestoned square in front of the Schloss. The machine guns were sited, the artillery pieces laid for firing over open sights at point blank range. To the apprehensive sailors inside the castle, it seemed as though the Guards were going about their business with no more concern than if they were setting up for some routine tactical exercise.

In the meantime, Ebert, by the promise of money, had persuaded leaders of the Naval Division to free the Chancellery and had been assured that Wels would be released from the cellar when the cash, some twenty thousand dollars, had been handed over. Ebert now tried to call off the Horse Guards, but the Supreme Command would have none of it; the Reds were just where they wanted them, trapped inside a large stone box under the guns of the last remaining loyal troops in Germany.

The battle opened in the gray dawn on the following morning with a crash of shellfire and the steady drumming of heavy machine guns. Holes were punched in the castle walls and stone chips and glass splintered from the windows and casements. Under this storm of steel and lead, assault units dashed across the cobbles and burst into the palace. It was deserted; the terrified sailors had fled into the adjoining imperial stables. Ninety more minutes of this redirected searching fire was all the sailors could stand. They ran up the white flag, begging for terms and for time to attend to their wounded. The firing stopped, and almost immediately the square filled with civilians who flooded in from the side streets, mixing inextricably with the astonished Horse Guards, grabbing at sleeves, standing in front of the guns, imploring them to stop the slaughter. No Guardsman was willing to club, shoot, or bayonet civilians, and in a haze of bewilderment, most of them dropped their carbines, abandoned the hunt and drifted aimlessly through the crowd and out of the square, soldiers no more, only wanderers seeking to salvage something out of Christmas Eve. Less than a hundred armed guardsmen gathered behind their officers, awaiting orders. Presenting as resolute a front as possible, they calmly worked their way through the milling mob and away from the spectre of Schloss Berlin. It was a humiliation none of them would ever forget.

The débâcle in the heart of Berlin left Ebert's government powerless to combat a threat far more serious than that posed by the People's Naval Division. The German Communist Party, whose members called themselves Spartacists, were led by a fiery little middle-aged lawyer named Karl Liebknecht who had devoted the entire energies of his working life toward social revolution and abolition of militarism as a political force in Germany. It was Liebknecht who smuggled seditious pamphlets into rations bound for the Front; it was Liebknecht who helped foment the naval mutinies; it was Liebknecht who offered aid to the Naval Division when the outcome was in doubt; and it was Liebknecht who now called for a general strike and arming of the workers for the final takeover of the Ebert government when the new year began.

Liebknecht and his uncounted thousands of followers were anathema to the German General Staff, still intact and functioning smoothly inside the turreted and crenellated walls of Schloss Wilhelmshöhe at Kassel, 180 miles southwest of Berlin. The General Staff remained a monolith of loyalty to the German nation. General Groener, himself a commoner and democratically oriented, was willing to go along with Ebert, and Ebert saw in the coldly efficient General Staff the only salvation of the new socialist republic and his own political aims. The Spartacists must be crushed—but how, and by whom?

The answer lay in the spontaneous creation of volunteer fighting units known as *Freikorps,* independently raised by professional army officers who knew no other trade and to whom warfare had become a way of life. The ranks were filled with tough veterans of the Western Front, most of them former elite assault troops who were bewildered and irritated after only a few weeks of civilian life. These Free Corps units were paid out of funds available to the Supreme Command and were uniformed and armed by the leaders who scoured villages and

towns looking for depots not already ransacked by the Spartacists. Early units mustered from a few hundred to as many as
four thousand men each.

The first major clash occurred during the second week of
January, 1919, when a Free Corps battalion of twelve hundred
men was called in to deal with the Spartacist takeover of Berlin,
crippled by a week-long general strike and torn by riots. The
battalion blasted the Reds out of a four-story building using
howitzers, trench mortars, flamethrowers and machine guns.
Some three hundred defenders gave themselves up; most were
hustled off to a nearby barrack, lined up against a wall and shot.
Three thousand more Freikorps troops were rushed into Berlin,
and for the next seventy-two hours the city echoed with the
sounds of combat. A dozen Alamos were fought in various parts
of the city as the strongholds were reduced one by one. Quarter
was frequently asked, but seldom given. By January 15, the last
pockets of resistance were cleaned out and Berlin was dominated by the Free Corps. Karl Liebknecht was captured and
shot dead deep in the gloom of the Tiergarten.

Heavy fighting followed in the port cities of Bremen, Cux-
haven, Hamburg and Wilhelmshaven. No sooner had these cities been secured than other revolutionary fires ignited all over
Germany, and Freikorps brigades were sent dashing to various
points of the compass to stamp them out. There was bloody
fighting in Erfurt, Gotha, Düsseldorf and Halle. Only last-
minute negotiations with steel workers and coal miners in the
Ruhr district avoided certain civil war. Now heavily outnumbered, the Spartacists could not risk another attempt at armed
insurrection inside the capital. A general strike was called instead, and on March 5 Berlin's two million inhabitants found
themselves once again without transportation or utilities.
Against Party orders, the revolutionaries hauled out secreted
rifles and took to the streets, swarmed over the city's thirty-two
precinct stations and managed to capture the city's police headquarters. The equivalent of two full wartime infantry divisions
were funneled into the city by Free Corps commanders, and for
the first time the volunteers could call upon airpower. While
the infantry took cover and the armored cars hid behind cor-

ners, biplanes swept down on the larger buildings and rained bombs through the roofs. The battle for Berlin lasted ten days, and when the smoke cleared, no fewer than two thousand revolutionary dead were dragged away for burial. The uprising had been decisively crushed, and with it any hopes for a Red Berlin in the foreseeable future.

The Communists achieved their greatest successes in the semiautonomous state of Bavaria and its capital city, Munich. But the achievements were only temporary. There was little difficulty in raising the Bavarian Red Army of some twenty thousand rifles, but the troops were workers who practiced close-order drill during their coffee breaks and who elected their own officers. They gained a certain amount of practical police experience by ferreting out and arresting known conservatives who wanted nothing to do with Russian-style government, and soon the prison cells were filled with Munich's best-educated and most affluent citizens.*

Thirty thousand Free Corps troops poured into Bavaria during the last week of April, preceded by Albatros and Fokker reconnaissance planes piloted by officers who had been unemployed and vilified during the past five months of "peace." They could now utilize their skills and their guns against men they regarded as traitors, men posing as soldiers defending an Asiatic ideology. Red Army units caught in the open were bombed and strafed without mercy. Initial opposition to the heavily armed columns was knocked aside and the Free Corps swept into Munich. Within seventy-two hours, the last red revolutionary banner was torn down, but the hunt for the remnants of the Bavarian Red Army went on for another week. When it was over, mass graves were dug for more than a thousand victims of Free Corps execution squads.

---

*On April 27, three Red Guards set out to arrest an outspoken opponent of bolshevism, a noncom living in the barracks of the Second Bavarian Regiment whose fiery nationalistic speeches had drawn the attention of communists and conservatives alike. When approached by the trio of would-be captors, old front-line fighter Corporal Adolf Hitler leveled his loaded and cocked carbine at them, glared, and watched "the three scoundrels . . . march off as they had come."

The events of winter and early spring made it abundantly clear to the Supreme Command and the new Socialist government alike that only a strong, vigorous and reconstituted *Reichswehr,* a national army, would permit Germany to survive in the difficult years that lay ahead. The flames of communism, temporarily damped within the frontiers, were bound to erupt again. Poland was rearming rapidly, greatly encouraged and helped with war materiel by the French, and the Poles offered no promise that their territorial ambitions did not include German land. Yet Germany had to tread carefully; nearly forty American, French and British divisions were deployed in the deep bridgeheads across the Rhine, poised, it seemed, to leap forward at the slightest displeasure occasioned by German actions aimed at keeping the fragmenting nation together. For Germany to become disarmed would mean risking dismemberment.

Accordingly, plans were drawn for a provisional Reichswehr whose function, the government was at pains to point out, was "to be the protection of the Reich's frontiers and the maintenance of [internal] order." As envisioned by the generals, the new army would total four hundred thousand men, including support and specialist troops, broken down into twenty-four combat divisions. The manpower would be handpicked from veterans of the old Imperial Army and from among the cream of the officers, noncoms, and men of the various Freikorps and, as before, fresh contingents would be drawn from volunteers from Prussia, Bavaria, Baden, Saxony, and Württemberg, all blended smoothly together under the command of the General Staff and the war minister. Volunteers would serve two years on active duty, then pass into an inactive reserve. A militia would be created in which young volunteers would be given ninety days' intensive training and kept current by mandatory field maneuvers for two weeks each summer. While the generals faced the fact that they would have to tolerate an army of democrats, they ruled out the idea of a democratic army, which is a contradiction in terms; there would be no election of officers by the men, no more of the soldiers' councils that had such a ruinous effect on discipline and efficiency. Remembering the final months of the war just ended in France, the generals included in their plans a healthy expansion of tank units—an area of military endeavor where they had been sadly eclipsed by the British and the French—and provisions were made for a much larger air force equipped with defensive fighters, reconnaissance machines and ground-attack planes.

The plans were sent to the government at Weimar for final approval. And here began the first of the skirmishes between the Socialists and the traditional Prussian military thinkers. The law creating the provisional Reichswehr was passed with several important amendments to the original plan. Although the soldiers' councils as such were not insisted upon, the government instead allowed the creation of a so-called Army Chamber made up of delegates from throughout the various divisions to redress grievances within the ranks. Military justice, the cornerstone of Prussia discipline for more than a hundred years, was abolished; instead, officers and men alike were to come under the jurisdiction of the civil law codes. Although these changes were looked upon by the generals as radical departures, they merely reflected the changeover from the nation governed by an emperor and the Great General Staff to a Socialist republic.

The Allied armies had confiscated the bulk of German heavy weapons following the signing of the Armistice Agreement, but it remained for a German civilian to point out that this could only be an advantage. Walther Rathenau's appointment in 1914 as head of the raw materials department of the War Ministry had created something of a silent wave of shock in the Wilhelmstrasse, especially among the Prussians. Urbane and well educated, Rathenau was the son and heir of the founder of Allgemeine Elektrizitätsgesellschaft—almost the direct equivalent of the American General Electric Company—and has been described as "a man who united the abilities of a great business leader with real qualities of philosophic wisdom." What was different about Rathenau among all those barons and the staff officers in their splendid uniforms was the fact that he was a Jew. When the war ended and the new government formed, Rathenau was named as head of the new Ministry of Reconstruction. He told the generals: "They have destroyed or taken your weapons, but these weapons would in any case have become obsolete before the next war. That war will be fought with brand-new ones, and the army which is least hampered with obsolete material will have a great advantage." Herr Rathenau could also point to a concurrent advantage of even a modest rearmament program: the unemployed skilled and semiskilled workers could be put back to work and the general economy would be greatly benefited.

Although the law promulgating the new army was passed with only minor faultfinding from the General Staff, it was not immediately implemented. The Allies were still sitting in deliberation over the actual peace terms that would include the vital clauses relating to Germany's military future. With the roar of the guns barely subsided, and with a full-scale civil war raging in Russia, the German generals hoped that the Allies would be realistic, if not generous.

But not many of them believed it.

The great failing of a logical mind is that it is not equipped for fathoming deep-rooted passions and hysteria aroused in others through past experiences. The Germans have long prided themselves on being able to proceed swiftly through the syllogistic process to arrive at logical conclusions without allowing unnecessary and embarrassing emotions to get in the way, and it is this clinical characteristic that was largely responsible for the shock they received at the outcome of the Peace Conference at Versailles—a conference the Germans were not invited to attend.

Even as the struggle for control of Germany's helm was being waged so bitterly, the Foreign Office's Bureau for Peace Negotiations speeded up work begun months before on a lengthy and detailed study of how best to confront the Allies when the day of reckoning came. Every conceivable posture was examined by staffs of experts in every field, and position papers were drafted and then polished with painstaking care, papers designed to meet any possible contingencies arising from what were assumed would be patient and sensible negotiations conducted among equals. The needs of the common man in Germany would be considered. The fact that Germany was rid of the despised Kaiser and his imperial entourage would be gratefully acknowledged and taken into account. The heroic fight waged by the new democratic government against the menace of bolshevism would be recognized and gratitude shown. Humanity would prevail. All these assumptions not only were predicated upon logic but, above all, were heavily influenced by the generosity promised in the many public statements presented to the world by the President of the United States. To most Germans, Thomas Woodrow Wilson was a messiah figure whose famous Fourteen Points might well have been engraved on tablets of clay, so sacred were they to German hopes for a just peace treaty and for hopes for the future.

"We have no quarrel with the German people," Wilson had said. "We have no feeling toward them except one of sympathy and friendship." Proceeding from there to the Fourteen Points —first pronounced on January 18, 1918—the Germans could see that Point Three offered "The removal of all economic barriers . . . establishment of an equality of trade." This augured well for a speedy economic recovery. With a resurrected merchant fleet, goods could be moved unhindered anywhere in the world, for Point Two promised "Absolute freedom of navigation of the seas, alike in peace or war. . . ." Under Point One, clandestine treaties and alliances would be outlawed; Germany would face no secret coalitions, say, between the French and the Poles, that would threaten her security. Wilson was seeking "Open covenants of peace . . . diplomacy shall proceed always frankly in the public view." Buttressing this first ideal, the final point proposed that "A general association should be formed [to] afford mutual guarantees of political independence and territorial integrity. . . ." This would mean that the nations would work out their differences in a civilized and gentlemanly manner; wars might well become a thing of the past. But until this utopian ideal was realized, Germany herself remained threatened from the East. What about arms to guarantee her safety? The German military advisors on the Bureau for Peace Negotiations could turn to Point Four for reassurance: "Adequate guarantees given and taken that national armaments will

be reduced to the lowest point consistent with national safety."
Who could better determine what the lowest point was than the
Germans themselves?

The Germans clung to these assumptions because they
seemed only logical, and because they had absolutely no other
guidelines to follow; the heads of state of the major powers and
more than one thousand delegates from thirty-two nations,
large and small, had been working on the peace treaty in Paris
since January 18, 1919, but no Germans had been granted permission to attend even the preliminary conferences sketching
out the broad outlines of the terms upon which the armistice
would be converted into an actual state of peace. Paris swarmed
with distinguished journalists, but so airtight were the security
arrangements and so closemouthed were the delegates that the
newsmen knew little more about what was being accomplished
than did the *clochards* drowsing in the spring sunshine along
the banks of the Seine. Whatever news about the peace conference did appear was little more than guesswork or was gathered by the frustrated reporters in bistros where they bought
drinks for minor delegates from such places as Montenegro
and Brazil. The real news, of course, could only come from
America's Woodrow Wilson, Britain's David Lloyd George, or
France's Georges Clemenceau. But all three were being exas-
peratingly political, issuing only the usual platitudes when they
bothered to comment on the endless meetings of the peace
delegates. A virtual blackout had descended upon the City of
Light, and the world was kept waiting, none so anxiously as the
Germans.

The Germans were essentially correct in surmising what Wilson might demand of them in the final settlement; he had made
his views known often enough. "No punitive damages," he insisted, "no annexations, no contributions." They were less sure
about David Lloyd George, although it was known that English
working-class sentiment was expressed in placards carried
through London streets demanding, "Hang the Kaiser!" This,
surely, was not meant to be taken seriously. But when gauging
the attitude of the French people and the savage-minded old

Premier, Georges Clemenceau, seventy-six, the Germans were living in what they call a "cloud cuckoo-land"; they simply could not comprehend the depth of fear and loathing harbored against them in every French heart. Nearly fifteen thousand square miles of once-lush, rolling farmland lay churned into muddy desolation; in the region of Verdun alone, unending shellfire had blown away the topsoil down to chalk, and nothing of beauty or value would ever grow there again. Peaceful little French villages had been erased from existence by the hundreds, their inhabitants rendered homeless, possessions reduced to what they could carry on their backs in flight from advancing floodtides of German troops. Churches were defiled and reduced to rubble; even the great cathedral at Rheims had been wantonly shelled. Paris, cradle of the arts and of everything civilized in the nineteenth and twentieth centuries, had first been bombed from nighttime skies, then subjected to a new terror in the closing months of the war—shells that plummeted randomly into the city, killing everywhere, fired by monstrous guns hidden in a forest seventy-two miles away. Only fearsome technology could produce such guns; only barbarians would use them against a beautiful city lying supine in summer's sun.

Most unforgivable of all was the fact that the promise of a nation's future lay rotting in the fields. More than a million and a half vital and irreplaceable lives had been consumed in the furnace of war to keep the Germans at bay. Four million men had been wounded, countless thousands of them mutilated beyond repair or rehabilitation. The legless, the armless, the sightless; the men who would spend the balance of their wretched lives coughing up lung tissue seared by German gas —who would care for them? Widows, parents and orphans of those vanished in shallow graves or blown to bits—who could dull their grief?

These fresh wounds inflicted upon the national soul and carapace were laid on top of older scars carved by Prussians. There were still those alive in 1919 who could recall how, forty-seven years earlier, Paris lay under siege by Krupp guns, and how dogs, cats and rats were sold at premium to alleviate the pangs of hunger. And how, when the city sagged into collapse, Wilhelm I arrogantly crowned himself Emperor at Versailles in the palace built by Louis XIV, the Sun King. Was France to live forever in the shadow of fear of its larger and aggressive neighbor? With the flower of her youth slaughtered on the battlefields, France could only look forward to Germany's greater recuperative powers which would see German men of military age double those of France within a generation. As it had happened in 1871 and again in 1914, it would inevitably happen again unless France, now at the height of victory, moved with ruthless and surgical speed to render Germany crippled and impotent, totally incapable of starting another war in the foreseeable future; only with the Prussian military malignancy excised could France ever feel herself secure. Moreover, the *Boches* must be made to pay heavily for the war's hideous cost in lives, property, and human spirit; reparations would not only help replenish France's drained treasury, but would be severely punitive, harsh enough to fit the enemy's unforgivable crimes.

To all this, Georges Clemenceau demanded acquiescence from the other Allied powers. When one of his cabinet ministers reminded him that his proposed terms ran sharply contrary to Wilson's Fourteen Points, Clemenceau growled, "Ah, so Wilson has Fourteen Points? God only needed ten." Then, shortly before the conferences began, Clemenceau finally found time to read a copy of the famous document, published nearly a year earlier.

The swollen corps of Allied delegates and experts in various fields labored but 102 days to produce a voluminous peace treaty whose aims were to justify the carnage of the preceding four years and, above all, to reshape the world into a safe and secure place in which to live. Considering the profound effects the peace treaty would have on the future conduct of human affairs of nations large and small and the lofty ambitions intended for it, the precipitate haste with which it was thrown together and the manner in which it was presented to the Germans can only be described as acts of folly. While the treaty, more than 75,000 words long, broken down into an astonishing 440 separate articles, was still being drafted, a German delegation of nearly two hundred plenipotentiaries, specialists, translators, and clerks was summoned to France. They were shunted to a hotel in Versailles, thirteen miles southeast of Paris, and placed in virtual house arrest while the querulous Allies tried to thrash out details of the peace settlement. The Germans were kept waiting futilely for a week, and when they threatened to pack up and go back home the panicky Allies ordered the treaty flung together, ready for presentation on the afternoon of May 7. So diffuse were the actual working arrangements and so hurried the assembling of the mass of individual articles that, unbelievably, not one of the major Allied leaders had a chance to read the treaty in its finished draft form until a few hours before it was to be handed to the Germans in a formal session at the Trianon Palace. Every American and British delegate who read the treaty in its complete form was shocked at the severity of the demands and the harshness of the language, but it was then too late to make changes. Clearly, they should have allowed themselves a few weeks more of sober and dispassionate study before springing such a document on the world, but the commitment was made.

At three o'clock on that afternoon of May 7, the primary German delegates were ushered inside the mirrored and varnished splendor of the Trianon to take their seats facing the gathered Allied leaders. The Germans realized instantly that they were seated not as negotiators but as accused prisoners in the dock. They were handed a single copy of the treaty, printed in English, and told they would be allowed just fifteen days to study the contents and make any written comments they had to offer before putting their signatures to the weighty document. The chief German plenipotentiary and Foreign Minister, lean, cold-featured Count Ulrich von Brockdorff-Rantzau, fifty, launched into a tirade even before glancing at the contents of the white-bound Conditions of Peace. He attacked the "inhuman" Allied blockade that had caused so much hardship among the civil population in Germany during the final year of the war, his voice strained with emotion and ill-concealed anger. Among those listening was a young British brigadier, John H. Morgan, seated across from the French delegation. He turned his gaze upon old Georges Clemenceau. "Under his beetling brows, his magnetic eyes sunk in a face yellow with age like an old parchment, he appeared to be watching intently, with a faintly ironical expression, every flicker of the German's eyelids, every telltale muscle of his face. Perhaps Clemenceau was living over again the days of France's agony and famine of 1870–71. Perhaps he was recalling, for he was an omnivorous reader, Bismarck's words as he gloated over the starvation of the people of Paris hemmed in as by a ring of steel with German troops and refusing to allow a single wagon of food from neutral countries to go through. *The French*, said Bismarck, *should be forced to an immediate capitulation by starvation. We are told to spare people out searching for potatoes on the outskirts of Paris. They should be shot, too. . . ."*

Clemenceau and the others listened to Brockdorff-Rantzau's outburst in silence, then the session was brought to an abrupt close. It had all taken less than an hour.

The treaty was in Berlin the following day, greeted by politicians, the General Staff, and the public alike with shock, outrage and incredulity. When summaries of the "Peace of Violence," as the treaty was called, were published across Germany in the newspapers, there were popular demonstrations in the streets. Harboring the delusion that the peace terms would be based solely upon Wilson's cherished Points, the Germans felt themselves tricked. They erroneously believed that Wilson was the chief architect of the damning document, and overnight he became an object of vilificaton. Even the most pessimistic among the Germans had never dreamed that the final terms would be so vindictive and ruinous of the Fatherland's chances to recover from the war and chart a new and freer passage into the future.

The treaty demanded, as a beginning, payment of the equivalent of $5 billion in gold within twenty-four months; but this was only a fraction of the total reparations bill to be submitted at a later date after the Reparations Committee had arrived at a reckoning based on every conceivable claim of damages to the civilian populations of England and France that arose. (The

United States made no such claims, but grudgingly backed those of her Allies, sharply deviating from Wilson's earlier pronouncements.) The bill would add up to approximately $130 billion, or almost half of Germany's total net worth in that year of 1919. Then, contradicting all logic, the treaty demanded the outright surrender of Germany's means to pay off this staggering sum: her colonies in Africa and in the Pacific must be given up; crippling amounts of iron ore and coal were to be turned over to the French; her blast furnaces were to be reduced by a third; the entire merchant navy of vessels exceeding small, sixteen-hundred tonners was to be handed over. How, then, could Germany be expected to meet these obligations? The French attitude was that this was no concern of theirs; the Germans would pay, with interest, even if it required fifty or a hundred years. David Lloyd George, when seeking reelection shortly after the Armistice, had promised the voters that he would see to it that Germany was squeezed like a lemon, although he knew at the time that Germany was a withered fruit. Observed Winston Churchill, "The economic clauses of the Treaty were malignant and silly. . . . The multitudes remained plunged in ignorance of the simplest economic facts, and their leaders, seeking their votes, did not undeceive them."

To the economic bloodletting were added what the Germans called "shame paragraphs," requiring Germany not only to admit sole responsibility for starting the war but to produce for trial before an Allied tribunal a host of individuals accused of war crimes. Leading the charge sheet was Article 227, calling for the arraignment of Wilhelm II for "a supreme offense against international morality and the sanctity of treaties." The Germans now had no doubt that if the Kaiser were somehow spirited out of Holland and placed on trial in England, he would be hanged in public view in Hyde Park.

Part V of the treaty stopped cold all planning then in progress for reshaping the Reichswehr. The Military, Naval and Air Clauses had been worked over more carefully than any others and had been scientifically designed to prohibit Germany from waging war as the twentieth century had come to know it. Article 160 excised the brain of the German war machine by ordering the permanent dissolution of the Great General Staff, and to inhibit inculcation of the traditional military spirit in future generations of German youth, all military academies were ordered closed. The new Reichswehr was not to exceed 100,000, including a maximum of 4,000 officers. This figure becomes significant when it is taken into account that Germany opened the war in 1914 with a total of 29,000 reserve and regular officers, ending the war in 1918 with 226,000 commissions. Seven infantry and three cavalry divisions would be allowed, but artillery was restricted to the smaller field guns and howitzers, less than 300 pieces in all. Possession of tanks and even armored cars was forbidden, and the manufacture of poison gas put outside the law. The treaty spelled out in meticulous detail how many machine guns, mortars, rifles, and carbines were allowed, and how much small arms ammunition could be stockpiled or manufactured—enough for about ten days' combat. Factories heretofore manufacturing proscribed goods would be either broken up or converted to production of farm machinery or other harmless goods. Importation of munitions of any kind was forbidden.

To prevent the accumulation of trained reserves, the new Reichswehr would consist only of volunteers agreeing to serve on a long-term basis—twelve years in the case of enlisted men, and twenty-five years in the case of officers—and once discharged, neither group could join any kind of reserve force as weekend soldiers. Conscription was outlawed, as were all the usual veterans' organizations that had any connection whatsoever with the War Ministry or any other agency of the state. Except for the undersized professional army, which would grow arthritic with time, Germany was to be demilitarized, body and soul.

The treaty reduced the German navy to a few ancient battleships and cruisers and a dozen each of destroyers and motor torpedo boats. Submarines were totally forbidden, and new ships of any kind to be built in the future could not exceed ten thousand tons. Naval personnel were limited to 16,500 officers and men, and all coastal fortifications within thirty miles of the sea would have to be dismantled. Article 185 stipulated that all

German ships outside the above limitations would be handed over to the Allies.* Coupled with the confiscation of her merchant fleet, the Naval Clauses effectively reduced Germany's sea power to a virtual zero.

Fewest of all the clauses were those pertaining to the air. So sweeping were they that only five were needed in the entire treaty to return Germany to the era of hot-air balloons, so popular in France in the nineteenth century. *No* air arm of any kind was permitted, and existing stocks of all air materiel not already handed over to the Allies were to be destroyed. Especially onerous to those in Germany who saw in wartime's spectacular technological leaps the promise of commercial aviation enterprise was Article 201, which read: "During the six months following the date on which the present Treaty comes into force, the manufacture and importation of aircraft, parts of aircraft, engines for aircraft and parts of engines for aircraft shall be forbidden in all German territory." Already the British and Americans were pioneering efforts that would lead to lucrative commercial business in the air. Only four weeks after the war ended, three Royal Air Force officers took off in a giant Handley-Page V-1500 bomber (designed to bomb Berlin and other targets deep inside Germany) and flew it from England to Cairo and on to Delhi, proving that long-range passenger and freight missions were entirely feasible. On March 1, 1919, the British inaugurated the first shuttle flights between Folkstone and Cologne, carrying mail to the Army of Occupation in the Rhineland. England created a new Department of Civil Aviation and opened the gates to civilians who wanted to fly for sport or pleasure. In May, the United States Navy managed to negotiate the unfriendly gray stretches of the Atlantic Ocean in Curtiss flying boats, reaching the coast of England from Newfoundland via the Azores and Lisbon. The British were readying for an attempt to fly the Atlantic non-stop in a war-surplus bomber

---

*England thus laid hands on 114 German U-boats, fifty of which were already interned at Scapa Flow, along with nine battleships, thirteen cruisers, and fifty destroyers. On the afternoon of June 21, 1919, almost the entire German fleet was scuttled before the astonished eyes of the British guard force.

and, using captured German airships, were setting up to prove the worth of lighter-than-air monsters in crossing the Atlantic first in one direction and then the other. These exciting adventures would be denied the Germans, who would be forced to watch their former enemies grab the lead in the exploration of the air and development of a whole new enterprise; not until July 1, 1920, six months after the treaty was to become effective, could they begin to resurrect their own aviation industry. By then—as the Allies had planned—Germany would be far behind.

To assure reparations payments at bayonet point, the French were going to occupy the ten thousand square miles of the Rhineland for a period of fifteen years, bringing five and a half million Germans under virtual French military rule. The Rhine would remain a Gallic waterway, its traffic strictly controlled. The Saar Basin, adjoining relinquished Alsace-Lorraine, contained a quarter of Germany's coal deposits; the treaty provided that the Germans could still mine the coal, but only under French supervision, and the proceeds were to be shipped directly to France to help meet the staggering payments.

Chancellor Philipp Scheidemann declared that the treaty was "unacceptable and impossible of execution," a sentiment echoed even by his political enemies.* But if the hated document were not signed, what, then, would prostrate Germany face? Intact French, British and American armies were poised along the Rhine, backed by enormous numbers of heavy guns, tanks, aircraft and unending reserves. The Americans who had arrived in France too late for the final big push were spoiling for a fight. Refusal to sign the treaty would mean—and this was almost impossible to conceive—that the war would start all over again. Debate raged back and forth between the Socialist Government at Weimar and the German High Command, still at Kolberg in East Prussia. The debate revolved around but two questions: Could the remnants of the Army and the scattered Freikorps physically resist an Allied invasion? Could the war-

---

*And in Paris, Woodrow Wilson admitted to one of his advisors, "If I were a German, I think I should not sign it."

sick and apathetic population be roused once again in patriotic fervor to offer itself up to further sacrifices? What finally emerged from Kolberg was a carefully phrased note over Hindenburg's signature.

"We can reconquer the province of Posen and defend our frontiers in the East," he stated, "[but] in the West we can scarcely count upon being able to withstand a serious offensive on the part of the enemy in view of the numerical superiority of the Entente and their ability to outflank us on both wings.

"The success of the operation as a whole is therefore very doubtful, but as a soldier I cannot help feeling that it were better to perish honorably than accept a disgraceful peace." For the archives, then, the crafty old man was for perishing honorably; but faced with the actual decision to fight or not to fight, Hindenburg dodged the issue and left the choice to the high civil servants at Weimar, who would bear the responsibility for either a peace of shame or honor salvaged at the price of ruin. Agonized and often violent arguments raged back and forth inside the National Assembly. The Foreign Minister, Brockdorff-Rantzau, resigned. The army threatened open revolt. Soundings throughout the country revealed that the general population was ready to ignite in insurrection should the new government plunge them yet again into war. The troops themselves were ready to fight, but they were outnumbered ten to one and had no heavy weapons. There was no choice, really. Only hours before the final deadline set by the implacable Allies for the resumption of hostilities and the investment of the rest of Germany, the harassed Assembly members voted to sign.

The questionable document was signed on Saturday afternoon, June 28, 1919, in the great Hall of Mirrors at Versailles in a ceremony marked by its brevity and lack of solemnity, which was made impossible by the continual buzz and hum created by the press and other invited spectators. When it was all over, David Lloyd George was heard to remark, "Well, we shall have to do the same thing all over again in twenty-five years, and at three times the cost."

With the *Diktat*, the dictated peace, in force on January 1, 1920, the Army of Occupation settled down in billets for a long stay, the officers of the Allied Commission of Control readied themselves to begin probing the state of Germany's self-disarmament, the German people looked forward to the years of peace that lay ahead—and a handful of dangerous career officers backed by fighting men who knew no other trade prepared for one final spasm of revolt against President Ebert and his republican form of government. No more reactionary group existed than the field-grade officers with hereditary titles who had devoted their lives to the profession of arms and their souls to a creed that placed the House of Hohenzollern before everything else and to the precept that the Great General Staff was the rock upon which the nation's destiny should be based. To these officers, words such as "democracy" and "republic" were alien. Those who had first agreed to the terms of the Armistice and then signed the Diktat were generally known as the "November criminals," a phrase that would see increasing use when needed, and it was against these "criminals" that certain old-guard officers now moved.

On the night of March 12, 1920, three Freikorps regiments and units of the regular Reichswehr occupied Berlin and proclaimed that President Ebert was to be ousted and that the current cabinet, having exhausted its mandate from the people, was dissolved. The insurgent troops were under the command of General Walther von Lüttwitz, sixty-one, the very figure of a modern Prussian general. Lüttwitz not only wanted the German army back in power as it had been in 1914, but had visions of reinstating the Hohenzollern dynasty. The figurehead for the new government was a fiery Nationalist named Wolfgang Kapp, sixty-two, who had once held a fairly high post as a civil servant with the Department of Agriculture, but whose qualifications for running a nation were totally unknown to everyone except himself. Kapp was not even a native German; he had been born in New York City, and later emigrated to the Fatherland and became naturalized. President Ebert and his cabinet fled to Stuttgart, and heard with amazement that Kapp had proclaimed himself Chancellor. A last-minute plea that the Reichswehr muster itself to crush the revolutionists was met with icy refusal. "The Army does not fight against the Army," was the reply.

The seizure of Berlin began quietly enough. From the window of the capital's famed Adlon Hotel, a British officer observed "four lethal-looking 77s, commanding all approaches. A few yards to the right, where the Wilhemstrasse deboûched into the Unter den Linden, was a machine-gun post and barbed-wire entanglements. Field kitchens were sending up wisps of smoke in the chill morning air. Jerries seemed to be everywhere—unmistakable Jerries in tin hats and full service kit. Each man carried a rifle, a pack and a brace of bombs. On their tin hats was a new and mysterious emblem . . . a [white] swastika. These were the irregulars of Erhardt's Marine Brigade, of von der Goltz's Iron Division of Baltic troops and the Lützow *Freikorps.*

"The first of a whole series of armored cars appeared in the Potsdammer Platz, followed by motor lorries mounted with machine guns. Three or four soldiers shed pamphlets which fluttered down like pigeons in the crowd. The pamphlets promised all things to all men, including a proclamation to the students of the University of Berlin that there should be no more examinations. From that moment the students were with the revolutionists to a man. All day long bodies of troops marched and counter-marched in columns of fours across the square, playing every tune in their repertoire from *Alte Kameraden* to *Deutschland über Alles.* Despite these demonstrations, the public appeared listless and unmoved."

Wolfgang Kapp's tenure in office lasted only one hundred hours. From Stuttgart, the temporarily exiled Republican government called for a general strike, a request heeded by every trade union in Berlin, and the city became cold, silent, and dark. Unwilling to crush the strike by force, Kapp instead permitted Lüttwitz's troops to demonstrate their powers to the general public. On Monday afternoon, March 15, Brigadier John Morgan was looking out the window from his Control Commission office on a floor of the Bellvue Hotel.

"I saw people suddenly flying across the square like autumn leaves driven by a strong west wind. Women fell, got up, stumbled and fell again. I heard a shot, and at that moment the head of a column of troops appeared from the mouth of the street on my right. The troops halted and opened fire. Men fell. One man was lying on the ground dragging his legs like a wounded hare. The next moment the square was empty of all living people. I went downstairs and found the staircase and hall choked with women who had rushed into our headquarters for cover. I heard triumphant music; a military band emerged, marching in perfect step across the square. The troops, having done their bloody business, fell into step behind them. *The bloodhounds!* exclaimed a civilian sheltering in our doorway. *First they shoot us and then they play music.*"

Kapp's efforts to establish a new government failed at every turn. The Imperial Bank refused him money to pay the troops; he could get no one to accept his cabinet posts; and the general strike continued. By the fourth day, it was clear even to Kapp that his vacillating thrashings amounted to little more than a putsch, which has been described in German as "a political movement which, aiming at a revolution, succeeds in achieving nothing more than a riot." General von Lüttwitz was informed that the British government had no intention of backing the so-called revolution and would not recognize the Kapp regime even should the revolution succeed. From Stuttgart, the Republican government sent a war-surplus reconnaissance plane winging low over Berlin, scattering leaflets in its slip-stream reminding Berliners that the real government still existed. The abortive putsch was called off on the morning of the fifth day, and Kapp took a taxi to the airdrome and flew off to Sweden and exile. The frustrated Freikorps troops formed up in an angry mood and marched out of Berlin after one last frenzy of firing and clubbing into the jeering crowds that lined the streets to watch them go.

The German Communist Party resurfaced with Spartacist zeal during the chaos, proclaiming that constitutions and parliaments were at an end, to be replaced by Moscow-style soviets. Arms depots at Spandau, Koepenick and Harburg were looted of weapons, and unsuspecting Reichswehr patrols were ambushed without mercy. At Harburg there occurred an incident typical of the workers' attitude toward any uniformed group defending the new Republic, and involving one of Germany's gamest, if least known, fighter pilots.

Rudolf Berthold was twenty-seven when the war ended and

he turned over his group's red and blue Siemen-Schuckert D.III fighters to the Allies. No pilot other than France's nearly immortal Charles Nungesser flew in combat in such terrible physical shape as did Hauptmann Berthold. One crash left him with numerous broken bones, and not long afterward his right arm was almost shredded by machine-gun slugs. The arm withered, but Berthold kept flying, even after the wounds reopened and began leaking while in the air. At night, without anesthetic, Berthold endured agonies while his medical orderly plucked bone splinters from the red flesh with tweezers. Berthold was awarded the Blue Max, gained his forty-fourth victory, and was shot down yet again shortly before the war ended. Like so many other pilots, Berthold could find no place in civilian life during the continuing upheavals that tore Germany apart following the signing of the Armistice. He was a commoner, the son of a forester, but he had no sympathy for the Left. He raised an infantry company he called the Iron Band, fighting the Communists wherever they threatened.

At Harburg on March 15, Berthold's unit blundered into a Red ambush and found themselves surrounded by great numbers of heavily armed strikers in an ugly mood. Berthold was for fighting to the last, as he had done so often during war, but reconsidered when the Red leader promised him and his men safe conduct out of Harburg if they would lay down their arms. Berthold, his Blue Max glittering at his throat, his right arm dangling useless at his side, reluctantly gave in. Weapons were dumped on the ground and Berthold ordered the Iron Band to march off. But he had taken only a few steps when he was felled by a rain of rifle butts; the strikers could not bear to allow an officer and holder of the Pour le Mérite to get away. While Berthold was lying senseless in his own blood upon the ground, someone bent down and twisted the ribbon of the Blue Max around his throat until he was strangled to death.

Berthold's murder was avenged on a massive scale. The government returned to Weimar, and the functionaries in Berlin could beat down the neo-Spartacists only by calling upon the Reichswehr and its handmaiden, the Security Police (SIPO), and giving them carte blanche. Again the streets rang with gunfire, and again the bodies piled up. Ruthless searches of homes, flats and factories were carried out by day and by night for hidden weapons and incriminating literature. Then followed a fast ride to the nearest caserne and quick execution. It did not escape President Ebert, his cabinet, and the members of the National Assembly that the troops who were so diligently stamping out the Communists were the same ones who had either participated in, or stood by and watched, the Kapp putsch. But it was either accept the officer corps as a strong partner in a marriage of convenience in order to preserve the hope of democracy, or abdicate from this ideal in the face of an armed and militant Left.

The fires of revolt were snuffed within a week, and the general strike brought to an end. The victory belonged neither to the people nor to their government, but to the Reichswehr, an army determined to weld itself back together as a potent political force despite the Treaty of Versailles and the Allied Control Commission sent to implement it.

You may strip Germany of her colonies, reduce her armaments to a mere
police force and her navy to that of a fifth-rate power; all the same in
the end if she feels that she has been unjustly treated in the peace of
1919 she will find means of exacting retribution on her conquerors.
—David Lloyd George

Surplus warplanes were converted to civilian use overnight. This L.V.G. observation craft became a mail carrier in 1919.
(Lufthansa.) □

Roland Rohrbach, innovator of the "stressed-skin" technique of aircraft manufacture which revolutionized the industry.

(Lufthansa.) □

An A.E.G. two-seater, once armed
and adorned with black crosses,
was later used by Germany's only
airline as a courier and freighter.
When fitted with a humped enclosure, it saw service as a passenger carrier.   *(Lufthansa.)* □

Sword into plowshare. The all-metal F.13, originally designed by Hugo Junkers as a ground-attack plane, was modified and became popular as a four-passenger liner on skis or wheels. *(Lufthansa.)* □

Hans von Seeckt, commander in chief of the Reichswehr from 1918 to 1926, was the creator of the new German army. *(The Bettmann Archive.)* □

Horsepower and manpower were used to launch German gliders in the 1920s. *(Peter Bowers.)* □

Fokker D.XIIIs were flown in Russia by future Luftwaffe pilots. *(Peter Bowers.)* ☐

The Junkers K.47, tested at Lipetsk, was a forerunner of the infamous Stuka. *(Peter Bowers.)* □

The Dornier 19, one of General Wever's Ural bombers, was scrapped by the Luftwaffe command, which saw no need for long-range aircraft. *(Peter Bowers.)* □

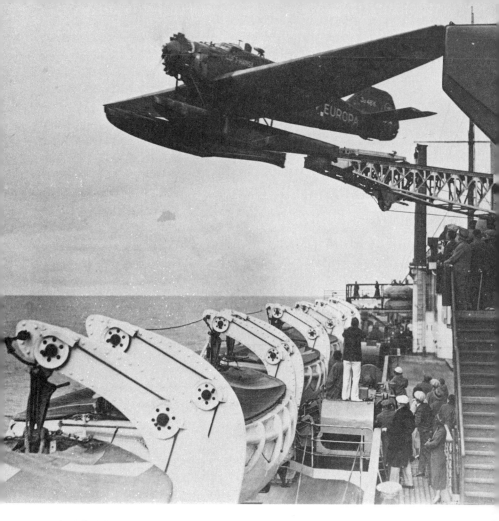

.Ju 46s like this one catapulted from the liner *Europa* in 1930 furthered Germany's bid to capture part of the trans-Atlantic mail service. This training was invaluable for later naval reconnaissance tasks. *(Lufthansa.)* □

Claudius Dornier.
(Lufthansa.) □

Dornier's twin-engined *Wal* made
lakes out of the North and South
Atlantic. These flying boats were
first built abroad to avoid restrictions imposed at Versailles, but
after 1933 Dornier's planes were
stamped "Made in Germany."
(Lufthansa.) □

Dornier's Super Whale, first built in 1926, became a familiar sight to South Americans and is seen here in the same sky as a postwar Zeppelin. *(Lufthansa.)* ☐

Right: Azores to New York, 1937. The gull-winged Blohm und Voss Ha.139 could be launched anywhere in the Atlantic, or take off on its own using a quartet of diesel engines.
(Lufthansa.) ☐

Hugo Junkers' leviathan G.38 transport, the wonder of Europe.
(Lufthansa.) □

Ernst Brandenburg.
(Lufthansa.) □

Erhard Milch.
(Lufthansa.) □

Ernst Heinkel.
(Lufthansa.) □

A Lufthansa Ju.46 floatplane airliner, flying the national colors.
(Lufthansa.) □

The venerable Ju.52: airliner, troop carrier, and bomber if necessary. *(Lufthansa.)* □

Heinkel's He.70, the fastest "transport" of its time and the test-bed for future fighter planes. *(Lufthansa.)* □

This Heinkel 112 lost out in the fighter competition to the Me.109. Its open cockpit was a concession to 1918-era judges.

(Peter Bowers.) □

The Arado 68 biplane fighter was a Luftwaffe mainstay until 1936.
(Peter Bowers.) ☐

Hermann Goering, now a bemedaled field marshal, confers with Hitler and his chief deputies. *(The Bettmann Archive.)* □

SEARCH AND DESTROY

We signed the Peace Treaty knowing we could never fulfill the terms
and believing no nation would ever expect us to do so.
—Gustav Noske

Despite the wastage and attrition of more than a thousand days
and nights of combat, prodigies of production by Germany's
thirty-five aircraft manufacturers and twenty aero-engine
plants enabled the *Luftstreitkrafte* to finish the war with 18,500
planes in inventory. In addition, the Austro-Hungarian air arm,
fed by eleven factories including Phoenix, Hungarian Lloyd,
Jakob Lohner, and Flieger Arsenal, wound up with 1,279 aircraft and 3,515 engines for which there was now no need. It
would be the task of the Inter-Allied Commission of Control to
seek out these twenty thousand-odd warplanes and trainers
and, after each country had taken its pick for transfer home for
future study, see to it that they were all broken up for scrap or
converted to ashes. Although the Control Commission would
not begin its work in earnest until more than fifteen months
after war's end, certain Allied officers were laying the groundwork long before that. Among them was Major Fred Zinn, a
U.S. Air Service observer from Battle Creek, Michigan, who was
in Koblenz as one of the representatives of the United States
Receiving Commission. Zinn's colorful military career began as
a private in the French Foreign Legion in 1914; he served as
gunner and aerial photographer with the *Service Aéronautique*
and member of the all-volunteer Lafayette Flying Corps, and
donned his own country's uniform after America entered the
war. Despite Zinn's long experience and expertise, his ignorance of the state of Germany's aircraft production and technical characteristics of the various late-model German combat

planes clearly reveals the skimpy intelligence efforts of his army's own air arm. While in Koblenz, Zinn pumped well-known
German fliers and factory executives for details of the equipment that had given the Allies such a hard time in the air,
details that might prove useful to his own country.

Zinn struck up an acquaintance with *Oberleutnants* Karl
Bolle and cocky little Ernst Udet, who, between them, boasted
a confirmed ninety-three victories. In talking to these veteran
war pilots, Zinn learned a great deal of technical information
that conceivably might be useful, but nothing that would con-
tribute to Germany's eventual disarmament. They discussed
the new Siemens-Schuckert fighters that appeared in the final
year of the war to earn the "hellish respect" of Captain Eddie
Rickenbacker. The Siemens planes were heavy-nosed, narrow-
winged, round-bodied, rakish-looking single-seaters with 200–
240 horsepower rotary engines fitted with four-bladed props.
When sent to Jasta 15 in early 1918, by *Idflieg—Inspektion de
Fliegertruppen* (Inspectorate of Aviation Troops)—one pilot
commented, "Highly sensitive on the controls, possesses excellent flying characteristics and climbs like a rocket!" This last was
certainly true; one Siemens left the ground and topped out at
19,685 feet just over fourteen minutes later. In September of
that year, a test pilot pushed another Siemens to the unprecedented altitude of 26,575 feet, and although the pilot was
groggy with hypoxia, he landed to report that even five miles
above the earth the stubby little fighter was still responding to
control inputs. Zinn learned, however, that neither Bolle nor
Udet were enthusiastic over the Siemens-Schuckert for the simple reason that a shortage of castor oil for the rotary engine
forced the use of mineral oil, and after eight to ten hours' running time, the pistons seized and the crowns ripped loose to fall
into the crankcase.

The problem was solved, the port wing was made four inches
shorter than the starboard to counteract torque imparted by
the whirling cylinders of the rotary engine, and the Siemens
D.IV model began trundling out of the factory. Strangely
enough, neither German pilot could tell Zinn whether or not
the improved versions ever reached the Front, when in fact two

full squadrons and parts of three fighter groups were equipped with the sensational new fighters for nearly three months prior to the end of the fighting. Neither was Zinn informed that the Siemens-Schuckert Werke—in between strikes, revolutions and counterrevolutions—continued leisurely to turn out fighters for many months after the signing of the Armistice, fulfilling the original wartime contract for 280 D.IVs and a prototype monoplane D.VI with great speed and a jettisonable main fuel tank hooked to the underside of the fuselage.

Zinn, who had flown under the flags of two nations whose governments had refused their fliers parachutes, discussed the problem of fire with Captain Bolle, who explained they had their own difficulties in this area, difficulties that had been virtually solved. Bolle recounted how, during the air fighting over Château-Thierry during the blazing hot summer of 1918, six Fokker D.VIIs caught fire on a single day when the wing-mounted fuel tanks overheated and burst into flame. Of course, Bolle hastened to add, the pilots saved themselves by going over the side under a canopy of silk, but such incidents were wasteful of equipment and deteriorated morale. Bolle handed Zinn a sheaf of photographs. Zinn saw how German engineers had fitted a flat, airfoil-shaped tank between the wheels of a D.VII, bolted to the axle. Incendiary bullets were fired into the tank, and, although the fuel ignited, the flames barely reached the underside of the fuselage. Zinn could only marvel, recalling the ingenuity of American-modified DH-4s that placed the large fuel tank between the pilot and the observer, in a position to roast them both, and in a flash of genius fixed the fuel overflow pipe adjacent to the extended—and red-hot—exhaust stacks running alongside the fuselage of that airplane, not without reason known as the "Flaming Four." Bolle seemed eager to explain what he could to Zinn, who put everything down in a report for his superiors, and Bolle said openly that his postwar job was "with Aviation Headquarters in Berlin, working on plans for the permanent organization of their Air Service."

At Dessau, along the Elbe north of Leipzig, ebullient Brigadier Billy Mitchell whipped through the Junkers Motor Works, accompanied by Hugo Junkers and a select team of engineers.

Mitchell, whose passionate views on air power would later cost him his job, his rank, and finally his life, was on another kind of search mission. Junkers proudly showed Mitchell the latest models of his all-metal, armor-protected ground-attack plane, explaining that 227 of them had been delivered to fighting units on both the Eastern and the Western Fronts, and not one had been shot down. Then Junkers took Mitchell to a separate corner of the factory and revealed to the American general, now Director of United States Military Aeronautics, the logical peacetime extension of this tough design. What Mitchell saw in prototype was the same square, ugly configuration in larger scale, but featuring a completely enclosed cabin accommodating pilot, copilot, four passengers, and ample baggage space. Mitchell's mind leaped at the possibilities of the F.13 used as a mail plane, a mobile tactical headquarters, a courier plane whisking himself and his staff from one echelon to another, an ambulance plane, a trainer for navigators, a trainer for military transport pilots. Mitchell placed an order or several of the exciting F.13s, shook hands with Hugo Junkers, and strode out of the factory with a head full of dreams.

But at the Fokker Flugzeugwerke at Schwerin in northern Germany, the dreams had vanished with the first ugly crackle of the rifles of revolution. Among the first to flee was the firm's owner and director, Tony Fokker himself, who had become a millionaire out of the war long before his twentieth birthday, which fell due in April 1919. Fokker, as a capitalist manufacturer of tools of war for the Imperial House of Hohenzollern, was a marked man. Although his house was under guard, Fokker managed to escape by donning the field-gray private's uniform belonging to the son of his concierge and striding past the similarly attired revolutionaries and into the darkened streets of Schwerin. A friend waiting in a side street on a motorcycle took him aboard and they bounced thirty miles across cobbled roads to the nearest functioning railroad station, where Fokker boarded a freight, hopping off in Berlin. He was back in Holland not long afterward, where he quickly renounced his wartime-acquired German citizenship and began scheming ways to smuggle his money and the contents of the factory out of Germany; the medals bestowed on him by grateful royalty he was willing to leave behind.* The bulk of his cash hoard was slipped into Holland by sea and by rail, in the latter case locked safely inside a trunk belonging to a cook with diplomatic privileges; but seeing to it that aircraft and engines escaped the Allied wrecking hammer was another matter.

Of all the German aircraft equipment, Fokker's products alone had been singled out by name in the terms of the Armistice agreement for surrender or destruction. Although 120 of his fighters had already been turned over to the Allies at Koblenz, there remained several hundred factory-fresh machines at Schwerin, and Fokker was determined to save what he could. Word was passed to his chief executives to disperse about half of the inventory throughout the countryside, away from the prying eyes of the inspectors sent out in advance of the Control Commission, whose weight could not be felt until some months after the signing of the Peace Treaty. The movers went to work. In this barn went a dozen wings belonging to the new D.VIII monoplane; into that cellar went a score of BMW engines; underneath the flooring of an unused plant were slid more wings and tail sections of D.VIIs; inside the tackroom of an abandoned stable, whose horses had long ago been taken by the army, went a score of Oberusel power plants for the D.VIIIs; remote sheds became temporary hangars for stripped fuselages. In this way, 220 Fokker aircraft and 400 engines were hidden away, leaving the rest for the enemy to discover in open view when they arrived in Schwerin.

Fokker arranged a deal with the Netherlands government to buy a certain number of fighters and spare engines; the others he would try to sell abroad, and the slim D.VIII monoplanes seemed likely prospects for private sport planes, if that market could be encouraged. To get what amounted to more than ten

---

*Wilhelm II awarded Fokker the Iron Cross, both First and Second Class, and the Grand Duke of Mecklenburg-Schwerin presented the Dutch businessman with the Mecklenburg Cross of Merit. The duke, with a surplus of such awards, distributed fifteen more among Fokker's eighteen hundred employees—including one to an awed and thunderstruck ancient with long seniority whose prime responsibility was maintenance of the factory lavatories.

squadrons of planes out of Germany, he needed two things: export licenses and transportation. Fokker's export manager, F. W. Seekatz, approached the Trade Ministry in Berlin and laid his cards on the table. If, explained Seekatz, we are allowed to move this equipment out of Germany to Holland—certainly a country that will never pose a threat to the Reich—not only will Germany receive the fees for licensing, but the Allies will be balked in their plans to burn all of those airplanes. Money will be saved and a measured amount of humiliation avoided. The logic was clear, and export permits for nearly half a million dollars' worth of materiel were quietly given. Pleas, bribes, and reminders of past favors secured the necessary rolling stock from the state railway, and the disassembled planes were removed from their secret hiding places, loaded onto trucks, and put aboard waiting boxcars and flatbeds. Within six weeks the move was completed, and everything shunted from Schwerin 350 miles to the Dutch frontier via Hannover. Included were tons of steel tubing, sheet aluminum, copper, rubber tires and tubes, turnbuckles, large bolts of silk and linen fabric, one hundred new parachutes, and everything else needed to fly and maintain a modern fighter force. Six trains of approximately sixty cars each were required for the move.

Flouting of this simple term of the Armistice agreement by one of the German ministries was a signal of what the Control Commission could expect when it moved in to implement the enormously more complicated Section V of the Peace Treaty; but it was a signal scorned.

To disarm a nation of some 65 million obstinate, querulous people spread across 182,000 square miles of territory, the victorious Allies sent a grand total of 383 officers and 737 enlisted men to Germany in the winter of 1919–1920, expecting these thousand-odd men to dismantle an armaments industry and an army that had been years in the making and that had come close to besting the military and industrial complex of the myriad nations ranked against them. Those who had created the Inter-Allied Commission of Control counted on the full cooperation of the German Socialist government, the generals, and the

arms merchants themselves to get the job over with as pain-
lessly as possible, but with so few men, and against manifest
opposition at every turn, the project was doomed from the start.
The first contingent of seventy officers arrived in Berlin on the
morning of September 15, 1919, and was put out of the train at
Zoo Station instead of at the Hauptbahnhof along the fashion-
able Friedrichstrasse. The newspapers, reporting the arrival of
the uniformed officers, referred to them as "our unwelcome
guests." Major General Sir Francis R. Bingham, chief of the
British mission, commented, "We felt like lepers on a leper
island."

When fully up to strength, the Control Commission was organized and quartered at the Hotel Adlon (later made famous by
Vicki Baum as *The Grand Hotel*), staffed by nine officers—four
French, two British, one Belgian, one Italian, and a diminutive
Japanese colonel fluent in several languages. The function of
the headquarters was to oversee the work of the three main
echelons deputized to exercise watchdog authority over armaments, personnel, and fortifications. These three echelons were
further broken down into twenty-two district commands scattered across Germany in the cities of Stettin, Königsberg, Bres-
lau, Dresden, Munich, Stuttgart, Frankfurt am Main, Kiel, Cologne, Münster, Hannover, Berlin, and the neutral-zone towns
of Karlsruhe and Duisburg. These district commands were
weighted eleven for armaments, eight for personnel, and three
for fortifications. The United States was nowhere represented
on the Control Commission for the simple reason that the Sen-
ate refused to ratify the Peace Treaty, repudiating the ailing
President Wilson's signature—and along with it the League of
Nations and any chance for the United States, then the world's
least-hated and potentially most powerful nation, to bring
enough pressure to bear to disarm Germany and indeed make
the country "safe for democracy."

In a major strategic blunder, later recognized and admitted
as such by General Bingham and his colleagues, the hierarchy
of the Control Commission insisted that the Germans provide
them with a liaison committee in order to facilitate the disarmament process. The Reichswehr seized upon this request with

alacrity, seeing the undreamed-of opportunity to create what, in effect, would be a committee of obstruction. Until the request came in out of the blue, the Reichswehr had accepted as a matter of course that the Control Commission would enter Germany in force and begin swift and arbitrary destruction and confiscation, handing out orders left and right, with sure punishment following any failure to heed the commands of the victors. To be *asked* to comply with military dictates was not in the Prussian handbook of procedures. The German War Department, now calling itself the Ministry of Defense in deference to Allied sensibilities, created the *Heeresfriedenskommission,* the Army Peace Commission, to deal with the Control Commission, and placed a Prussian general named Cramon at its head. General von Cramon had spent the four years of the war attached to the Austrian General Staff and was rabidly against the Treaty of Versailles and its every clause pertaining to disarmament.

On January 29, 1920, the officers of the Allied Control Commission and Cramon's cohorts clashed head-on in the first plenary meeting, a confrontation that would set the tone for "cooperation" between the two sides in the embattled years that lay ahead. Cramon, learning in advance that the commander of the Allied Control Commission, a French general named Nollet, was bringing only six of his officers to this initial conference, loaded the meeting with fourteen ranking German officers, all in full dress uniform ablaze with decorations. The opposing teams took their seats at the long table in stony silence. Nollet and Cramon faced each other. Observed Colonel John Morgan, "The two protagonists presented a striking contrast in types. Cramon a typical Prussian of huge physique, tall, thick, with cropped hair, a swollen face, prognathous jaw and a bulbous nose, his hands like hams; Nollet shorter by a head but compact with resolution in every line of him, the full broad brow of a thinker, a delicately chiseled nose, sensitive nostrils and finely shaped hands."

Cramon said with dramatic suddenness, "I proclaim this sitting open," and prepared to take his seat.

"Stop!" called out General Nollet. "It is for *me* to declare this sitting open. *We* are in control here." Nollet's words sounded to Colonel Morgan "like pistol shots."

Cramon, who was in a semicrouched position before Nollet's command was barked out, rose upright and stood at attention. "You are a foreign mission," he said, "on our territory in time of peace. By all diplomatic precedents it is for *me* to preside."

"There are no precedents," Nollet snapped back. "The Treaty has made one. The Treaty has placed us in control, and control means supervision."

"Very well," Cramon came back, "then that ends it. I must report to my Government."

"And I to mine," said Nollet. Then the officers swept up their briefcases and marched out of the room without another word. The first plenary session ended before anyone had time to sit down. No more attempts were made to have another, and from then on, whatever progress the Control Commission was to make would be outside of the council chamber.

Back in the shabby offices at the Hotel Bellvue, General Nollet stood in the center of the room with his hands thrust deep inside the pockets of his long, horizon-blue coat and said, "I have beaten them four times in the field on the Western Front —but von Cramon has never fought a battle!" However, the battle now beginning was one that Cramon was not going to lose.

At first, the Control Commission could report encouraging results in seeing to it that the seven thousand factories in Germany capable of producing war materiel were being rendered harmless. Krupp's, the largest armaments complex the world has ever known, shrank energetically. The maximum work force of 180,000 was cut by more than two-thirds. The great shell house at Essen, five hundred yards long, was stripped of its presses—capable of turning out 36,000 shells every ten-hour working day—and was being converted to production of sewing machines and farm implements. The largest gun shop in the Krupp domain, and hence in the world, sprawled across nineteen acres, and here the workers, almost all of them Spartacists, worked with a will to dismantle the tons of machinery to make way for conversion to the manufacture of locomotives. More than three million artillery rounds were destroyed in open fields using the fastest, if the most dangerous, method possible. Near Frankfurt, General Bingham watched as German workmen piled shells in rows, then lighted fires near the nose fuses in order to melt the charge. "But haven't you killed men doing it that way?" Bingham asked.

"No, Herr General," came the reply. "Not so many." Of course, the safest and most expeditious method would have been to load the shells aboard ships and dump them at sea, but because the German merchant marine no longer existed, disposal in the ocean was not possible.

The smaller arms makers complied just as methodically with the treaty, dealing correctly and even politely with inspection teams sent out from Berlin, and this is not to be wondered at. If the new Reichswehr was being cut back to less than a twentieth of its wartime peak, then the drastic reduction in materiel requirements would force the conversion to manufacture of peacetime goods in any case. Then, overnight, German attitudes hardened, cooperation vanished, and the work of the Control Commission was brought to a standstill.

On February 4, 1920, the Allied governments presented to the German Foreign Office in Berlin the names of nine hundred German officers, noncoms, and privates accused of a variety of war crimes. This Black List, as it was known, included the names of Hindenburg, Ludendorff, and other figures looked upon as national heroes. The Allies demanded that all nine hundred be extradited and handed over to the Allies for judgment before a military tribunal. Reaction was swift and negative. Trumpeted the *National Zeitung:* "Extradition is out of the question. Does the Government really think that Reichswehr officers are prepared to see their former comrades handed over to foreigners for trial?"

Just as the Allies had no success in persuading the Dutch to surrender the Kaiser, so they had none with the Germans. In an astonishingly short time, the Allies capitulated to what the Germans called a compromise: only nine days after the submission of the Black List and the extradition demand, the Allies in Paris accepted a German proposal to conduct a token trial of 113 of the accused before a civil court in Leipzig. Charges against the other 797 were dropped, including those against General von Kluck, accused of the massacre of 674 civilians in the small Belgian town of Dinant in 1914. Nor were those responsible for the sacking of Louvain, the destruction of its medieval library and the shooting of civilians there brought to trial. Regarding Louvain, Major General von Disfurth wrote for all the world to read in the pages of the *Hamburger Nachrichten:*

"We have nothing to explain, even as we have nothing to excuse. If all the monuments and all the pictures in the world be destroyed, the fact is of no importance so long as their destruction facilitates a German victory. War is war and should be conducted with the utmost harshness. The rudest stone that marks the tomb of a German grenadier is more glorious and more to be worshipped than all the cathedrals in Europe. We are called barbarians. I hope in this war we have done our best to earn the epithet."

Bearing in mind that Disfurth's attitude was by no means uncommon among the German Officers' Corps, and that even after the war civil servants held Prussian officers in awe, the outcome of the Leipzig trials was predictable—especially so, since a German general named Fransecky was on hand, holding a "watching brief" on behalf of the German Officers' Corps. "The Court," recalled a British legal officer present throughout the proceedings, "treated him with almost servile deference."*

Three generals were indicted, but the public prosecutor

---

*A servility dating back for more than a hundred years. The great English novelist Thomas Hardy produced a yellowing letter written by a friend of the family, datelined Berlin, June 1815. The writer, a well-to-do gentleman from Dorset, fulminated against Napoleon's legacy: "Buonaparte has rendered Germany completely military; at inns and post-houses a private Gentleman commands not half the respect exacted by a soldier. This contempt for those who wear no swords displays itself in no pleasant manner to travelers. About three weeks ago I might have died of damp sheets if my German servant had not taken upon himself to assure a brute of a Postmaster that I was an English general traveling for my health. . . . I have since girded on a sabre, got a military cap, and let my moustache grow. Soldiers now present arms as we pass." Hardy's keepsake letter was quoted to Colonel John Morgan, who had expressed his disgust at the farcical proceedings at Leipzig.

asked the court to dismiss the charges, and this was quickly done. Two enlisted men, guards proved guilty of brutally mal- treating prisoners of war, were let off with sentences of two and ten months, respectively. General von Fransecky did nòt dis- pute the fact that the guards had kicked and clubbed prisoners, but pointed out that Private Neumann and Sergeant Heynen were only "doing their duty," that "obedience in camps must be preserved at all costs." A major named Mueller, convicted of riding down prisoners on his horse, clubbing them, and tak- ing snapshots of sick men while they were using the outdoor camp latrines, was let off with six months. The major explained that he took the photographs "with no ill feeling, but only to commemorate my service as Commandant." Two U-boat offi- cers, Lieutenants Boldt and Dittmar, were convicted of tor- pedoing the British hospital ship *Llandovery Castle* on June 27, 1918, and machine-gunning the occupants of the three lifeboats that managed to be launched before the ship went under, carry- ing down nearly two hundred medical personnel. Only one of the lifeboats escaped the U-boat's fire; the other two vanished, one of them with fourteen nurses aboard. Dittmar and Boldt were handed the stiffest sentences of the lot—four years each —but a few weeks later they "escaped" from prison and were never rearrested.

Thus ended the Leipzig trials. The general feeling was that the German army had been vindicated, and because the Allied governments acquiesced to the outcome, showing lamentable weakness, the work of the undermanned Control Commission was even more frustrating. Factory managers became hostile and evasive. Cramon's liaison officers began quibbling over ev- ery point, their objections founded, said Colonel Morgan, on "elaborate arguments based on textual interpretations of the Treaty, upon which the Reichs War Ministry now got to work with the misplaced ingenuity of a German professor editing the corrupt text of a classical author." One depot officer refused to turn over a supply of new Zeiss rangefinders, arguing that they were indispensable for determining the heights of clouds for use in meteorological work. Another defended his stock of flamethrowers, saying they were vital to the growth of the nation's agriculture because they were perfect for spraying crops and burning insects off fruit trees. "Anyhow," he added, *"flammenwerfer* are humane weapons of war." The white-coated officials at the Mauser *Waffenfabrik,* located in an old monastary at Oberndorf-am-Neckar in the Black Forest, argued against the destruction of their lathes and other expensive tools, pointing out that the making of sporting rifles, for which Mauser was equally famous, was nowhere prohibited under the terms of the treaty. This was true enough, and the Control Commission officers had to be satisfied with confiscating the stock of rifles and carbines left inside the factory for just that purpose. Throughout Germany, a total of four and a half million rifles were uncovered and destroyed; but there were another million and a half that could not be found. The War Ministry claimed that they had all been "lost" during the retreat of November 1918.

When it came to inspection of Reichswehr units to make sure that platoons were not indeed companies and battalions regiments, the drawback of the liaison system became painfully evident. Two Control Commission officers decided to visit the Potsdam barracks, and so informed Cramon's office. Accompanied by the inevitable liaison officer, the Control Commission officers presented themselves at the barracks only to be met by a tough-looking noncom who gruffly explained that the CO, his staff, and even the adjutant were all missing. At Duisburg, Allied officers arrived to be greeted by the commanding officer and his entire staff standing at attention, but the inspection could not be carried out because the liaison officer had unaccountably failed to show up. "No doubt," commented one of the Allied officers, "the comedies had all been carefully rehearsed on the telephone before the Control officers arrived."

Tiring of practical jokes, the Reichswehr turned to physical intimidation in an effort to discourage the Control officers. At Bremen, two French officers were flung to the ground and threatened with bayonets when they insisted upon seeing the unit's muster roll. At Prenzlau and at Ingolstadt, officers were jeered and became targets of a stone-throwing crowd. At Bremen, a British naval officer was thrown off a pier and into the water. These antics cost the German government a quarter of a million dollars in fines, and although physical abuse on the part of Reichswehr troops practically ceased, the hostility remained.*

The Control Commission had the easiest time of it when faced with the problem of dissolving the German aviation industry, although the task required far longer than anybody had imagined at the time. Under the terms of the treaty—which seemed more and more to have been concocted in some kind of a dream world as the months dragged by—every piece of aeronautical equipment should have been delivered to the Allies or destroyed by April 10, 1920. Given the state of the railroads and the internal chaos that followed on the heels of the armistice, complying with Article 202 was manifestly impossible. As late as August of that year, four months past the arbitrary deadline, Control officers reported the discovery of six thousand German aircraft, intact and ready for flight. Understandably, the various manufacturers made every effort to unload substantial amounts of inventory wherever they could. Aircraft and engines were sold to Norway, Sweden, Denmark, Finland, Turkey, Latin America and Holland, and active negotiations had begun with Japan. In all, about 1000 planes and 2500 engines were gotten out of Germany—equipment the Allies had rights to as part of the huge reparations bill.

The clause prohibiting manufacture and importation of even peacetime aviation equipment severely discouraged many of the German airframe and engine makers, who put themselves out of business and saved the Control Commission the trouble. As we have noted, Fokker got out early, leaving his staff and a

---

*The French were special targets for abuse. A large, heavy parcel arrived at the French Embassy in Berlin by registered post, addressed to the ambassador. Inside was the carcass of a dog, described as being in "an advanced state of decomposition." An accompanying note written by the anonymous sender read, "The first and the last payment of Reparations!" The imperturbable French counsellor, the Comte St. Quentin, merely forwarded the dead dog to the German Foreign Office, noting that the original sender had failed to comply with the required German veterinary regulations.

few workers to struggle unsuccessfully with making and distributing canoes, household scales and welded bedsteads. Gotha, Friedrichshafen, and DFW (Deutsche Flugzeugwerke) in Berlin folded, as did the aviation department of the giant AEG corporation. The Pfalz works in Speyer went under, and so did the Siemens-Schuckert plant after completing its run of D.IV fighters. Only two of the D.IVs eventually survived, one going to Switzerland, the other eagerly taken over by a clandestine aviation detachment at Aldershof for high-altitude research. The Control Commission protested in vain at the retention of this fighter, but were never able to force its surrender or destruction. The remaining major manufacturers—Junkers, Heinkel, and Dornier—decided to hang on somehow, hoping the air would clear so that Germany's aviation future would not be forfeit.

Despite the agonizing slowness with which Germany was being disarmed, the Control Commission was halved in the summer of 1921, leaving only 174 officers and 400 men of other ranks to deal with the recalcitrant Reichswehr. Moreover, the Allies' "big stick," the Army of Occupation, was whittled drastically that same summer, until by August only 106,000 troops of all classes remained on German territory, and more than two-thirds of them were French. Although the German air force was officially dissolved in the spring of 1920, it was not until September 24 of the following year that the Control Commission was able to submit a list that detailed the stripping of Germany of virtually everything that could fly. The account, as rendered to the Air Ministry in London, was a reminder of just how industrious the Germans had been right up to the end:

In a seeming paradox, it was the remaining handful of German aviation industrialists who impatiently awaited the total destruction of the warplanes they had helped create. The Versailles Treaty had originally specified that not even commercial aviation could commence inside Germany until the six-month period had elapsed, that is, until April 10, 1920. But because the schedule of destruction lagged so far behind, the Allies, in a conference held in Boulogne on June 22 of that year, set this time period back until three months after the Control Commission had satisfied itself that the Air Clauses had been executed. Only then could commercial dreams, born and nourished during the final year of the war, begin to materialize.

Among those who fidgeted, while watching wartime profits dwindle, was Adolf Rohrbach, one of Zeppelin's chief designers at Staaken, near Berlin. One of Rohrbach's confrères described him as "tall, slim, a grand seigneur, very popular with women, a man of the world, elegant, charming. He made others around him look *petit bourgeois.*" Rohrbach was also considerably ahead of any other designer and visionary, and in the interim period between the Armistice and the arrival of the Control Commission, he had created the world's first prototype of a true passenger airliner. Rohrbach's creation, known as the E.20, was an all-metal craft, as elegant and slender as the man who designed it. The single, cantilevered wing was set high on the narrow fuselage, and was so thick in airfoil section that a mechanic could crawl between the ribs to service the engines while in flight. It carried four of these engines, 260 horsepower Daimler Mercedes inline and water-cooled, and the multiwindowed passenger cabin was fitted with eighteen seats. Rohrbach and his co-workers envisioned nation-spanning arcs through the sky from Berlin to Paris, Rome, Moscow, and beyond. The English Channel would be reduced to its proper proportions as a saltwater ditch. Flights between the capital cities of Europe would become commonplace for tourist and businessman alike. Since nothing like the E.20 existed anywhere in the world, air-minded countries would be standing in line for deliveries of an airliner that was years ahead of its time.

The E.20 never flew. Flushed with the eventual success in seeing Germany's wartime inventory or planes and engines put to the torch, and lacking firm guidelines as to what constituted the significant difference between civil and military multiengined aircraft, officers of the Control Commission ordered the E.20 destroyed. Rohrbach pointed out that the E.20 had been designed as a purely commercial ship from the time the first line was sketched in on drafting paper, that had he wished to design a bomber, he would have done so. But neither his charm nor his logic made the difference: torches went to work on the gleaming metal, cutting the wings loose from the fuselage and excising the engines from the mounts. Axes smashed in the windows. The upholstered seats were ripped out. The tail section was removed. The resulting junk was shoved into a corner of the factory and forgotten.

So energetic had the Control Commission become in the one area where it was effective, aviation, that it countermanded its own orders. Earlier the Commission had given permission for the German government to retain possession of a hundred and fifty surplus two-seaters to be used for a variety of civilian purposes; but when these aircraft appeared in Riga and Vienna, Control officers were waiting with new orders for their demolition. They even descended upon the Junkers factory and seized the enclosed cabin monoplanes ordered by General Billy Mitchell, although this mistake was rectified soon afterwards.

By the beginning of 1922, almost the only things German that could be seen flying in German skies were birds and homemade gliders. In two years the executors of the Versailles Treaty had rendered Germany barren of wings; but there was no formula for robbing the German will to fly, and fly armed.

4
TO HIDE AN ARMY

The fame of the Flying Corps engraved in the history of the German
armed forces will never fade. It is not dead; its spirit lives onl
—General Hans von Seeckt

With Prussian officers, correct behavior had been a point of honor. With
German officers, it must be a point of honor to be sly.
—General Werner von Blomberg

Just frequently enough in a nation's history, the right tool comes
to hand when the government gropes for the means of continued survival. Following the abortive Kapp putsch, the point
was driven home to President Ebert's Majority Socialists how
imperative it was for the new national army to be welded together by a man whose devotion to his trade exceeded political
ambition, a thorough professional who would create the finest
possible armed force within the limits of the Treaty of Versailles. Moreover, this commander should be a man of the times;
forward looking, yet not unmindful of worthwhile tradition. He
would work with the government, not against it, and would
know how to deal sensibly with reactionary and republican
alike. He would manifest strength, but not obstinacy, and would
have a far broader outlook on the turbulent, changing currents
of world affairs than the average Prussian officer of the old
Imperial Army.

This paragon was found in the form of General Hans von
Seeckt, whose name was almost unknown outside of German
military circles, but who had been the architect (as a brilliant
staff officer) of severe defeats handed to the French in the early
months of the war, and against the Russians at Gorlice in the
spring of 1915. Seeckt was fifty-four when, in March 1920, he was
appointed *Chef der Heeresleitung,* Chief of the Army Com-

mand, but he had a figure any prima ballerina would envy: erect, narrow waisted, lean hipped, elegant in every line. Above the stiff uniform collar, glittering at the throat with the Pour le Mérite, Seeckt's somewhat oversized head rested on a slender neck. The eyes were wide-spaced and thoughtful, marked with the downward-slanting fold of lid that is characteristically Prussian. A monocle rested naturally over his left eye. Seeckt had retained his hair, brushed to either side to reveal a broad forehead, buttressing the opinion of one of his contemporaries "that [Seeckt] is too intelligent to be a general."

The British Ambassador, Lord d'Abernon, upon seeing Seeckt for the first time, thought the German's face "severe . . . reminding one of 'General into Fox.'" After several encounters with the new Chef der Heeresleitung, however, Lord d'Abernon was moved to observe that Seeckt "has few of the fox characteristics, being an honorable man and even a punctilious man." He exhibited "a broader mind than is expected in so tight a uniform; a wider outlook than seems appropriate to so precise, so correct, so neat an exterior." Seeckt's broad perspective was gained partly through wide-ranging travels throughout the Continent, to Africa, and as far east as India, where he struck up a friendship with Lord Kitchener; and partly through a naturally curious mind whose interests transcended the boundaries usually imposed by aristocratic birth into a Pomeranian family with a largely military tradition. Hans von Seeckt was as adept in discussing music, literature, and painting as he was in outlining the strategic deployment of armies, and could converse in French or English with ease. An officer of the Emperor Alexander Guards Grenadier Regiment at nineteen, named to the General Staff Corps at thirty-three, Chief of Staff of the Third Corps when the war began, defender of the *Reich* frontiers against the Bolsheviks and the Poles when the war was over, conqueror of Riga, military member of the Peace Commission at Versailles, Seeckt was better qualified than any other German general to be Hindenburg's replacement. Economical with words, a commander given to keeping his own counsel, The Sphinx—as he was known to those who worked with him—did not reveal publicly until years afterward that his primary mission was to "neutralize the poison contained in the disarmament clauses of the Treaty." To this end Seeckt now moved.

From the moment he assumed command, Seeckt knew precisely what kind of Reichswehr he wanted to build: a hand-picked, elite force of officers and men mentally equipped and rigorously trained to perform a multitude of roles. Truck drivers would know how to service field guns; cooks and bakers would be proficient with machine guns; quartermaster clerks could be quickly formed into rifle squads; sergeants would be able to lead platoons, and lieutenants, battalions. "The whole future of warfare," noted Seeckt in 1921, "appears to me to be in the employment of mobile armies, relatively small but of high quality, and rendered distinctly more effective by the addition of aircraft." What was not realized at the time, nor for a long time afterward, was that The Sphinx was outlining the basis for *Blitzkrieg* warfare as the world would later know it; Seeckt, the intellectual strategist and tactician, was already thinking in warfare's second dimension, dynamics, and in its third dimension, the air. Seeckt's grasp of air power's potential function in the kind of mobile army he envisioned was perhaps greater than that of any other Prussian general officer; but his vision was tempered by the knowledge that the re-creation inside Germany of an operational air arm would be impossible to conceal from the Control Commission. His first move to keep the spirit of the defunct air service alive while he worked on a scheme to resurrect its body was to choose three experienced squadron and group commanders to work directly under him in the *Truppenamt,* the Troop Office, whose function was almost precisely the same as the outlawed General Staff. These three aviators were shortly afterward joined by a dozen others, and acted as a general brain trust for the entire Reichswehr. This corps of airmen formed the *Fliegerzentrale,* Flying Center, a name carefully hidden from the Allies. Seeckt, over the objections of the jittery Personnel Office inside the Defense Ministry, pulled in another 180 pilots and distributed them in the various military districts, creating air cells throughout the major commands. The function of these men without wings was to somehow inculcate air-mindedness throughout the army, while reminding ground commanders on maneuvers to take into account the actions of warplanes, friendly and enemy, when planning their tactics. Thus the framework of future German air power was knit together, with a skeleton invisible from the outside.

These air officers discovered that Seeckt was effecting a radical change in the atmosphere and the way of life in the new army; Prussian discipline, as they had known it, had all but vanished. The relationship between officers and men remained strictly correct, but the oppressive and even brutal discipline resulting in senseless abuses that had prevailed since the time of the Napoleonic Wars was a thing of the past. Seeckt had studied the psychology of the German fighting man and knew that the old rules simply would not do in a compact, elite force where there would not be such qualitative differences between officers, noncoms and privates.

When the old Imperial German Air Service had its beginnings in 1915, it was common practice for the observer to be an officer seated in the rear cockpit, leaving the donkey work of piloting to a sergeant. A rough ride—usually occasioned by low-level atmospheric conditions about which the officer understood nothing—or a mistake in navigation, or failure to observe the military amenities while aloft was sufficient cause for vilification and a thrashing with the officer's riding crop while still airborne; these measures were hardly conducive to efficient teamwork. It was far worse for the ground troops.

In the old Army Penal Code, the *Militärstrafgesetzbuch,* which Seeckt was having rewritten, the enlisted man was totally at the mercy of his superiors, especially at the hands of the noncoms. Close arrest meant up to a month in a cramped cell that was totally dark, on a diet of day-old bread and tap water. Physical abuse of enlisted men by officers and noncoms was not only tolerated under the Army Penal Code, it was encouraged in the interests of discipline. A French innkeeper's wife in the little village of La Ferté sous Jouarre on the Marne recounted to a British liaison officer what happened when a German cavalry private forgot to hang a lantern outside his troop commander's quarters as ordered. "Von Bülow knocked him down, and then, as he lay prostrate, jumped upon him, kicked him, and finally beat him about the head and face, alternately with saber and riding whip. The soldier lay quite still and never uttered a word—*pas un mot!*"

Recruits, as in any army, were victimized, but in ways not permitted in the Anglo-Saxon forces. A one-time Prussian trooper named Kape, a large, cropped-hair youth, described to Colonel John Morgan how his *Unter-Offiziere,* his noncoms, amused themselves when Kape was caught in some minor infraction of barrack rules. "They used to make me dance on top of a hot oven with bare feet in my shirt while they whistled the tune of 'Little Marie Sat Dreaming in the Garden.' The oven was so hot that I had to dance the whole time."

The astonished Morgan said, "But, good heavens, man, why didn't you complain to an officer?"

"That wouldn't have been any good," Kape said impatiently. "I could only have complained to the *Feldwebel* (the Sergeant-Major), and he would have said, 'What! You *Schweinhund,* you complain of an *Unter-Offizier!* Take that!' And he would have boxed my ears soundly."

Morgan pursued the subject of Prussian discipline, so alien to his own twentieth-century British code prohibiting any kind of physical maltreatment, and once induced an officer of the 25th Dragoons to defend the system. Major Wolff confessed that, except for the Saxons, "N.C.O.s were often very brutal . . . but officers did not approve of that sort of thing." He explained how "paternalistic" most German officers were, calling to mind a commanding officer who always offered delinquent soldiers their choice of punishment: three days' confinement to barracks, or a box on the ear, *eine Ohrfeige.* Morgan explains that "a box on the ear from the heavy fist of a Prussian officer was a knockout blow, calculated to break the ear-drum." He learned later that any soldier foolish enough to opt for close confinement would be dealt both sentences.

It was the immeasurable gulf between the officer class and the other ranks, coupled with the smoldering resentment against draconian punishments meted out for the slightest infractions, that had helped ignite the flames of open rebellion within the army during the final soul-draining weeks of the war. Seeckt was determined that the seeds of hatred sown among the soldiery by nineteenth-century attitudes toward discipline would have no chance to take root in the Reichswehr of his making. Any discipline worthy of the name is based upon respect running a reciprocal course, and this means willing soldiers led by totally competent superior officers, the chain of command linked together by literate noncoms who realize that shame is a sharper remedial tool for honing inherent pride than a blow on the side of the head.

In choosing officers and men for the microcosmic army, there was an embarrassment of riches. The Reich totaled more than sixty million people, of which some eight million were of military age, and only four thousand officers were allowed. The disguised Great General Staff, the Truppenamt, could be especially ruthless in its selection of officer trainees for staff work. Applicants were required to possess not only great skills in the military sciences, but a thoroughgoing knowledge of languages, history, political science, communications, railway systems and a general familiarity with cultural subjects. Because the War Academy had been closed by order of the Control Commission, entrance examinations were held instead. The first aspirants for the exalted Truppenamt included 164 officers who sat through the grueling examinations. Four months later, only the top 20 were passed into a special school for leader's assistants, the *Führergehilfsenausbildung,* from which only six emerged as contenders. Three years later, one of the six was finally posted to Berlin with the privilege of wearing red tabs on his collar. Qualifications for field officers were almost as rigorous, and any man who could not qualify in a written and oral examination for the next higher grade was summarily dismissed to make room for one who could.

Through a major oversight on the part of those responsible for drafting the Disarmament Clauses of the Treaty, no limitation was placed on the number of noncommissioned officers allowed in the new Reichswehr. Seeckt seized upon this piece of carelessness and filled the ranks with forty thousand NCOs, or almost one noncom to every private, about eight times as many as are required. Every one of these noncoms was officer material, with an educational background far exceeding that of the world's average. The cream of the noncoms were installed in the Reichswehr, and other tough and experienced squad leaders were hidden in the Prussian Police and in the ranks of the Security Police, or SIPO. The Prussian Police numbered eighty-five thousand men, equipped with machine guns, rifles, pistols, rubber truncheons and armored cars, who were trained along military lines. The Security Police had been formed out of the remnants of the Prussian Guard in Berlin during the frantic days following the revolution and numbered nine thousand men, equivalent to a full infantry division. The Control Commission tried in vain to have the *Sicherheitspolizei* disbanded, but the demands were either met with silence or with explanations that the SIPOs were needed for internal security.

There was no lack of volunteers to be ordinary privates in Seeckt's new army. For every volunteer, ten could be turned away. Jews were automatically put into the same category as Marxists, and anyone even suspected of leftist sympathies was rejected. Young men of peasant stock were shown preference over those from cities and industrial areas, and sons of former noncoms were welcomed most of all. Only superb physical specimens were considered. Postwar recruits entered a world their fathers had never known. The barracks were larger and more cheerful; each man had a bunk on the floor and no one sleeping above him; the army cooks were reeducated, and the recruits found that the food was not only ample but tasty; officers and NCOs were sometimes loud, usually stern—but never mindlessly cruel. Curfew was far more lenient, and mandatory church parade was abolished. There were constant challenges in learning how to field strip and operate every light weapon in the Reichswehr inventory, and the emphasis was upon field exercises and vigorous sports programs instead of mind-dulling, spine-jarring hours of close-order drill known by the British as square bashing.

Probably in no other army was morale so high, especially

since not one of the recruits was actually required to sign up for the full twelve-year hitch, as laid down by the Versailles Treaty. While making his rounds of the various units, Colonel John Morgan discovered that the men were being recruited on a six- and twelve-month basis, then illegally passed into a masked reserve. A kind of double-entry bookkeeping was maintained, but when Morgan chanced upon the genuine muster roll of one unit, he discovered that a great number of ostensible privates were actually being paid incomes due an NCO. Morgan, as head of the Effectives Subcommission, routinely reported his findings, which were routinely sent to the German Defense Ministry with a complaint, which was just as routinely explained away or ignored.

Seeckt's job was made easier by the replacement of Gustav Noske as Defense Minister on March 24, 1920, by Otto Karl Gessler, forty-five, a wooden-faced, drowsy-eyed, bullet-headed lawyer from Nuremburg. Unlike Noske, Gessler was not a doctrinaire Republican, but a self-styled Democrat; in the political alignments of the time, this put Gessler much further to the Right than his predecessor. His chief value to the German Truppenamt, however, lay in his lack of character. Contemporary military men referred to Gessler as a "man of straw," a "purely ornamental being." The Control Commission's General Nollet said of Gessler: "He confined himself to signing the decisions of General von Seeckt. . . . It was under the cover of his name and of his political authority that von Seeckt carried out his work of reorganization." In short, Gessler was a rubber stamp, a man of no integrity whose sole ambition was to remain in his post, which he managed to do through numerous changes of government in the coming eight years. To Seeckt, Gessler was almost beneath contempt—but he was the Reichswehr's most valuable civilian handmaiden, and The Sphinx took care not to let his true feelings show.

By the beginning of 1921, Hans von Seeckt was able to feel a justifiable pride in his creation, and knew his position was secure. To the Reichswehr, he announced, "The army is finally formed. A new chapter in the history of the German army begins. . . . we vow to stand together in devotion to our profes-

sion. We want to keep the sword sharp and the shield shining.
. . . Called upon to protect the Fatherland, the army and every
soldier must be filled with a burning love of the Fatherland,
willing to sacrifice his life, loyal to his oath and in the fulfillment
of his duty. The army," he reminded Germany, "is the first
instrument of the power of the Reich."

To keep the sword sharp, Seeckt forced the battalions on the
move in a series of field maneuvers designed to test the efficiency of divisional staff work and to discover any lack of cohe-
sion in the newly organized combat units. Keenly aware of the
value of military tradition, Seeckt assigned to each unit the
battle honors, banners, customs and traditions of one of the old
Imperial Army regiments; thus one of the new infantry companies numbering less than three hundred men was charged with
the duty of maintaining the glory of, say, the Prussian Grenadier Guards Regiment that once mustered three thousand and
which could trace its heritage back to the eighteenth century.
In line with his beliefs that the next war would be fought by
highly mobile armies, Seeckt created the closest thing to motorized divisions the Versailles Treaty allowed, and sent them on
realistic mock invasions of the rugged Harz Mountains in south-
central Germany. The troops, burdened only with the lightest
combat loads, were carried to their jumpoff points in trucks, and
a handful of thin-skinned armored cars represented tanks.
While the regimental commander deployed his forces to seize
this or that objective, one of the aviation advisors attached to
the division stood by to remind him to take into account the role
air power would play in actual combat. Somebody would cry
out, *"Achtung! Flugzeug!"* and the troops would dive for cover
while machine guns were elevated to spray imaginary attacking
aircraft. The air officer, recalling his own experiences in the
skies over France, reminded the younger men to cut undergrowth and camouflage their vehicles, so visible from the air.
The battalion commander placed imaginary telephone calls to
nonexistent airdromes requesting reconnaissance over enemy
lines, then invented invisible artillery regulating machines
wirelessing back coordinates to ghostly batteries so that strong
points could be shelled. They imagined fleets of bombers wing-

ing overhead, on their way to bomb the enemy's lines of communication, protected by squadrons of swift and well-armed fighters.

It was a pathetic way to practice air-ground cooperation, and the impossibility of rebuilding Germany's air arm inside the partially occupied and controlled national frontiers caused Seeckt to turn his gaze to the east—across the Elbe, the Bug, the Don, and the Volga—to Moscow, the heart of Communist Russia, where the immediate problem could be solved.

Russia was not a signatory to the Treaty of Versailles, nor had it been invited to join the League of Nations; obligated only to self-interest, it was beyond Allied control or sanctions. Russia's limitless spaces, remote from Western observation or interference, offered factory sites, proving grounds, and tactical training areas for an air force as large as Germany wanted or could afford. Germany and Russia had in common the status of world outcasts, and even more binding, an expedient fear and hatred of Poland, another loathesome child of Versailles. Polish forces, encouraged by the French, were trying to push their way deeper into Upper Silesia, fighting against twenty battalions of illegal German volunteers, and were driving to the east against the distinctly unhomogenized Red Army.

In a private memorandum, Seeckt made his feelings about the future of Poland crystal clear: "Poland's existence is intolerable and incompatible with the survival of Germany. Poland must disappear, and will disappear through her own inner weakness and through Russia—with our help. With Poland collapses one of the strongest pillars of the Peace of Versailles, France's advance post of power. Poland is more intolerable for Russia than for ourselves. The attainment of this objective must be one of the firmest guiding principles of German policy; it is capable of achievement—but only through Russia or with her help. Poland can never offer any advantage to Germany, either economically, because she is incapable of development, or politically, because she is a vassal of France. The restoration of the frontier between Russia and Germany is a necessary condition before both sides can become strong. The 1914 frontier between

Russia and Germany should be the basis of understanding between the two countries. . . .

"We want two things: Firstly, a strong Russia, economically, politically, and therefore militarily; thus indirectly [we create] a stronger Germany inasmuch as we would be strengthening a possible ally. We also want, cautiously and tentatively at first, a direct increase of strength for ourselves by helping to build up in Russia an armaments industry which in case of need would be of use to us.

"Our first aim would, of course, be directly promoted by such an armaments industry carried out by private German firms and would follow our instructions. The extent of this development would depend upon how the situation in Russia progressed, and upon the efficiency and goodwill of German private industry. . . ."

In an astonishing few sentences, Seeckt revealed his true feelings regarding the ascendancy of the General Staff over the civilian government. "In all these enterprises," he cautioned, "participation and even official recognition by the German government would be absolutely out of the question. The detailed negotiations could only be conducted by military authorities. . . .

"The German nation, with its Socialist majority, would be averse to a policy of action, which has to reckon with the possibility of war. It must be admitted that the spirit surrounding the Peace Delegation at Versailles has not yet disappeared, and that the stupid cry of 'No more war!' is widely echoed. It is echoed by many pacifist-bourgeois elements—but among the workers and among the members of the official Social Democrat party, there are many who are not prepared to eat out of the hands of Poland and France. . . . The clearest heads, when considering the pros and cons of war, will be those of the military, but to pursue a policy means to take the lead. In spite of everything, the German people will follow the leader in the struggle for their existence. Our task is to prepare for this struggle, for we shall not be spared it. . . ."

Tentative overtures were made to the Soviets early in 1920, but it was not until the Red Army's defeat before the gates of

Warsaw late that year that the Russians clearly saw the need for some kind of Russian-German alliance in order to reorganize the Soviet forces. Lenin, then fifty, stated his feelings realistically. "I am not fond of the Germans by any means," he told his followers, "but at the present time it is more advantageous to use them than to challenge them. An independent Poland is very dangerous to Soviet Russia: it is an evil, however, [that] also has its redeeming features; for while it exists we may safely count on Germany, because the Germans hate Poland and will at any time make common cause with us in order to strangle Poland. . . . Germany wants revenge, and we want revolution. For the moment, our aims are the same." Then Lenin cautioned, "When our ways part, [however], they will be our most ferocious and our greatest enemies. Time will tell whether a German hegemony or a Communist federation is to arise out of the ruins of Europe."

The new Russian leaders certainly held no illusions concerning German magnanimity when they were victors: The Treaty of Brest-Litovsk that had ended the tsarist war with Germany in 1918 had stripped Russia of its breadbasket, the Ukraine, and other territory with a population of 56 million; a third of its rail lines; more than five thousand factories; almost 90 percent of Russian's coal and 73 per cent of its iron ore; and a huge indemnity amounting to 6 billion marks, about 1½ billion dollars. The ruthless and bloody suppression of the German Communist movement and the murder of its leaders left no doubt as to the Reichswehr's feelings toward Lenin's revolution. Yet, where else could the Bolsheviks turn? Principles and ideals were shelved for the sake of political and military expediency, and the two natural enemies moved toward rapprochement.

In the early spring of 1921, Lenin made formal application to the Reichswehr for help in overhauling the Red Army. Within less than four weeks, on May 6, the German-Russian Commercial Agreement was signed. In preparation for the more detailed military arrangements to follow, German agents in mufti visited Russia and were given tours of the major industrial works and Red Army and Red Air Force training centers. They returned to Germany unimpressed, but brought back the news that the Bolsheviks, according to Karl Radek, thirty-six, the Leninist go-between, "intended to attack Poland again and needed, above all, airplanes." The pilot officers inside Flieger-zentrale in Berlin were not surprised that aviation should be given priority by the Soviets; tsarist pilots with whom they had dueled along the Eastern Front had been almost suicidally brave, but they flew mainly obsolescent craft, were chronically outnumbered, and obviously were backed up by pitiful mainte-nance, repair, and production facilities.

Tsar Nicholas II was an enthusiast and patron of Russian avia-tion, and when the war began in 1914, the Imperial Air Services, army, and navy shared between them 224 aircraft, a dozen small airships, and a number of captive balloons. One of the world's top designers, Igor Sikorsky, was busy sketching new plans, and his work had so pleased the tsar that he had been presented with a handsome gold watch by Nicholas in person. Besides Sikorsky, there were three other major air frame manufacturers in Russia—Dux, in Moscow; Russo-Baltic, near Riga; and the V. A. Lebedov concern, at Petrograd—but the dismal atmosphere of graft and general inefficiency prevalent inside the court filtered down to factory level, and by the time the Red Revolution broke out in 1917, only 4700 aircraft of all kinds had been turned out (less than a tenth the number pro-duced by Germany at war's end), and a great proportion of these were French and British designs built under license, sometimes with disastrous results. The Russo-Baltic Wagon Works was licensed to build spare wings for the handy little Nieuport fighters, but when they were fitted to fuselages built by Dux, inexplicable and usually fatal crashes occurred. A French technical mission finally discovered the reason: the Im-perial War Office, for reasons best known to itself, had altered French plans and passed them on to the Russo-Baltic factory. Built with these alterations, wings were fitted to the supporting struts with only one-half the required angle of incidence; thus, when pilots put the nose down with reduced power to enter a glide, the planes simply nosedived into the ground. The Rus-sians ordered a variety of completed, but disassembled, planes from France, Britain and America, but they had to come via the distant ports of Archangel and Murmansk, and so chaotic were rail conditions that few of the crates ever reached their destinations in the interior.

The Russians produced at least three great pilots and three woman military aviators. However, none of the great pilots was a revolutionary, and their services were not available to Lenin's Red Air Force. Staff Captain Alexander Alexandrovich Kazakov, a giant, blue-eyed former cavalry officer sporting an eight-inch moustache, shot down seventeen Germans before the Revolution; afterwards, gazetted major in the Royal Air Force, he shot down an unknown number of Red Russian pilots during the civil war. Ivan Smirnoff bagged a dozen Germans before a friendly mechanic of Smirnoff's 19th Squadron warned him to flee before he was murdered by the outfit's revolutionary-minded enlisted men; this he did, and eventually became an airline pilot for the Dutch. Lieutenant Commander Alexander Procofieff de Seversky, a graduate of the Imperial Naval Academy, became one of the world's best-known aviation experts, both as prophet and as designer. His first night bombing mission very nearly proved his last. On the night of July 2, 1915, de Seversky's two-seater seaplane was shot down in the Baltic. He happened to be carrying a small bomb inside the cockpit, and when the airplane struck the water, the bomb exploded. The observer was killed outright, and de Seversky's right leg was blown off. He survived to become, first, Inspector of Aircraft Production; then he was transferred to fighters, and shot down thirteen German planes in fifty-seven missions. In September 1917 de Seversky was sent to Washington as part of the Russian naval air mission—and stayed there after the Bolsheviks seized power.

The female pilots, oddities at the time in the Imperial Russian Air Services, included Princess Sophie Alexandrovna Dolgorunaya, attached to the 26th Corps Air Squadron by permission of Kerensky; Princess Eugenie Shakhovskaya, who, by the grace of the Tsar, was posted to the front as a reconnaissance pilot after she pointed out she had been flying since 1911 on good American equipment built by Glenn Curtiss, and under expert German instruction; and the untitled—but nonetheless noble—

Nadeshka Degtereva, who managed in the rush of the 1914 mobilization to slip fully clothed through a Russian army physical and was accepted as an aviation cadet at the training center near Sevastopol. Wounded in action by Austrian gunfire in 1915, Nadeshka's masquerade came to an end when the doctor stripped off her flying clothes to treat wounds in an arm and a leg.

The war with Germany, the disruptive Revolution, and the civil war had left Lenin and his military overseer, Leon Trotsky, virtually nothing with which to build up a Red air force. Almost all of the top pilots had either been killed or, as we have noted, gone over to fly under Western ideology. Morale among even the regulars had begun to crack as early as the summer of 1917, when some Russian squadrons were logging an average of only six hours per month per pilot. On June 11 of that year, an old German LVG marked with Russian roundels set down on a British field in Macedonia. The pilot, Staff Captain Smolianinov, explained to Captain H. A. Jones that he had flown from Rumania across hostile Bulgaria to join the Allies "in the hope of getting more fighting." Jones went on to say that Smolianinov "had been flying almost continuously since the beginning of the war, mostly on captured German machines. . . ."

During the civil war between the Whites and the Reds that began in 1918, those Russian fliers who sided with the Revolutionists found themselves facing not only White Russians, but experienced Royal Air Force pilots sent over by the British as part of the abortive joint Allied Expeditionary Force to help quell the uprising. Russians, flying a heterogeneous collection of captured Fokkers, homebuilt Nieuports, and imported Spads, went up against such men as Raymond Collishaw, the Canadian with sixty-three kills, and other aces of the 47th Squadron flying the latest Sopwith Snipes. The resulting casualties further whittled down the corps' number of experienced—and politically secure—Russian pilots, leaving no Richthofen-like characters alive upon which to build tradition. Skilled factory workers had abandoned their tools to join one side or the other, and the factories lay mouldering. Facing what they considered to be their greatest enemy, Poland, with her French-equipped squadrons and advisors, it is little wonder that the Soviets were ready to embrace the Reichswehr air officers and the recent enemy's almost limitless number of technicians, designers, and experienced industrial supervisors.

To deal with the Russians and to prepare the way for what was bound to be the painfully slow re-creation of the German air force on foreign soil, Seeckt organized *Sondergruppe R,* Special Group R[ussia], within the Truppenamt in Berlin. At its head was the former German Chief of Intelligence, Colonel Nikolai, and the higher echelon included Colonel Oskar von Niedermayer, whose daring wartime forays into Afghanistan and Persia earned him fame as the German T. E. Lawrence; Major Fritz Schunke, who had served with Seeckt in Turkey in 1918; General Otto Hasso, and Major Kurt von Schleicher, a former Freikorps commander and generally considered to have one of the finest brains in the Reichswehr. With Sondergruppe R functioning, Seeckt not long afterward established a German military mission in the Russian capital, known as *Zentrale Moskau.* The ubiquitous Niedermayer was attached to Moscow Central, under the command of Colonel von der Lieth-Thomsen, onetime Chief of Air Staff for the old Imperial Air Service. Both Niedermayer and Lieth-Thomsen were ostensibly put on the retired list during their sojourn in Russia, but picked up back pay and uniforms when they returned to the Fatherland. To all intents and purposes, these stiffly erect, cropped-headed men in tightly cut gray suits were merely German civilians engaged in some kind of business activities requiring long periods away from home.

All that was needed was an official treaty between Russia and Germany to sanctify the union—a treaty that would not, of course, spell out the military details of the new alliance. This was accomplished in the Italian town of Rapallo on April 16, 1922. The Treaty of Rapallo reestablished commercial and diplomatic relations between the two countries, which had been sundered by the war, re-created by the Treaty of Brest-Litovsk, and resundered by the Treaty of Versailles. The Allied Powers, then holding their own conference up the coast at Genoa, were understandably disconcerted at this unexpected turn of events.

They were already looking ahead to their own rapid disarmament, as set forth in the Covenant of the League of Nations, and the realization of a Russo-German entente was no promise for stability in Europe or for peace in the world.

5

CRADLE OF DECEIT

We young Germans who traveled to the Rhoen, starving and freezing,
did so without any idea of a war of revenge in the future. We did it
because we did not want to give up our dream of flying.
—Captain Hermann Steiner

But the Control Commission, I said. Where are we going to build our
kites?
—Ernst Heinkel

The understanding with Russia and the clandestine exchange of
military missions between Moscow and Berlin augured well for
the future of German military aviation. But the Rapallo Treaty
was an augury only; everything had to be built from scratch,
and it was not until three years after the treaty was signed that
German pilots first began training in Russian skies. However,
meaningful ferment continued at home during the interim.

The impetus to somehow maintain the self-indulgent uplift of
spirit that flight brings—in the discouraging and depressing
conditions prevailing in Germany in the first years after the war
—was explained by an ex-Gotha pilot, Captain Hermann
Steiner, who had destroyed his bomber on the ground by exploding a fuel tank only minutes after word was passed that, as
his observer put it, "The Armistice had broken out." Said
Steiner: "We had had a better living than the rest of the army;
we had better uniforms, better food, and we had more time to
ourselves. We were an aggressive sort—and we felt ourselves to
be an elite. The fact that our morale was excellent, while the
mass of the German Army was in a state of demoralization, did
not have so much to do with material things as with our mentality, the special mentality of fliers everywhere in the world.

Flying somewhere in the immense ether, often alone, made us feel superior to the little beings down below, to the small business being enacted miles beneath us. . . . We had a special sort of pride.

"And now that the war had ended, our superiority, although perhaps imaginary, seemed to come to an end as well. What were we going to do? Most of us were very young; in fact, most of us had left school to become fliers. Now we had no place to go, we had nothing to do. . . . we felt nostalgia. We looked for and object for our dreams, an object for our idealism. Most of us determined to go on flying, no matter what the peace conditions might be, no matter what would be allowed or forbidden in the future. . . . This nostalgia for something better, for something higher (in the best sense of the word), this passion for flying—which with many of us was almost a sickness—grew stronger and stronger during the next few years of revolution, inflation and unemployment, when life became all but hopeless and without point for a great part of the German people. For many of us, flying became the very meaning of life."

Steiner, whose interest in military aviation went up with the black smoke from his blazing Gotha, entered a university in the Rhineland to pursue a career in aeronautical engineering. Like so many other ex-officers, he had no civilian clothes, nor money to buy any on the flourishing postwar black market. He cut the brass military buttons from his tunic, substituted ones of bone, and reported to class looking like so many others—like officers who had been stripped of honors and drummed out of service. The longing among Steiner and other flying men to once again break the shackles that bound them to earth grew to be an obsession. They coupled practical experience in aerodynamics with textbook theory to design man-carrying gliders which were hardly more sophisticated than the ones flown by the great German pioneer, Otto Lilienthal, himself killed in a glider crash in 1896, victim of imperfectly understood control forces. Students who were fortunate enough to find nighttime jobs in nearby factories managed to scrounge wood, wire and fabric, and community efforts in abandoned sheds resulted in small, crude-looking gliders: a pod to encase the pilot up to his shoulders, a narrow wing overhead, narrow booms running to his back to carry the tail assembly. Because of the terrific freight charges on railroads to ship fully assembled gliders, they were designed to come apart in sections, and packed in more manageable crates and transported to the Rhoen mountain region in central Germany. "We took them ourselves into the freight cars," Steiner recalled, "and hovered over them, defending our contraptions passionately against the mistrustful stares of the railway employees who were pretty sure we were crazy. In a way, we probably were."

The gliders were assembled at the base of the Wasserkuppe, a mountain towering over the town of Gersfeld, and laboriously dragged to the top and launched into the wind for a few heady, precious moments of flight—then hauled all the way up again with a tow rope. There was, of course, no question of the students' being able to afford a room at the inn in Gersfeld; they slept outside under the stars on the first night of a delicious summer holiday from the university—then under a sodden blanket of fog and rain for two weeks straight when the weather broke and moisture rolled down from the sky and from the flanks of the brooding Wasserkuppe. Some of the pilots slept inside eiderdown bags, others curled awkwardly inside the coffinlike shipping crates; what blankets and tarps had been brought along were used to protect the precious gliders from the rain.

When the skies cleared and the sunshine flooded the valley again, the competitions began in earnest. Steiner was lofted from the mountain and remained airborne for an entire minute. A man named Klemperer beat this time by thirty seconds, only to have the record toppled by Steiner's two minutes flat. Klemperer regained the title with two and a half minutes aloft, a record that held in Germany until the following year. Among the many onlookers who gathered in the valley near Gersfeld to witness the resurrection of a sport dead for more then twenty years was a young, good-looking wartime flier, Captain Kurt Student, and his stunning wife. Student exhibited keen interest in the gliders and in the men who labored so hard to earn brief moments in the air. Unknown to the others, Student was one of the hidden air officers in the Truppenamt, handpicked by Seeckt as that department's technical advisor. Steiner recalled that not long afterward, many of the more enthusiastic glider pilots were provided with money and materials with which to extend their experiments in powerless flight. The subsidies were provided by the innocuous-sounding Ministry of Transport, but the funds were actually withdrawn from the Reichswehr budget. No strings were attached to these windfalls, other than strong suggestions that future experiments "be conducted along half-military lines," an ambiguous request that was difficult to comprehend or to implement.

Other Truppenamt emissaries fanned out through the remains of Germany's industrial empire, seeking support for the various secret rearmament projects. One of the most enthusiastic collaborators was Gustav Krupp von Bohlen and Halbach, who had been forced to stand by and watch as the Control Commission dismantled more than half of his production facilities, worth at least fifty million dollars. "If ever there should be a resurrection for Germany," he confided, "if ever she were to shake off the chains of Versailles, then Krupps would have to be prepared. The machines were demolished, the tools were destroyed; but one thing remained—the men, the men at the drawing boards and in the workshops, who in happy cooperation had brought the manufacture of guns to its last perfection. Their skill would have to be saved, [along with] their immense resources of knowledge and experience." He boasted how "even the Allied spying commission was fooled: padlocks, milk cans, cash registers, rail-mending machines, refuse carts and similar rubbish appeared really innocent, and locomotives and motor cars appeared perfectly peaceful." When the manufacture of heavy tractors began, Krupp's officials saw in these heavy-tracked vehicles nothing less than test beds for tanks to be built for tomorrow's army to help win what was looked forward to as the "war of liberation." Even though camouflaged, and against all obstacles, Krupp "had to be maintained as an armaments factory for the distant future."

The Truppenamt exacted aid from another German giant of industry, Professor Hugo Junkers, whose motives were altogether different. At sixty-three, Junkers remained a visionary, a quixotic scientist who, not long after the war was over, enthusiastically told one of his officials, "The airplane will become a weapon of happy humanitarianism carrying blessings to all peoples and all nations, and returning blessings from all people and all nations." Junkers was small, wiry, and energetic. Thick white hair swept back from a broad forehead, and bright blue eyes, now dreamy, now cynical, danced behind his spectacles. He loved to wear old clothes and crumpled hats, turning a deaf ear to Frau Junkers' pleas to dress befitting his station in life. A sun worshipper, Junkers was prone to strip to a pair of trunks and stretch his aged but still supple frame on a terrace outside his office; his executives grew used to sudden calls for important conferences at midday, held in the fresh air on the terrace and presided over by the little professor dressed only in shorts and waving a small black notebook crammed with random jottings. No gourmand, Junkers dined habitually on only an apple and a slice of buttered bread, forcing his guests to share this frugal menu. Despite his eccentricities, Junkers was well loved by those who worked for him; he never used the word "employee" when talking about the hundreds who worked for him at the factory at Dessau—all of them were to him "collaborators" or "friends." Disliking the industrial star system, of whom he considered the flown Tony Fokker a prime example, Junkers once said of himself, "I'm only a trustee."

Junkers had sired twelve children, and loved nothing better than to gather them in the family room and inject some provocative remark into the conversation, getting a discussion started and fanning the flames of controversy until the children had involved themselves in violent argument. Junkers believed that his sons and daughters in being made to fight for their own points of view became stronger personalities, and what evolved from the verbal melee was usually a fresh train of thought and clearer attitudes. It was a tactic he carried into the factory. When Hermann Steiner completed university training, he was taken on as one of Junkers' chief engineers, and describes his patron's approach to conferences. "Meetings with him were not nice, quiet gatherings—they were extremely stormy. With almost fiendish joy he would incite us to prove each other wrong; to prove that the plans of this, that or the other one were impossible, and why. He would induce us to go to extremes. Then, when we were all excited and pled our cases passionately, he would listen to us carefully, only to get excited himself, to start shouting and banging his fist on the table.

"Then, suddenly, he would grow calm, take out his notebook, make a few entries, smile, and very lucidly sum up the situation. He never carried a personal grudge against any of us, no matter how heated the disagreement, no matter how far out we pushed ourselves on the limb. He pointed out that the presentation of an absolutely unworkable idea often led to one that was workable. Junkers had the courage of his convictions. When he sent one of his F.13 passenger planes to South America for demonstration flights, his son, Werner, went along. When Werner was killed in a crash shortly afterward, Junkers felt the loss as keenly as any father, but later commented: 'Have I the right to risk the life of other men's sons if I don't want to risk the life of my own?' "

Junkers' background was in thermodynamics, but while he was teaching at a university in Aachen, the new field of aerodynamics exerted its appeal, and on February 1, 1910, he took out a patent on a full-cantilevered flying-wing kind of powered aircraft; biplanes, with their maze of struts and wires, made no sense to him at all. A tireless investigator, Junkers created the first reliable instrument able to calculate the calorific value of fuel. A profound understanding of economics led him into researches on the value of natural gas as a fuel, and he designed a gas engine with two pistons moving against each other in the same cylinder. The principle was adapted by Junkers to Diesel engines, and he opened the Jumo works to manufacture these new Diesel engines for trucks and aircraft. He later developed the then revolutionary free-piston engine Diesel compressor which, without crankshaft, valves, connecting rods or ignition, was considered the simplest and most trouble-free piston engine ever designed. The Jumo works, a smaller enterprise, Iko Bathroom Heaters, and his wartime profits building planes had made Junkers one of the wealthiest men in Germany; he could have retired in comfort for the rest of his life without building another airplane. But airliners such as the F.13 and the lamented Rohrback E.4/20 were important tools with which the world could mend itself in harmony, vehicles to knit nations together with understanding and goodwill.

Despite his wealth, Junkers felt that the capitalist system was bankrupt and unethical; when business was slack, he refused to indulge in the common practice of layoff, but kept his men on the payroll. He referred to bureaucrats and politicians as "parasites on the body of creative and productive humanity." In referring to the problems of Germany—and, indeed, the world —in the immediate postwar period, Junkers said to Steiner, "The only basis from which to start is responsibility. And those politicians don't know what that means."

In July 1921 Major von Niedermayer visited Dessau and broached the subject of building airframe and aero-engine plants in Russia to Hugo Junkers. The old man, intensely distrustful, was noncommittal, but he did not turn Niedermayer down. Four months later, Junkers was again visited by the Truppenamt, this time in the persons of Otto Hasse and a general named Wurtzbacher; they pointed out that the secret talks with the Russians looked promising, and that there was bound to be a treaty agreement with their late enemies rather sooner than later (as indeed happened at Rapallo during the following April). Junkers, who recalled his recent experiences with the Control Commission when the F.13 transports ordered by General Billy Mitchell had been temporarily confiscated, and still without firm guidelines from the Commission as to exactly what kind of aircraft Germany would be permitted to build, saw in the Russian scheme the removal of all fetters and the opportunity to design as large as his imagination dared. On March 15, 1922, Junkers signed a contract in Berlin with Sondergruppe R. The terms stipulated that the Sondergruppe would pay Junkers $10 million to begin with, and would put at the firm's disposal another $25 million as a capital sum; moreover, Junkers would be under no obligation of repayment. When it was suggested that Junkers design his new passenger planes so that they could be easily converted into bombers, Junkers flew into a rage and

said that the suggestion not only violated sound design principles, but that he had no further interest in military aviation
whatsoever; it was swords onto plowshares he was after, and not
the other way around. What the disguised General Staff did
with his civilian creations was their own affair. Sondergruppe R
did not press the point; they had no intentions of honoring the
contract as drawn, and once Junkers swung into action and
began building small factories at Fili, not far from Moscow,
Sondergruppe R considered the mission practically accomplished.

Running parallel with efforts to re-create military flying out
of sight of Allied watchdogs were overt moves to bring German
civil aviation up to a competitive position in Europe. In 1920,
after the Control Commission had confiscated a hundred surplus aircraft originally freed for civil use, the authorities relented and allowed the Germans to buy them back. Small companies were formed for ferrying bags of mail and the occasional
passenger. The government offered a subsidy of $3 million in
1920, increased to $6.5 million in 1921. The main airmail routes
ran from Berlin to Bremen, Hamburg, Dortmund, Munich,
Dresden and Königsberg; subsidiary routes were flown from
Hamburg to Magdeburg and Dresden, while the southern part
of Germany was served by a line running from Munich to Constance.

Once the Allies had satisfied themselves that the air disarmament of Germany was complete, attention was turned to the
problem of drawing up guidelines for the manufacture of
purely civil aircraft. The process was drawn out to ridiculous
lengths and when completed, the results lacked imagination;
moreover, they were totally unrealistic. On January 31, 1921, an
Allied council informed Berlin that they were in the process of
forming a set of "definitions" to which German aircraft manufacturers would have to adhere in order to resume business.
Four months later, on May 10, Berlin agreed to accept the definitions, whatever they might be. Nearly a year went by before
the Allies were able to agree on specifics; thus, it was not until
April 14, 1922, that the long-awaited definitions were published.

Understandably, the German aviation segments were incredulous at the limitations: no airplane could be manufactured whose speed was greater than 105 miles per hour, whose range exceeded 170 miles, whose ceiling was above 13,000 feet, whose payload was greater than 1,300 pounds, and whose endurance was greater than two and one-half hours. Working inside these parameters would mean that the best German design brains would be put to work creating aircraft with performances limited to those of the vintage of 1916. Although the air officers inside the Truppenamt and the leading manufacturers protested against these crippling restrictions, the politicians accepted them with haste, enacting legislation on May 5 requiring that any importation or manufacture of aircraft in the future would have to comply strictly with the new rules.

The Liberal and Center Party members of President Ebert's *Reichstag* had good reasons for accepting the airpower definitions with such alacrity. The next installments of the massive reparations payments were due, and galloping inflation made it evident that the bill could not be met. The hope was that by accepting docilely demands on such minor points as how high and how far German airplanes would be allowed to fly, they might gain major concessions concerning the really ruinous provisions of the Treaty of Versailles. To pay for the war launched by the Kaiser and the Great General Staff, the Weimar Republic faced an initial statement of five billion dollars in gold and in goods. Normally pegged at four to the dollar, the *Reichsmark* had slipped to seventy-five to the dollar at the beginning of 1921, plunged to four hundred in 1922, and, by the end of the year, stood at seven thousand and was still plummeting downward.

Although German airframe manufacturers were willing to consider producing aircraft that would conform to the Allied definitions for use as trainers and sport flying, they were by no means content to stop there. Rohrbach, who had vaulted to fame with his short-lived E.4/20 passenger liner, opened a business office of the Rohrbach Metal Aircraft Company in Berlin, subsidized with both government and private funds. The Berlin office was a blind for Rohrbach's research and development plant, which he opened in Copenhagen with help from the Danes, whose own aviation industry was as barren as that of the rest of her Scandinavian neighbors. Rohrbach was a firm advocate of Junkers' cantilevered wing methods of building, but Rohrbach realized that the corrugated metal surfaces favored by Junkers, although strong, added unnecessary drag. He began working with smooth metal surfaces for wings and tail, which were laid over spars and ribs, thus forcing these supporting members to share some of the load carried by the wings themselves. Although this new technique was looked upon as revolutionary, it came to be generally accepted for the major technological advance it was, and influenced international aircraft design through the years. Rohrbach called his technique "stressed-skin" construction, a term that would remain in aviation's lexicon. Rohrbach built a number of huge flying boats using the stressed-skin method, aircraft whose specifications far exceeded those allowed by the Allies, but since they were all built and flown in Denmark, there was nothing the Control Commission could do.

No German designer had more ambition or took more chances with the Control Commission than did Ernst Heinkel, who at the age of thirty-two in 1920 believed that his career as an aviation designer was at an end. Heinkel, short, chubby and already balding, was the son of a Swabian tinsmith, and had worked for LVG, Etrich, and Albatros before settling as a designer for Hansa-Brandenburg, makers of a successful two-seater fighter and reconnaissance plane mounted on floats. The company went under with the end of the war, and Heinkel moved back to his hometown of Grunbach and opened a small factory which turned out household electrical fixtures. He bought a small house, a vineyard and a fruit orchard, but after the excitement of the war, life as a socket-maker and tree-pruner seemed stultifying.

Heinkel's chain of boredom was broken one summer afternoon in 1921 with the unexpected appearance at the front gate of Friedrich Christiansen, a weatherbeaten, bushy-browed character with a ringing laugh, a sailor's gait, and, at forty-two, one of Germany's oldest surviving aces. A Pour le Mérite winner, Christiansen had flown Heinkel's floatplanes to score twenty-one kills—including British aircraft, flying boats, the Royal Navy's coastal airship, the C.27, and the British submarine C.25. This old salt had obviously earned his decoration and his sobriquet, "the Fighter of Zeebrugge." After the war, Christiansen managed to smuggle a Hansa-Brandenburg floatplane to Norway and promoted himself a job with the fishing industries scouting schools of herring and sardines from the air. He returned to Germany full of ideas, and sought out another naval flyer named Carl Caspar, who had bought a small plant at Travemünde, where he was making cabinets for phonograph players. Christiansen convinced Caspar that they would have little difficulty in selling aircraft not only to the Norwegians and the Swedes, but to the Americans and the Japanese as well. Would Caspar take the risk of converting his plant to the manufacture of aircraft? Yes, said Caspar, provided they could attract some well-known designer whose name would provide the necessary lure. Hence Christiansen's sudden visit to Heinkel.

He had not forgotten Heinkel's experimental folding plane designed to fit aboard a special hangar on the deck of a U-boat, an innovation that had not had time to be developed by war's end. Christiansen told Heinkel that he had already given details to the American naval attaché in Berlin, who was "crazy about it." Christiansen said that he also knew some Japanese officers, and "if the Americans get one of the U-boat planes, the Japs will want one, too." Heinkel pointed out that the Control Commission was still active and asked where they would build their planes. "At Caspar's, of course," Christiansen replied. "Under the counter, you know, simply under the counter." Heinkel sold his factory and his house in Grunbach, moved to the coastal town of Travemünde, and went to work building airplanes again.

Through the naval attaché in Berlin, Heinkel was given the American requirements for the submarine plane to be built illegally at Caspar's plant. The craft would have to be constructed so that it could be stowed in a metal tank 18 feet long and 4½ feet wide. The design that emerged, the U.1, was a cantilever biplane with a 50-horsepower engine, a top speed of 87 miles per hour, and the ability to climb to 3,300 feet in six minutes. Four men, without tools, could dismantle the U.1 in twenty-two seconds and stow it inside the submersible tank, ready for diving; another thirty-three seconds were required for the plane to be reassembled, ready for takeoff. Christiansen's prophecy came true: two weeks after the enthusiastic acceptance of the U.1 by the United States Navy, the Japanese appeared at Travemünde and ordered two of the craft, willing to pay "any price." It bothered the Japanese as little as it did the Americans that they were in collusion with the enemy in flagrantly circumventing the disarmament clauses of the Versailles Treaty. The Japanese, after all, were members of the Inter-Allied Control Commission, while the Americans could plead a technical—if not an ethical—not guilty.

It was not a time, however, when ethics flowered. Through an ex-fighter pilot named Clemens Bücker, the Caspar firm obtained a contract with the Swedish air force, with whom Bücker had received a captain's commission. What was needed was a new seaplane, designed and partly fabricated in Germany, but assembled in Sweden in order to increase employment there. The design for a low-wing monoplane with floats was completed, and the secretly constructed parts were smuggled out of Travemüde and shipped across the water 160 miles to Malmö. Under German supervision, the Swedes assembled the S.1, as it was called, and then flight trials began. Heinkel's representative was a wartime co-worker named Jupp Köhler, and the Swedish air force was represented by an untutored naval officer named Angström who, according to Heinkel, "was an honorable man, but no match for Köhler."

The plane, as flown by test pilot Christiansen, met the required speed of 122 miles per hour, but was deficient in ceiling. Angström, whose knowledge of German was slight, allowed Köhler to assist in drawing up the performance charts from flight data supplied by the pilot. "Needless to say," Heinkel boasted later, "they far surpassed all requirements." Thus did Heinkel land the contract for the S.1 from the gullible Swedes, plus a 10 per cent bonus for a fictitious 20 per cent increase in performance requirements.

When, on May 5, 1922, the definitions were published allowing resumption of limited kinds of aircraft manufacture in Germany, Heinkel spent a sleepless night. By 8 A.M. he was at the factory, talking to three of Caspar's top engineers. He talked to Bücker, who assured him that the Swedish contract was only the first of many to come. Moreover, Bücker added, he had certain lines leading to the inner circles of the Reichswehr, hinting that soon there would be business from that quarter. Heinkel knew to the pfennig how much his share was of American dollars, Japanese yen, and Swedish kronor—currency in no danger of being devalued in the foreseeable future—so he unhesitatingly walked into Caspar's office on the morning of the seventh and told him that he was quitting and taking some of Caspar's best men along to set up a competing firm.

While casting around for a workshop, Heinkel moved his design team into a large room at the rear of a Travemünde beer hall and went to work on plans for a racing seaplane to enter in a Swedish competition to be held in the shipbuilding city of Göteborg. The He.3 was derivative of former models, but Heinkel's innovations included plywood-covered wings and fuselage and a self-starter that eliminated the familiar and fatiguing swing-through of the heavy propellor blade to get the engine running. At Warnemünde, sixty miles east along the coast and just above Rostock, Heinkel located an abandoned shed, once part of the German navy's seaplane testing station, and moved in. On December 1, 1922, work began on the He.3 under discouraging circumstances. There was, at first, neither heat nor light nor any windows. Doors were propped open in order to admit the pale rays of the winter sun, but icy Baltic breezes turned men's hands cold and stiff. Heinkel ordered windows cut in the shed—in violation of a Versailles Treaty stipulation against any modification of any German wartime building—and installed wood-burning potbellied stoves that threw out little heat but much blinding smoke. Despite these handicaps, the He.3 was finished on time and put aboard a truck for Lübeck for shipment by ferry to Göteborg. Although the only power plant available was an old 100 horsepower Siemens-Halske, the He.3 managed 90 miles per hour and proved so maneuverable that it captured first prize at the Göteborg trials. Heinkel returned to Germany elated at the promise of incoming hard Swedish currency.

Heinkel by now had demonstrated that he was the kind of stuff the clandestine side of the Reichswehr was seeking. One afternoon following the Swedish triumph, a visitor calling himself Herr Seebach was announced at Heinkel's new home in Warnemünde. "Although he was in civilian clothes," Heinkel recalled, "every gesture betrayed the officer." Seebach, of course, was Kurt Student. He was at first cagey with Heinkel, never mentioning his previous deal with Junkers or revealing the secret agreements with Soviet Russia. He asked if Heinkel was prepared to carry out work on one or two sample designs. Needed was a land biplane with a minimum speed of 140 miles per hour and a ceiling of not less than 20,000 feet. The plane, Student hinted, would be needed for the future air arm of the Reichswehr to fulfill short-range reconnaissance missions. Student admitted that, for the time being, no financial guarantees could be made, but suggested that Heinkel nonetheless owed certain obligations to the Fatherland. Heinkel was intrigued; playing hide-and-seek with the Control Commission would be "a great challenge."

While Heinkel was at work on the Reichswehr's first all-new reconnaissance plane, the He.17, he was approached by the same Japanese officers who had bought two of the submarine planes, a Captain Kaga of the Japanese delegation in Berlin, and an engineer named Yonezawa, who was the chief European representative of the Aichi Tokei Denki aircraft firm in Japan. The Japanese wanted from Heinkel land planes with performance characteristics similar to the one ordered by Student, and, in addition, they needed modern torpedo carriers. Heinkel was eager for the business, but he pointed out to Captain Kaga the obvious difficulties in hiding so many military prototypes from the Control Commission. Heinkel observed that Kaga's "friendly, sphinxlike smile" grew broader. "Herr Heinkel," Kaga said, "you work for us and all your troubles are over." The Japanese officer explained that their naval attaché in Berlin was a member of the Control Commission, and therefore would know the scheduled dates and places of inspection; it would be a simple matter, Kaga said, for Heinkel to be tipped off in plenty of time to hide incriminating evidence. With this assurance in hand, Heinkel hired additional staff and began work concurrently on designs for both his own country and for Japan.

He rented a second shed, known familiarly as the "hot works," where work was done on the planes ordered by Student and Kaga. The Japanese were true to their word, and at infrequent intervals, a mysterious caller would ring up Heinkel with a simple, coded message that meant the inspectors were on their way. Like a well-drilled team, the workers swung into action clearing the hot works of airplanes and parts of airplanes, which were loaded aboard waiting trucks and driven off to be hidden among the desolate sand dunes a few miles away. Thanks to this Japanese perfidy, Heinkel was not once caught in his illegal activities. More annoying than the control officers, however, was Student, who assumed the role of counterintelligence agent and began unannounced penetrations of Heinkel's defenses, appearing at the factory gate—and as often as not, over the high-wire fences surrounding the assembly sheds—at odd hours of the day or night. Student once managed to get over the wire guarding the hot shop at dawn one morning, causing tremendous excitement. Student chided Heinkel for the lapse in security, pointing out that he might well have been an Allied Control officer. Heinkel could only reply that the Allies had never been known to show such enterprise, and besides, the Japanese naval attaché's office had never failed him yet.

With several other German designers opening up small aeronautical firms at home and abroad, the Truppenamt plans for a meaningful aviation industry began to assume a definite, if fragile, mold. But 1923 was a year which saw a political event that first threatened to unravel, but then tightened firmly, the military fabric Seeckt had so laboriously knitted together.

At the close of the old year, the German government informed the Allied Reparations Commission that the Weimar Republic could see no way in which the installment due could be met. Instead, it was proposed that reparation should be reduced to "tolerable dimensions," that Germany should be released from all payments, both in cash and in goods such as coal and lumber, for a period of several years, given a bank credit, and restored to trade equality. To these demands, reactions varied. The British government, short on troops and money and facing labor difficulties at home, remained passive. The United States government, having ratified its own separate peace treaty with Germany on November 11, 1921, reacted to the approaching crisis by withdrawing its full contingent of occupying forces, numbering 1,199 officers, warrant officers, men, and nurses, and entraining them for France to await shipping space for home, far away from any further European embroilment. The French, however, under the new premier, Raymond Poincaré, were outraged at this new turn of German "perfidy and arrogance," and acted decisively. Five combat divisions under General Degoutte, equipped with light and heavy tanks, field artillery and aviation detachments, moved into the coal-rich Ruhr district on January 9, prepared to extract by main force all its coal as a protective pledge and as a sanction. Degoutte was joined by a division of Belgians, while Italy contributed a party of civil engineers. In a comment that reveals the quickly changing attitudes of the times, the British Official History recorded that, with the Americans gone from the Rhineland, "This left the small British Zone isolated in the midst of French and Belgian troops." That is, the British were surrounded by their allies.

The sudden move of the heavily armed French divisions into the Ruhr not only created an acute mental crisis within the German government, but revealed sharply differing attitudes as to the stance the nation should assume. The more liberal members of the Reichstag pleaded that the reparations payments should somehow be met in order to mollify the French and to prove honorable intent in living up to the Versailles Treaty. But these voices were few, and easily drowned in the general shouts of nationalist outrage at the Franco-Belgian invasion. Lieutenant Colonel Edwin von Stülpnagel submitted a memorandum to Seeckt, reminding the general that "from the national and soldierly point of view, it is the duty of the soldier to act." Such an

automatic reaction, conditioned among the German Officers
Corps by four years of warfare against the French and the
British, had not been tempered by four years and two months of
what was called peace, and there were many in the Reichswehr
who felt as did Stülpnagel: mobilization must begin, if not to oust
the enemy from the Ruhr, then certainly to fight against any
further incursions on German soil.

Seeckt realized that precipitate action with the forces at hand
—still ill-equipped, lacking trained reserves in quantity, and
backed by no true military air force—would mean only that his
handpicked Reichswehr, the cradle of Germany's future power,
would be ground to dust within less than thirty days, if for no
other reason than that there was a desperate shortage of small-
arms ammunition. Moreover, a renewed war against the west
would automatically bring the Poles and the Czechs pouring
inside Germany from the east. Following the brief, gallant
struggle would come lightning defeat, with Germany reduced
to a French vassal in perpetual bondage to eternal reparations.
Yet, if Seeckt took no soldierly act of any kind, there was no real
guarantee that he would not be prematurely retired to make
room for someone less restrained—or even murdered by the
extreme Nationalist Organization Consul, responsible for the
murder of the brilliant foreign minister, Walther Rathenau, on
June 22, 1922. In broad morning light on the Königsallee, a
horrified witness saw a large, gray, six-seater limousine plunge
out of a sidestreet and draw up alongside Rathenau's chauffer-
driven car, one of three men wearing long leather coats slip an
automatic pistol out and empty the clip in Rathenau's direction,
another of the leathercoats fling a hand grenade, the long gray
car screech out of sight up a narrow street leading out of Konigs-
allee, and Rathenau's car bump to a stop on the sidewalk. The
screech of tire rubber, the sharp cracking of the Luger, the loud
crash of the grenade—all were sounds typical of a Chicago
gangland killing. But dying in the rear seat of the sedan, his
body holed five times, was no beer baron or rum runner, but an
urbane diplomat who had been disposed to negotiate with the
Reparations Commission, a moderate who had committed

other socialist or democratic transgressions against nationalism, and, not least of all, a Jew.*

At risk, then, depending upon his decision, was the ruination of the Reich or Seeckt's own career—and possibly his life. Seeckt chose a course that would have been approved by even the most ancient of Oriental minds—passive resistance. Working closely with President Ebert and the latest chancellor, Wilhelm Cuno, Seeckt convinced the government that this was the only sensible course. Within twenty-four hours of the appearance of the French army in Germany's industrial heartland, orders were sent down from Berlin that brought thousands of German coal miners up the shafts to scatter to their homes, caused the blast furnaces to die down and cool, saw the miles of railroad track go empty and the marshaling yards become packed with engines and cars. Added to the winter gloom of the Ruhr was now a profound and ominous silence.

Furious at this unexpected show of defiance, the French expelled or imprisoned the recalcitrant German officials and corporate directors, and proceeded to evict entire households in order to make room for imported labor. Then, on January 19, the Allied High Commission issued ordinances that placed the German coal companies in the Ruhr (and elsewhere in occupied territory), the financial and customs offices, and the forestry departments under operational control of the Inter-Allied Commission of Factories and Mines. More than 15,000 French and Belgian engineers, signalmen and guards were brought in to replace the 170,000 German railway workers who had walked off the job. French troops with bayoneted rifles were stationed at strategic points along the rails to guard against possible sabotage. It was a thorough, pervading and tough military occupation of a part of Germany that had not seen an armed enemy soldier since the time of Napoleon.

---

*Two members of the murder gang, Fisher and Kern, were trapped by police three weeks later and died in the ensuing shootout. Both were former naval officers of the Erhardt Brigade. Three more, also ex-officers, named Tillessen, Techow, and Ernst von Salomen, and two right-wing students named Günther and Stubenrauch, were later captured and brought to trial. Sentences ranged only from two to fifteen years, little of which were served.

Brigadier John Morgan witnessed German popular reaction to the French presence in the Ruhr. "In the State elementary schools," he recalled, "the teachers suddenly began teaching their pupils to lisp in unison, *Frankreich is unser Feind,* France is our enemy. In public places notices appeared overnight, in identical terms, offering a reward of two thousand marks to the first German to spit in the face of a Frenchman. In restaurants the incitement was slightly varied by an invitation to spit in a Frenchman's plate. . . . Bülow, in his *Memoirs,* informs us that honorable members of the Bavarian Parliament spat at one another when words failed to express their political differences." The French officers on Morgan's staff were unmoved, and certainly not intimidated, agreeing with Bülow that "to a race denied the gift of debate, expectoration is perhaps the easiest form of repartee."

The reaction in the Ruhr went far beyond primary-school truculence. Organized bands of saboteurs roamed throughout the countryside, blowing up bridges, cutting lines, and derailing troop trains in the best tradition of T. E. Lawrence and his Bedouin irregulars. Famous for his daring as one of the leaders of the Heinz Organization was a young ex-officer named Leo Schlageter, who was finally caught in the act of setting a charge underneath a bridge carrying rail freight from the Ruhr to France. He was stood against a wall and shot by the French— and became a martyred hero overnight; friends came to mourn at an obelisk erected in his memory. Captured saboteurs who were shot found themselves in fetid holds on ships bound for Devil's Island.

Denied four-fifths of the normal coal supply, Germans endured another freezing winter almost without heat or hot water. With much of the rail traffic disrupted, even in the unoccupied zones, there were severe shortages of almost everything —at least among the common run of German humanity. A special Ruhr Fund was set up by the government to subsidize the passive resisters, but the money was practically worthless. On January 11, the mark slipped to 18,000 to the dollar; by July 1, it stood at 160,000; a month later it took 1 million marks to buy a dollar, 4 billion on November 1, and before the year was out, the amount zoomed into the trillions. Wheelbarrows piled high with marks were trundled into the baker's to pay for a loaf of bread. Farmers who got their produce to market discovered that by the time they returned home, the proceeds had been quartered in value.

The opportunities afforded the Reichswehr in the turmoil of the Ruhr were considerable. In asking Seeckt's advice, the government had made him—and therefore the army—a partner in matters of policy-making. To prepare for a theoretical French advance to the Weser and a potential thrust from the east by Czechs and Poles, the Truppenamt was heavily engaged in full-scale tactical and strategic planning exercises, providing badly needed training in general staff work. Seeckt also had ample opportunity to test the possibilities of incorporating the bewildering number of so-called patriotic organizations that had proliferated throughout Germany during the preceding five years. Included was the oldest and best-known, the *Stalhelm* (Steel Helmet) Organization, the *Jungdeutsche Orden,* (Order of Young Germans), the Battalion Hindenburg, the Vikings, the Werewolfs, and literally dozens of others. Attempts to convince the leaders of these largely paramilitary groups to agree to place themselves under the mobilization plans of the Reichswehr were largely fruitless, however; too many of them believed that Germany's greatest enemy was the current Republican government, not France, and only wished to see its downfall. And many of those less fanatical still refused to amalgamate unless Seeckt could promise that they would be attached to—but not absorbed by—the Reichswehr serving as self-contained units under their chosen leaders.

Among the few veterans' associations that were willing to back the Reichswehr wholeheartedly was one that could provide only moral support during the Ruhr crisis. This was the *Ring Deutscher Flieger,* the Society of German Flyers, which had been formed not long after the war. A comprehensive file was kept on every surviving pilot, observer and gunner with operational or training experience. The chief advisors were General von Hoeppner, the first Chief of the German Air Service (who died at the age of sixty-two on September 25, 1922), and Colonel Wilhelm Siegert, Hoeppner's chief of staff and an active pilot whose specialty was bombing operations. The Ring drew attention to itself in Britain's semiofficial *Royal United Services Institute Review*, whose RAF correspondent reported in mid-1922: "The fact that as far as possible each link that forms the 'Ring' is to consist of the combatants who served together in one squadron or unit, coupled with the violent invective used by the chief speaker at its opening meeting, shows that the future activities of this society will probably be directed towards keeping in being, though in a disguised form, an air force imbued with the ideals of the old one. No entrance fee or subscription is asked for from the members; this may indicate that strong financial and industrial interests, if not the government, are offering their support."

The willingness of the Ring to support Seeckt only pointed up the painful fact that Germany was shamefully naked in the air. Suppose the Ruhr crisis should ignite another war? French aircraft could roam at will the length of Germany. This was the argument put forward to President Ebert by Seeckt, who strongly advised the immediate purchase abroad of the latest fighters, which, as the President knew, were purely defensive weapons. And the Control Commission? Its activities stopped abruptly the day the French began rolling into the Ruhr. Cramon had informed General Nollet that he was not actually refusing his duties of liaison, but that under the circumstances, the Germans could not guarantee the safety of French or Belgian inspection teams anywhere in Germany. With the snoopers virtually confined to quarters, here was an opportunity to be seized and exploited. With the blessing of Ebert and Cuno, Seeckt issued orders to General Hasse to buy a hundred new fighter planes, to be paid for out of the Ruhr Fund. In addition, a contract was let to Ernst Heinkel for ten of the new He.1 low-wing monoplanes, equipped with floats, to be built in the subsidiary plant in Sweden.*

The deal for the fighters was brokered through the offices of

---

*Seeckt realized at the time that the orders probably could not be filled in time to be of any use inside Germany, but he was looking ahead to the time when the planes would be needed for training German pilots in Russia, planes openly paid for in advance.

one of Germany's largest industrialists, Hugo Stinnes, estimated to hold control of 20 per cent of the country's postwar resources. Stinnes's great fortune included interests in cellulose and shipping, and a vast publishing empire. Stinnes, whose attitude toward politics was described as childlike, was already involved in the financing of the Russian venture, and was willing to lend his resources to help along air rearmament because whatever was good for the Reich was good for business. From Stinnes's impressive office in the port city of Hamburg, a call was put through to Tony Fokker in Amsterdam, two hundred miles distant. Fokker was in Hamburg that same afternoon, excitedly discussing details of the windfall offer to buy a hundred of his finest fighters—to be paid for in hard currency.

The first design Fokker could offer was the D.XI, strongly derivative of the famous D.VII, but larger and improved in several ways. The cantilevered wings were covered with plywood and equipped with balanced ailerons. Powered with the Spanish-designed 300-horsepower Hispano-Suiza eight-cyclinder engine, the D.XI could top 140 miles per hour and exhibited the usual Fokker excellent climb characteristics. Then Fokker showed the Germans designs for an even better fighter, the D.XIII, designed around a British Napier-Lion power plant of 450 horsepower. The D.XIII was heavier, with a gross weight of 3,637 pounds, but when built proved to be the fastest fighter in the world, clocking 171 miles per hour in level flight. Uncharacteristic in a Fokker design, the D.XIII was rounded and smooth looking everywhere, promising easy passage through the air. Where, asked Fokker of Stinnes's manager, Captain Hormel, were the fighters bound for? "For the Argentine," Hormel replied.

As it turned out, the Ruhr crisis was over long before either fighter could be delivered to Germany. The fifty D.XIs ordered were later sold to Rumania, but Fokker completed the fifty newer D.XIIIs, which were accepted by the Reichswehr after a wringing out in the air by a test pilot named Hans Leutert, and again by the bird dog, Kurt Student.

Events in the Ruhr reached stalemate with the discovery by the French and the Belgians that, in the phraseology of the time, it was not profitable to dig coal with bayonets; and the German government realized sadly that you cannot subsidize industry, pay the working class for not working, without paying court to economic ruin. On August 12, Wilhelm Cuno was ousted as chancellor and replaced by the director of a chocolate combine and amateur politician named Gustav Stresemann— a monarchist at heart, but a Republican in reality. On September 26, Stresemann announced the end of passive resistance, and Germans went back to work in the Ruhr, resigned to the continuing and sullen occupation and happy to be earning the billions of marks a day that enabled them to provide at least one hot meal for their families every twenty-four hours.

Almost immediately afterward, Seeckt was granted extraordinary powers under Article 48 of the Weimar Constitution to deal with yet another series of internal crises. Through the puppet defense minister, Gessler, Seeckt became what can best be called a benevolent dictator during a state of emergency arising from attempts in both Bavaria and the Rhineland to separate from the Reich and form independent republics. Then he confronted a revolt by some six hundred officers and men of the so-called Black Reichswehr, renegades bent upon abolishing the Republic. They rashly seized three old forts on the outskirts of Berlin and held out for forty-eight hours before surrendering, sheeplike, to Reichswehr regulars.

It was in November, however, that gunfire in a Munich street halted what would become the most famous putsch in German history, an outdoor drama featuring a legendary field marshal whose reason was beginning to dissolve, a retired, much-decorated air service captain whose soul was corrupting with political ambition, and a one-time lance corporal who afterward would be described by a distinguished British journal as an "Austrian carpenter."

6

THE BRIDGE

The man who is born to be a dictator is not compelled. He wills it.
—Adolf Hitler

Munich. November 9, 1923. 11 A.M.

Underneath a heavy gray sky, three thousand men file out of the cavernous Bürgerbraükeller, a beer hall on the eastern outskirts of the city. Most are armed with the short infantry carbine. They stream through the garden in an orderly column, and, once clear of the building, an army truck filled with machinegunners attaches itself to the rear of the column and bumps along slowly. At the head of this booted and light-brown-uniformed brigade is Erich Ludendorff, imperious looking even in his somber suit of civilian clothes.

At the beginning of 1919, Ludendorff fled to Sweden, his mother's birthplace, disguised in false whiskers and blue-tinted sunglasses. He returned not long afterward, began writing his memoirs, and inadvertently provided a generation of Germans with a catch-phrase that absolved the military of the blame for defeat. At lunch one day with the British General Sir Niall Malcolm, Ludendorff was having difficulty in finding words to explain the depressing effects the Revolution had upon front-line soldiers. General Malcolm suggested a phrase to Ludendorff, who seized it and cried, "Stabbed in the back? Yes, that's it exactly. We were stabbed in the back!" Ludendorff, who admitted to his wife that it would make him far from unhappy to see "Herr Ebert and company hanged," agreed to lend his name and his presence to a putsch aimed at the overthrow of the Republic and the restitution of Bavaria's former privileged and semiautonomous state.

The column boots its way toward the center of the city and reaches the first tactical obstacle at the entrance to the old Ludwig Bridge, arching across the swift-running Isar that divides the city. Solid ranks of police in black leather helmets and green uniforms block the way. Ludendorff halts, perhaps expecting a salute, and the brown column halts behind him. A square figure dressed dramatically in a steel helmet and a long leather coat pushes past Ludendorff and addresses the chief of these green police, threatening to kill the hostages brought along for the purpose if the field marshal and his followers are not allowed to pass. The chief hesitates, uncertain of where his duty lies, then orders his men to clear a passage. Ludendorff resumes his stately walk, and the column picks up the pace behind him. Marching just to Ludendorff's left is a tense figure wrapped in a crumpled trenchcoat, one hand gripping tightly a small Walther automatic pistol, the other arm linked to the man on his left. Adolf Hitler is marching along the road to glory.

Hitler remained in the army until 1920; he was never promoted in rank, but was elevated to an investigator for the Reichswehr's political department. He attended dozens of meetings held by myriad small organizations, left and right, one of which proved fateful. In September 1919, he went to a gathering of the German Workers' Party. Someone passed a political tract into his hand and Hitler took it back to his barracks. He awoke next morning at five, and while listening to the mice feed on breadcrumbs he had scattered on the floor next to his bunk the night before, he read the tract through. Hitler joined the organization, which had at the time less than two dollars in the treasury and numbered 140 members. He left the army in 1920 to begin a full-time career in politics. He quickly gained control of the party he had impetuously joined, changing its name to the National Socialist German Workers' Party and choosing the ancient rune, the *Hakenkreuz,* the swastika, as the NSDAP symbol. To break up meetings of other parties—and to protect his own from molestation—Hitler recruited strong-arm squads from the flotsam and jetsam of Free Corps fighters. These men were specialists in back-alley brawls and street fighting, methods necessary for political survival in the bitter months following the outbreak of peace. Hitler's aims were the destruction of the Republic, the elimination of the "November criminals," and the abrogation of the Treaty of Versailles. The unrest in Bavaria and in the Rhineland, coupled with Stresemann's "shameful" action in ending passive resistance in the Ruhr, convinced Hitler that November 9 was not a day too early to strike.

The mixed force of storm troopers and the more colorfully uniformed officer cadets from the infantry school flow down Zweibrückenstrasse, leaving behind the bridge and the river. Silent crowds gather on the street to watch them go. The column keeps formation as it swings through the Marienplatz, and closes up even tighter as it funnels itself into the narrow Residenzstrasse leading into broad Odeonsplatz, near the War Ministry and the ultimate goal. Those at the head of the column hesitate, then move forward again, then halt: they see at the end of the street at least a hundred armed green police, carbines ready. Standing in the second rank, just behind and to the left of Adolf Hitler, is Hermann Goering, the collar of his black leather coat pulled apart to reveal the Pour le Mérite glittering at his throat. It was Goering who had gotten them through the first police line at the bridge, and it is time to act once more.

Goering had never forgotten the vilification he suffered as a member of the officer class in the weeks immediately following the breakup of the Richthofen Group. At a meeting inside the Berlin Philharmonic Hall late in December 1919, in which the Prussian minister of war, Colonel Walther Reinhardt, pled for support of the Republican government's policies, Goering shot up from his chair and shouted Reinhardt down. He called Reinhardt's compliant attitude shameful, and implored the audience to "cherish a profound, abiding hatred of those animals who have outraged the German people." Goering handed in his resignation immediately afterward and went to Copenhagen as a demonstration pilot for Fokker, earning money on the side as a one-man barnstorming act. His fame as a wartime air hero enabled him to work his way into the middle echelons of Danish society, but his popularity was fleeting; not only did he embarrass his new friends by overtly attempting to seduce another man's wife, but violent explosions of temper over the Versailles Treaty and diatribes against the November criminals were out of place during dinner or in the salon, where Goering usually chose to unleash his barrages.

He moved to Stockholm and managed to get a job with Svensk Lufttrafik as a charter pilot making short-haul runs; on the side he acted as an agent for Heinicken, manufacturer of an automatically opening parachute. It was a charter flight that accidentally landed Goering in the lap of nobility and altered the course of his life.

Adventuresome Count Eric von Rosen sought out Goering one winter afternoon at Stockholm's airport and hired him to fly him to his estate near Sparreholm, a half hour away from the capital. The field was blown with snow and visibility was poor, but there had never been anything wrong with Goering's personal courage, so he stuffed his elegant passenger in the rear cockpit and trundled the Fokker onto the white, wet field and took off. Goering managed to find Rosen's estate, a place of medieval magnificence, and landed on a nearby frozen lake. Impressed with Goering's performance and his hearty manner, the count invited the German pilot to stay the weekend, sheltered from the storm. Goering was introduced to Rosen's sister-in-law, the Baroness von Kantzow (née Karin Fock), daughter of an officer, estranged wife of an officer. At thirty-two, she was five years Goering's senior and the mother of a five-year-old boy, but her gentle manner, quiet beauty, and doelike eyes captivated Goering. The attraction was reciprocal, and Goering determined to improve his station in life so as to be worthy as a husband. He abandoned aviation, returned to Germany in the summer of 1921, and enrolled in the University of Munich to study political science. Karin secured an uncontested divorce, and with the money her husband provided, she and Goering were able to marry. The ceremony was performed in Munich on February 3, 1923.

By this time, Goering had become a crony of Adolf Hitler, whom he met at a political rally in the autumn of 1922. Hitler's words of denunciation of the Versailles Treaty, Goering recalled, "were spoken word for word as if from my own soul."

Hitler offered Goering command of the SA, the storm troopers, and Goering accepted immediately; the challenge of converting undisciplined rabble into an efficient street-fighting force was one he could not resist.

Before Goering could step forward to deal with the commander of the police, Hitler's personal bodyguard, burly Elrich Graf, shoved through and shouted, "Nicht schiessen! Don't shoot! His Excellency Ludendorff is coming!" Then Hitler barked, "Surrender! Surrender!" A nervous finger squeezes too hard on a trigger and a rifle shot cracks. The police level their carbines and a ripple of fire slams into the tight ranks of the storm troopers. The man with whom Hitler's arm is linked, Scheubner-Richter, is struck and jerked away and falls dying to the street. Hitler, his old front-soldier instincts working, dives for the curb and painfully dislocates his shoulder. A high-velocity 7.9 millimeter slug rips into Goering's upper right thigh, inches from the groin, and he sits down on the street holding his leg with both hands, his face white with shock. The firing dies out within sixty seconds, leaving sixteen National Socialists and three green police dead or dying at the entrance to the Odeonsplatz. The storm troopers flee, but Ludendorff marches straight ahead, shoving aside carbine barrels as he goes, until, alone, he reaches the center of the square. The putsch has failed, and only Ludendorff has kept his honor.

Like a member of an unsuccessful gang of bank robbers, Adolf Hitler scampered to the rear and was hustled into a waiting getaway car and driven to a hideout in the country, where he was arrested two days later. Loyal storm troopers dragged Goering out of the street and into a building variously described as a pharmacy, a bank, and a furniture store, where Frau Ilse Ballin, a Jew, did her best to bind up the hideous wound with towels. She allowed Goering and his helpers to remain hidden until nightfall, when a car was secured and Goering was driven first to a clinic for professional treatment, and later to a friend's house near Garmisch-Partenkirchen, seventy miles south of Munich. Goering's wound became badly infected, necessitating a series of operations to remove fragments of lead and dirt embedded in his thigh muscles. He was put on morphine to relieve the pain, but without success. Wrote Karin, "He bites the pillow because it hurts so much, and he moans all the time. . . . His mind seems to wander and he dreams of street-fighting."

Two months passed before Goering could get around without the use of crutches or a walking stick. He volunteered to stand trial with Hitler, who refused, saying Goering would be more use to the party outside of jail than in. The Goerings, almost broke and cut off from aid, remained in Austria for several months, until authorities asked them to leave. They made their way to Florence and to Venice. Goering met Benito Mussolini, whose own putsch in 1922 had secured Fascist control of Italy. Goering, still limping, an outcast from his own land, suffering the indignities of being short of cash, would have to wait almost ten years before his own ascent to the power he dreamed of.

Thus ended the ultimate putsch, the last insurrectional crisis of the decade. The chaotic year, with its economic blizzard, witnessed the phenomenon of the elimination of Germany's huge middle class—their savings, pensions, and bonds turned to smoke by the fires of inflation. Introduction of a new mark— backed by Germany's agricultural future and by banks holding gold reserves, and afterward the inauguration of the Dawes Plan whereby the United States lent Germany great sums of money to put the economy on its feet, brought a sense of stability to the country unknown for nearly six years. Chancellor Stresemann's policy of reaching for an understanding with the French with promises of picking up reparations payments brought peace and full German control to the Ruhr. With the Poles turned quiescent, the threat of conflict receded in the east. Through it all, Seeckt had kept the Reichswehr politically uninvolved, a state within a state, but he was in a stronger position than ever to guide Germany's destiny.

A positive material gain was the acquisition of sixty modern warplanes. And with the Control Commission temporarily paralyzed, Fliegerzentrale in Berlin could with increased haste develop civil aviation along lines useful to an air force in the making.

7

BREAKING THE SHACKLES

The judge . . . when it was alleged that the prisoner could fly, remarked
that there was no law against flying.
—Dictionary of National Biography
(on Jane Wenham, accused
of witchcraft in 1712)

The achievements of civil aviation in Germany during the past two years
when a commission of control has been destroying or confiscating
material, when construction has been prohibited, and when commercial
stability has frequently been threatened by violent political upheavals,
give some index as to the development which may be expected in the
future when comparative freedom will be enjoyed.
—Royal United Services Institute Journal, Volume LXVII, 1922

Readers of the national newspapers and subscribers to the
monthly journal issued by the Ring der Flieger were kept current on developments in aviation in the rest of the world,
events that created among the young the frustration of being
excluded and an aching desire to take part in the exciting con-
quests of space and time. In 1923, during Germany's calamitous
twelve months, foreigners had accomplished significant leaps
forward. On January 9, near Madrid, Juan de la Cievera astonished onlookers with the first successful liftoff, flight and landing
of a gyroplane, his C.3 Autogiro. The Germans, limited to building aircraft with a range of under 200 miles, could only read
about the flight on May 2–3 of two American lieutenants, Or-
ville Kelly and John Macready, in an ungainly Fokker T.2
monoplane that jumped across the continent from coast to
coast, nonstop, covering 2,520 miles in just under twenty-seven
hours. German planes were permitted a time aloft of two and
a half hours; on August 27–28, the Americans, flying a wartime

DH-4B, experimented with air-to-air refueling using a long rubber hose and gravity feed and succeeded in keeping the two-seater bomber in the air continuously for thirty-seven hours, fifteen minutes, and fourteen seconds. Over Germany soared passenger-carrying airliners of Daimler Airways, outbound from London to Berlin via Bremen and Hamburg, a once-daily schedule in operation since early spring. Out of the south roared huge Farman Goliaths, modified French bombers with twin engines and fully enclosed passenger compartments, arrogantly plowing through German airspace, overshadowing the smaller Junkers F.13s on their short hops. The will to participate and the drive to compete are inherent in the young, and came easily to the surface in postwar Germany.

More outlets for the obsession for flight were needed in addition to the increasing gliding activity in the Rhoen mountains. This outlet was provided by a thirty-three-year-old wartime pilot named Friedrich Wilhelm (Fritz) Siebel, an energetic planner who had been to Russia following the signing of the Treaty of Rapallo and had gauged—correctly—that the establishment of a German training command and test facility there would be no overnight matter. Fritz Siebel decided that no time should be lost in training enthusiasts right in Germany, ostensibly working within the infamous definitions established by the Conference of Ambassadors in Paris. Both of Heinkel's new biplanes, the He.18 and the He.21, had performance characteristics within Allied limitations and could be used openly. Siebel suggested to the Defense Ministry in Berlin that civilian flying schools be opened in Germany where not only serving and former officers could keep their hand in, but where an entire new crop of students could be given the equivalent of basic and primary training. On January 1, 1924, Sportflug G.m.b.H. (Sportflying, Ltd.) was founded, and a training center was set up at Warnemünde, almost next door to Heinkel's factory.

Within a year, Sportflug G.m.b.H. expanded to include nine other flight training centers at Böblingen, Berlin-Staaken, Königsberg, Osnabrück, Hanover, Stettin, Schkeudnitz, Schleissheim, and Würzburg. Out of a total budget allocated to the hidden air arm of the Reichswehr of $2½ million in 1925, almost half was funneled to these ten schools as a subsidy, including airframe and engine costs, maintenance, and primitive air-raid protection measures. Another three-quarters of a million dollars went into research and development, while the remainder was turned over to Special Group R and its Russian program. The ten flight training schools were strategically located, intentionally sited throughout the seven military districts so as to be convenient for wartime officers to undergo refresher training; very few of them indeed had put boots to rudder bar or hands to stick during the previous six years. The Paris Air Agreements allowed only six active-duty officers to be trained each year, but Seeckt got around this provision easily: officer cadets were provided the basic training and licensed as civilians before being passed on to active duty. In this way, five times as many officers as were legally allowed underwent flight training during the first year of Sportflug's operation, and a reserve of pilots slowly began to accumulate.

This groundwork had been laid during the time the Control Commission was in a state of enforced hibernation. On January 1, 1924, however, General Nollet announced that the Conference of Ambassadors in Paris "would tolerate no further delay," and that the inspections would recommence forthwith. Stresemann objected, claiming that the disarmament of Germany was complete. In a countermove, the Allies offered to replace the Commission with a so-called committee of guarantee—an inspectorate under another name. The stiffening attitude of the government regarding inspection teams had suddenly coalesced from mere evasion into outright defiance. This spark of aggressiveness prompted the German Officers' Corps to pop to the surface with the issuance of a manifesto that appeared, on March 12, on the front pages of *Der Tag* and all the other Nationalist newspapers in Germany.

"The National Union of German Officers, the German Officers' League, the Naval Officers' Union," it ran, "take the strongest exception to the latest Note of the Ambassadors' Conference in Paris. Our Associations demand of the Government of the German Reich that the Note be decisively rejected. The unanimous shout of the German people must ring in the ears of the foreigner: Out with all these Control Commissions! Clear them out of Germany!"

Stresemann did indeed reject the offer of a Guarantee Committee, claiming that henceforth only the League of Nations should have the authority of delving further into the state of German disarmament. Stresemann nonetheless permitted two small teams to carry out inspection visits on January 10 and 12; however, since Control officers were allowed inside factories for verbal interrogations only, results were nil, and Commission headquarters in Berlin again halted any efforts to penetrate the military and industrial cloak of subterfuge. It was not until June that the Germans agreed to a general inspection on the part of the Control Commission, and then only because Stresemann did not want to trouble the atmosphere surrounding negotiations leading to talks in London concerning the evacuation of the Ruhr by the occupying forces. Even so, the general inspection did not begin until September 8, and so contentious were Cramon's liaison officers and factory managers that the tours did not end until January 25 of the following year. Only once was a real coup delivered by the Commission, and that because of an informer. In December 1924 a pacifist-minded workman tipped off Control officers to a cache of arms hidden in a factory at Wittenau. A surprise visit by a British team uncovered a store of 113,000 rifles. Unfortunately for the workman, he was found out, and a German judge sentenced him to a long stretch in prison for what he called betrayal of the Reich.

The Commission submitted its comprehensive five-hundred-page report, pointing to the discovery of the re-created General Staff inside the Truppenamt, to the fact that the police had more than thirty thousand men over the specified number, that new and mobile guns had been erected in the east facing Poland, that the budget for replacement of infantry weapons was about ten times that required for an army of the size allowed by the Treaty, that nonauthorized firms were engaged in producing munitions, that illegal enlistment procedures were being carried out, and that some kind of air arm was being resurrected. Stresemann referred to the charges in the Commission's report as "petty details." He stood before the assembled members of the Reichstag and proclaimed, "Germany, by the conditions of the Peace Treaty, is disarmed to a degree that she is no longer a military factor in European politics."

Stresemann's astute choice of words drove the nail home. Armies, after all, are only political hammers, and not even the most rabid Frenchman could claim that the Reichswehr of 1925 was able to exert influence on European political events. England, facing rising labor troubles at home born of unemployment, was anxious to disconnect from European affairs that were a drain on the treasury, and only too glad to reach for an amicable settlement with all European powers. The sooner the disarmament thorn could be withdrawn from their sides, the sooner the Army of Occupation could be brought home. A way must somehow be found to knit the European community of nations together into a confederation of trust and understanding.

These thoughts led to the dreamy Italian resort town of Locarno, where a pact was signed by representatives of the governments of Germany, France, England, Italy and Belgium the essence of which was an agreement that none of the contracting powers would wage war against any of the signatories for a period of thirty years—which was about as long as Seeckt figured it would take Germany to be ready for another major European war. Moreover, it was agreed that Germany and France would negotiate their differences, although the pact left the Versailles Treaty intact. This new spirit of Locarno went abroad in the land, reducing the Control Commission to a high-ranking clerical staff whose functions withered to feeble written protests against one or another violation.* The Locarno agreements were signed on December 1, 1925, and nine months later Germany was admitted to the League of Nations with a permanent seat on the Council. There were few who did not believe that it was peace in their time.

---

*The Inter-Allied Control Commission lasted until February 28, 1927, when the last officer was withdrawn from Germany and the Commission was dissolved.

Even before these formal political moves to ease national tensions got underway, an outstanding young staff officer in the Aviation Department of the Transport Ministry, Captain Ernst Brandenburg, had already found ways to help Germany throw off the straitjacket binding the development of civil aviation by using a clause of the Versailles Treaty. Brandenburg, as commander of *Bombengeschwader* 3, had pioneered Gotha raids over London and against targets in the south of England, earning the Pour le Mérite for leadership qualities and personal courage. Following one of these missions, Brandenburg's Gotha crashed heavily while landing, crushing one of his legs. Complications developed later on and the leg was amputated. When Brandenburg, a short, clean-shaven, reticent-looking man with a receding hairline, assumed the post of Deputy State Secretary for the *Abteilung Luftfahrt* in 1920, he was still on crutches; but co-workers soon discovered that Captain Brandenburg had lost none of his energies.

Brandenburg set as his first task bringing Germany's civil air fleet up to the level enjoyed by the French and British companies already entrenched in the Continent and beyond. The beginnings of German commercial aviation dated back to 1917 when victory over the Allies seemed within reach. The AEG company, makers of a series of medium-range bombers, created on paper the *Deutsche Luftreederei*, the German Air Transport Agency, primarily in order to assure markets for its own postwar designs. Defeat did not flatten the idea, and, using converted twin-engined bombers, the Luftreederei began a Berlin–Weimar, Berlin–Hamburg service, carrying ten thousand passengers and ten tons of mail between these cities during 1919. With healthy government subsidies in 1920, additional routes were established linking Germany with Sweden, Denmark and Holland. Despite restrictions laid down by the Control Commission, another thirty airline companies had been formed by 1922, some of them little more than one- or two-man operations flying short hops in a single surplus plane.

The mass of largely independent operators were amalgamated into one corporate entity, German Aero-Lloyd, with the blessings of the Traffic Ministry and with backing from several sources, including Hugo Stinnes's empire and the powerful Deutsche Bank. One of the prime movers in the merger was the bank's president, Emil Strauss, who was well connected with the Postal Ministry and had cultivated the friendship of Ernst Brandenburg; the possibilities of lucrative contracts and continuing subsidies were obvious.

Aero-Lloyd faced stiff competition from the start. Hugo Junkers was already solidly established as Germany's largest air carrier, and certainly his operation was the best integrated; Junkers not only held an early lead in concessions, but designed, built and maintained the planes to service these handpicked routes. The driving power behind the old man's dream of "making the airplane a tool of a happy humanity" was Gotthard Sachsenberg, who, like Brandenburg, had been a well-known wartime hero. Sachsenberg, at twenty-five, was commanding the 1st Naval Fighter Group on the Flanders front when the war ended, and was one of the few German pilots to fly Fokker's new high-wing monoplane fighter, the D.VIII, in combat. Sachsenberg's thirty-one kills earned him the Blue Max, but his days of air fighting did not end with the Armistice. Along with Theo Osterkamp, Sachsenberg journeyed to the Baltic and flew Junkers armored fighters against the Bolsheviks in support of the Iron Division. When the campaign ended, Sachsenberg managed to keep one of the two-seater ground strafers and went into business as a solo charter operator. As a concession to foul weather, he fabricated a crude folding hood over the rear cockpit of the J.10/CL-1. The effect, however, was claustrophobic, and passengers unused to the nose-searing stink of gasoline fumes welling up inside the enclosed space, the ominous creaking of the metal wings in flight and the unmuffled roar of the engine seldom returned to pay for a second experience. Sachsenberg got rid of his jury-rigged airliner and went to Dessau, where he had no trouble landing a job as one of Junkers' directors.

Sachsenberg's ambitious plans for expanding inland traffic across international frontiers to a worldwide network could never be met as long as Germany was forbidden to fly over occupied Rhineland and the Allied-imposed restrictions on aircraft performance were in effect. It was on January 1, 1923, that Ernst Brandenburg—with a copy of the Versailles Treaty at hand—went into action inside the Traffic Ministry to hoist the Allies on their own petard.

On the first day of the year, by law, the aerial navigation clauses of the Treaty ceased to be operative, which meant that Germany regained sovereignty over her own air space and could forbid foreign aircraft the right of passage over unoccupied territory. Brandenburg soon demonstrated that he meant to apply the letter of the law, put on the books by the Allies themselves four years earlier. The first victim was France, whose Franco-Roumaine Airline continued to weave paths across German skies without the formality of permissions. Engines being what they were, forced landings were common, and, one after another, no less than thirteen of Franco-Roumaine's airliners were impounded by the authorities when they put down on German soil. The British were just as concerned, for their air routes to India were in jeopardy unless they had free passage across the Reich. Other clauses in the treaty allowed Brandenburg to tighten the screw.

Article 313: " . . . Allied aircraft shall enjoy the same privileges as German aircraft. . . . "

Article 314: ". . . Any regulations which may be made by Germany . . . shall be applicable equally to the aircraft of Germany and to those of the Allied and Associated countries."

Article 315: ". . . Aircraft of the Allied and associated Powers . . . shall be treated on a footing of equality with German aircraft. . . ."

All of which meant, said Brandenburg, that henceforth any Allied plane flying over unoccupied Germany must have the same reduced performance characteristics imposed on German craft by the definitions laid down in Paris. In conforming to their own rules, British and French service outside the Rhineland and the Ruhr was severely crippled. To chagrin was added alarm at falling profits. Carriers on both sides of the Channel petitioned and pressured their respective governments to change the rules. Negotiations were slow to get underway, and deliberations among the Conference of Ambassadors in Paris were desultory. It was not until May 21, 1926, that the Paris Air Agreement, which legally removed the last of the technical restrictions on Germany's civil air industry, was signed. Further concessions were gained by the stubborn German air representatives, who gained the right to fly over the Rhineland and were permitted access to three airfields in the French zone. Of course, none of the manufacturers waited until the restrictions were lifted to begin work on prototypes designed around the most powerful engines available and within the limits of existing technology, nor did the carriers hesitate to plan routes stretching beyond the horizons.

The Junkers-Sachsenberg international outlook on the future of commercial aviation held wide appeal throughout Europe, drawing the continent's leading airmen and manufacturers to Dessau to explore the tantalizing possibilities offered by mutual planning and cooperation. The favorite watering place of the youthful Junkers engineers was Papa Rossow's *Gasthaus* in the Dessau suburb of Ziebigk; here, over pilsner and bratwurst, could be found stimulating discussions between the Junkers men and a galaxy of European postwar air pioneers. Hermann Steiner, a habitué of Papa Rossow's, called to mind "Karl and Adrian Florman, the directors of the great Swedish airline company, charming Herr Deutelmoser of the Austrian airlines, the Wygard brothers from Warsaw, Renato Morandi, of the Italian company, Señor Moreno from the Spanish Aero Union in Madrid, the Swiss flyer Walther Mittelholzer, and General Kuksin of the Red air fleet." On Rossow's polished wooden tables, pencils flew across random paper, spinning air routes over the face of the earth. A line was flung from Moscow to Turkestan; another leapt from Stockholm to Baghdad, via Moscow, Rostov, Baku and Teheran. Junkers men even stretched their lines— and their imaginations—to create an air bridge from Berlin to China. Many of these projects were realized by Sachsenberg, especially the pioneering efforts in South America; others remained only schemes.

Sachsenberg launched a barnstorming campaign inside German borders in response to popular demand. Explained Steiner: "The mayors of practically all the towns in Germany visited Dessau and waited in line to see Sachsenberg. They all brought money along and insisted that Sachsenberg take it and put their town on the airline map. He took their money. Then, on a Sunday a few months later, a Junkers [G.31] three-engined passenger plane would appear at the town's newly built airport and be duly baptized. The following Sunday our plane would appear at another new airport and again be baptized. I suppose that the populations of those towns always thought it was 'their' plane—and had a lot of fun. The entire development inside Germany was somewhat unsound, to say the least, and had all the earmarks of a gold rush. . . . Had Junkers been given a few years' time, something permanent would have come out of it, something the world had never before seen—an airline independent of state subsidies, and therefore independent of power politics." The pendulum, however, was to swing in the opposite direction.

Ernst Brandenburg's farsighted planning inside the Traffic Ministry included operational training of tomorrow's bomber crews in long-distance navigation and night flying in multiengined aircraft. The quickest way this could be accomplished would be through the growing airlines system, and under dictatorial ministerial authority. The scheme fell into place almost by default, with only a little Machiavellian execution on the part of Brandenburg to make acquisition complete. Mismanagement at Aero-Lloyd and miscalculation by Junkers plunged the fiscal affairs of both companies deeply into the red, rendering their foundations weak. Withdrawal of government subsidies and pressure on Herr Strauss at the Deutsche Bank to halt credit extensions could have toppled Aero-Lloyd at command, but this was not what Brandenburg and his superiors wanted; not yet.

The Junkers concern was another matter. Although Hugo Junkers had been willing to venture into Russia against uncertain Reich guarantees, he remained obdurate in his refusals to dilute principles by allowing his design and planning staffs to splice military requirements into the purely commercial texture of his operations. If the old man could not be bent, then he could be broken, and Brandenburg found a way.

By the end of 1924, the Junkers Russian plant at Fili was completed, and the German staff and work force of ninety-one men were turning out reconnaissance planes for the Red Air Force. But Soviet orders fell far short of expectations. Meanwhile, the accountants at Dessau were charging off their own overhead and losses to Fili, worsening the debit there by nearly 50 per cent. The result was that the books showed a net loss of some twelve thousand dollars for each aircraft manufactured inside Russia, a loss the Weapons Procurement Office in Berlin termed "almost grotesque." Junkers nevertheless considered that he had fulfilled his part of the bargain with the Traffic Ministry by getting the Russian plant in operation, and requested that he be paid the rest of the money due him. Moreover, he reminded the government that his plant at Dessau had been promised an order for two hundred aircraft. This order would go a long way in pumping fresh capital into the company, enabling the accounts to climb again into the black. Junkers was informed that inflation had so eaten into the Reichswehr funds that no more money was available, nor would the promised order for two hundred new planes be forthcoming. Junkers, who had made the mistake of investing large amounts of his own capital both in the Russian venture and in plant expansion at home, expecting prompt reimbursement from the government, now faced ruin.

Brandenburg offered Junkers two options: bankruptcy, or partial settlement that would allow him to keep his Dessau manufacturing concern and his airlines concessions abroad— including the new route opened in Persia—and would provide a cash settlement. All Brandenburg wanted in return was the entire Junkers airlines operation inside Germany. Junkers, in helpless fury, decided to bring suit against the government for breach of contract. However, his original agreements with Niedermayer and Genral Hasse had been verbal only; the contracts Junkers had secured later proved insufficient—at least in the eyes of the judges who tried his case—and the short hearing held on January 12, 1926, saw Junkers' claims disallowed. In order to save his other interests, Junkers turned over his airline to the Traffic Ministry and watched it disappear; that same month, his former firm was merged with Aero-Lloyd and the residue of remaining independent operators into a state monopolied airline named Deutsche Lufthansa. With this one act, private airlines competition ceased to exist, and the Reichswehr gained its bomber training command.

The benefits arising from the sudden flush of government money made available by the Ruhr crisis, and the further deterioration of the effectiveness of the Control Commission were not confined to the Reischswehr, but spread to the skeleton of the German navy, enabling the bones to be covered with a defensive skin if not full sinews. A naval captain named Lohmann was entrusted with $2½ million, for which no account needed to be rendered. Captain Lohmann funneled part of the money to the Travemünder Yachthafen, A.G., and ordered prototypes and testing of small, fast motorboats capable of firing torpedoes. Lohmann spent more money to subsidize a Dutch firm in The Hague, Ingenieurskantoor voor Scheepsbouw (I.v.S.), where foreign orders for five- and six-hundred-ton submarines were obtained—especially from Japan, Turkey, Spain and Finland. Although none of the U-boats was destined for the German navy, the experiment in Holland enabled German engineers to keep up with current developments by studying the latest design and construction techniques.

The ten Heinkel seaplane fighters authorized for purchase at the same time money was provided for the Reichswehr's far larger number of Fokker D.XIIIs, which were being built in the Swedish branch factory, accrued to the navy free and clear. To provide training for crews to man these airplanes, and for others Lohmann planned to buy in the future, a cover organization was created with offices in Berlin and facilities in Warnemünde. Known as Severa, Ltd. (short for *Seeflugzeug-Versuchsabteilung*, Seaplane Experimental Testing Service), the bogus firm was allotted three hundred thousand dollars a year for operating expenses. Severa was ostensibly created to provide aerial target-towing for the navy's antiaircraft gunners, but Lohmann combined this activity with pilot and observer training, turning out six of each during the first year. Spending more money, Lohmann acquired the Caspar works at Travemünde, and opened a flying training school at List, on the island of Sylt, near the Danish border. Classes were upped to twenty-seven cadets, enrolling for a two-year curriculum. The Japanese, who, more than any others, manifested continuing interest in German naval aviation developments, followed Lohmann's progress throughout; and it was the Japanese military attaché, Captain Komaki, who informed Lohmann that he was not really putting anything over on the Allies. In February 1925, Komaki paid a visit to Naval Command and reported that the Control Commission "was doubtless well informed about the construction of airplanes at Warnemünde and Copenhagen, especially since the British had an extensive espionage service in Germany." Komaki's remarks were delivered only a short time after the Commission's so-called general inspection had ended, at a time when that body's effectiveness was ebbing fast, and in any event, whether informed or not, the British made no decisive moves to halt the production of warplanes or cancel the training of naval flyers. (Nor did the French; however, the British later admitted that they did not pass along all of their intelligence to France at the highest government levels.)

While Komaki was reporting his findings in Berlin, his naval counterpart, Captain Kojima, was at Warnemünde with a contract for Ernst Heinkel. What Kojima wanted was a launching device that could hurl a reconnaissance plane from the forward section of the new thirty-thousand-ton Japanese battleship *Nagato*. Kojima had brought along an enlarged photograph of the new dreadnought, mounting sixteen-inch guns, and he pointed to a clear space forward of the bridge and on top of the massive turret. Here, the Japanese said, is where the plane will be carried and from where it must be launched. He explained that the floatplane would have to be clearly airborne within a sixty-foot run. Heinkel tackled the problem with typical energy, and within ninety days was ready for testing. Manufacturing the two floatplanes—the two-seater He.25 and the single-seater He.26—had been easy enough, but no engines were available in Germany that would provide the necessary takeoff acceleration. Through a Dutch company, however, he easily purchased two new British-made Napier-Lion aircraft power plants of 300 and 450 horsepower. The launching device was simple in theory, simple in construction. Heinkel built iron rails on a wooden girder. On top of the girder rested a small, lightweight trolley. Resting on the trolley was the plane itself. With the pilot strapped in the cockpit, and with the launching rails turned into the wind, the plane was braked while the engine was started and run up to full rpm. With the tachometer needle holding steady just at the edge of the red line, the pilot signaled go, the plane was unbraked, and the sheer acceleration provided by the propellor chewing and pulling through the air started the trolley whizzing on its wheels down the rails. At the end of the run the plane had achieved flying speed and rose into the air, while the trolley merely flipped off the end of the rails.

The Warnemünde test was a success, but Heinkel was invited to Japan to demonstrate that the device would work aboard the *Nagato,* and at sea. Heinkel was piped aboard the great ship where he "was received like an admiral, with six hundred Japanese sailors in snow-white uniforms paraded on deck." His launching rails had been anchored to the top of the number two turret, and could be turned through about sixty degrees. In September 1925, the *Nagato* put out of Yokosuka and stood for the open sea. Heinkel was invited to the flying bridge to see that the great prow was pointed dead into the wind, and watched his company pilot, Bücker, climb into the He.26 and prepare for launch. The Napier-Lion roared into life and held. Freed, the biplane shot forward and was airborne into a freshening wind before reaching the end of rails. "She flew over the foc's'le of the *Nagato,* and away," Heinkel remembered. "Bücker then circled the ship while the whole crew cheered."

Heinkel was back in Germany in time to oversee his company's entry in Germany's first large-scale seaplane competition, sponsored by the Civil Air Transportation Association, but in reality backed by the German Naval Command. The competition was for the purpose of selecting the finest aircraft possible for the navy's armed reconnaissance role, that is, a combat plane to be built in open violation of the Versailles Treaty, whose clauses forbidding the construction of military planes had in no way been affected by the 1926 Paris Air Agreements. By early summer of that year, seventeen different designs had been readied to compete for prize money totaling ninety thousand dollars and the almost certain guarantee of contracts for series production that would follow. By June 24, when the competition began, seven of the designs had been withdrawn, and in the speed heats that followed, Heinkel's He.5a and He.5b took first and second place, with speeds of 130 miles per hour. Although the He.5s were new designs, three-seater monoplanes, Heinkel again had to rely on foreign engines, including the Napier-Lion and a 420-horsepower French Gnôme-Rhône. The seaworthiness tests were held near Warnemünde on August 5, and Heinkel watched angrily as one of his pilots, Dewitz, in an attempt to make what he described as an "elegant and classy" landing, smacked the water flat, crushed the floats, and managed to get rammed by the rescue launch, which caused the He.5 to capsize and sink. The other floatplane, flown by Wolfgang von Gronau, made a gentle splash onto the surface of the water by stalling in from a few feet in a nose-high altitude. Heinkel took first and third place, while Junkers placed second with his W.33, a seaborne descendant of his famous F.13.

So successful were the German navy's beginnings at resurrecting its air arm that the higher echelon could afford to turn down every Russian offer of cooperation. The Soviets offered to help train navel pilots at their base in Odessa, by the warm waters of the Black Sea, where flying conditions in the winter and during the early spring were far better than those prevailing on the Baltic, but the offer was refused. The German Chief of Naval Service, Admiral Hans Zenker, stated in an official memorandum dated July 22, 1926, that "military cooperation with Russia could only be undertaken with great caution . . . [but] the thread [was] not to be cut, so as to be able to put pressure on the Anglo-Saxons occasionally." One of Zenker's subordinates, Captain Wilfried von Loewenfeld, expressed the majority opinion of the traditionally conservative navy when he said: "Britain is at the moment the leader of Western culture, and if she is destroyed by communism, or by a revolt of her colonies, the danger of the Bolshevization of Europe becomes burningly acute." Loewenfeld urged, above all, a gradual understanding with Great Britain—an understanding that could never come to pass if the German navy openly began cooperating with the Russians. To Loewenfeld and Zenker, what the Reichswehr did was not the navy's concern. The captain's advice to Zenker as to how best to handle the Bolsheviks was worthy of the French. "Only play with the Russians," he suggested. "Deceive them amicably, without their noticing it." In the years that followed, almost all that the German navy was willing to give the Russians were plans for obsolete submarines.

The stepped-up activity in powered flight served to intensify the interest in gliding throughout Germany. The Traffic Ministry continued to pour in subsidies to encourage experimentation. Two new glider schools were established, one at Darmstadt and the other at Rositten. Gliding, which was relatively inexpensive, not only infused German youth with air-mindedness, but provided an outdoor research laboratory where design engineers could study drag as it affected flight characteristics. Gliders evolved from the rather chubby-bodied, square-winged affairs of the early 1920s into slender, gull-like craft stripped of every excess protuberance. Lessons learned from these elegant wooden birds were applied to coming generations of German warplanes.

And at Rhoen, where German postwar gliding began, a slender monument was erected near the summit of the Wasserkuppe. Chiseled into its base was an inscription that was both a tribute to the past and a signpost to the future:

> *Wir deutschen Flieger*
> *Wurden Sieger*
> *Durch uns allein.*
> *Volk, flieg, Du Wieder*
> *Und Du wirst Sieger*
> *Durch Dich allein.*

We German fliers
Became victorious
Through ourselves alone.
German nation, you must fly
And you will be victorious
Through yourself alone.

8

MADE IN RUSSIA

Lipetsk was a child's toy and gave us no great benefit.
—Erhard Milch

On May 28, 1925, the last of the fifty green and gold Fokker
D.XIII fighters was stowed safely aboard the freighter *Edmund
Hugo Stinnes,* then lying in port at Stettin on the river Oder
leading into the Baltic Sea, and only eighty miles from the new
Polish frontier. From Stettin, the freighter nosed into open
water and steered for Leningrad, nearly eight hundred nautical
miles away. At Leningrad, the disassembled planes were loaded
into boxcars, the doors were sealed, and armed guards climbed
aboard to mount precarious perches on top of the cars for the
long, open-air journey to Moscow and beyond. With a pause at
the capital for coal and water, the train chugged on to the
southeast, across the Don basin, to arrive finally at Lipetsk, 220
miles from Moscow, 600 miles from Leningrad, and more than
1,000 miles from Berlin. It was here, in this alien and Asiatic
sweep of land, that the Reichswehr had such high hopes for
creating the nucleus of Germany's new air force.

Although the first advance party of German technicians and
construction experts had arrived in Lipetsk early in 1924, it was
not until a year later than the field could be made ready to
receive its full quota of flying personnel, ground crew, and
technicians needed to make Lipetsk Airdrome fully operational. Lipetsk itself is located on the Voronezh River, a flat
town whose small one- and two-story buildings were almost
submerged in the sea of green trees crowding every vacant
space of land. From the air, it seemed that fully half of the city
had been given over to a mammoth square, inside which, glowing like a jewel, sat a many-cupolaed Russian Orthodox church,

walled in, and itself surrounded by a cushion of green. Lipetsk had been a favored spa of Peter the Great, but to the Germans confined to the rawly finished airfield some distance away from the center of town, life was monastic.

Trainees discovered, however, that Lipetsk was equipped to serve almost all military needs. When finished, the complex was described by Helm Speidel, one of the flying officers who trained there, in this way: "Around two runways there came into being a large complex of hangars, wharfs, production and repair shops. . . . There were administrative and living quarters, a hospital equipped with the most modern clinical apparatus, wireless and telephone installations, railway connections and so forth. The German flyers' colony was quartered in the wide area of the airdrome, which was highly modern according to the standards of the time, camouflaged on the outside to give the impression [that the buildings belonged to] the Fourth Squadron of the Red Air Force. . . . The whole complex was sealed off and guarded by Soviet militia.

"The German personnel consisted of the permanent party that remained at Lipetsk throughout the year, numbering about sixty men. In addition there were about fifty men making up the personnel of the military training courses, held during the summer months; and finally, there were between seventy and a hundred men engaged in technical experiments. Thus there were, on an average, about two hundred Germans always present during the summer. The Red Air Force was represented at Lipetsk by a fairly large number of soldiers who were trained in special technical courses by German instructors, both foremen and mechanics. . . ."

With the arrival of the long-awaited Fokkers, it was at last possible for training to begin, although on a limited scale. A sense of urgency emanated from Berlin, where a top-secret list of available military pilots carried only 180 names—and the Reichswehr planners were looking forward to a mobilization potential of one thousand aircraft by 1930, in just over four years' time. But before organized classes of student pilots could be put through the training mill, a cadre of instructors had to be created, experienced airmen able to teach themselves the idiosyncrasies of the new Fokkers and so be able to instruct others. At the same time, they would have to put together a workable syllabus, based partly on their own hard-earned experiences in aerial warfare, but mostly upon educated guesswork as to what might be required in the future.

Among the very first instructors assigned to Lipetsk were Karl von Schönebeck and Werner Junck, both wartime fighter pilots with experience in combat against the Bolsheviks in 1919 on the Eastern Front, and therefore considered politically reliable by the Reichswehr. They shared thirteen victories between them; they also shared a dislike of the infantry, which both had joined after their respective squadrons were disbanded, preferring that to civilian life in postwar Germany. Like every other German who would go to Russia, these pilots traveled the underground route out of Stettin to Leningrad and from there on to Lipetsk. They were dressed in ordinary civilian suits and carried no army paybooks, and their incoming mail was handled through a circuitous route that began with a Berlin box number and ended at the field after being channeled through the German Embassy in Moscow. Thus Germans would spend an entire season beyond the Volga while their relatives believed them to be still in their own country.

Relations with the Russians were strained at first, but the German instructors discovered a way to ease the tension and make Russians friendly: be tough, beat them at their own game. Junck has described how he and the others challenged the Soviet pilots to an aerial duel to see who were the better fliers. The challenge was accepted, and the Russians went aloft in their seven- and eight-year-old British-built planes to face the Germans in their factory-fresh, 450-horsepower Fokkers. Understandably, the Russians were trounced, but the ice was truly broken when the Germans traded aircraft for a second round and still managed to outfly the Soviets. After that, the Germans were shown enormous respect and the instructors, who were allowed off the base, seldom had to buy their own vodka when visiting the casino in Lipetsk, one of the town's few diversions.

The weather closed down early in the autumn, and all that was accomplished by the instructors at Lipetsk was feeding a handful of older fliers through the improvised course, but even refresher training proved overdemanding for these veterans, most of whom discovered that a seven-year layoff combined with an extra 250 horsepower was almost too much for their advancing years. When the snows came, the instructors returned to Germany to submit their opinions to Fliegerzentrale. From the Commercial Pilots' School at Stettin, and from a number of the private flying clubs elsewhere in Germany, an even dozen of the younger and more promising pilots were selected. In the spring of 1926, these handpicked men were sent to Lipetsk, and in the six months of good weather that followed, Junck and the others turned them into instructor pilots. They returned to Germany in time to witness the sacking of a hero and a ripple of revolution within the Reichstag aimed at dismantling the structure of the Russian enterprise with which they were so newly involved.

When, on February 28, 1925, President Ebert died and was replaced by Field Marshal von Hindenburg, then seventy-eight, Seeckt's stature began to shrink. He worsened his position by continually bypassing Defense Minister Gessler in open breaching of the chain of command. His worst blunder was approving a request by the crown prince that his son, the Kaiser's grandson, Prince William of Prussia, be allowed to participate as a uniformed officer in fall maneuvers held by the 9th Infantry Regiment. This was a clear affront to the Social Democrats, and the leftist press flayed Seeckt unmercifully. On October 9, 1926, Seeckt handed in his resignation and was replaced by the man of his own choice, Colonel General Wilhelm Heye. There was no danger that Heye would slow the wheels of rearment set in motion by Seeckt, but what happened next in Berlin was, from the Reichswehr point of view, outrageous and embarrassing.

When Hugo Junkers was forced against the wall by Brandenburg with the consequest loss of his airline system within Germany, the Junkers design and production staff gathered to pledge that none of them would accept posts with Lufthansa, no matter how lucrative the offer. The one exception was a former captain in the Imperial Air Service, Erhard Milch, thirty-four, who had ended the war as commander of Fighter

Group 6, a replacement training unit. Technically oriented and with driving ambition, Milch quit Junkers Airways, Ltd., to join as one of the directors of Lufthansa, and within a short time had shoved others aside to become top man. Those who remained with Junkers were as embittered as men who feel they have been betrayed can be, and they suspected that Milch had been the Reichswehr's man within the organization as a kind of Judas leading the firm into a trap. (Milch and Brandenburg were, in fact, quite close.) Simmering with frustration, one of the Junkers directors—and it may well have been Sachsenberg—prepared a lengthy memorandum detailing the secret negotiations between Junkers and the Traffic Ministry concerning affairs in Russia. The memo was given to the liberal Social Democratic deputy Philipp Scheidemann, who made extracts which were read aloud to the Reichstag in open assembly on December 16, 1926. To most of the Social Democrats there, who were ignorant of the labyrinthian connections between the various ministries and the Reichswehr, the contents exploded like a howitzer shell.

I would like to prove through several pertinent facts [Scheidemann began] that the Reichswehr has become more and more a state within the State, obeying its own laws and following its own politics. Based on a memorandum from the house of Junkers which has come to our attention, it seems there exists within the Reichswehr Ministry a special section known as [Sondergruppe R] whose members are, for the most part, serving army officers. They have spent since 1923 sums mounting in the neighborhood of eighty million gold marks.
Hear! Hear!
And there exists in a large Berlin bank an account upon which one of the Reichswehr functionaries, Herr Spangenburg, executes the necessary payments. . . . This Spangenburg is in close contact with the so-called Society to Promote Industrial Enterprise, or *Gefu*, among whose directors one finds a certain Otto zur Leien, who resides always abroad, notably in Russia. Through Spangenburg, several millions of marks have been paid into the treasury of *Gefu*, clearly demonstrating the collusion between the Reichswehr and this society.
The task of *Gefu* is the building of an armaments industry

abroad, chiefly in Russia. Contracts have been signed with false names. The go-between for the Junkers contracts, signed on March 14, 1922, was none other than General Hasse.

Tumult on the right, diverse cries directed against Scheidemann: Traitor! Louse! Throw him out!

We know for a certainty, [Scheidemann continued, not to be intimidated] that Russian-made munitions have arrived [here] by boat from Leningrad at the end of September and in October of this year. . . . The communist cell at the port [of Stettin] is perfectly aware of these things.

Embarrassed laughter from the left.

It is neither clean nor honest to see Soviet Russia preaching world disarmament on one hand, while at the same time she is actively rearming the Reichswehr.

Interruptions from the left; diverse cries.

We must put an end to this scandal! We can no longer tolerate a state of things contrary to the creation of a truly republican and democratic army. The Reichswehr needs to be completely shaken up and reformed.

Applause from the center and from the left. Tumult on the right.

Repercussions from this tempest were not what the airmen feared. Public disclosure of the hitherto secret Russian dealings, including front-page articles in such liberal German newspapers as *Vorwärts,* and England's respected *Manchester Guardian,* accomplished little more than forcing the closure of the Gefu organization—but only after some three hundred thousand Russian-made artillery shells were distributed and stored safely inside Reichswehr bunkers. The aviation program continued to gather momentum.

In the spring of 1927, Junck, Schönebeck, and the other instructors received the first input of aspiring fighter pilots at Lipetsk. They were the cream of the cream. Under a new scheme formulated by the training command, no fewer than sixty pilots destined for the Reichswehr were to be turned out each year. Of this number, half could be serving officers, and of these, ten could be without previous flying experience. The remaining thirty hopefuls were, in effect, officer candidates who would go through preflight and flight training as civilians, eligible for commissions after graduation. All sixty student pilots were passed through the year-long course at the German Commercial Flying Academy at Schleissheim, and those who made the grade received B2 certificates, the equivalent of a commercial pilot's license. Only the top ten graduates, youths on fire with the spirit of the hunter, were selected for the fighter pilots' course at Lipetsk.

The transition from Schleissheim's low-powered trainers to the new Fokkers, which were nearly twice as fast, was smoother than even the most sanguinary instructor had expected. The D.XIII, like its famous predecessor, was light on the controls, stable in level flight, and forgiving of all but the grossest of student mistakes. Fast and sensitive, the D.XIIIs offered to the student the sensation of being mounted aboard a thoroughbred; but to their instructors, the new Fokkers were sadly lacking in the two characteristics that had made the old ones great: the D.VIIs' elevator-like climbing ability and low stalling speed, which permitted the dreamy stall turns that led Allied pilots to believe the D.VIIs could "hang on their props" while firing into the bellies of French and British planes. Other than these handicaps, serious only in a plane intended for an active role as a fighter-interceptor, the heavy (3,637 pounds maximum gross, more than 1,600 pounds heavier than the D.VII) Fokker was not otherwise faulted as an advanced combat trainer. There were initial problems with the Napier-Lion engines when it came time for periodic overhauls; the power plants had to be crated and shipped the long distance to Holland, and from there to the factory in England and back again. British Napier believed the work was being done for the Dutch, and never had an inkling they were contributing to the maintenance of the secret German air arm. But once the necessary nonmetric tools had been imported and mechanics trained, overhauls were carried out in the extensive workshops at Lipetsk.

The training inside Russia did not differ radically from that given in Germany during the last year of the war. The major difference between the 1918 and the 1927 syllabus lay in the emphasis upon low-level tactical exercises designed to teach effective cooperation with ground forces. The fighters were fitted with bomb racks and release mechanisms, converting the Fokkers into airborne artillery seeking pinpoint accuracy against simulated supply dumps, troop concentrations, transport columns and other tactical targets. The climax of the intensive air-to-air work came toward the end of the course, when two squadrons of nine aircraft each were formed of students and instructors alike and sent to stalk each other out of the sun. These eighteen-ship melees over the Russian plains resembled the classic dogfights waged over the Western Front nine years earlier, but at Lipetsk the victories were awarded on the basis of grainy gun-camera film run off on a clattering projector inside one of the darkened classrooms.

The high caliber of the instructors, the surprisingly adept Russian fitters, riggers and machinists employed in the maintenance shops, and the fact that the student pilots were hand-picked and already had commercial licenses all combined to keep the accident rate at an unprecedented low. During the war it had not been considered unusual to lose 30 per cent of a training class killed or maimed in flying accidents, but in the six years that Lipetsk served as an operational training base, fatal crashes took the lives of only three pilots, just 3 per cent of the whole. The trip home for the dead lacked any sense of military dignity or flourish: to pass the corpses through Russian customs points undetected, they were simply packed inside elongated wooden crates stamped "Spare Parts" and run from Leningrad to Stettin in the holds of a ship.

The perversity of Russian attitudes baffled the Germans. While on the one hand there was respect and even friendliness among the Germans and the Russians working together at the airdrome, and while profitable exchanges were made between visiting Russian general officers in Berlin and their counterparts in Moscow, the Soviet customs officials, on the other hand, proved obstinate, suspicious and contentious. Shipments of vitally needed parts were subject to long, frustrating delays. Until the problem was finally ironed out with the grudging permission of Moscow for the Germans to establish their own customs station right at Lipetsk, much equipment was simply smuggled across the Baltic in small boats, sometimes laden dangerously to the waterline with bombs and live machine-gun ammunition.

In the summer of 1928, the chief of the Truppenamt, General Werner von Blomberg, took several of his staff officers on an inspection trip of the German operations inside Russia, a trip that included participation in the joint maneuvers held on the rolling plains near Voronezh, sixty miles south of Lipetsk. Blomberg watched with pleasure the tight formations of Fokkers and new Heinkel observation planes zooming over the heads of Russian infrantry and Russian tanks advancing through clouds of dust. The German officers visited the new tank school at Kazan, and went to Orenberg, where experiments in poison gas were being carried out. Blomberg returned to Berlin in an enthusiastic frame of mind and dictated a detailed fifty-four-page report of what they had seen.

"The reception of the German officers was everywhere friendly," he wrote, "often cordial and very hospitable. The War Commissar, Voroshilov, had given instructions to show everything and to meet all our wishes. . . . The value of the cooperation to the Red Army was emphasized time and again, as was the wish to hear the verdict of German officers—which is considered authoritative—about the achievements of the Red Army." Blomberg was especially impressed with the operational efficiency of Lipetsk, which was "of great value to our armament program." He told how Voroshilov pressed him on the point of German support in case of a Polish attack on Russia, but here Blomberg had hedged, pointing out that the decision could only be reached at a higher level.

Lipetsk was not only a school, but a testing ground for prototypes of combat planes, reflecting the significant aviation developments inside Germany where the industry was flexing its experimental wings. On September 30, 1929, Fritz von Opel strapped himself deep in the narrow cockpit of a rocket-powered glider and launched his creation from atop the Wasserkuppe for a fiery flight lasting ten minutes, clocking 100 miles per hour before burnout. Three weeks later, designer Claudius

Dornier watched apprehensively as his ambitious project, the twelve-engine Do.X flying boat, lumbered into the air from Lake Constance packed with 169 passengers, 9 of whom were stowaways. The American-built Curtiss Conqueror engines were mounted in tandem on pylons atop the wing; six propellers pulling, six propellers pushing. Three of these freakish craft were built, ostensibly as Lufthansa's bid to capture the market for transoceanic air traffic, carrying a normal load of seventy to eighty passengers; but in reality the Do.X was financed by the German navy as an experimental long-range reconnaissance plane to be equipped with torpedoes. In 1930, in the experienced hands of Friedrich Christiansen, a Do.X completed a 28,000-mile goodwill and propaganda flight reaching from Germany to Lisbon, from the Bahamas to South America, Miami, and New York, and from Newfoundland to Spain—then home to dead storage inside a German museum.

More practical and longer lived was Hugo Junkers' leviathan G.38. Designed purely as a passenger liner carrying thirty-four and a crew of seven, the G.38's monstrous wing, 144 feet 4 inches long and more than 3,200 square feet in area, dwarfed the fuselage and the double-decker tail. The only German airframe manufacturer capable of producing his own engines, Junkers mounted four of his 750-horsepower Jumo power plants in streamlined nacelles in a wing so deep a man could stand erect near its leading edge. These engines, the most powerful then available in Germany, were still shy of the horsepower ideal for a plane weighing twenty-six tons, yet the cruising speed of 115 miles per hour was respectable, and the oversize fuel tanks provided a range of 2,150 miles—enough to fly nonstop from Munich to Tunisia and back. Lufthansa bought two of these durable transports, naming them *Deutschland* and *General Feldmarschall von Hindenburg*, crowd pleasers that crisscrossed European skies for nine years.

At Lipetsk, remote from the Disarmament Committee of the League of Nations and watchdogs of the Left among Reichstag deputies, nine different war-oriented aircraft were put through strenuous testing programs between 1928 and 1932. The Arado works contributed their Ar.64 and Ar.65, deep-bellied biplane fighters; Ernst Heinkel sent an HD.38 seaplane fighter equipped with wheels for tests on land, the He.45 reconnaissance bomber, and the He.46 parasol monoplane two-seater. The most provocative and innovative tactical aircraft sent to Lipetsk for testing was the Junkers K.47, built in the Swedish factory near Malmö. Ahead of its time, the K.47 was a fully cantilevered, all-metal monoplane offering exceptionally smooth lines. The rounded monocoque fuselage rested on an extra-sturdy landing gear, part of which was designed to carry a pair of 120-pound bombs slung just behind the wheels. The pilot sat five feet behind the 480-horsepower British Jupiter radial engine, and behind him was the observer-gunner, equipped with a newly developed gun mounting ring offering exceptionally easy traverse and a wide field of fire. The K.47 was conceived as a ground assault craft, and its performance was all that even the greediest commander could ask for: speed, 168 miles per hour; range, 404 miles; ceiling, 26,000 feet. Here was an aircraft that could have gone into series production as the Reichswehr's basic infantry and tank cooperation machine. Pilots loved to fly it. But when pitted against biplane fighters with their shorter turning radius and lower wing loading, the K.47 appeared to be no match, and the promising design was passed over. Junkers, however, was convinced that he was right and the evaluation board wrong, and the concept was one his designers would not give up, and determined to improve.

In the quest for workable tactical aircraft, the need for strategic bombers was not overlooked. The Billy Mitchell of Italy, General Giulio Douhet, whose book, *The Command of the Air*, published in 1921, had made him an outcast at home but a Nostradamus abroad, was Europe's air-power prophet. Douhet, with Latin passion, envisioned a war of tomorrow when the industrial plants of whole cities and nations would be left in smoking rubble by blows delivered from the air. He warned that "in the future no state will be able to win a war unless it has at its disposal a completely independent air force of such striking power that it can obtain absolute air supremacy in a short space of time." Thoughts of a separate air force were still debatable inside the Reichswehr, but there was no question that big bombers were needed.

Three prototypes were constructed and sent to Russia for

testing. Unknown to the Polish government, these long-range aircraft penetrated their air space en route to Lipetsk; this was a calculated risk undertaken to save the time and labor involved in transporting crated parts by sea and by rail, and the Reichswehr was as careful to hide these illegal flights from the Reichstag as from the Poles or the French. Sometimes at night, and always at maximum altitude, the missions were staged from Germany across the Danzig corridor to East Prussia and from there through Polish skies a second time in order to reach Lipetsk. Not one of these overflights was detected.

The Rohrbach Roland was nothing more than a standard Lufthansa three-engine transport modified by the addition of defensive gun emplacements, one located far aft atop the fuselage and two others stuck underneath the trailing edge of the wing as extensions of the engine nacelles. This design was rejected for series production, a decision that coupled with the general world economic slump to put Rohrbach out of business. Dornier submitted a four-engine bomber with a crew of six, but the Do.P, like the Do.X, had its engines mounted in tandem atop the wing, a system that was never wholly satisfactory. Finally, a sensible compromise was reached in Dornier's Do.11, a replica of Dornier's successful freight carrier, the Do.F.

There was never any question of German designers' ability to come up with a successful four-engine plane designed only for the bombing role; the almost insurmountable difficulty lay in the capacity of the industry as it then stood to turn out civilian and military aircraft simultaneously. Added to the problem was the chronic shortage of suitable power plants, worsened by the sudden folding of the Bavarian Motor Works. And in any case, open manufacture of heavy bombers inside German plants was such a flagrant violation of the Versailles Treaty that Germany might easily lose her place on the League of Nations Council, unthinkable to the majority Social Democrats in the Reichstag. Thus the Reichswehr accepted the Do.11 as its heavy bomber, despite the fact that it had only two, and not the desired four, engines. Since it had been designed to carry freight and not passengers, its conversion to bomber posed few problems, and when completed planes rolled out of the plant, the Do.11 looked very much the innocent workhorse to which it owed its existence. To cut drag, Dornier engineers equipped the Do.11 with a hand-cranked retractable landing gear, praised by the pilot when it worked, but cursed by the sweating crewmen who had to operate it.

In 1931, the Reichswehr made up its mind to begin phasing out Lipetsk as an operational pilot and observer training center, a decision partly influenced by an agreement reached on the part of the German ministers of defense, transportation, and foreign affairs on November 30, 1930. The decision was no less than the waiving of that section of the Versailles Treaty prohibiting the stockpiling of aeronautical equipment. This decision, made unilaterally and *in camera*, was passed along only on a need-to-know basis. It marked the beginning of Germany's buildup of an organized air arm within its own frontiers. A secret technical test station was already functioning at Rechlin, in Mecklenburg, and plans were being continually updated for its expansion. Lipetsk could be abandoned within twenty-four months, the training and testing program transferred in easy stages back to the homeland.

And this is precisely what happened. The Fokker D.XIIIs that had seemed so precious a short time ago were scrapped after sustaining airframe damage requiring more than routine repair. They were not replaced. And when, during the fall maneuvers of 1931 in Silesia, the new defense minister, General Wilhelm Groener, flew into a rage because the army used small, free-floating balloons to represent aircraft roaring overhead, a dozen top instructors were hurriedly withdrawn from Lipetsk, equipped with new Ar.65 fighters and formed into three showcase squadrons of four machines each. They were never returned to Russia, but were stationed in different parts of Germany—Königsberg, Berlin, and Nuremberg—where their active status was camouflaged in an ingenious, if demeaning, manner: the fighters were hired out to commercial firms as towplanes, dragging behind them gaudy banners exhorting Germans to drink Dortmünder Union beer or to invest in a variety of other consumer goods and services.

The observers' school at Lipetsk-Voronezh was closed down late in 1931, and the last class of fighter pilots was passed through the course at Lipetsk in the summer of 1932. Although the relationship between the German and Russian high commands had never been more cordial—Marshal Tukhachevski and his staff had even been invited to attend the Reichswehr's 1932 maneuvers, where they were warmly received by President von Hindenburg—the phasing out of Lipetsk caused sharp reactions. From Moscow, the demand came for reactivation of the field to its former intensive pitch; to bring this about, the Russians suggested, it would be necessary to return the instructors of the showcase squadrons, along with their newly acquired fighters. Moreover, the Russians insisted upon witnessing a demonstration of German "massed night bombing operations." The request was legitimately turned down on the ground that outside of the three or four prototype bombers parked on the field at Lipetsk, no night bomber force existed. Russian insistence on keeping Lipetsk open as a tactical training area and test center is easy to understand: Red Air Force pilots had been allowed to fly every new German plane sent to Lipetsk, and their engineers had been soaking up the expertise freely offered by German technicians and master mechanics; in return, the Russians, committed only to the lease of ground and air space, hid their own developments in aircraft design.

After hard bargaining, the Russians relented. The permanent fixtures on the field were turned over to the Red Air Force, and the experimental bombers were allowed to be flown back to Germany. The Russians claimed the Fokker D.XIIIs, less than two-thirds of which were still flyable, a claim the Germans were quick to grant.

The Lipetsk venture, from inception to final closure in 1933, lasted ten years, six of which were given over to active training of air crews. An even 100 pilots were graduated from the fighter school, and 120 air observers were commissioned and added to Reichswehr's active list. The cost worked out at approximately thirty thousand dollars per trained airman, or one-three-hundredth of the total Reichswehr budget. Events would prove it to be rock-bottom cost accounting.

9

COMMAND

It is quite a mistake to suppose that Hitler has seized power. All that has
happened is that we have given him a job.
—Franz von Papen

I cannot share control of the aeronautical industry with any outside
agency, any more than I could share control of my air force.
—Hermann Goering

At fifteen minutes past eleven, on the morning of January 30,
1933, Adolf Hitler marched up the steps of the Reichs Chancellery in Berlin. Waiting to receive him was President von Hindenburg, only four years short of his ninetieth birthday. Less
than a quarter of an hour later, Hitler swept back through the
massive Chancellery portals and into the wintry air outside. He
moved quickly down the steps and climbed into the back seat
of a waiting black sedan. The door slammed and the car shot
across the square and pulled up in front of the Kaiserhof Hotel.
Hitler hurried inside and was escorted upstairs to a suite where
waited most of the Nazi party chiefs who had battled at his side
in turbulent political meetings and in bloody street brawls during the past ten years to bring about this moment of glory. The
door was flung open and Hitler strode inside, surrounded by a
sea of brown-shirted men. At forty-three, Adolf Hitler had just
become Chancellor of Germany. The little intellectual, Joseph
Goebbels, observed in this hour of triumph, "He says nothing,
we all say nothing; but his eyes are full of tears."

Hitler's ascent to the throne of power was not greeted with
universal enthusiasm in the Reichswehr, nearly 25 per cent of
whose officers were members of the archly conservative aristoc-
racy. Active socialism had even less appeal than the failed offer-

ings of democracy of the now-dead Weimar Republic, and the uninhibited use of truncheon, fist and rifle butt by the Nazis to discourage political opposition was abhorrent to officers brought up by a code of behavior that allowed gentlemen to duel but never to brawl. However, the new chancellor compensated for his socially repellent background and his obnoxious cohorts in significant ways, especially on the crucial questions affecting the future of the Reichswehr.

The peculiar structure of Seeckt's creation—a cadre army top-heavy with rank—resulted in an elite force necessarily stagnating for lack of expansion and promotion. Officers had long ago ceased to be towering figures of respect among civilians, and enlisted men felt outcast from society, their lives dull and mean. (Despair is not too strong a word to describe the general feeling; the army's suicide rate fluctuated between four and five times that of the general population.) A disillusioned Reichswehr lieutenant named Scheringer explained the apathy that had settled over the army after the first flush of exultation had drained away. Writing for the Nazi weekly *Völkischer Beobachter* (People's Observer), Lieutenant Scheringer commented, "Soldiers turn into officials, officers become candidates for pensions. What remains is a police troop. People know nothing of the tragedy of the four words, Twelve years as subalterns."

The new chancellor promised to change all that, offering the resurrection of the deep-running pride in the profession of arms and the infusion of purpose in his vow "that out of the present Reichswehr shall rise the great Army of the German people." Following a night-long torchlight victory parade that seemed to the French ambassador to turn the streets of Berlin into "rivers of fire," Hitler's first act on the morning of his second day in office was a surprise visit to the barracks of the Berlin garrison force. The startled and not wholly pleased commanding officer hastily assembled the troops in the square. Hitler put them at ease, and the cold was forgotten in the torrent of heated words that were flung at them during the next exhilarating hour. Hitler addressed them not as just another in a long and dreary succession of politicians, but as an old *Frontsoldat*, a trench rat who had earned his Iron Cross, First Class, under fire. Two days later, having successfully wooed the ranks, Hitler won converts among the generals and the admirals by accepting a formal dinner invitation at the home of General Kurt von Hammer-stein-Equord, where a two-hour harangue left the guests groggy with fatigue, yet encouraged by what Hitler had said. Henceforth, the armed forces of the Reich would be able to develop along lines of their choosing, unhindered by a pacifistic Reichstag and without regard to the Treaty of Versailles.

The least of Hitler's worries was finding a candidate for the important cabinet post of Reichswehr minister—equivalent to the old American secretary of war; one had already been ap-pointed only the day before Hitler was made Chancellor. At fifty-four, Lieutenant General Werner von Blomberg was the very figure of a classic Prussian general: tall, erect, robust, blue-eyed, strong-chinned, immaculately uniformed, a holder of the Blue Max for brilliant staff planning during the war, adept at moving with the times, impetuous, gifted with humor, radiating command presence wherever he went. Werner von Blomberg possessed one quality above all others that endeared him to the chancellor—an almost slavish devotion to Hitler's person and ideals. This idolatry was so obvious to officers less mesmerized by Hitler that Blomberg was jokingly referred to by them as the Rubber Lion. But the new Reichswehr minister had good rea-sons for putting his faith in Adolf Hitler. He had just left his previous command in East Prussia, where his outnumbered Reichswehr forces faced a sudden resurgence of Polish bel-licosity. Blomberg's field intelligence units reported strong cav-alry reinforcements pouring into the area, concentrating along the Danzig corridor and the German-Lithuanian border. The buildup had been going on for months, and even before Hitler was sure he could come to power, he had ordered his private army, the SA, to back up the Reichswehr with everything it had. Since the *Sturmabteilung* formations throughout Germany numbered more than two million men, its support had real meaning. Moreover, Hitler assured Blomberg that he was al-ready at work on a political solution to the Polish question; the solution, he hinted, would allow Blomberg to keep the Reichswehr intact until it was ready for combat—and when that time came, they would both see the new army a power to be reckoned with in Europe. For a start, he could begin planning to add another two hundred thousand men.*

The logical choice to man the newly created post of Air Commissioner was Major General Helmut Wilberg, fifty-three, who had been installed as the top airman in the Truppenamt as early as 1920. It was Wilberg who had singled out the energetic Ernst Brandenburg and put his organizational talents to use, and it was Wilberg who fully understood Seeckt's concept of an army in miniature as applied to the secret air arm. Wilberg was one of the few prewar pilots still on active duty during the early struggles to form an air cadre, and there was no faulting his wartime service with the First and Fourth Armies as commanding air officer. Wilberg had helped organize the training and testing procedures in Russia and was abreast of aviation developments throughout the world. More importantly, he was familiar with the capabilities and limitations of the staff, field and company officers making up the Reichswehr's air units. Unfortunately for Wilberg and, as it turned out, for the German air force, General Wilberg was a Jew, or partly so, and had the true military man's disdain for politics. Although not denied an active role by Hitler from 1933 onwards, Wilberg was shunted aside from the top job, which went to Hermann Goering.

Hitler's elevation of Goering from retired captain to cabinet member was expedient, and probably inevitable, despite the glaring deficiencies in Goering's background that would have eliminated another, politically uncommitted man from seeking the ultimate job involving the realm of the air. Goering had neither engineering nor technical grounding, and was totally without corporate managerial experience. He was not a student of economics or history and lacked strategic grasp. He was nei-

---

*The gathering of Polish forces was no idle threat. Only two months after Hitler came to power, in March 1933, Marshal Józef Pilsudski urged the French to join him in a preventive war on Germany, a suggestion the French were quick to veto.

ther visionary nor prophet, and did not have a whole-souled dedication to aviation and a deep awareness of the function of air power as a political weapon. His tactical experience was fourteen years in the past, and the nine years that had elapsed since the fiasco in Munich had produced dissolution, not strengthening, of his moral fiber.

The ricocheting carbine slug fired by the Munich policeman did more than tear a gaping hole in Goering's leg—the wound (his first) was a shocking reminder of mortality, and it bled his will. The wound healed and the pain vanished during the long recuperation in Austria, but morphine syrettes remained part of the Goering baggage. During their purposeless stay in Italy, financed largely with borrowed funds, his wife watched Siegfried dissolve. Goering's hard body turned flaccid. His skin drained of color and became fish-belly white. Violent outbursts or temper were more frequent, lapsing into a moroseness that was followed by opium-induced euphoria. Normally ascetic in eating habits, Goering developed an obsession for rich, flaky, cream-filled pastries, and the calories piled up below the waist, leaving his face still angular and hard and cruel. When Goering applied for amnesty for his part in the 1923 putsch and was refused, his anger erupted, uncharacteristically, on racial grounds. In a letter to his mother-in-law in Sweden in which he confessed to "the wounds in my soul," he wrote that "I only want to go back to a strongly Nationalized Germany, not to that Jew-run Republic. . . ."

Goering had no intention of following his *Führer*, his leader, into the dock and thence into languid imprisonment at Landsberg, where Adolf Hitler was at leisure to work at his turgid prose summing up his political testament, a work entitled simply *Mein Kampf.* Goering's own battle was one of survival, no more. The sudden illness of the elder Baroness von Fock provided the excuse for the long journey back to Sweden, where, conceivably, Goering could have kicked the dope habit and gone to work for Rohrbach, Heinkel or Junkers in one of the branch factories busy turning out prototype aircraft for the clandestine German air arm. Instead, he installed himself and his wife in a cheap flat in Stockholm and lived on the slender proceeds of the sale of their house in Austria. When this money ran low, his wife was placed in the humiliating position of borrowing from her family to pay rent, buy groceries and feed Goering's habit. By now, Karin Goering's own frail constitution had given way and doctors ordered her to bed. As for the former air hero, whose explosive temper tantrums culminated in physical violence in an attempt to secure morphine, doctors stepped in and had him certified as a dangerous addict. On September 1, 1925, Hermann Goering was committed to a state asylum at Langbro.

Goering spent three months inside asylum walls under intensive treatment and observation before doctors felt that there was sufficient remission for him to be released. However, Goering was back again in the early part of 1926, a year that ended with a kind of victory for him when he achieved the status of an outpatient no longer considered dangerous. When, in 1927, Hindenburg declared a general amnesty for all those who had taken part in the 1923 putsch and Goering was free to go back to Germany, his spirits rose to subdue the acute need for drugs. After four years of idleness, he sought out the sales manager of Tornblad Parachutes, Ltd., and secured a job as a straight-commission salesman with Germany as his territory. Once back in Berlin, he was able to drum up other representational jobs, including one with Ernst Heinkel, and at last was actually able to pay rent on an apartment. In 1928, with Hitler's help, Goering managed to secure a seat as a Nazi deputy in the Reichstag. Goering's fire-and-steel speeches so pleased Hitler that he presented him with a new black Mercedes sedan, long-nosed and powerfully engined. Hitler, who was generally cold to airplanes, had a high-school boy's fascination with high-performance automobiles, and enthusiastically accepted Goering's offer of a ride in the twelve-cylinder gift. Hitler was aghast at Goering's wild swings of the wheel that put the heavy car on both sides of the road, his lead-footed lunges at the accelerator pedal and his manic delight in sounding the klaxon-like horn to warn others of his meteoric approach. If Goering's driving was no indication of his former piloting skill, it was clearly a manifestation of personality traits that Swedish psychiatrists had found so disturbing.

In the predawn hours of October 17, 1931, Karin Goering died in Stockholm, worn out at the age of forty-three. Goering was in Berlin at the time, summoned there by Hitler. He rushed back to Sweden for the funeral—overcome, his friends said, by grief and remorse—and returned immediately to Germany. Ten months later, on August 30, 1932, Hermann Goering, with the help of the Central and the Bavarian People's Party, was elected Reichstag President.

From Hitler's point of view, Goering's psychiatric history and his general estrangement from German affairs for four years weighed little on the scales when balanced against the ease with which Goering moved in social circles in order to extract contributions from wealthy industrialists for the party fund, and Goering's undoubted fealty to his liege lord was beyond price. Goering proclaimed publicly that the love for Adolf Hitler rose from the deep belief "that God has sent him to us to save Germany." Goering not only associated the new Chancellor with the Deity, but likened him to England's legendary King Arthur. Hitler's myriad virtues were "mystical, inexpressible, almost incomprehensible." Hitler could expect no such sentiments from, for example, General Wilberg. Goering had mentioned that because he pledged total loyalty to Hitler, Hitler in return offered "unqualified confidence" in him. There was no doubt of this fact; Goering not only was named Reichs Air Commissioner by the Führer, but was appointed Minister of the Interior for Prussia—which gave him total control of the police forces there—and Minister without Portfolio, an omnibus title that effectively made Goering the Chancellor's personal ambassador.

With a liberal helping of state funds, Goering had built for himself an ornately furnished townhouse near the center of Berlin, renaming the street that ran past the front door Hermann-Goeringstrasse. He hired a personal valet named Robert Kropp, who discovered that his new master was a man of erratic hours and bizarre habits. Goering, swamped with the organizational problems connected with his manifold duties, including the creation of the *Geheime Staatspolizei*, the Secret State Police, the Gestapo, often stayed up until one or two in the morning bent over a stack of fat file folders. He would go to bed only to be assaulted by hunger, whereupon he would shout down the servant's line for Kropp to bring up beer, sandwiches and cake. Kropp would appear almost instantly with the required heavy snack at Goering's bedroom door, to be greeted by the master dressed for sleep in what has been described as a "silk night-gown with puffed sleeves." The mind boggles at the vision of Goering's 280 pounds stuffed inside.

Like any other politician, Goering needed proficient cronies as subordinates, and his early choices were astute indeed. He needed someone to organize the increasingly irritating amount of office paperwork as badly as he needed Kropp to help him get dressed at home. The job fell to Karl Bodenschatz, who was appointed Adjutant and general upper-echelon factotum. Bodenschatz, still lean and darkly handsome, had served Goe-ring in the same capacity in 1918 and had been Richthofen's adjutant before that. He was not only a diligent organizer, but an author as well, having published *Hunting in Flanders Skies* a few years after the war. To standardize civilian training proce-dures under one administrative control, Goering merged the profusion of flying and glider clubs into one organization called the German Air Sport Association. Named president of the new federation of enthusiasts was Bruno Loerzer, Goering's pilot in 1915 when Goering was learning the art of aerial observation. Loerzer became a cigar salesman after the war, but unlike Goering retained his zest for flying and was an active weekend light-plane pilot. Having commanded a fighter group, JG3, in 1918, Loerzer was acquainted with managing the man-machine combination, and his Blue Max and forty-one kills ensured awe and respect among Germany's youthful fliers.

The most critical selection was that of State Secretary for Air; the man who filled this post would have to be proficient where Goering was not, knowledgeable in fields where Goering was ignorant, and energetic where Goering was slothful. Goering unhesitatingly chose Erhard Milch. At forty-one, Milch was known throughout the European and Asian aviation industry as the man primarily responsible for Lufthansa's surge of growth, which had established Germany as preeminent among nations with airlines; in 1932, Lufthansa controlled the largest civil air fleet in Europe. Sixty-five lines ran as far as Moscow, Barcelona, London and Athens. Lufthansa organized a trunk route from Madrid to Morocco. As early as 1930, barely four years after its founding, Lufthansa set up an airways system in China called Eurasia. In 1932, Milch's last year as Lufthansa's director, the line flew six and a half million miles of scheduled service, meeting 93 per cent of scheduled departures. While working with Junkers, Milch was remembered as intelligent, ambitious, a born organizer, cherubic-faced, cold-voiced and friendless. Adolf Hitler endorsed Goering's recommendation of Milch, partly because Goering assured him Milch was the man for the job, and partly because the new Chancellor owed Milch a heavy favor—it was Milch who put a new three-engine transport plane at Hitler's disposal during the big 1932 National Socialist campaign, enabling the party leader and his chieftains to cover twenty-three thousand miles free of charge. The irony, of course, was that the state-owned airline was helping to bring down the Republic that financed it. Despite Milch's obvious qualifications, his appointment to high position within the National Socialist regime raised a legion of eyebrows. Erhard Milch was a Jew, or partly so—enough in any case to disqualify him under the so-called Aryan paragraph just drafted as part of regulations to be applied to the appointment of officials in the Hitler government. The regulations were published on April 7, 1933, and promulgated not too vigorously early in the following year with the dismissal of thirty-nine officers and men from the army. The paragraph in question read as follows:

3.1. Officials who are not of Aryan descent are to be retired. In case of honorary officials, they are to be dismissed from their official positions.

There was an escape clause in the regulations that would have gotten Milch across the barricades:

3.2. does not apply to officials who have been officials since 1 August 1914, or who served at the Front for Germany or her allies in the Great War, or whose fathers or sons fell in the war.

Any German who had either one grandparent or parent who was non-Aryan—especially Jewish—was considered a non-Aryan himself, and this applied to Milch, whose father, Anton, was a Jewish pharmacist with long service in the navy. Milch opted not to point to the escape clause that would obviate his non-Aryan stigma, but instead made himself an accomplice to a scheme that provided job security by renouncing his father and branding his mother an adulteress all in the same odious document. Frau Milch, eager to help her boy get ahead, willingly signed an affidavit stating that she had dallied in bed with another Aryan while her husband, the Jew, was away at work. The result was Erhard, who thus was not tainted after all. In case the question should ever arise, Milch's original birth certificate on file in Wilhelmshaven was quietly withdrawn and a forgery slipped in its place. The father, four decades later, magically became Baron Hermann von Bier, a minor aristocrat, replacing the familiar, inoffensive commoner, Anton Milch. This patricide-by-document at once placed Milch in the same league with his Führer—who saved the pornographic drawings he had made of his niece, Geli Raubal, a suicide in 1931 at the age of twenty-three—and with Milch's immediate superior, the junkie.*

The task facing Goering, Milch and the other newcomers was not to prepare for Germany's rearmament in the air, for the foundations were laid ten years earlier, and the structure as it existed at the beginning of 1933 was imposing enough. Besides the pilots, observers and technical people trained at Lipetsk, there were an additional fifteen hundred private pilots in Germany, and the large number of soaring associations listed fifteen thousand glider pilots. Loerzer's organization absorbed more than three hundred private flying clubs already well organized on a unit basis, and more than a hundred airfields of varying

---

*The Aryan paragraphs immediately gave rise to an underground joke: *What kind of a woman does a German like to possess most? A blonde? A brunette? A slender one? A buxom one?* The answer was, *An Aryan grandmother!* After 1942, only the most sadistic found it funny.

quality were receiving aircraft daily. General Wilberg and Ernst Brandenburg, working with Lufthansa, had already set up experimental stations to improve existing ground-to-air communications, and the meteorological stations scattered throughout Germany were as good as any in the world. The fighter manual, derived largely from tactical training exercises conducted in Russia, was already in general distribution, designed for easy editing and changes as equipment improved and squadrons grew to groups, and groups to wings. The first step on the road to an independent air force had already been taken by General von Blomberg, who, six days before the Nazis came to partial power in the Reichstag, had separated the Air Inspectorate from the Weapons Inspectorate. An Italian financier named Castiglioni had stepped in with a massive infusion of funds to resurrect and gain operational control of the Bayerische Flugzeugwerke, thus giving German airframe industries access once again to the respected BMW engines. German aircraft designers were already engaged in improving models wrung out at Lipetsk and had on the boards or in jigs fighters, bombers, trainers, reconnaissance planes, and transports designed to be built in parallel as machines of war and machines of peace. Reichswehr generals had already witnessed, in 1931, the first Russian demonstration of airborne infantry at Voronezh in the world's premier of the parachute drop of armed men, and were giving this new dimension deep consideration; Major Kurt Student thought parachutists were ideal additions to the kind of lightning wars General von Seeckt saw in Germany's future. And as for the strategic implications of the war of tomorrow, Mitchell and Douhet had said it all ten years before—and had paid the penalty.

The mission, then, of Goering and his expanding staff was not to develop concepts, but to implement the ones already in existence and to provide the right tools to see the job through. In another move toward autonomy, the Air Inspectorate became the Reichs Air Ministry, and Goering hired architects to design a monumental building to house his burgeoning staff and to physically separate airmen from the others. Both the army and the *Kriegsmarine*, the navy, became alarmed at Goering's siphoning away of control of the air; the navy's operational requirements were related to tactical roles peculiar to sea warfare, and the army all along was geared to depend upon close support from an air arm under army tactical control. Hans Siburg, a wartime naval pilot who later would transfer to the air force with the rank of general, commented, "Both the Army and the Navy were well aware of the fact that Goering would not be content to restrict himself to civilian aviation. Neither branch of service—and this applied especially to the Navy—felt it could afford to get along without an air service of its own. In order to be able to confront Goering's desire for power with a united front, the Army, whose most important officers were in the Aviation Inspectorate, the majority of whom were in favor of an independent air arm, considered it advisable to concentrate at least the development of all air equipment in the Army Ordnance Office. The Navy agreed to the proposal in an attempt to salvage what it could. . . ."

Thus the development of German military aviation was transferred to the Wehrmacht's weapons-testing branch. The reaction of the navy can be imagined when the transfer included its own test station at Travemünde. Goering was not altogether pleased with the arrangement, and within the year, he would have back control of aircraft development, making good his boast that "Everything that flies belongs to me!"

While Milch and his staff bent their efforts to working up a production scheme for the expansion of Germany's air arm, Europe was treated to one of Joseph Goebbels' feats of fabrication, although few recognized it as such at the time. On March 16, 1933, Hitler had proclaimed the right of air sovereignty, but made no mention of aerial rearmament. Three months later, on June 24, millions of *Völkischer Beobachter* readers were shocked at the paper's headlines and at the lead story covering the front page. RED PLAGUE OVER BERLIN! shouted the banner head, followed by a dramatic description of how, the day before, unknown but obviously foreign warplanes had arrogantly penetrated German air space, circling the capital before forming up for the unhurried flight back to the east. Goering, a study of mock outrage and helpless innocence, contacted the British Embassy and complained of Germany's defenselessness in the air. Could not the British, Goering asked, grant export permits for engines with which to equip "a few police planes" for the Reich's defense? The plea came at a time when the RAF was waging an unsuccessful battle for more squadrons, and British manufacturers were engaged in seeking orders from abroad. Goering suggested that if the permits were granted, Lufthansa was bound to be a steady and reliable customer.

Not only were the permits granted, but Sir John Siddeley, managing director of the Armstrong-Siddeley works in England, flew to Germany for a personal conference with Hitler and Goering at the Eagle's Nest above Berchtesgaden. Hitler, who had an abiding respect and admiration for almost everything British, was at his charming best with the English aviation pioneer and industrialist, who was delighted to receive an order for eighty-five aircraft engines of the latest type. The Führer was vague concerning technical specifications and delivery dates, but Siddeley assumed the German leader knew what he was doing, or had discussed the matter beforehand, and thought no more about it. On the broad terrace overlooking the stunning sweep of mountains guarding the German-Austrian frontier, Sir John conferred with Hermann Goering about the possibilities of Germany's buying British military aircraft for Goering's police planes, should the Red Plague again threaten German skies. However, the Air Ministry bought no British planes, and when the eighty-five Siddeley engines were delivered, Milch and the others were incredulous; they would fit no German aircraft then under manufacture, and when they were palmed off on Lufthansa, the procurement director only ordered them into a warehouse. Lufthansa could not use them, either.

This was the first—and it would be by no means the last—instance of Adolf Hitler's meddling in air force technical affairs, but the results far outweighed the waste: Britain had proved yielding, despite angry French protests at the informal entente established between the English and the Germans, and for the moment Hitler wanted more than anything else to draw closer to the British. In any case, Goering was flushed with a new triumph. After a long campaign, he succeeded in persuading doddering old Hindenburg to promote him from his wartime rank of captain. On August 31, 1933, Hermann Goering shot up near the top of the Reichswehr list with the rank of General der Infantrie, equivalent to the three-star appointment of lieutenant general. Although still outranked by Blomberg in both badges and command function, Goering more than made up for the slight discrepancy politically, for he was able to end-run around Blomberg directly to Hitler when the occasion arose.

On October 14, Hitler sprang another first on the world and on his own generals. He withdrew Germany from the League of Nations and from the rhetorical disarmament conference at Geneva. Anticipating the move, Hitler had prepared in advance secret orders for the defense minister. When he read them, Blomberg was stunned: Hitler, assuming the duties of commander in chief of the armed forces, ordered Blomberg to take the necessary steps to defend the frontiers of the Reich on the east and the west against expected League sanctions—and by sanctions Hitler meant armed invasion. Not only was the Reichswehr outnumbered on all sides by twenty to one, but Blomberg could muster barely two hundred aircraft against seven times that number possessed by the French, and should the British agree to go along with French sanctions (which was not really likely), the RAF stood ready with more than eight hundred planes. Krupp was busy making tanks, but the production line was barely underway. Blomberg thought it would be madness to challenge France. And so it would have been, except that neither the French, nor the British, nor the Czechs, nor the Poles reacted. It was the Chancellor's first exercise in power politics without the power, and it had worked. But Blomberg and every other professional soldier of field rank had had a good scare thrown into them—a fright that was only partially alleviated when, ninety days later on January 26, 1934, Hitler pulled another surprise by announcing the signing of a ten-year nonaggression pact with Poland. With the Reichstag dissolved for the second time, and with a plebiscite revealing that 92 per cent of the German people stood behind Hitler and his new

National Socialist policies, there was no question in military minds that the Chancellor was in to stay. Hitler was demonstrably a gambler, and there was no way to tell where he would next put the nation at risk. A new urgency developed within the Wehrmacht to create an air force worthy of the name, and as fast as possible.

Erhard Milch had not been idle. His first move, of course, was to examine the country's aviation production potential. At the beginning of 1933 there were fewer than four thousand aircraft workers employed in eight airframe and five engine manufacturing plants. Milch, offering contracts, added nine new works to the air-armament industry, including two newcomers, Henschel and Blohm und Voss, both willing to add aircraft manufacturing to their standard lines of locomotive-making and shipbuilding respectively. He visited the Junkers plant at Dessau and asked how many of the ugly, three-engine Ju.52 corrugated workhorse transports could be turned out annually. A maximum of nineteen, was the reply. Milch ordered two hundred, to be delivered without fail before twelve months passed. Milch sent a representative from the Air Office to see Ernst Heinkel. He was Albert Kesselring, a Reichswehr colonel in mufti who had been drafted out of the army to serve as Milch's chief of administration. Kesselring came straight to the point: to meet the expansion plans, still to be kept secret from the rest of the world, Heinkel would be required to build an altogether new plant capable of employing three thousand workers. The little works at Warnemünde would not do, and anyhow, they were to be turned back to the navy. Kesselring came equipped with plant specifications meticulously worked out in advance. The site should be at Marienehe, near Rostock, in the secluded 750-acre Mecklenburg State Park. A river, the Warnow, ran through the fields, so Heinkel could test his seaplanes. Looking ahead to a time when Germany's enemies would be able to wage strategic war from the air, a dispersal plan had been worked out. No new building, regardless of function, could exceed 64,500 square feet of floor space. Each building would, wherever possible, be separated from its neighbor by a distance equal to two buildings of the same size. Profiles were required to match that of the surrounding terrain, and deep shelters must be provided for the workers. The cost? Heinkel would be given so many hundreds of aircraft orders, plus fees for Heinkel designs to be built at other plants, that a quick return on profits would be guaranteed.

By the end of the year, the aviation work force stood at twenty thousand, a figure Milch forecast would be nearly quadrupled within another twelve months, and Project Rhineland, as the crash program was called, was gathering momentum. Milch's detailed specifications called for 4,021 aircraft to be manufactured within Germany between January 1, 1934, and September 30, 1935. Within the Air Ministry and inside the Wehrmacht High Command, Milch's projected flood of airplanes was commonly referred to as the Risk Air Force, a name with a double meaning; it was necessarily to be made up of existing designs, some of them already obsolescent and therefore expendable, and its sheer weight of numbers was designed to inject a feeling of risk to any foreign power attempting to frustrate National Socialist ambitions, whatever they might turn out to include.

Milch's figure of 4,000-plus aircraft to be turned out within twenty-one months only assumes its correct proportions when broken down; not all of these aircraft would be intended for combat. The figure included 1,760 primary trainers, 40 per cent of the whole. Planned were 822 bombers, but only 245 fighters. And the bomber figure included 450 Ju.52/3M transports, lumbering along at 150 miles per hour, armed with one free-firing machine gun on top of the fuselage near the tail and another in a deep metal bucket lowered through a hole in the deck aft of the wheels. The bomb load of 3,300 pounds was respectable, however—provided the plane could reach a target under fire. Indicating that the new air force had neither forgotten the lessons of 1914–1918 nor changed the concepts developed at Lipetsk, Milch's production list included 590 reconnaissance planes designed to work in close cooperation with the army. These were He.45s and He.46s, already tested in Russia. The total figure also included an insignificant 153 planes of various types for the navy, less than 3 per cent of the whole, and 115 planes to be siphoned off to Lufthansa should war not intervene —and the staff prayed that it would not. There were twenty different types of airplanes scheduled for production, and of these only three designs were considered capable of wresting air superiority from the French and the British in their given roles; two of them, the Dornier 17 and the Heinkel 111, were still prototypes, and Milch could count on only nine each being available by the target date.

The most prestigious aircraft on Milch's list was one he had earlier helped develop to maintain Lufthansa's superiority in Europe. In the spring of 1932, Swissair introduced an American-built Lockheed Orion passenger plane capable of 162 miles per hour on the Zurich-Vienna run. Milch summoned Ernst Heinkel to Berlin and asked if he could produce, quickly, a plane to counter the American export threat. Heinkel put his chief designers to the task, and thirty days later Seigfried and Walther Günther came up with blueprints and specifications. Just twenty-one weeks afterward, the He.70 Blitz was rolled out of the hangar at Warnemünde. Nothing like it existed anywhere on the Continent. The fuselage was made of lightweight Duralumin, round of contour, and with every drag-inducing rivet countersunk. The 48-foot 6-inch wings were elliptical, made of stressed wood that faired into the fuselage with gull-like elegance. In the interests of time, wind-tunnel tests were bypassed in favor of a crude but workable air-flow study created on the spot: small pipes attached to the cowling sprayed soot back with the slipstream, covering every square inch of fuselage and lifting surface. Irregularities were seen at once, and the rough spots smoothed over with balsa. The Blitz could carry pilot, co-pilot, four passengers, baggage and mail. The engine, beautifully cowled, was a new 630-horsepower BMW VI liquid-cooled inline mounting a three-bladed propeller. The undercarriage retracted with manful pumps on a handle actuating the hydraulic system. With all this, and fully laden with fuel, the He.70 weighed under eight thousand pounds. The Blitz was first test-flown on December 1, 1932. Before the year was out, the plane lived up to its name by clocking a flight of 225 miles per hour, then one of 234 miles per hour—faster than even the latest RAF operational fighter, the Hawker Fury II, by almost 10 miles per hour. Between March 14 and April 28, 1933, the He.70 captured no fewer than eight international speed records. The Günther brothers had created a triumph, and in record time.

Lights continued to blaze inside the Air Ministry until all hours of the night, but seldom, now, in Goering's office. His initial burst of martial enthusiasm waned in favor of more pleasurable pursuits. He asked the Führer to name him Master of the Hunt and Master of the German Forests. Garbed in medieval costume more suitable for Sherwood Forest than for twentieth-century Germany, Goering roamed the fields and forests north of Berlin, taking stock of wildlife. He appropriated a hundred thousand acres of land in the Schorfheide and set to work building a manor house that can best be described as part Gothic and part Early European Farmyard; the enclosed forecourt led directly to a massive door opening into an entrance hall 150 feet wide. He named the place Karinhall, and built a granite mausoleum to house the body of his wife, brought back from Sweden in a pewter coffin large enough to accommodate them both. He filled the ever-growing number of rooms with paintings by Cranach and Gobelin tapestries. The banqueting hall was forested with columns of red marble. The servants were dressed in doublets, green breeches, and buckskin boots. He built an indoor swimming pool, a sauna bath, a gymnasium, and a motion picture theater. In the great attic under the deep mansard roof, Goering laid out an elaborate miniature electric railway with a track more than sixty feet long, operated by remote control from a baronial red leather chair. A flick of a switch on the control panel started in motion scale model bombers, moving under the ceiling in electric jerks, dropping tiny wooden bombs on the train below. Goering was frequently away from Berlin, bound on diplomatic missions for the Leader. Gorgeously outfitted in a general's uniform of blue, hung with medals and armed with ceremonial dirks and swords, he visited Mussolini in Italy and General Pilsudski in Poland, and attended the funeral of King Alexandria of Yugoslavia in Belgrade. While in Berlin, his social life whirled; he was everywhere accompanied by an attractive brunette named Emmy Sonnemann, an actress from Weimar, whom Goering preferred to introduce as his private secretary. More ominously, he was forced to plot the blood purge of his own SA command, a showdown that could no longer be forestalled.* And there remained black periods that occurred with clockwork regularity when he would simply disappear inside a clinic or his bedroom at Karinhall in futile attempts to purge his system of morphine's demand.

An armed force with a commander so fragmented in personality and in responsibility needed, above all, a skilled and smoothly functioning staff headed by a chief whose character and sense of mission were beyond question; that is, a man totally unlike Goering. The choice settled upon a forty-six-year-old Reichswehr colonel with no flying experience—but with plenty of other qualifications.

Walther Wever came to the German Air Ministry with twenty-eight years of unbroken service marked by brilliant performance and agonizing slowness in promotion. At eighteen, Wever left his middle-class home in the eastern province of Posen to become an officer candidate in the infantry. A year later he was commissioned second lieutenant, a rank he held until the age of twenty-seven and the outbreak of war. Distinguished front-line service as a platoon commander earned him a captaincy and a post as staff officer. Early in 1917, two years later, Captain Wever was handpicked to join the elite staff of Ludendorff and Hindenburg. It was partly Wever's brain that was responsible for the concept of elastic defense—allowing forward areas to be temporarily abandoned during bombardments, leaving the strategic mass deep in dugouts and secure —that was responsible for breaking the back of the French

---

*On Saturday, June 30, 1934, black-uniformed *Schutzstaffel* troops swept down on the unsuspecting Brownshirts in Berlin and in the Tegernsee resort area and shot to death suspected plotters in numbers estimated anywhere from two hundred to a thousand. Included in the SS toll was the SA's nominal leader, the porcine homosexual Ernst Roehm.

army in the abortive Chemin des Dames offensive. It was some of Wever's energetic and meticulous planning that was responsible for the early successes of the great, last-gasp Ludendorff offensive of the spring of 1918. And it was partly due to Wever that the defeated German army was able to effect the miraculous withdrawal from occupied France and Belgium beginning on November 11, 1918—Wever's thirty-first birthday.

Wever remained on active duty with the Reichswehr, posted to the Truppenamt, where he earned the respect of Seeckt and —at last, after eleven years a captain—promotion to major, age thirty-nine. By 1932 Wever had advanced to full colonel and was in charge of the Truppenamt's training branch. It was from there that Wever was pulled to serve as Chief of the Air Command Office, which in effect was only a camouflaged name for chief of the Air General Staff. Wever's name was put forward by Colonel Hans-Jürgen Stumpff, himself a Reichswehr officer transferred to aviation and an intimate of Wever's for many years. General von Blomberg, while approving of Wever's transfer, complained, "You're taking my best man!" To Stumpff, Wever was "outstanding." Milch, who was not easily impressed, said of Wever that he "possessed tremendous professional ability [and] was the most significant of the officers taken over from the Army." To Goering, Wever was simply "tremendous. . . . Tireless by day, tireless by night." To Colonel Wilhelm Speidel of the Operations Branch, it seemed that Wever, "this realistic and uncompromisingly clear-headed man had a second soul in his breast—a soul that indulged in fantastic and unrealistic goals."

The goals Wever had in mind far surpassed even Milch's ambitious plans for four thousand-plus aircraft by 1935; he looked ahead to an air force of ten thousand aircraft of every kind. To answer the question, What kind of planes?, the planner must first ask What kind of war? Lacking any kind of strategic directive from Goering, Wever's Rosetta stone was a well-thumbed copy of *Mein Kampf.* Surfacing through Hitler's awful prose were two clear beacons: the Führer wanted no war of revenge against France, and he certainly wanted none with England, for the British were "Aryan brothers," to be cultivated as allies. But Bolshevik Russia stood squarely in the way of Germany's historical avenue of expansion to the east, and Hitler was rabid on the subject of communism as a political reality. Wever assumed office when German-Russian relations were peaking out after several years of increasing friendliness and cooperation; Lipetsk had been closed as a German training base, and Hitler had just ordered the shutting down of the tank and gas warfare schools inside Russia. Given Hitler's ideology and the downward turn in military cooperation, it was clear to Wever that National Socialism's primary strategic enemy was the Soviet Union, and that eventually a major clash would occur. Wever believed that it was far more economical to destroy the enemy's weapons at the source than on the battlefield; why wait to knock out aircraft and tanks piecemeal in combat when the factories can be blown apart? What Wever wanted was an aircraft designed to reach out for Russia's industrial heartland beyond the Ural Mountains, more than fifteen hundred miles away.

No such design appeared on Milch's production list to fulfill the Rhineland Program, but Wever had at hand a memorandum prepared by Colonel Wilhelm Wimmer, a wartime pilot and member of Fliegerzentrale's technical office. Wimmer outlined the need for a four-engine strategic bomber in any future war. Wever concurred wholeheartedly, and ordered preliminary design studies to be speeded up on what he named the "Ural Bomber."

Although Wever had spent almost all of his adult life in a traditionalist army, his grasp of the function of air power was immediate. Soaring enthusiasm for the task at hand was revealed in nearly every phrase of a speech delivered to the handpicked first class of staff aspirants to the new Air War College and Air Technical Academy which Wever opened two years after assuming command as Chief of Staff. Said Wever: "The realms of the air are not restricted to the fronts of the Army; they are above and behind the Army, over the coasts and seas, over the whole nation, and over the whole of the enemy's territories. . . . Mountains, rivers, forests and swamps are natural defense lines, imposing certain restrictions upon the move-

ments of armies and, in the period of massed armies, sap the
strength of a nation and bleed it to death in the mud of shell
craters and trenches. . . . but a modern army, cooperating with
the air force, will find the means of preventing positional warfare of massed armies. In the air force we have a weapon that
knows no such boundaries. . . ."

Wever explained what he meant by strategic air war: "The
destruction of the enemy air force, his army, his navy, and the
source of supply of the enemy's forces, the armament industry."
He cautioned that "only the nation with strong bomber forces
at its disposal can expect decisive action by its air force." To
bring into being an air arm capable of its proper dual role,
Wever warned against ambitions directed toward "coveted
promotions or honors," and exhorted to "moral steadfastness,
boldness of spirit, imagination and determination."

With plans put forward to create not one but two kinds of air
force, tactical and strategic, Wever demonstrated his own bold
spirits and determination by presenting himself, at the age of
forty-eight, at a training school near Berlin dressed in coveralls,
gloves and leather helmet, requesting that he be put through
the necessary part of the curriculum that would enable him to
put up his wings as a pilot. By this time Wever was a two-star
general, but he took orders from his instructor just like everybody else.

10

THE WEAPONS GAME

Except for a few flower pots on the balcony I have never cultivated anything. But I am ready with all my heart and soul, and with firm belief in the greatness of the German nation, to devote all my energies to this mighty task.

—Hermann Goering

With all of Germany humming after twelve years' stagnation, the Rhineland Program moved swiftly toward completion. By the end of 1934, with another nine months in hand, approximately half of the four thousand planes ordered by Milch had emerged from the factories and were delivered to the proliferating units activated by Wever. There were forty-one organized formations scattered throughout six *Luftkreis* (air district) commands, units whose military functions were concealed under innocuous code names. The bomber unit equipped with Dornier 11s at Fassberg, for example, was camouflaged under the name Hanseatic Flying School. The bomber training station at Lechfeld operated its Ju.52s undercover as research planes of the headquarters, German Flight Weather Services. The familiar German Commercial Pilots' School at Braunschweig hid the activities of the Heinkel 46 reconnaissance outfit. And at Prenzlau, student bomber pilots took refuge as crop dusters, their Ju.52s merging with the State Agricultural Pest Control Unit.

The first fighter unit was activated on April 1, 1934; it was known unofficially as Squadron 132, but officially as one of the so-called advertising squadrons that had been parading across German skies for more than a year. The unit designation, 132, was not meant to imply that Germany possessed a hundred-plus squadrons, but was a simplified code; the first digit indicated that the unit was squadron one, the second revealed that it was equipped with fighters, while the third digit showed that the squadron was based within Air District II (Berlin.) Chosen to command was Major Robert Ritter von Greim, a grizzled veteran of the skies over the Western Front, a dead shot with twenty-five kills to his credit, a wearer of the cross of the Pour le Mérite, and, until his return to Germany, one of the organizers of Chiang Kai-shek's Chinese air force.

To meet the immediate needs of the expanding air units for men to perform the less glamorous chores of air base duty, thousands of NCOs and enlisted men were summarily transferred from the Reichswehr and put into new blue uniforms as they became available. Because most of them were volunteers, and because of Seeckt's policy of quality when he could not have quantity, the airmen, almost without exception, were of high caliber and well qualified to learn quickly the technical aspects of their new career field. It was after August 1, 1934, that incoming airmen were presented with a new oath to swear, an oath far more personal than existed during the Weimar period. On that date, President von Hindenburg died and Hitler assumed his title as well as that of chancellor. Instead of swearing loyalty to the Constitution, recruits henceforth chanted, "I swear by God this holy oath, that I will render to Adolf Hitler, Leader of the German nation and people, Supreme Commander of the Armed Forces, unconditional obedience, and I am ready as a brave soldier to risk my life at any time for this oath."

The Nazi Party was not mentioned, but soon its symbol began to appear on every naval and military uniform. General von Blomberg, although adamant against allowing Wehrmacht members to join the NSDAP, nonetheless wanted to show his commander in chief that the Wehrmacht was as loyal to him as were the SS and other purely party organizations. He ordered new cloth badges from the quartermaster, a design featuring a straight-winged eagle clutching a small swastika in its claws. These were sewn on the uniform jacket just over the right upper pocket. Goering ordered badges with more sweeping lines, a soaring eagle looking downward, talons clutching the party symbol as though a bird of prey was dragging its victim through the sky. The order was placed in anticipation of the Führer's next big moves, which were not long in coming.

On February 26, 1936, Adolf Hitler signed a decree that established the air force as an independent branch of the armed forces. At last, the shadowy air arm had a name given it by the Führer himself—the *Reichsluftwaffe*. Nobody liked it, and in general parlance the name was shortened to *Luftwaffe* (air weapon), which soon became accepted official usage. The new command structure ranked the Luftwaffe equally with the army *(Reichsheer)* and the navy *(Reichsmarine)*, answerable through Goering to Blomberg and through him to Hitler. On March 1, the decree was implemented. Independence! A dream British military airmen had realized in 1918 after three years of hard political infighting, and a dream their American counterparts had despaired of achieving, and would not realize for another twelve years. On March 10, Goering summoned the correspondent of the friendly London *Daily Mail* and presented Ward Price with the scoop of the year. Goering told Price he had created a new German air force, but with no intention of threatening the rest of the world; his Luftwaffe, Goering said, was purely defensive. Four days later, Major von Greim's J.G.132 was christened *J.G. Richthofen 2*, and squadron mechanics got busy painting the cowlings red and adding black crosses to wings and fuselages of the new Arado 65 and Heinkel 51 biplane fighters. Roaring over German towns in warpaint, the slender, elegant Heinkels looked menacing and businesslike —and from the ground the carefully kept secret that the resurrected Richthofen Circus had no guns could not be discovered. Shortly afterward, yet another fighter wing was created out of the equipment pouring from the factories. The party influence was clearly revealed in the choice of names for J.G.134, known as *Jagdgeschwader Horst Wessel*. For those officers and men who believed the official version of Wessel's death in February 1930—that he "died on the barricades in the struggle against Bolshevism"—the name was acceptable, even though Wessel had never been connected with flying in any way. To those who knew the truth, it was something else. Wessel, in fact, was a twenty-three-year-old storm trooper living in a Berlin slum,

earning pocket money as a part-time pimp. He was shot to
death by another party member, also a pimp, over possession
of the chattel, Erna Jänicke.

When Goering made his announcement, the Luftwaffe
strength stood at sixteen squadrons; by August 1, five months
later, the figure had trebled, and the first-line strength stood at
1,833 aircraft, broken down as follows:

372	bombers (Do.11 and Do.23)
450	auxiliary bombers (Ju.52)
51	dive-bomber trainers (He.50)
251	fighters (Ar.64, Ar.65, He.51)
320	reconnaissance (long-range He.45)
270	reconnaissance (short-range He.46)
119	naval (He.38, Do.16, He.59, Do.18, He.51W)

There was more. On Saturday, March 16, Hitler announced
that he had signed a decree reintroducing compulsory military
service; conscription would enable the army to field thirty-six
divisions, about five hundred thousand troops. On top of the
news of the Luftwaffe as a force in being, this latest pronounce-
ment torpedoed the already foundering ship of Versailles, leaking violations at every seam. Reaction to this German truculence on the part of the treaty signatories was pitiful: Great
Britain, France, and Italy met at Stresa, under a League of
Nations mandate, and spent their time concocting notes of
pious outrage and condemnation. France signed a mutual-
assistance pact with Russia; Russia signed one with Czechoslovakia; England kept quiet about her own plans for a treaty with
Germany that would allow the potential enemy to greatly increase the Reichsmarine—an agreement reached only two
months later, and one that included the British approval of
German submarine building. Sir John Simon, Whitehall's new
foreign minister, was received by Adolf Hitler in the Reichs
Chancellery in Berlin and listened while Hitler, now gracious,
now scowling, stressed his desire for peace. Then came the
sword thrust. The Luftwaffe, said Hitler, with the surety of a
poker player holding a full house, has achieved parity in the air

with England. This was not true at the time, but with Berlin's streets filled with columns of marching men in brand-new blue uniforms, and with the skies overhead alive with the thunder of Luftwaffe formations of bombers and fighters, there was no way to disprove it.

Generalleutnant Wever, as he now was, having seen the Rhineland Program heading toward completion, bent his energies to the Luftwaffe's second-generation force. Wever assigned highest priority to the development of a basic four-engine strategic bomber design. Through the technical chief, Colonel Wimmer, General Wever pressed development contracts on the Junkers works at Dessau and on Claudius Dornier at his Friedrichshaven plant on Lake Constance. Both Wever and Wimmer were satisfied with the preliminary drawings, and work proceeded to the mock-up stage. In final configuration, both bombers were remarkably similar: broad wings exceeding one hundred feet in length, four engines grouped closely together, deep-bellied fuselages, twin rudders. The Do.19, typically Dornier, was cleaner of line than its competitor, the Ju.89, which (typically Junkers) was brutish and robust. Both featured retractable landing gear housed inside the inboard engine nacelles; both bombers' noses rode high off the ground.

Wimmer recalled how, in the spring of 1935, he persuaded Goering to accompany him on a visit to Dessau. They marched through the crowded Junkers workshops, shouting to be heard above the crash of hammers, the whine of plane saws, the stutter of riveting guns and the crackle of arc welding equipment. They passed through the great sliding doors leading into a cavernous building where the only sounds were the gentle scraping of sandpaper, the desultory slap-slap-slap of paintbrushes, and the creak of wood being fitted to wood. Goering gazed upward at the full-scale mock-up of the giant Ju.89, its bulk seeming to fill the hangar. Goering turned incredulously to Wimmer and, still shouting, yelled out, "What on earth's that?"

Wimmer explained that it was the final wooden study of the much-discussed Ural bomber, about which the Minister must surely have been informed. Wimmer remembered that Goering turned suddenly furious and bellowed, "Any such major project as that can only be decided by me personally!" Then Goering stamped out of the building. Wimmer was at a loss, but decided that Goering's blast was only another temper tantrum, probably forgotten by the time he got back to Berlin. Work on the Ju.89 continued.

Next, Wimmer escorted Blomberg through the Dornier works and explained in detail about the hoped-for capability of the Do.19. The War Minister listened patiently, then asked Wimmer when he thought the Do.19 could become operational. Wimmer replied, "In about four or five years." Blomberg, along with every other German officer of field rank, believed that the next war could not possibly begin before 1942 or 1943. Therefore, if the strategic bombers, the Ju.89s and/or the Do.19s, were ready for combat by the spring of 1939 or 1940, that would be soon enough. His somewhat abstract comment to Colonel Wimmer in response to the time lag Wimmer mentioned, "Yes, that's about the size of it," was interpreted to mean that he was favorably impressed with the Do.19. Work on the big bomber was ordered to proceed.

The dual-purpose Luftwaffe envisioned by Wever required not only a strike force with extended reach, but a tactical sword whose importance lay not in the weight of the blade but in the speed of the stroke. Even before Wever's installation in the command structure, airmen in the old Fliegerzentrale used to theorize endlessly about the kind of bombers they would some-day build. What emerged from these serious daydreams was the concept of bombers so fast they would outrun fighters, obviating the need for heavy defensive armament whose weight—plus that of the men needed to serve the guns—could be better utilized in payload or fuel. It was a concept with which Wever did not argue. Fortunately for the development section of the Luftwaffe's Technical Office, such a bomber already existed in prototype, a reject found in Lufthansa's passenger-plane bin.

Late in 1933, Lufthansa presented Dornier with a require-ment for a new mail plane capable of hauling six passengers; because the airlines wanted the plane for use on express runs between European cities only, range was not important, but speed was paramount. The most powerful engines then available were BMW VIs, twelve-cylinder, liquid-cooled inlines developing 660 horsepower at takeoff, and around this power plant, with its low frontal area, Dornier designers planned to build the most aerodynamically advanced aircraft in the world. The fuselage was as slim as a pencil, the nose shaped like a bullet. The round-tipped wings, fifty-nine feet long, were set in the shoulder of the fuselage, some distance aft of the flight deck, and faired so smoothly that the wing-body structure seemed to have been poured molten into a mold and allowed to set. The rudder was small and nearly triangular. The wide-track landing gear folded neatly backward into the curve of the engine nacelles, and, as a final triumph over drag, even the small tail wheel retracted into the fuselage where it was so narrow a large man could encircle it with both arms.

Lufthansa took delivery of three prototype Do.17s for evaluation. Test pilots were enthusiastic about control response and general handling, the traffic chiefs agreed that the two hundred-plus miles per hour exceeded performance requirements, and Lufthansa's flight engineers were keen on the new power plants. But those responsible for passenger ticket sales vetoed the Do.17 on the spot. Because the plane had been designed for speed, and only speed, accommodation for fare-paying passengers was only an afterthought: a tiny cabin for two people was fitted immediately behind the flight deck, making the clients almost part of the crew; but unlike the crew, their visibility was extremely restricted. Room for four others was made just aft of the wing, providing a good view downward—along with the full benefit of the noise of the engines and the propellers. Ingress and egress to the seats required contortions not possible except to the young and the athletic, and women hobbled with the skirts of the time would have refused the attempt. All three prototypes were returned to Dornier.

At this point, Flight Captain Untucht stepped into the picture. Untucht, Lufthansa's chief pilot and a former test pilot for Dornier, had friends in the Air Ministry, and he suggested that the elegant Do.17, with only a few modifications, would make

an ideal quick-dash bomber. The forward passenger box was
ripped out and replaced with radio equipment and a seat for
the operator. Portholes were eliminated. The fuselage was
shortened by twenty-two inches, and the single rudder was
replaced by twin rudders to eliminate the plane's only evil, a
tendency to yaw left and right. A sixth prototype, the Do.17V6,
was fitted with different engines, twelve-cylinder Hispano-
Suiza inlines developing 775 horsepower at takeoff, and, thus
modified, the new bomber entered flight trials in the fall of
1935. With the throttles bent all the way forward, the V6
clocked a sizzling 243 miles per hour, faster than Heinkel's
famous He.70 Blitz, and 13 miles per hour faster than Britain's
latest biplane fighter, the Gloster Gauntlet.

The argument was advanced within the Luftwaffe Technical
Office that since chance had provided the long-discussed high-
speed bomber, production should commence without further
modifications; no armament was needed; speed alone was proof
against interception. Sagely, the suggestion was vetoed. After
all, it was only a question of time before tomorrow's enemy,
whoever that might be, produced faster fighters. The Technical
Office ordered guns installed. The Do.17 went through yet two
more prototype versions, ending with the V9; then full production began for the Luftwaffe with model Do.17E-1. Armament
included a 7.9 millimeter (.30 caliber) machine gun firing downward and another gun mounted on top of the fuselage just aft
of the wing. The maximum bomb load was 1,650 pounds, i.e., a
pair of 550-pounders and four 110-pound general-purpose
bombs. Speed was reduced to 220 miles per hour at sea level,
and the thin, low-drag wings accommodated fuel enough for a
tactical range of barely 310 miles—enough, however, for a high-
speed run and back from the Oder to Warsaw, from the Rhine
to Paris, or from Düsseldorf to London. With a quantity order
in hand, Dornier produced an innovation in the manufacturing
process: the Do.17's airframe was broken down into component
parts for ease in subcontracting, a technique that not only resulted in early dispersal of the German aircraft industry, but made
it easier for replacement of damaged airframe parts at group
and even squadron level.

The other major contributor to the Luftwaffe's plowshares-into-swords scheme was Ernst Heinkel. Even before the last of the seventy-two He.70s ordered by the Air Ministry rolled off the line at Warnemünde, its derivative big brother was being assembled in the new plant at Marienehe. Unlike the Do.17, Heinkel's 111 was laid out on the drawing board as both a bomber and a transport right at the start. In civil dress, the He.111 carried ten passengers—four forward and six aft. In between was an improvised space Lufthansa called a smoking compartment, but which was in reality the bomb bay. The He.111, powered by the BMW VI engines, was a much larger airplane than the Do.17—the wings, broad and elliptical, spanned fully eighty-two feet—and was nearly a ton and a half heavier unladen. Even so, the first test flight on February 24, 1935, produced a top speed of 217 miles per hour, and a pilot verdict that the handling characteristics were delightful, even superior to those of the famous He.70 Blitz. The Luftwaffe ordered ten He.111s in full military configuration, including three machine-gun positions, a longer fuselage, and a many-windowed plastic nose section for the bombardier. Ballasted for the maximum bomb load of 2,200 pounds, the gross weight of the bomber shot up to more than six tons, and the cruising speed dropped to under 170 miles per hour. Luftwaffe test pilots at the Rechlin proving center complained that the He.111 required excessive stick pressures and, in general, was mulish in flight. All ten were rejected—but Heinkel later sold them at a handsome profit to Chiang Kai-shek.

Now Daimler-Benz came forward with a new engine that not only saved the He.111 program, but boosted the dreams of fighter plane designers, who were frustrated at the meager horsepower available inside Germany. The new power plant, an inverted V, twelve-cylinder inline, boasted 1,000 horsepower at takeoff, and this made all the difference. Powered with the DB 600A engines, the fifth prototype of the new bomber reached 224 miles per hour in trials at Rechlin despite the extra 838 pounds added to the gross weight by the bigger engines. Could Heinkel have all the new Daimler engines he wanted for series production of the He.111? He could not; they, and improved variants already in the works, were earmarked for the fighter program, but the Luftwaffe was so keen on the prospects of the He.111 that Daimler was asked to provide similar, if slightly downrated, power plants for the new Heinkel bomber. With certain structural modifications—including altering the pure ellipses of the wings to a more straight-line shape in the interests of simplifying and speeding up shopwork—and equipped to mount DB 600C engines offering 880 horsepower, the He.111B-1 was ordered into full production.

Heinkel's production capacity was strained to the limit, but relief was promised with the visit of Colonel Fritz Loeb, a young Luftwaffe officer attached to the Technical Office. Loeb told Heinkel that the air force wanted yet another factory built, one devoted exclusively to the output of He.111s at an initial rate of one hundred a month. Heinkel, already heavily overspent on the new works at Marienehe, asked where the funds were coming from; he had no intention of going into hock with the moneylenders. Loeb told him the Luftwaffe would pay for everything, that money was no problem. Indeed it was not; the Luftwaffe budget was increasing by quantum jumps. Under Special Plan XVI for fiscal 1933–1934, the Luftwaffe was allotted $30 million, of which $10 million was siphoned from funds available to the army and navy. For fiscal 1934–1935, the amount was increased to $52 million, and from 1935 onward, the Luftwaffe had at its disposal $85 million in one budget and a whopping $750 million in a separate black fund financed through interest-bearing notes sold by the government to the Reichsbank. This scheme was concocted by the Reichsbank's president, financial wizard Hjalmar Schact, who kept the transactions secret in order to avoid inflation at home and loss of confidence in the reichsmark abroad.

Colonel Loeb specified that the new plant must be located near Berlin and made it clear that the factory must be laid out with war in mind. He told Heinkel, "Not in a city—no compact block of buildings, but everything scattered in case of attacks from the air." Heinkel pointed out that dispersion resulted in production inefficiency with consequent loss of profit margins. "Don't worry about it," Loeb said, "it isn't your money."

Heinkel's scouts roamed the countryside near Berlin and

came back with the report that the hilly, wooded stretch of heath near Oranienburg seemed ideal. Oranienburg was only eighteen miles north of the heart of Berlin, and an electric tramline connected the two places. The major drawback was the absence of water. Heinkel sent for a diviner, who plodded across the vacant spaces with a forked stick, and shortly afterward reported a strike. Sure enough, ample water was found only six feet beneath the surface. Heinkel consulted Hitler's architect, young Albert Speer, and plans for the Oranienburg works were completed at the beginning of April 1936. The plant was broken down into eight major workshops, many of them hidden under the trees. Despite the possibility of air raids, Heinkel later boasted of the plant's "vast areas of glass framed in steel and red-glazed brick." Deep shelters were dug, however, and the factory ran its own large fire department. New track was laid connecting the complex with the main line running from Berlin to Oranienburg, but rail traffic was necessarily intended for delivery of raw materials, and Heinkel realized that dependence upon the tram for getting workers back and forth from Berlin was only asking for trouble. A workers' town was built on the site, comprising twelve hundred homes, a school, a town hall, theaters, shops, laundries and a swimming pool. Ground was broken on May 4, 1936, and a year to the day later, the first He.111 bomber taxied out of the assembly shop to the cheers of thousands of workers and invited guests. Oranienburg was the German aviation industry's showcase, and the Luftwaffe used it to impress—and intimidate—visitors from abroad.

The high-speed medium bomber program was purely a Luftwaffe idea, but the concept of pinpoint bombing of highly selected, individual targets using specially constructed dive-bombers releasing loads along the plane's near-vertical axis of flight was borrowed from the United States Navy. That the concept was hammered into operational reality over stubborn opposition and at great personal risk to its prophet was due to the fiery dedication of one man: a civilian barnstormer, Germany's greatest living ace from the war, Ernst Udet. When the war ended, Udet was twenty-two and unemployable. His only trade was combat flying, his only reward the Blue Max, his only yearning, the sky, and freedom, his only need. He turned down a posting with the Reichswehr, married his wartime girl, Zo Link, and borrowed money to start a small aircraft factory. He built and demonstrated neat biplane sport planes with such evocative names as Hummingbird and Flamingo. His marriage dissolved, then his interest in manufacturing. His partners wanted to move into the four-engine airliner business, and big planes interested Udet not at all. He was a born Bohemian, blessed with wit and a knack for mimicry and caricature with pen and ink. Udet was sociable without being social, and expansive without being garrulous. Parties in his Berlin flat were famous in a time when every kind of behavioral barrier had been let down, and chance callers were always assured of a glass of champagne or brandy, or the two mixed together served in a shell case, the famous concoction dreamed up by a Lafayette Escadrille pilot and known as a Seventy-five. Udet was a drinker without being a drunk, and a raconteur who was never a bore.

Udet, second only to Manfred von Richthofen on the victory list, could have bartered his name and his personality on the marketplace; but Udet was neither politician nor prostitute. He was a pilot, a technological man of his times needing to use his craft—a narrow skill at best—to pay his way in life. Like most bon vivants, Udet was at heart a realist, sensing that heroism in war does not necessarily qualify a man to administer the affairs of commerce. He would not sell his name for promotion, but when approached by twenty-six-year-old Leni Riefenstal, painter and ballerina turned actress and film director, to put his courage and piloting skill to hire in film work, Udet accepted readily. He worked both in Africa and in the Arctic, where his best-known footage was shot for the 1929 feature, *The White Hell of Pitz Palü*.

Udet, barnstorming in the United States, made friends wherever he went, including wartime air service pilots he had dueled with over the western front more than a decade earlier; among them were Eddie Rickenbacker and Elliott White Springs. Thousands of Americans thrilled to Udet's seemingly harebrained stunt flying, and only pilots in the crowd realized that what laymen took for madness was but consummate skill pushed to the limit by personal courage.

Among Udet's admirers was the American pioneer airman, Glenn L. Curtiss, who invited the German to visit the Curtiss-Wright plant in Buffalo, New York, while Udet was touring America in 1933. On September 27, a date that would have fateful repercussions for the Luftwaffe, Curtiss asked Udet if he would like to fly a factory-fresh F2C Hawk, a robust single-seat biplane designed for the U.S. Navy as a carrier-borne dive-bomber. Twenty minutes later Udet and the Hawk were wringing each other out, man versus machine in a brutal contest to see which would come apart first under the punishing G-loads imparted to both frames as Udet hurled the plane at the ground again and again, hauling the stick back sharply against his stomach only seconds before the earth rushed up to claim them. When Udet landed and taxied up to the hangars he was drained and thrilled. Aiming the nose of the plane at one of Curtiss's factory buildings and howling down at over 250 miles per hour was like riding a shell on its downward plunge to the target. Here was a plane to thrill the crowds and, it occurred to Udet, one with which the German air arm should experiment. Few targets are harder to hit from the air than ships underway on tho opon occan, and if the U.S. Navy was working on the idea of the dive-bomber as the solution to the problem, then so should his own people in Berlin. Udet immediately wrote Erhard Milch with a glowing description of the Curtiss Hawk, wondering if there were some way he could bring a pair of them back to Germany. Milch wired back agreement, adding that funds to cover purchase cost were on the way. Curtiss, happy to make the sale at a time of depressed markets at home, received no problem with export licenses from the U.S. government.

Two months later, Udet was at the Rechlin test center with the assembled American Hawks. Gathered on the field whipped by cold December winds, Milch, Goering and others from the Air Ministry watched Udet scream down on them in four successive power dives, pulling out a little closer to the ground each time. Through the fog of near blackout, Udet rolled off the top of the zoom and treated the fighter pilots among the critics below to an exhibition of acrobatics, proving that the thirty-seven-year-old pilot and the new machine could take it. Udet was invited to a conference in Berlin at the beginning of the new year, the only civilian among the galaxy of brass, and the upshot was an order from Goering to develop some kind of vertical bomber. Wever, as chief of staff, was a supporter of the idea because it did not interfere with his ideas of a mixed force: the strategic bombers then being developed by Dornier and Junkers, the medium Do.17s and the He.111s then in the planning stage, and now the *Sturzkampfflugzeug*—literally, the plunge-battle aircraft. It was not envisioned that the *Stuka* would be used primarily as a naval attack weapon, but rather as a kind of extreme-range piece of heavy artillery. None of the German bombsights then under development, the Goerz-Visier 219 or the Lofte 7 and 7D, were considered sophisticated enough to achieve acceptable accuracy in horizontal bombing except by the most experienced crews; Stukas, with their inherent accuracy, would solve the problem of putting bombs on small targets in the field: bridges, power stations, fuel and ammo dumps, roads, tanks, enemy airfields. Moreover, Germany's raw-material reserves were limited and production of Stuka-type aircraft would eat into these strategic reserves sparingly.

The most outspoken opponent of the dive-bomber concept was Major Wolfram von Richthofen, thirty-eight, Manfred's younger cousin. Wolfram flew his first patrol on the day that Manfred flew his last, and finished the war in 1918 with eight kills. A tall, heavy man with a porcine face and narrow eyes, he based his objections to the Stuka on his wartime experiences as a fighter pilot and upon his studies for a doctorate in engineering after the war. Richthofen believed that it was suicidal for aircraft to operate below three thousand feet in the face of ground fire, and jettisoning a bomb load vertically any higher would nullify the pinpoint accuracy claimed for dive-bombers. Nor did he believe that aircraft could be built that would withstand the cumulative effects of stress absorbed by airframes in day-in, day-out operations. On July 20, 1934, a near disaster at Berlin's Templehof field seemed to prove his theory correct. Udet had been practicing during the spring and early summer, and was no doubt the most proficient dive-bomber pilot in the world by the time July rolled around. With almost the entire Luftwaffe General Staff watching, Udet rolled the Hawk on its back and plunged for the earth. He hauled the stick back at the last moment, the Hawk began its agonizing pullout—then the tail section fluttered wildly, finally wrenching loose. The Curtiss plummeted straight down, engine running full out. Udet, who had been through all this before, unstrapped and went over the side, hauling on the D-ring as he went. The chute popped just before he slammed into the ground. The Hawk exploded at the far end of the field.

Despite the disintegration of Udet's plane, the Luftwaffe high command was convinced of the practicality of the Stuka idea, and development orders went out to Arado, Blohm und Voss, Heinkel, and Junkers. To Junkers's chief designer, Wilhelm Pohlmann, the order seemed almost coincidental; already sketched out on his drawing board was a study for an advanced, all-metal, low-wing dive-bomber based on the K.47 that had been built in Sweden and tested at Lipetsk. The Luftwaffe specified dive brakes, and while templates were being cut for the new plane, brakes were fabricated and fitted to the K.47 and given a thorough testing. The K.47's twin-ruddered tail offered the gunner a wide field of fire to the rear, and so the twin tail was retained on the new prototye. Fitted with a 600-horsepower Rolls-Royce Kestrel engine, the prototype Stuka, the Ju.87V-1 was rolled out of the assembly hangar at Dessau in the early spring of 1935, ready for flight. The Ju.87 was square, angular, awkward, and unwieldy looking—in fact, it was ugly; but it looked strong. Test pilots felt few qualms about putting it through its paces, gradually increasing the steepness of the dive and the G-levels as flight testing progressed. What were its limits? Nobody knew. Determined to find out, one pilot pushed the Ju.87 past the limits of endurance, and although the wings held, the twin tail tore loose before pullout and the Stuka exploded against the ground. A standard rudder was fitted to the next prototypes, as well as an automatic pullout device connected to the elevators and actuated by the altimeter; blackout at five and six Gs, caused by gravity's draining of the blood from the brain down to (it seemed) the pilot's boots, was not to be taken lightly in an airplane at speed close to the ground.

While Junkers was busy pinching out the bugs in the Ju.87 and the others were working hard to catch up, Udet was being drawn into the Luftwaffe's web. Milch, Wever, and the Luftwaffe's personnel chief, Hans-Jürgen Stumpff, decided that Udet's passion for flight was needed more in a rearming Germany than at air shows. He was offered the rank of colonel and a post as inspector of the fighter and dive-bomber forces. Udet hesitated; throwing away his personal freedom after seventeen years was something he must think about. Besides, he was all but oblivious to the precepts of National Socialism, and the Luftwaffe was being bent strongly along those lines. Udet was no political animal, and he admitted it. What would the Führer say? In point of fact, the matter had been cleared all the way up to Hitler, whose admiration for Udet's record far outweighed his objection to placing politically unoriented officers in key positions. Udet was won over with a simple, clear and honest argument: if he wanted to see Germany equipped with the finest dive-bombers in the world, he could not do so as a civilian—but with the rank and the title offered, nobody could oversee the job better. On June 1, 1935, Ernst Udet was sworn in.

A Berlin tailor outfitted his now portly figure in a new Luftwaffe uniform, in which he appeared only infrequently at his office; paperwork was not for Udet. Most of his hours were spent in the cockpit of his private staff plane, a little Siebel Beetle, rushing from one aircraft factory to another, urging speed in the dive-bomber developmental program. Early in 1936, the Luftwaffe was notified by the four prime contractors that each was ready for the trials to be staged at Rechlin.

Arado missed the boat by submitting a biplane design, and the Ar.81 looked, and was, obsolescent from the beginning. Designers at Blohm und Voss had apparently not read the Luftwaffe specifications, for their Ha.137, a low-wing monoplane,

was a single seater, and the Technical Office had distinctly
called for a two-place aircraft. Heinkel took off on his already
successful He.70 design and fielded the He.118, a slick-looking
metal monoplane with retractable gear and powered by the DB
600 engine of 900 horsepower, giving it a top speed of more
than 250 miles per hour. It looked to be a sure winner. Then the
worked-over Ju.87, the fourth prototype, was unbuttoned for
inspection. The Junkers Jumo 210 engine was fitted with a three-
bladed, controllable-pitch prop designed by the American firm
of Hamilton-Standard and built under license in Germany. The
elongated greenhouse provided almost unrestricted visibility
for the pilot and rear gunner. The oversize wheels were covered with huge metal spats. The ugly square tail was heavily
braced. A heavy crutchlike strut was fastened flat underneath
the belly; just before bomb release, the pilot actuated the
crutch, which swung down and out so that the falling bomb
would clear the arc of the propeller blades. Inboard of each
wheel spat was a small round housing with fanlike blades. One
of the inspecting officers asked Udet, "What's that?" Udet said,
"You'll see!"

The flights of the Arado and the Blohm und Voss were quickly
dispensed with. Then the Junkers test crew got aboard, were
quickly airborne, and began diving. To the shattering roar of
the Jumo engine and the three-bladed prop was added an
uncarthly scream, boring into the eardrums with almost un-
bearable intensity. The Ju.87 pulled out of its dive so close to the
field the watchers instinctively ducked. Again and again Rechlin vibrated to the banshee wail of the assaulting Stuka. When
the Ju.87 wheeled around to shoot its landing, only Udet and
the Junkers engineers were smiling: what Udet had done on one
of his many trips to Dessau was to suggest attaching sirens to the
underside of the Ju.87 as an experiment in psychological warfare. He called them "trumpets of Jericho," and they had had
their effect.

It was a tough act for the sleek He.118 to follow. Unknown to
Ernst Heinkel, the new test pilot named Heinrich had an av-
ersion to power dives, although he was reliable in every other
way. The He.118 took off, reached altitude, then tentatively

dropped its nose toward the ground. Heinrich swept gracefully down in gentle swoops, his flight parabola resembling that of a glider with a throttled-down engine. Dive he would not, and the trials at Rechlin ended with the Ju.87 as the obvious choice. Heinkel unleashed his Swabian temper on his test pilot, but cooled down when Udet walked over and said, "Heinkel, I won't make up my mind at the moment. I must dive your damned plane myself. I'll come out to Marienehe."

Udet showed up unexpectedly at Marienehe some weeks later on a day when Heinkel was busy giving the red-carpet treatment to an American visitor, Charles Augustus Lindbergh. Milch had rung through from Berlin, telling Heinkel "to show Lindbergh everything." In halting English, Heinkel answered the Lone Eagle's penetrating technical questions about all of the plant's latest designs. Lindbergh had already toured the other German aviation factories, and it struck Heinkel that the American flyer "knew more about the Luftwaffe than anyone in the world." While they were inspecting the third-floor workshops, Udet was aloft preparing to put the He.118 through its paces. Heinkel and Lindbergh missed witnessing what happened next.

Udet hauled the light bomber up to ten thousand feet in the clear blue early summer sky and unhesitatingly rammed the stick forward. The 900-horsepower engine wound up tight, and Udet's ears were pierced with a high-frequency scream. Too high. Udet, forgetful of Heinkel's warning, had neglected to check the pitch setting on the controllable prop. The He.118 bucked and vibrated, plunging straight for the deck out of control. Udet fought to get his bulky frame clear of the cramped cockpit. He got half out, battered by the slipstream, but one foot was wedged against the rudder pedal and the airframe. The prop wound up past its limits and flew off into space. The tail assembly tore loose and fluttered away through space. Udet wrenched his socked foot from the jammed oxford and flew backwards out of the cockpit. His chute cracked open while his body was moving downward at more than 200 miles per hour, and he crashed heavily against the earth in a cornfield. Unconscious, Udet did not hear the explosion as the He.118 tore itself to pieces not far away.

Udet, bruised and sore but otherwise uninjured, spent a few days in a Rostock hospital, managing to stay pleasantly tight on champagne smuggled in by friends. Heinkel's hopes for the He.118 were buried in the wreckage of prototype, branded by Udet as no more than "a damned deathtrap." The contract for the Stuka was let to Junkers, and shortly afterward, the first of nearly five thousand production models began rolling off the lines at Dessau.

On the day following Lindbergh's visit to Marienehe, a formal reception was held in the U.S. Embassy in Berlin for the American pioneer aviator who, if he held second place at all in the affections of an air-minded public at home, ranked next to Eddie Rickenbacker. Almost every Luftwaffe pilot and command officer of note was present, and so were the leading designers. The American military attaché, Truman Smith, hoped Lindbergh would not make a pacifistic speech, for the state of the world deeply troubled Lindbergh, and what he had seen of the Luftwaffe impressed and disturbed him. Goering, as usual, turned up late for the reception, and breezily handed Lindbergh a small leather case holding a decoration. "From the Führer!" boomed Goering. Ernst Heinkel, standing nearby, observed that "Lindbergh looked mockingly at Goering, shook his head, and put the decoration in his pocket without bothering to look at it."

Lindbergh made no embarrassing speeches, but before he left Berlin he did field a prophecy. He said to Heinkel, "It must never come to an air war between Germany, England, and America. Only the Russians would profit by it."

The era of the biplane fighter was ending even while He.51s and improved Arado 68s were coming out of the factories in fulfillment of the quotas established under the Rhineland Program. In the summer of 1934, the Air Ministry invited tenders from the aviation industry for a new fighter, specifying that the speed required must be no less than 280 miles per hour. This would require adroit approaches to aerodynamics and the keenest scrutiny to every weight-saving trick known to the engineers; at the time the various designers bent over their boards to begin initial design studies, there was no engine available for the competititon that exceeded 700 horsepower. Two of the manufacturers were handicapped from the start. Arado was told their entry could assume any configuration the designers could dream up—but they could not submit a plane with a retractable undercarriage, which was not yet considered foolproof. Focke-Wulf at Bremen was instructed to produce a high-wing monoplane based on its successful FW.56. Heinkel was told he could build what he liked, and so was the newcomer, Willy Messerschmitt, of the Bayerischeflugzeugwerke at Augsburg. BFW was given free rein because Messerschmitt was considered to stand little chance, and those in the know inside the Air Ministry considered it astounding that the tall, scowling, heavy-jawed, ruthless-looking builder should be a contender at all. Messerschmitt and Milch had disliked each other on sight, and during the years Milch was running Lufthansa, Messerschmitt succeeded in selling the airlines very few passenger craft, Messerschmitt's entire stock in trade. In 1935, Messerschmitt was thirty-seven and had been involved with aviation design for twenty years. Messerschmitt and his mentor, Friedrich Harth, built and flew a glider in 1916 that stayed aloft for two and a half minutes, and after the war the team was a familiar sight on the Wasserküppe. Between 1925 and 1928, Messerschmitt built a number of light airliners, biplanes, and sport machines, but it was in the summer of 1928 that he made his move to enter the ranks of major German industrialists. As the son of a Frankfurt wine merchant, he had no resources of his own, but as the son-in-law of the wealthy Strohmeyer-Raulino family, he was able to secure backing to buy the shares of the BFW company owned by the Bavarian government. The company failed in 1931, but Messerschmitt saved it by selling personal possessions and lining up contracts with a Rumanian firm to build his designs under license.

Messerschmitt's fortunes changed dramatically when he sold one of his trim-looking M.23 racing monoplanes to Hitler's favorite deputy, Rudolph Hess. Money was soon made available to restructure BFW as a going firm, but Milch frustrated Messerschmitt's hopes by consigning the Augsburg works to building Heinkel's He.45 reconnaissance planes. And even in this Messerschmitt faced a ridiculous situation: Heinkel liked Messerschmitt as little as did Milch, and when BFW technicians appeared at Warnemünde to inspect the aircraft they were to manufacture, Heinkel refused them entrance to the factory. The absurd stalemate was sorted out, but Messerschmitt was not a man content with realizing other men's designs; he found buyers in Rumania for a new airliner and set to work. It was at this juncture that the Luftwaffe's Technical Office, in the form of Wilhelm Wimmer, offered Messerschmitt a clear shot at the German fighter competition.

The odds against him were considered high because, of the twenty-four different designs Messerschmitt had created, only one had been militarily oriented, and that one a lusterless stab at a biplane bomber back in 1928. But both Wimmer and Hess, an avid amateur pilot, knew that Messerschmitt had a new thoroughbred in stable, the finest plane of its kind in Europe, and little imagination was required to visualize its quick evolution into the kind of fighter the Luftwaffe needed. The design in question, a four-place, low-wing, all-metal craft—the first Messerschmitt had ever built—known as the Bf.108, had been created to satisfy the need for a light, high-speed touring plane, and, more specifically, to equip German teams competing in the annual European *Challenge de Tourism Internationale.* Although power was limited to 220 horsepower, the 108's exceptionally clean lines and light weight provided a speed of just under 200 miles per hour and a range of just over 600 miles. Independently operating Handley-Page slats mounted on the outer portion of the wing leading edges provided adventuresome pilots with unprecedented control at low speeds and at unusual flight attitudes. With, for instance, the nose up and the wings vertically banked, the slats popped outward (at from 63 to 68 miles per hour) to impart lift, retarding stall until the last moment—and giving the pilot advance warning before the craft stalled absolutely. The 108 had a roll rate of sixty-four degrees per second and was vigorously acrobatic.

Using the tourer as a design base, Messerschmitt and his designers created a slimmer, more angular version with a narrow cockpit for one man, a shorter wing and fuselage, and room in the nose for guns. Engineers mounted the British Kestrel V engine, the Bf.109 was test flown in September 1935, and three weeks later, Messerschmitt pronounced it ready for competition.

Designer Kurt Tank's Focke-Wulf 159 high-wing monoplane was the most beautiful plane entered in the final trials at Travemünde. It was about twenty years ahead of its time in light-plane design, but it was not a fighter. Eliminated. The handsome, gull-winged Arado 80 looked promising, but the mandatory fixed gear produced excess drag with a consequent loss in required speed. Eliminated. This left the Bf.109 and Heinkel's entry, the He.112, another gull-wing, low-wing monoplane with retractable gear and the only open cockpit among the four entrants—a concession to those World War I pilots in the Luftwaffe high command who did not believe a fighter pilot could see unless his head was exposed to the blast of propwash. Heinkel's problem with the 112 stemmed from his design chief, Heinrich Hertel, an inveterate tinkerer cursed with the typical German industrial disease of overengineering. *Is the airframe strong enough here? Better add another brace and some more rivets. This former does not look right. Tear it out, strengthen it, replace it. The oleo struts for the gear are too long. Take them out, shorten by seven centimeters, and put them back. But this means the wheel wells in the wings will have to be moved inboard. We'd better . . .*

The result was a heavy fighter made up of 2,885 individual parts, and no fewer than 26,864 rivets. In his obsession for last-minute alterations, Hertel had no time left over to install mechanically operated hydraulic retraction gear, and the Luftwaffe engineer who carried out the test wore a blister on his hand cranking the gear up manually. Heinkel watched as the engineer "climbed out of the machine covered with sweat and cursing roundly."

The test pilot who flew the 109 reported that the plane was fast and responsive in the air, but ill-mannered on the ground. To lessen the strain on the wings and to avoid clutter between the ribs, Messerschmitt had the gear struts attached to the fuselage instead, which resulted in splaying out the wheels and reducing the track. This made ground handling tricky, and when the 109 was on takeoff roll, it exhibited a maddening tendency to swerve abruptly to the left before becoming airborne. The pilot said you had to keep pressure on right rudder at the moment the stick came back to raise the tail, otherwise ground looping was inevitable. The 112 was tighter in the turns, but at 292 miles per hour, the Messerschmitt was faster. The competition ended in a Mexican standoff, and Udet threw up his hands and ordered ten each from Heinkel and Messerschmitt for the final acceptance tests.

Heinkel's subsequent prototypes were cleaned up aerodynamically, equipped with automatic retraction gear, fitted with an enclosed canopy, and emerged with elliptical wings four feet shorter than the original. Powered with a different engine, the Jumo 210-D rated at 690 horsepower, the He.112V4 weighed in at 4,894 pounds loaded, but speed shot up to 317 miles per hour. Messerschmitt's fourth prototype boasted stronger landing gear, slightly improved ground manners, and a Jumo engine that did nothing for its maximum speed. Udet flew the He.112 himself, and admitted that he liked the fighter's superior rate of climb and sturdier gear, but the final approval was going to the competition. He explained why: the Bf.109 was already earmarked to receive the new DB 600 engine that would push it to past 340 miles per hour, its straight-line wings were easier and cheaper to manufacture, and, besides, Messerschmitt's Augsburg plant was ready to roll in series production, while Heinkel was burdened with bomber contracts and handicapped by Heinrich Hertel's manic production techniques. Puffing on a cigar, Udet suggested to Heinkel, "Palm your crate off on the Turks or the Japs or the Rumanians. They'll lap it up."

Heinkel was bitterly disappointed, and especially so because he lost the order to Messerschmitt, whom he considered an upstart as far as military aircraft were concerned. Heinkel also admitted that in "turning down the He.112, Udet had hit my deepest striving—to build the fastest possible airplane." Heinkel was far from ready to admit defeat in the fighter field, and would resurface dramatically two years later.

The Luftwaffe was called on to play a major role in a Hitlerian gamble for high stakes when it was barely a year old, still raw with unassimilated growth, and with its supporting industries only beginning to tool up for modern weapons. On February 12, 1936, Adolf Hitler summoned to the chancellery General Werner Thomas Ludwig von Fritsch, commander in chief of the army, and told him he had decided to reoccupy the demilitarized Rhineland. General von Fritsch hesitated, saying that he agreed in principle with the Führer that the Rhineland had the greatest strategic significance in case of war with the West, but pointed out that the Wehrmacht was still in the throes of organization and was far too weak to deal with an estimated 110 divisions the French could mobilize. Hitler said he wanted the Rhineland, but he did not yet want war; the operation was to be a major bluff, probing the willingness of the Locarno Treaty signatories to back up their convictions by force of arms. General Alfred Jodl described the atmosphere prevailing inside the General Staff as "like that of the roulette table when a player stakes his fortunes on a single number."

The operation was mounted with frantic haste. The directive for Operation *Winterübung*, Winter Exercise, was drawn by General von Blomberg only sixteen days after the Führer's decision, and was not released until March 5, just forty-eight hours before the army was ordered to cross the Rhine. The Luftwaffe was alerted, and General Wever began shuffling his scattered units around like pawns on a chessboard. Two under-strength fighter wings, JG 132 and JG 134, were pulled from their bases and sent south. A bomber wing, KG 4, was ordered to stand by, its unwieldy Ju.52s fuelled to the limit for a possible mission to Paris. The few fully operational tactical training schools were stripped of instructors and planes, hastily formed into impromptu squadrons, and moved to bases all up and down the Rhine. On the cold, wet dawn of March 7, three small battalions of German infantry, about three thousand men in all, armed with nothing more than rifles, carbines, and machine guns, crossed the Rhine and occupied Aachen, Saarbrücken and Tier. The helmeted men, their capes dripping with rain, were greeted with cheers by Germans who had not seen friendly troops in more than a decade. Overhead buzzed the Heinkel and Arado fighters of the Richthofen and Horst Wessel squadrons. The pilots kept glancing toward France, expecting to see massed formations of the *Armée de l'Air*. The German airmen were understandably apprehensive: not one fighter could give combat; those who had ammunition lacked guns, and those who had guns lacked the synchronization gear necessary for firing through the prop. If French planes appeared, they would have to be rammed.

Tension in the Reichs chancellery, in Army High Command, and inside the Air Ministry had never. been so high. Hitler paced the carpet, and General von Blomberg's aides noted that the Rubber Lion had developed a facial twitch. Luftwaffe staff officers hovered over the telephones, half expecting the next call or the next would bring word of crushing French reaction, wiping out the Rhine bridgeheads and massacring the carefully hoarded—and quite harmless—fighter aircraft. French Intelligence, usually among the world's best, grossly miscalculated German armed strength inside the Rhineland at 265,000 troops. The British more realistically believed Hitler had sent in 35,000 men, nearly four divisions, and they erroneously accepted Hitler's boast made a year earlier that the Luftwaffe had achieved air parity with the RAF. Reaction was not what Hitler and the others feared; the French prepared for defense by manning fully the subterranean Maginot Line and mobilizing thirteen divisions, and the British pleaded for calm. And outside of anguished cries in the Chamber of Deputies, calm indeed prevailed. Hitler had gotten away with it. Neither the British nor the French public believed that the Rhineland, characterized by Lord Lothian as "after all, Germany's back garden," or the principle that lay behind its occupation, was worth fighting over. Hitler later admitted to Blomberg that he "hoped he would not have to go through another such ordeal for at least ten years."

The Luftwaffe's rapid deployment revealed the luster and fine-toothed gearing imparted to the Air General Staff by Walther Wever during his thirty months in office. His gift of motivating men to reach for the best within themselves—to feel shame at any lesser effort—created an electric air of striving for total efficiency; nobody wanted to let Wever down. When the general planned war games in conjunction with the army, his staff performed prodigies of planning in order to make good Wever's promises. If Colonel Heinz Guderian expected a simulated bombing attack in front of his 2nd Panzer Division at 0845 hours, he could be sure of the arrival of the Ju.52s at the required time. If a corps artillery commander needed air spotters to call strikes for his new Krupp guns, he could be sure the He.45s would be buzzing over the range at the time the shoot was scheduled to begin. Wever created not only an efficient staff but, what is rarer, a harmonious one. And since Wever had originally distinguished himself in staff operations of the army, both in combat and during the difficult days of the hundred-thousand-man peacetime Reichswehr, no one in the Wehrmacht felt that he was dealing with an air specialist blind to the requirements of other branches. In recalling Wever's crusade for a strategic strike force, one of his operations deputies, General Paul Deichmann, noted Wever's state of mind during the first large-scale war game carried out by the Luftwaffe late in 1934.

"During the course of the war game the bomber units were employed deep in the heart of enemy territory. At that time, most of these units were equipped with provisionally armed Ju.52s, which were completely inferior to the French fighters [in use at the time]. Officers in charge of the maneuver suggested to General Wever that he assume a loss of 80 per cent of the bomber force, but Wever refused brusquely with the words, 'That would deprive me of my confidence in strategic air operations!' Although the maneuver leaders pointed out that the percentage of losses would presumably be that high only until the Luftwaffe had more modern bombers at its disposal, Wever insisted upon a lower percentage."*

Hitler's Rhineland adventure directed Wever's thoughts to

---

*During the strategic air offensive over Germany conducted by the RAF and the USAAF from 1943 to 1945, losses above 10 per cent of the raiding force were considered almost prohibitive.

the west and to the north. Although Wever remained convinced that Russia was Germany's greatest potential enemy, he could not discount the possibility of England's springing to the aid of France, the traditional enemy. It was all very well for Hitler to proclaim his desire for friendship with the British, but it is the function of the General Staff to base its plans for the future upon pragmatic considerations and not upon political desires, no matter how fervent. There was no question of the ability of the German naval building program, then accelerating, to provide the Reich with parity at sea with the Royal Navy. Wever believed that strategic bombers could play a decisive role not only in laying waste Britain's industries, concentrated as they were on an island only five hundred miles in length, but in maritime operations designed to deny the British economy raw materials, and the people, food. Bombers with a radius of action of even twelve hundred miles could range from Germany far out over the North Atlantic as far as Iceland; the central Atlantic approaches to the ports of France could be covered and so, too, could the entire Mediterranean, almost as far as Suez. With the medium bombers and the Stukas and the chosen German fighter now coming off the production lines, Wever pressed for completion of strategic bomber planning.

The Ju.89 prototype rolled out for flight tests. The wings spanned an inch under 115 feet, and the deep-bellied fuselage could hold 2,600 pounds of bombs. The great drawback of the Ju.89 was lack of power; the only engines available were 620-horsepower Jumos, enough only for a maximum range of 1,240 miles and a top speed of 192 miles per hour. The Do.19, harnessed to the same power plants, was 15 miles per hour slower, but had a range of 1,800 miles—still not enough for the demands Wever intended to impose later on. Wever had not expected greater performance figures for either bomber, and believing that in the next air war God would be on the side of the greatest horsepower, ordered further testing to be carried out, pending availability of newer, more powerful engines. He was not to live long enough to see his dream realized.

Although Wever's rank entitled him to a courier plane with stand-by crew, he insisted on piloting his own flights to various corners of Germany. He had less than two hundred hours in his logbook, but chose the fastest plane of its type for his personal aircraft, the single-engine, three-ton He.70 Blitz. On June 3, 1936, Wever and his flight engineer climbed into the Blitz and flew from Berlin to Dresden, where Wever was scheduled to give a talk to the cadets at the new Air War Academy. Wever finished his business at the *Luftkriegsakademie,* then ordered his driver to hurry him back to the airfield; he was due back in Berlin to attend the funeral of General Karl von Litzman, hero of the war on the Eastern Front in 1914, and Wever was never known to be late. Wever slipped his flight suit on over his dress uniform and looked around for his flight engineer. Where had he gone to? Wever guessed he had gone into Dresden on some errand. He paced the tarmac, shooting glances at his watch, impatient to be off. His mind on the 105-mile flight back to Berlin, Wever failed to make the customary walk-around pre-flight check of the He.70, an airplane he had only recently acquired and with whose eccentricities he was not thoroughly familiar.

Finally the flight engineer hurried across the runway, apologized for the delay, and without further ado the two men got back into the airplane, strapped in, and started the engine. Observers on the ground watched the Heinkel move down the concrete strip, gathering speed. The tail lifted, then the wheels left the runway and Wever got the nose up in takeoff attitude. One wing dipped slightly, and instead of being picked up with a quick movement of the ailerons, the wing dropped lower still, lost its grip on the air, and the heavy He.70 plunged into the ground with the engine running full bore at takeoff rpm. The Blitz, heavy with fuel, exploded on impact, killing Wever and his tardy flight engineer instantly. Enough of the wreckage was left to determine the cause of the crash: failure to disengage the aileron lock prior to takeoff, a matter of a simple hand movement.

According to the Luftwaffe intelligence chief, Major Josef "Beppo" Schmid, who was in the Air Ministry in Berlin when the news was telephoned through, Goering "broke down and wept like a child."

And well he might have: with Wever were buried the Luftwaffe's chances of winning a war spread beyond the narrow frontiers of continental Europe.

We bombed it, and bombed it and bombed it, and *bueno* why not?
—Nationalist staff officer

Wever was replaced by Major General Albert Kesselring, forty-eight, a stocky, balding, open-faced professional army officer known for boundless energy and expansive humor. Kesselring served throughout the war, and remained in Seeckt's Reichswehr afterward. He transferred into the Luftwaffe in the fall of 1933, following on Wever's heels, and although the two men got along well together, Kesselring was surprised at being named Wever's successor; Wever had his eye on Major Hans Jeschonnek, only thirty-seven, a pilot, ardent National Socialist, clearly a comer in grasping the intricacies of air staff work. It was Jeschonnek, as chief of the Luftwaffe Operations Staff, who had prepared the plans for the deployment of the Luftwaffe during the Rhineland adventure. Kesselring had no quarrel with the Luftwaffe's rearmament program as set in motion by Milch and Wever, and only six weeks after taking command of the Air General Staff, Kesselring was presented with the unexpected opportunity of putting selected Luftwaffe units through trial by combat. He was delighted; all the tactical theories and the new weapons could be proven in a foreign cauldron, using somebody else's country as a battleground, and with negligible risk of becoming prematurely embroiled in a war with any major power. The proving ground lay across the Pyrenees.

On the evening of July 26, 1936, Adolf Hitler and the greater part of his entourage were in Bayreuth, attending the annual music festival. That afternoon Hitler had been treated to the full orchestral treatment of Wagner's *Ride of the Valkyries*, and was in a soaring mood when he received three emissaries from the Spanish mainland, then in its ninth day of a bloody uprising against the Republican government. The visitors, Adolf Langenheim and Johannes Bernhardt, both Nazi party officials resident in Spain, were accompanied by a Nationalist air force officer, Captain Francisco Arranz, bearing a letter from his commander in chief, General Francisco Franco. The Falangist leader's request was modest enough: purchase of "ten transport aircraft with maximum seating capacity" so as to airlift his troops in Morocco across the Strait of Gibraltar to join in the revolt. Republican sailors had seized thirty-nine of Spain's fifty warships, slaughtering the officers in the process, and the straits and the Alboran Sea were effectively closed to Nationalist maritime traffic.

Hitler agreed immediately to supply the needed transport planes, and added that he was willing to do a great deal more. He gave numerous reasons for springing to Franco's aid, any one of which would have sufficed: it was an opportunity to thwart the "danger of the Red Peril overwhelming Europe"; Germany needed Spanish iron ore—which would not be supplied by a left-wing regime; and a Fascist victory would be a strategic defeat for Britain and France, who would face a power friendly to Germany across their sea communications in the Mediterranean. Admiral Wilhelm Canaris (code name "Guillermo"), head of Germany's counterintelligence branch, the *Abwehr*, urged help for Franco so as to protect the lives and the property of some fifteen thousand German nationals living in Spain, and because if Germany became involved in a war with France and England, the German U-boat fleet would need Spanish bases for refueling. Goering urged Hitler to "give support under all circumstances. Firstly, to prevent the further spread of Communism; secondly, to test my young Luftwaffe. . . ."

Hitler ordered Goering to send not ten but thirty of the Luftwaffe's three-engine Ju.52s to Franco. Extra fuel tanks were hurriedly fitted for the long haul from Stuttgart to Franco's staging area at Tetuán, 1,250 miles distant, a few miles inland from the Moroccan coast. Violating five hundred miles of

French air space worried the transport pilots far less than did the prospect of forced landing inside Republican territory, and in fact this occurred only once; the crew was eventually released unharmed and allowed to go on their way. The first Ju.52 cleared for Africa twenty-four hours after the conference at Bayreuth, and twenty-four hours after that, a Lufthansa senior pilot named Hencke was winging his way across the Strait of Gibraltar with his Junkers packed with armed Moroccan troops. Thus began the first major airlift. The rest of the Ju.52s arrived almost immediately afterward and were organized in a shuttle service that saw them in the air from dawn to dusk, pausing only long enough to load and unload and to refuel. Out of Tetuán, the destination was Jerez de la Frontera, ninety miles northwest, just above Cádiz and fifty miles below Seville. With the help of some old Dornier Whales and Savoia flying boats on Nationalist inventory, the Ju.52s and their tireless German crews ferried 10,500 Moroccans to Spain from Africa within thirty-three days, delivering another 9,700 during the month of September, along with forty-four pieces of artillery, ninety machine guns, and five hundred tons of ammunition and other equipment, all without loss. This prodigious feat of endurance on the part of the German air crews and skilled maintenance on the part of German engineers enabled Franco to re-form his Army of Africa and get it moving up the Portuguese frontier to link up with General Emilio Mola's Army of the North.

Although Generals von Blomberg and von Fritsch protested to Hitler that Operation Magic Fire, as the German aid program to Spain was code-named, was "militarily wasteful," preparations for its execution on an expanded scale went rapidly forward. Franco's pressing need was for aircraft and pilots. When the uprising began, the rebels could muster only 88 pilots and 50 airplanes; the figure included 33 French-made Bréguet XIX two seaters of post-World War I vintage (7 of which were useless,) 3 old Dornier Whales, 3 Fokker D.XIIIs, and half a dozen light planes belonging to the Seville Aero Club and pressed into service as battlefield reconnaissance planes. On the other hand, the Republican government retained 214 aircraft of somewhat more modern vintage, including 26 British-made Vickers Vildebeests, 36 Savoia flying boats, 3 Douglas DC-2 transports, and 3 British Hawker Fury fighters. The balance was made up of 60 of the Bréguet XIXs and various other old bombers. To man this hodge-podge air arm were 155 pilots loyal to the government.

While the first of the Ju.52s were headed for Spain through French nighttime skies, things were moving inside the German War Ministry in Berlin. Special Staff W was formed, with Major General Helmut Wilberg at its head; Wilberg's recent experience with running the clandestine training scheme in Russia qualified him for the job of gathering so-called volunteers and the dispatch of war materiel. A holding corporation, the Spanish-Moroccan Transport Company, was created to handle outgoing sales and incoming pesetas, gold, and ore. Eighty-six Luftwaffe pilots, mechanics, and other support personnel donned civilian clothes, and under the command of Colonel von Scheele, boarded a steamer at Hamburg on the night of July 31. Locked in the holds were six He.51 fighters. They unloaded at Cádiz five days later, having run the Republican blockade. From then on, cargo ships laden with German men and weapons—including tanks—slipped out of Hamburg, Stettin, and Swinemünde on an average of five per week, while other goods were flown into Spain from Germany in Ju.52s on a four-times-weekly schedule.

By November 6, no fewer than 6,500 German fighting men and support troops were assembled at Seville, the composite group known as the *Legion Kondor,* under command of General Hugo von Sperrle, fifty-one, a World War I aerial observer, member of Freikorps Lüttwitz in 1919, and afterward one of the organizers of the secret Reichswehr air service during the days of the Control Commission. Sperrle took along as his chief of staff Wolfram von Richthofen, who wanted to see for himself how Luftwaffe equipment worked in action. The pilots, for the most part, were volunteers, most of them under twenty-five, who believed they were on some kind of crusade. The ardent Nazis among them saw in the Spanish adventure an opportunity to live up to the promise of their marching song: *We shall be marching onwards, if all else crashes about us. Our foes are the Reds, the Bolshevizers of the world.*

Aside from the combat role, the Condor Legion was charged

with operational training of Spanish air crews. One of the aspirants was the aristocratic José Larios, the Duke of Lerma, who found the Germans "extremely competent" in every field of endeavor. Larios has described how the Germans requisitioned part of the notorious red-light district near the Alameda de Hercules gardens in Seville, organizing everything on military lines. "The men," recalls Larios, "were marched up in formation, and if the houses were full the overflow was lined up in the street, ready to advance in single file, waiting patiently for orders from the commander inside who was clocking them in with mathematical precision."

The Condor Legion was organized roughly in wing strength, broken down into Bomb Group K/88, composed of thirty Ju. 52s made up of four squadrons; Fighter Group J/88, equipped with twenty-seven He.51s; and Reconnaissance Squadron A/88, whose pilots flew a mixture of six He.45s and a dozen He.70 Blitzes. The North Sea Group, AS/88, flew at squadron strength, equipped with one He.60 and nine He.59s, large twin-engine biplanes. Additionally, Flak Detachment F/88 came under Sperrle's command to protect the legion's airfields with batteries of 20-millimeter and the new, high-velocity 88-millimeter antiaircraft guns. To these were added numerous searchlight detachments and a signals unit. In all, there were seventy-eight aircraft, of which an average of 85 per cent could be found serviceable at any one time, excluding temporary drops due to attrition in combat.

German pilots and aircraft were in action before the Condor Legion was fully organized. The Republican fleet, thirty-nine ships in all, was scattered from Tangiers, thirty miles across the tip of the peninsula from Tetuán, through the Alboran Sea and into the Mediterranean. On August 14, while the great airlift was still in progress, Lufthansa Flight Captain Rudolf Freiherr von Moreau bombed up his Ju.52 and joined a small formation of Spanish planes in an attack on the enemy ships hiding in the port of Tangiers. Picking out the largest ship he could find, Moreau dropped down to fifteen hundred feet above the water and flew through inaccurate antiaircraft fire and let the bombs fly. Hauling the clumsy transport plane around in a shallow bank, he saw that he had scored hits; plumes of smoke were rising from the ship. He landed back at Tetuán and excitedly reported that he had put out of action the Republic's only battleship, the sixteen-thousand-ton *Jaime Primero,* mounting eight 12-inch guns. Later Moreau learned that his bombs had struck something else; on the day in question, the *Jaime Primero* was lying off the west coast of Mallorca, five hundred miles away, assisting in a landing operation designed to regain control of the island for the government. Nonetheless, the persistent air attacks on the Republican fleet, manned as they were by crews without officers, had the desired effect, and by the close of September, the Republican fleet had been nullified.

Although the Republicans were heartened at the promise of early delivery of both French and Russian planes to counter the increasing flood of materiel flowing to the insurgents from Germany and Italy, government wireless-intercept services began picking up Nationalist messages in October whose cryptic contents were interpreted as ominous warnings of impending assaults from the air on a scale hitherto not experienced. On October 17, three intercepts were made, one from León and two from Seville, directed to General Alfredo Kindelán, commander in chief of the Nationalist air force at Salamanca. The first intercept ran:

Received four Bredas, six Junkers, two Fokkers, one Dragon, thirty-six Heinkels Ammunition, D, 16955; 379 A bombs; 230 B bombs. Hundred kilograms of 15. Fuel, A 36939; B 4532.

From the commander, Second Air Group, Kindelán learned that the base at Seville had received three Ju.52s, two Italian Savoias, and three Heinkel reconnaissance planes. From the same source a little later in the day, the following information was pulled out of the air:

Received and in stock 295 incendiary 12397 Italian high explosive. German weight: Ten kilos—172; Fifty kilos—107; 250 kilos—139; 500 kilos—9.

The stockpiling of bombs and the gathering of planes was to satisfy General Mola's request for air bombardment heavy enough to throw decisive weight against Loyalist forces still stubbornly defending Madrid against artillery and infantry attack, and to satisfy Sperrle's and Richthofen's curiosity in an experiment of terrorizing the population of a great city in "a carefully planned attempt to set fire to the city, quarter by quarter."

On the morning of November 16, Junkers and Savoia squadrons began lifting off from their bases west of Madrid. Some of the flights had to cross the Sierra de Gredos to reach the rendezvous point with the fighters, and they found the long mountain chain that begins in Estremadura blanketed with dazzling snow. The highest point of the Gredos extends above eight thousand feet, and the Ju.52 crews were frozen during the long, slow trip over the mountains and under the cloud ceiling that, here and there, dipped down to scrape against the peaks. Pilots flew with one hand, while beating the other against their thighs to restore circulation. Once across the Gredos, the bombers swung south to rendezvous with the He.51 escort fighters above Torrijos, then, in arrowhead formation, the strike force droned across the Guadarama River and reached Madrid. Avoiding the northwestern outskirts of the capital, where Nationalist troops were locked in battle inside University City with militia and the International Brigades, the forty-odd bombers flew on to unload in the heart of the city. Richthofen, who had carefully studied the photographs brought back by the He.70 reconnaissance planes, had directed the German crews to concentrate on public buildings first, so as to create the greatest possible panic. The huge telephone exchange, the Telefónica, was hit again and again by 110- and 550-pound bombs, as were a great number of hospitals. With the loads of high explosives gone, hatches were opened and crewmen began dumping out hundreds of slim, two-pound thermite incendiaries. When the formation flew away, Madrid was ablaze in several quarters. The raids continued, despite worsening weather, for the next seventy-two hours. For those who came by night, it was easy to tell where the next cargo was to be showered down—in those darkened areas of the city where no fires blazed. As an exercise in formation flying and area targeting, the raids could be counted a success; fires raged almost unchecked throughout the city, and an estimated one thousand *Madrileños* of varying ages and of both sexes lay dead under the rubble and in the streets filled with glasss, bricks and puddles of water from burst water mains. But as an exercise in subjugation, the raids failed dismally, serving only to harden attitudes of hatred; although twenty thousand people were out in the streets, with now no place to live, it was noticed by Nationalist troops that resistance inside University City was stiffer than ever.

Madrid was not going to fall that year or the next, and Franco ordered General Mola and his staff to prepare for a major offensive in the north. By the beginning of 1937, Nationalists controlled approximately 65 per cent of the Spanish earth, the stain of conquest spreading eastward from Portugal and Finisterre on the Atlantic to Granada on the Mediterranean. So far denied them were the Basque provinces in the north, which, after the fall of Irún and San Sebastián, were reduced to an area two hundred miles long and forty miles deep. The Basque coastal provinces are among the loveliest in Spain. Mountains, rounded with age and forested with green pine, reach upward with peaks topping five thousand feet, and their rolling foothills drop right down to the sea. Millennia of winter storms have sculptured the coastline in erratic, tortured configuration, providing innumerable coves and inlets. In spring and summer, the shoreline and outward along the Bay of Biscay is dotted with color; hundreds of deep blue and rich green and vermilion trawlers and two- and four-man oared craft rakishly trimmed in white slide through the blue water to harvest from the sea. The Basques are, first of all, fishermen, and after that, foresters. They are their own people, with their own language and a tradition of independent-mindedness exceeding that of any other group on the Iberian peninsula. Nationalism means nothing to a Basque—unless you are talking about a kind of Basque nationalism that would free them of any Spanish government. Lacking autonomy, the Basque prefers to think about *la República* as a compromise to be lived with, but the concept of life under a Fascist regime was—and is—abhorrent. What was to be

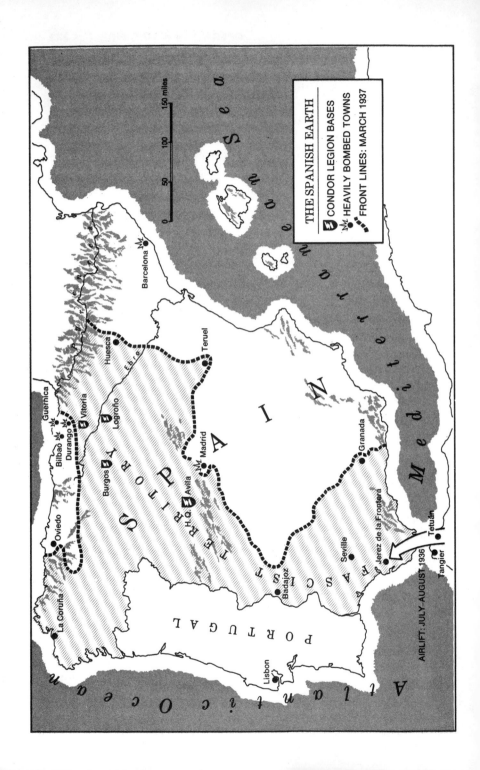

protected from the onrush of Nationalist armies, and especially the alien Moors, was not only independence of the Basque provinces, but particularly the most important city of the north, Bilbao.

The city, whose population had swollen to more than 300,000 by the war, lies eight miles up the Nervión River that runs into the sea, navigable all the way. Bilbao was not only the most populous and heavily trafficked port in the north, but was a center of shipbuilding and supported profitable iron mines. The beginnings of a small-arms industry was founded in Bilbao not long before the uprising, and a new 81-millimeter mortar was being readied for world markets when the war began. To protect Bilbao, sturdy Basque woodsmen and grain farmers from the tablelands fanned out in a circle surrounding the city, constructed dugouts, bunkers and trenches on the tops of the green hills, and, when they had it, strung barbed wire. Enthusiastically but amateurishly built, the defensive circle surrounding Bilbao was hopefully called the Ring of Iron. The positions were manned largely with volunteers uniformed in corduroy pants, checkered lumberjackets known as canadianas, and topped with the dark blue Basque beret. They were armed with rifles and machine guns bought in Germany, held up in France, and finally stolen by a Basque pirate named Letho, who ran them up the Nervión to be delivered into the waiting hands of the Republican troops.

Until the end of October 1936, Bilbao was defenseless from the air, and the city had already been the target of attacks by Condor Legion Ju.52s that had been moved to the legion's advanced airdrome at Vitoria, thirty air miles to the south. The bombers appeared over Bilbao on the morning of September 25, during the afternoon, and again at night. They were over again the next day. Unopposed, they bombed at will and flew back to Vitoria. The He.51 fighter pilots had come along merely for the ride, and returned full of triumph to the Hotel Frontón, where they were quartered, to celebrate the imminent collapse of the northern front. To crown an eventful day, one of the Heinkel pilots returned to the airfield, climbed into the fighter, and took off to thrill the people of Vitoria with his skill at low-level acrobatics learned at the fighter school at Schlessheim. The exhibition ended spectacularly when the pilot's wine-dulled judgment led him to fly into the stone tower of the parish church to become the legion's first fighter-pilot fatality.

During the last week in October, Russian merchantmen from the Baltic moved slowly up the Nervión and tied up along Bilbao's wharves. The most welcome cargo aboard were a dozen large crates containing Russian Polikarpov I-15 biplane fighters, stubby-bodied copies of an American Boeing, and powered with a 750-horsepower license version of the nine-cylinder Wright Cyclone. The I-15's top speed of 230 miles per hour put it 30 miles per hour up on the He.51s, and it had double the firepower, mounting four light machine guns. Only the year before, a modified I-15 had captured the world altitude record when a Russian pilot lofted the light (3,100-pound) fighter to 47,818 feet. Even in standard operational rig, the I-15's maximum ceiling of 32,800 feet gave it greater performance at altitude than any airplane being used in Spain by either side. The I-15's flat nose gave birth to its Republican nickname, *Chato*. The fighters were accompanied by experienced Russian pilots, observed by London *Times* correspondent George L. Steer to be "oldish men of thirty-six and thereabouts, who kept very much to themselves and neither drank nor smoked." They brought with them a mascot, a large Russian fox terrier the Basques called *Ruso*. The fighters were assembled on the polo grounds outside Bilbao under Russian supervision, the dark green surfaces enlivened with bright red wingtips and the Republican colors on the rudder. Four of the I-15s were sent up the coast to Santander, and the other eight were kept at Bilbao. The polo field was converted into an airdrome, where the Russians patiently worked with an eager few Basque advanced amateur pilots to turn them into combat fliers before the expected Nationalist offensive began.

The advance guard of the Condor Legion was joined at Vitoria by an additional Ju.52 squadron and another of He.51s. On the afternoon of January 4, 1937, elements of K/88 and J/88, nine bombers and a dozen fighters, roared off the field and formed up for the first major aerial assault on Bilbao. The Ju.52s got off first, followed by the much faster He.51s, which took up station three thousand feet above the bombers, perfectly formed in an arrowhead of three flights of three planes each. Inside the lead Ju.52, Karl Gustav Schmidt made his way amidships and began cranking down the dustbin gun turret aft of the wheels. Encumbered by his seat-pack parachute and sheepskin-lined flight jacket, he had difficulty in squeezing himself into position behind the machine gun, and once there thanked God that the target was only a few minutes away; the blast of winter air buffeting the dustbin at 150 miles per hour chilled him to the bone. The roar of the engines was deafening. Peering down at the undulating hills guarding the approaches to Bilbao, Schmidt could see first the workers on the Ring of Iron scurry for cover inside bunkers and under heavy canopied trees, then the silver glint of the Nervión as the pilot began letting down for the run-in to the target when the formation entered the gentle valley. Schmidt pulled the charging handle of his gun back and fired a warming burst. He forgot the cold in his intense concentration on the sky around him.

In Bilbao, sirens emptied the streets of all except firemen and leather-jacketed police. At the polo grounds, the Russian fighters leapt into the air, four piloted by Russians, and four flown by recently trained Basques. Tactics had been carefully worked out in advance: four of the Chatos split away and went for altitude to deal with the German fighters, while the others bored through the sky straight for the bombers. Leading the attack was Felipe Del Río, age twenty. He picked the Ju.52 at the point of the German formation and went for it just as his Russian mentors had shown him with their hands: a head-on attack just slightly above the line of flight of the enemy machine, the Junkers' blind spot. No forward gun turret could be mounted there because of the nose-mounted third engine. Del Río peered through the gulled top wing and watched the bomber fill his sights. He opened fire and saw the four streams of tracer hitting true. They were closing at more than 400 miles per hour, and Del Río had time for only one long burst. It was enough. Flames and heavy smoke erupted from the shot-up engine and swept through the bomber. Del Río banked away from the falling Ju.52 and saw that the remaining eight were jettisoning their bombs into the river and along its banks. Above, the German pilots were having a hard time with the I-15s. The Heinkels attacked in tight groups of three, maintaining flawless formation as though they were performing an acrobatic display. Although badly outnumbered, the Russian and Basque pilots lost only one fighter, while bagging one of the Heinkels, which spun away and crashed into the hills.

The combat that began at three fifteen ended seven minutes later. The Condor Legion task force wheeled away and flew back to Vitoria, having never reached the center of Bilbao. Their bombs had killed three civilians and injured three more.

Only Karl Schmidt and the copilot, Lieutenant Adolf Hermann, escaped from the blazing Ju.52. Hermann landed in a village upriver from Bilbao, where a pistol duel with a militiaman left a woman bystander and the militiaman dead, and Hermann stomped to death by an angry mob. Schmidt banged to earth in a field outside the village of Encuri. He struggled out of his parachute harness and pulled his pistol from its holster to deal with an armed group streaming toward him from nearby towns. Then Schmidt was amazed to see a Russian fighter put down on the rough field not a hundred yards away. The Russian pilot climbed out of the cockpit and ran over to where Schmidt was standing. He waved off the crowd with his own gun, and shortly afterward Schmidt and his Russian benefactor were in a staff car on their way to Bilbao, where the German was interrogated and put in protective custody. He told them he had been sent to Spain in September by the Nazi party, of which he was a member, and that he had come to Spain "to suppress Communism." At which, recalled correspondent Steer, "the Basques laughed heartily."

The reaction to the abortive raid on Bilbao was out of all proportion to the casualties sustained. Anarchists, carrying their black-and-red flag before them, were joined by mobs of homeless refugees who stormed the Larrinaga prison and two convents where political prisoners were held. Before order was restored late that night, 194 Nationalists were killed, and another 30 died of injuries.

With the ground battle around Madrid facing a winter stalemate, General Mola was determined to keep up Nationalist morale by a resounding victory on the northern front, delivering a quick knockout blow using the greatest concentration of air power yet seen in the civil war. Intimidating leaflets were scattered by the thousands inside Republican lines, and Mola's intentions made clear with the words, ". . . if submission is not immediate I will raze all Vizcaya to the ground, beginning with the industries of war. I have the means to do so." And indeed he had. Sperrle and Richthofen asked Berlin for reinforcements, and they came. Thirty new He.111B-1s were sent from Germany in February, 1937, to join K/88 as two operational squadrons. Shortly afterward, fifteen of the 225 mile-per-hour Do.17F-A Flying Pencil bombers were added to the bomber group's strength. Additional crates of He.51s arrived in Cádiz and were forwarded to the north. The Condor Legion field at Vitoria was improved, beginning with new and longer runways and the installation of 88-millimeter flak guns. German fighters were taken from Talavera and from the legion's HQ airdrome at Ávila and sent to take part in the coming offensive. Vitoria was the main airdrome, but German fighters and the new bombers were scattered behind the lines at Burgos, Soria, and Logroño. Added to these were Ju.52s and the old Bréguets of Franco's *Argrupación Española* and Fiat CR.32 biplane fighters and Savoia Marchetti S.81 bombers of Italy's *Aviacion Legionara*.

There was hardly a square meter of Republican ground with which the pilots of the air task force were not familiar. He.70s and He.45s were prowling over Republican defenses every clear day, bringing back detailed photographs. These reconnaissance missions were unopposed because the Republican fighter force at Bilbao had dwindled to only six I-15s, and these were hoarded for use against the bombers. A German Nazi long resident in Spain, "good-natured, flossy-haired old Paul Freese," joined the Condor Legion at Vitoria as interpreter and intelligence specialist, poring over the unit's series of Michelin maps and pointing out the important communication centers and the locations of the smaller factories. A Condor Legion flyer, Captain Carsten von Harling, was assigned by Richthofen to act as liaison officer with the attacking ground troops.

The Condor Legion, with its subsidiary Italo-Spanish squadrons, was required to fulfill four primary missions in support of Mola's grand offensive. First, to hammer at the Basque frontline positions with bombs and machine-gun fire. Second, to bring to a standstill all traffic on Republican roads. Third, to raid Basque villages serving as headquarters immediately behind the front. And fourth, to demolish the town of Durango by saturation bombing on a scale unprecedented in modern war.

At seven sharp on the morning of March 31, the air assault began. Along a front more than sixty miles long, great fountains of fire erupted as the bombers swept over in wave after wave, unloading 110- and 550-pound bombs. Fighters roamed the back areas, often at deck level, strafing vehicles and bringing traffic to a halt. The villages of Ochandiano, Elgueta, and Elorrio were hit again and again. Mola's infantry followed on the heels of the planes and captured three mountains, whose defenders were dazed by the weight of the assault, and whose communications were shredded by bombs gouging the earth and cutting the lines in a hundred places. Only in front of Ochandiano did Basque resistance prove too stiff to overcome, and when one attack after another was bloodily repulsed, airpower was concentrated there, culminating on April 4 in an afternoon-long attack by relays of bombers making the short run from Vitoria and back. Survivors reported that from noon to 5 P.M., there were never less than forty planes overhead, and from then until dusk, the number increased to fifty-seven. It was calculated that five thousand bombs were dumped on the village itself and upon the trenches and dugouts defending it. When one attack ended, Basque troops who crawled from their blasted positions to give aid to the wounded were forced back to ground by Heinkels and Fiats strafing at ground level. When it was all over, Mola's men discovered six hundred Basque dead lying on the churned earth, but nobody could guess at how many others were buried in caved-in trenches. It was a frightening demonstration of what unopposed air power could accomplish against ground defenses.

The fiasco of the first large raid on Bilbao was not repeated when the Condor Legion struck at the rail and road center of Durango, a typical Basque country town sixteen miles south of Bilbao. Against no aerial opposition, K/88 decided it would be safe to employ Ju.52s, escorted by a squadron of He.51s, equipped for the occasion with racks holding 22-pound fragmentation bombs. The first Ju.52s appeared over Durango at 7:20 A.M. on the day the offensive opened, and dropped down to the altitude of a thousand feet to assure better aim. The Ju.52s were using 550-pound bombs, hopefully to blast Durango's buildings into the streets in such big heaps that all traffic there would be blocked for days to come. The raid caught Durango at the time of early mass, and the town's three large churches were filled. One bomb plummeted through the roof of the Church of the Jesuit Fathers, killing everyone inside except the vicar. Another ripped into the roof of the Santa Susana chapel, killing fourteen nuns. Santa María was hit just as Father Don Carlos Morilla was elevating the Host; he was crushed underneath tons of rubble. The bombs poured through the rest of the town, and when the Ju.52s had emptied themselves, the He.51s swooped down and scattered their own light loads throughout. At 7:50 A.M. the raid ended, and Durango tried to dig itself out. It was bombed again the next day, and the day after that, and again on April 4. The fighters added new touches to their technique by machine-gunning the streets after scattering their fragmentation bombs, and two Sisters of Charity were thus killed while running for safety. When it was all over, 127 corpses were dragged from the ruins, and another 121 died later in Bilbao hospitals.

Bilbao itself was raided on every clear day during April, the planes coming over in small packets at low altitude at irregular intervals. Fourteen alarms were sounded during one ten-hour period on a day in early April, but the worst day of all was Sunday, April 18. Three of the new Do.17s and a pair of He.111s hit the city three separate times, managing to demolish the shoe factory and a whole block of flats in the old town, leaving 67 dead and 110 badly injured. But on the third sortie, the Do.17s found four Russian fighters waiting for them in the low-lying clouds over the valley. Led by young Felipe Del Río, the Russian fighters tore into the fast-flying Dorniers from astern, and Del Río got one and a wingmate bagged another. Del Río's victim crashed north of the town; two of the crew jumped too late and were killed by the impact of striking the river with partially open parachutes. The pilot, Hans Sobotka, went down with the flaming bomber. Crowds rushed to the site of the crash, where the Do.17 was blazing in a field of heather, and gazed at Sobotka, thrown clear of the wreckage. An observer recounted how "Sobotka lay on his back, half carbonized, stiffly curved upwards along the spine. Part of his intestines, which were fried into a good imitation of sausages, hung out of his rather corpulent body. His two arms were held in dead stylized terror across his face, as he must have raised them in the last agony before he hit the hillside. . . ." Papers discovered on the corpse revealed that the Do.17 and its crew had been in Spain only thirteen days, having left Rome on April 5 for the flight to the zone of operations across the Mediterranean.

Sobotka's Do.17 was Del Río's seventh and last kill. The German gunners on the fast bombers were put on the *qui vive* after the eighteenth, and a few days later when they were bounced by the I-15, the gunners were waiting and shot the Basque down over the mouth of the river. This fact, coupled with the sure knowledge that Bilbao was to receive no more reinforcements, broke the morale of the others. What use were three overworked fighters against the Germans' apparently limitless supply of bombers that were nearly as fast as they were?

The aerial massacre of Durango had prompted other villages that lay behind Republican lines to improvise shelters, usually no more than cellars or basements surrounded by sandbags and marked with a cardboard notice proclaiming *Refugio.* Guernica, or as the Basques spelled it, Gernika, was one town that had so provided for itself. By Monday, April 26, more than three weeks had passed since the devastation at Durango, which lay only ten miles to the south, and since the bombers had not been seen over Guernica, it was hoped the city might be spared. Located but a mile from an inlet leading to the sea, Guernica offered only an insignificant small arms factory, a bridge and a railway terminal as strategic targets. Its normal population of seven thousand was swollen by an estimated three thousand refugees—some of them from Durango—and quartered near the town were two understrength battalions of Basque infantry. Thus, on April 26, Guernica was filled with some eleven thousand people in a town constructed densely, so that one building butts up against its neighbor.

At Vitoria, ten minutes' flying time away, Condor Legion ground crews began loading up the bombers in the early afternoon. The He.111s were filled with a mixture of light and heavy bombs, suspended in the dark bays nose up, hanging like sleeping bats with folded wings. At four thirty, the first Heinkel, glinting silver in the warm rays of the sun, appeared over Guernica. The heavy bell in the great tower of the parish church began to peal. The oxen drivers seated on the high wagons looked up, and so did the hundreds who jammed the market square buying and selling farm goods, as they had done every Monday since Guernica was a town of any importance. The HE.111 flew for the railway station and unloaded half a dozen bombs near the tracks, then zoomed loudly over the top of the town, machine-gunning as it went. A few minutes later another He.111 appeared and scattered its load in the same area. Then silence. A quarter of an hour passed. People emerged from shelters to look at the damage, thinking that they had been luckier than those who lived in Durango. They came out just in time to see numbers of the big ugly Ju.52s appear in the sky over the heart of the town. Tons of high explosive turned the narrow streets of Guernica into cauldrons of death, and those who scrambled out of weakened *refugios* to seek stronger shelters in, above all, the churches, were gunned down by flights of He.51s spraying the village with machine guns. At five fifteen, the serious and methodical effort to erase Guernica quarter by quarter, as had been attempted at Madrid, began. Survivors say that from that hour onward, flights of from three to a dozen bombers appeared overhead at twenty-minute intervals. Mixed in with the high explosives that were gutting buildings from top to bottom was a new weapon of terror, cascades of slender, two-pound thermite incendiaries. The Church of San Juan blazed up, and so did the chapel of Andra Mari. Clouds of smoke and grit so obscured Guernica that succeeding waves of bombers were forced down to six hundred feet in order to distinguish the town from the countryside. The last of the shuttle bombers disappeared in the red sky three hours and a quarter after the first bombs fell, leaving the once pleasant Basque village totally unrecognizable. The roseate glow could be seen fifteen miles away, reflected in the nighttime clouds hovering over the valley.

Seventy per cent of Guernica's buildings were totally destroyed, and another 20 per cent badly damaged. Estimates of the dead ranged from only a hundred to as high as sixteen hundred; based on the experience at Durango, and considering the weight of the attack and the density of population, a figure of three hundred dead at Guernica would not be an exaggeration. At first, Franco's information services denied all Nationalist responsibility for the bombing, claiming that the town had been set alight by "Red" arsonists. This fiction prevailed for weeks afterward, until a visiting correspondent for the London *Sunday Times* was told by one of General Fidel Dávila's staff officers that the Nationalists had indeed bombed Guernica, and *bueno* why not? The press officer accompanying the *Times* reporter never mentioned Guernica again, but when George Steer repeated the quote for his own paper, he received threats from two different sources abroad that if he were caught alive, he would be shot at once. Corroboration, if any were needed, was provided three weeks later by a Condor Legion pilot whose He.51 was shot down by ground fire near Vizkargi. The uninjured pilot, a twenty-three-year-old Silesian named Hans Joachim Wandel, had written in his diary opposite April 26 the word *Garnika*. At first Wandel said that this was the name of his girlfriend in Hamburg. He would not admit to having strafed the town, but boasted of accompanying He.111s on missions in which incendiary bombs were used on Basque pine forests as a defoliation measure and as a means of driving defenders from cover. Wandel said he had been recruited on the Wilhelmstrasse in mid-April, had arrived in Seville via Rome, and was paid the equivalent of $125 a month.

The military effectiveness of the bombing of Guernica was without question. Its usefulness as a rail and communications point vanished. Because this ancient town was the citadel of Basque law and customs, its ruin cast gloom throughout the province of Vizcaya. Intense bombing of the defensive positions east of the town further weakened the power to resist, and three days after the merciless air raid, Guernica fell to Nationalist troops.

Throughout May and the early days of June, the Condor Legion was kept in the air harassing Basque defenders in the shrinking perimeter around Bilbao. The city, blockaded by sea, defenseless in the air, starving, blasted by bombs and now by artillery fire—twenty thousand rounds in one day—finally gave in. On June 19, the last militiaman had left Bilbao, moved west to Asturias for a last, hopeless stand. Before the ultimate battle could be fought, the Condor Legion was suddenly withdrawn from the northern front to deal with an unexpected Republican offensive unleashed toward Brunete, fifteen miles west of Madrid. Between July 7 and 26, a see-saw air, infantry, and tank battle raged in the hills and across the plains, at first in favor of the Republicans, and then in favor of the Nationalists. The Republicans lost about 100 of the 150 aircraft with which they opened the battle, while the Nationalists, Germans included, lost only 23.

The Legion flew back to the north, where the offensive had stalled due to lack of air support. The Republicans were now confined to a pocket barely ninety miles wide and fifty miles deep. Their ragged positions were bombed and strafed for hours on end, and in mid-October the dazed troops were treated to yet another experiment in tactical air support of ground operations. Using maps and aerial photographs, the Legion staff plotted a key sector of Asturian trenches. Then a group of bombers and fighter-bombers swept around the enemy lines and approached the marked target area from the rear, roaring up valleys at low altitude to make their bomb run in a predetermined formation. The next thing the Republican troops knew was a sudden thunder of engines, then a thunderclap that tore the ground from under their feet; the German fleet had unloaded their high explosives simultaneously on signal from the leader, and the entire weight of bombs struck the earth in pattern. Coming on top of six weeks of hard combat, this blow from the air was shattering. A new phrase, carpet bombing, was added to the lexicon of war, and a week later, on October 21, organized resistance in the last pocket ended. The Condor Legion could rightly claim that much of the Nationalist victory in the north was undeniably stamped "Made in Germany."

From its formal organization in November 1936 until the end of the war, the Condor Legion remained operational in Spain for twenty-nine months. To assure that the maximum number of Luftwaffe personnel—pilots, navigators, engineers, gunners, mechanics, clerks, and staff—would receive the benefit of field experience, sections were rotated back home periodically to make room for others sent out from Germany via the Berlin-Rome-Seville line. Thus, approximately fourteen thousand Germans of all ranks served with the Condor Legion, including the flak troops, or about as many civilians as were killed in Republican areas by air bombardment.

The Luftwaffe had the opportunity not only to test its personnel and theories of modern war on and over Spanish battlefields, but every kind of aircraft on inventory as well, just as the Russians on the other side of the line were doing. In addition to the 550 biplane I-15s sent to Spain, Russia exported 475 newer I-16 low-wing, monoplane fighters that provided stiff competition for Germany's best. The fat little I-16, nicknamed *Mosca* (fly) by the Spanish and American volunteers who flew her, was good for 283 miles per hour in short bursts and cruised handily at above 220 miles per hour. The Mosca, four gunned and quick turning, earned the respect of even Messerschmitt 109 pilots, and they could make hash of He.51s, which were relegated to ground-strafing duties.

By December 1938, the Condor Legion was stocked with 106 aircraft. The figure includes 40 He.111s and 5 Do.17s, the latter having replaced all the Heinkel Blitzes as reconnaissance machines, and no fewer than 45 Bf.109B-2 and C-1 type fighters.

These were ostensibly the finest fighters in the world, and when dealing with anything except Moscas, they ruled the skies over Spain. German pilots discovered that the rotund I-16s had a higher rate of roll, were faster flat out than they, and could turn inside them. Needed were superior tactical formations, and they were worked out by such coming Luftwaffe fighter stars as Adolf Galland, Werner Mölders, Herbert Ihlefeld, Walter Oesau, and others. The rigid, three-element attack formation as used by He.51 squadrons in 1937 during the early stages of the battle for Bilbao was thrown out. Instead, the basic tactical unit was reduced to an element of two, with the leader trailed some two hundred yards aft by another Bf.109 riding his port or starboard wing. This two-ship attack formation could be combined with another to form a *Schwarme*, leaving the element leaders free to concentrate on the target ahead, knowing their tails were protected. This basic combat formation proved itself again and again with the flexibility and security it offered, and was one of the major contributions made by the Condor Legion's fighter group, J/88, during the civil war. Occasionally, He.51s were sent out as bait, stacked a few thousand feet below the Bf.109s, and when the Heinkels were jumped by Moscas, they in turn were bounced by the 109s, who used their superior diving speed to great advantage.*

Richthofen, promoted to general and elevated to command of the Condor Legion in 1938, had all of his previous doubts concerning the value of dive-bombing removed while in Spain. Three Ju.87As were sent out from Germany, later replaced by three Ju.87Bs, and after initial teething troubles were worked out, Richthofen was ecstatic about them as pinpoint bombers for use against bridges and even Russian tanks.

Considering the military benefits that accrued to the Luftwaffe from the Spanish adventure, the cost was not high. The Condor Legion lost 96 aircraft (56 of them through accidents, chiefly in winter-weather flying), while bagging 277 Republican planes in air-to-air combat. Another 58 Republican planes were

---

*This "finger four" formation was later adopted by the RAF and USAAF during World War II, and remains basic with both fighter arms to this day.

shot down by Condor Legion flak batteries. There were a few German pilots who grew to feel that they were fighting for the wrong side, and one admitted that the Legion had not always fought to the hilt. When he returned to Germany, a fighter pilot named Lützow explained why in a letter. Wrote Captain Lützow: "The fact that we were fighting for a people other than our own, carrying out sorties deep into enemy territory, and the responsibility for irreplaceable, highly qualified personnel, all this inhibited the keenness and natural élan of the German fighter pilot. He could only operate all-out when his own force's aircraft were in danger. . . ."

Which is a natural enough reaction.

12

THE CONFUSION FACTORY

I am now the Commanding General and the Front has to accept the
planes I send them.
—Ernst Udet

Ever since Foreign Secretary Anthony Eden had returned to
London from Berlin in March 1936 with Hitler's suave (and
totally false) assurances that the Luftwaffe had achieved air
parity with Britain, no opportunity was lost to exploit the gulli-
bility of the rest of the world concerning Germany's overwhelming superiority in the air. The seismic shockwave generated by the destruction of Guernica traveled around the world,
giving military men a new insight on air power, stirring alarm
in European capitals, and inspiring Pablo Picasso to create a
large painting immortalizing the ruined Basque town. Even as
German bombers were, in the words of the British periodical
The Aeroplane, "doing good work in Spain," Europeans were
given their first opportunity to witness the Luftwaffe's wizardry
in peaceful Switzerland.

Goering, who by now was fully aware of the political benefits
to be reaped through propaganda concerning "my Luftwaffe,"
easily obtained the Führer's permission to send the newest
fighters, bombers, and reconnaissance planes to the Fourth International Air Meet, held at Zurich from July 23 through August 1, 1937. The outcome of the competition was everything
they had dreamed about. The real stunner of the meet was the
appearance of an all-silver Do.17, eighth prototype version, in
full military markings. This particular Flying Pencil had been
specially fitted with a pair of the scarce DB 600A, 1,000-horse-
power engines, and handily won the Alpine Circuit competition with a maximum speed of 280 miles per hour—faster than

any of the foreign fighters present. The Do.17's performance astonished French and British air observers, who had no way of knowing that production versions of the bomber were coming off the lines with lesser engines and speeds 30 miles per hour less than those demonstrated at Zurich.

Heinkel displayed the fast He.112; Fiesler awed the crowd with a preproduction Fi.156 *Storch,* a high-wing monoplane with short takeoff and landing characteristics, able to near-hover at 32 miles per hour without stalling out; Kurt Tank's F.W.58, a swift, twin-engine courier plane, was much admired, as was the record-holding Bf.108 *Taifun;* but the greatest honors were won by Messerschmitt's 109 fighters. Of the five Bf.109s sent to Zurich, two were powered with new Daimler engines. Although there were ample numbers of young Luftwaffe fighter and test pilots available, Udet, now forty-one and a brigadier general, insisted on flying one of the high-performing 109s himself in the Alpine Circuit race. Of course, there was nothing wrong with Udet's piloting skill, but his luck was generally atrocious. His record attempt was barely underway when the Daimler lost revs and the new three-bladed experimental prop slowed, then stopped. Udet frantically sought a clear patch of earth on the foothills leading up to the glittering Alps, found one, and smacked down for a spine-jarring crash landing that broke the 109's fuselage in half just behind the cockpit. Udet disentagled himself from the wreckage and watched the others roaring across the Swiss sky. Udet's crash was the only piece of misfortune suffered by the Germans during the meet. One heat of 228 miles was won easily by another of the 109s in a time of 57 minutes 7 seconds, averaging 233.5 miles per hour, closely trailed by two other 109s placing second and third. Then the Alpenflug circuit, four times around a 31.4-mile course, was won by a 109 with an average of 254.54 miles per hour. The climb-and-dive competition was again taken by one of the German fighters, which was shot up to 9,840 feet and back down to 1,060 feet in only 2 minutes, 5.7 seconds. It was a clean sweep for the Luftwaffe, followed on November 11 by yet another triumph when a Bf.109V13 equipped with a special DB 601 engine captured a new world speed record of 379.4 miles per hour.

In August 1938, five months after the *Anschluss* had dragged Austria into the Third Reich, Hermann Goering invited the heads of the French Armée de l'Air to Germany for an inspection trip of selected Luftwaffe installations. Goering hoped to impress, and indeed, to intimidate, his old adversaries—especially the stocky chief of the Air General Staff, General Joseph Vuillemin, a Spad pilot of the 1918 war with seven victories. Vuillemin and key members of his staff were shown massively built and lavishly furnished Luftwaffe barracks, training fields, operational units and factories. General Milch, the Frenchmen's beaming guide, made it a point to take his guests to Berlin-Döberitz, where the reconstituted Richthofen Wing awaited inspection. Vuillemin walked past long lines of new Messerschmitt fighters, and past tall, stern-faced pilots dressed for combat standing rigidly at attention on the grass. Milch next took the French airmen to Germany's showcase industrial complex at Oranienburg, where Milch, Heinkel, and Udet had laid an impressive trap.

When Heinkel's 112 fighter design lost to the Bf.109 at the trials at Travemünde, the decision acted as a spur and not as a deterrent. He determined not only to build a better fighter than the 109, but an airplane to capture the world's absolute speed record. The new fighter was built around an improved Daimler engine, the DB 601, normally developing 1,100 horsepower, but modified to a special high-compression ratio and designed to burn suporootane fuel so as to provide up to 1,800 horsepower in a short, furious burst. The He.112's finicky engineering was eliminated, replaced by every weight-saving and drag-reducing technique Heinkel's designers could dream up. The He.100, as the new plane was called, could be built from only 969 parts instead of the He.112's 2,885. Rivet consumption was cut to less than half that of the 112, and Heinkel boasted that 1,150 man-hours were thereby saved on the wings alone. A new kind of explosive rivet was developed to further speed the building process, for which licenses were later sold to Japan and to the Du Pont company in the United States. Faulting Messerschmitt's chronically weak landing gear, Heinkel insisted on a wide-track gear folding inward. Even though the wingspan was cut to less than twenty-seven feet, there was room in the fighter for two cannon and four machine guns. The greatest engineering advance, however, was in the cooling system. Heinkel designers calculated that by eliminating the usual drag-evoking radiators, speed could be increased by as much as 50 miles per hour. The DB 601 engine tolerated higher-than-normal temperatures, able to withstand 230 degrees Fahrenheit without steam forming in the engine itself.

"We decided to experiment with evaporative cooling," Heinkel explained. "The cooling water around the engine was pressurized in various ways, [and] after being ducted away from the engine this water was depressurized, and steam formed. Steam and water were parted in a steam separator, and the water returned to the cooling circuit and the steam was piped to the wings, where it was condensed to water by cooling, and this water was again returned to the engine circuit by centrifugal pumps."

The slick-looking fighter was first flown on January 22, 1938, and two more prototypes were completed shortly afterward. On Whitsunday, June 5, Heinkel believed that the He.100 was ready to assault the hundred-kilometer closed-circuit record. As the fighter was being prepared for flight, with the Heinkel test pilot standing by, Udet's all-red courier plane appeared overhead and landed. Udet, dressed in baggy flannels, a bowtie, and flying jacket, stepped out and said he would like to fly the He.100V3, confessing to Heinkel that he had already flown the V1 prototype while it was at Rechlin proving center. If Udet did not crash this expensive and beautiful plane, which would be no surprise, and happened to beat the record, it would go far to help Heinkel in wresting away from Willy Messerschmitt his virtual monopoly on fighter contracts. Heinkel agreed, and Udet, still dressed more like a Sunday golfer than a test pilot, climbed into the He.100 and strapped in.

He took off at four twenty-seven that afternoon, climbed like a rocket, and disappeared from sight. He landed back at Marienehe at four fifty-three, having clocked 394.6 miles per hour for a new sixty-mile closed-circuit record. The Monday morning papers in Germany were filled with enthusiastic accounts of the blue-ribbon flight, and by that afternoon, the story was picked up and featured in every paper in Europe. However, the Goebbels press release did not describe the plane as a custom-built experimental model, but as a production version of the He.112U —a design that did not exist. It was this phantom that the Germans were going to use to haunt General Vuillemin.

The French Chief of Air Staff was shown through the humming workshops at Oranienburg where dozens of He.111 bombers were coming off the line, through the new hangars, and even deep in the earth to inspect the spotless air-raid shelters, where he found "everything in readiness, even down to ten sharpened pencils on every desk," and then back outside to watch an He.111 being put through its paces using only one engine. Then Udet invited the French general up in his light, slow courier plane for an aerial view of the sprawling works. Then, in a carefully rehearsed drama staged for Vuillemin's benefit, Udet brought the plane in for a landing at just above stalling speed. At that moment, test pilot Hans Dieterle flashed past in an He.100 with the throttle almost fire-walled, streaking across the Frenchman's line of vision in a blur too fast for the eye to see details, but with a sound like the hiss of lightning. With both planes down, Vuillemin and his staff walked over to examine the "He.112U." Through an interpreter, Milch explained to the French that they were looking at the newest German production fighter. "Tell me, Udet," said Milch, "how far along are we with mass production?"

"Oh," Udet replied casually, "the second production line is ready, and the third will be within two weeks." Vuillemin, thinking of his far slower and clumsier-looking Morane and Dewoitine fighters sluggishly coming off the production lines at home, looked crestfallen. He admitted on the spot to Milch that he was "shattered."

Afterward, the French airmen and their ambassador to Berlin, André François-Poncet, were invited to a lavish breakfast at Karinhall. Goering asked General Vuillemin point blank what France would do in case war broke out between Germany and Czechoslovakia, and Vuillemin replied that "France will keep the promise she has given." But in the car on the way back to

Berlin for the return to France, Vuillemin admitted privately to François-Poncet that he was depressed by what he had seen, and commented, "If war breaks out at the end of September, as you think it will, there won't be a single French aircraft left after fourteen days."

Vuillemin's visit had been strategically timed, coming as it did during a period of French agonizing over whether three million Sudeten Germans and the principle involved were worth the risk of war. On September 30, a month after the French air chief's trip inside the dragon's mouth, the British and the French handed the Sudetenland to Hitler. The victory was made complete six months later when the new Czech president, Dr. Emil Hácha, sixty-seven, was summoned to Berlin and had his nation threatened with destruction at the hands of the Luftwaffe unless the rest of his country, this creature of Versailles, Moravia and Bohemia were turned into Reich protectorates. Goering, pushing a pen at the old man, boomed that unless Hácha signed, "Half of Prague will lie in ruins within two hours. Hundreds of bombers," stressed Goering, "are waiting the order to take off. . . ." At this point, Hácha fainted. He revived, and with visions of beautiful Prague reduced to fire and rubble, signed away his nation.

Ten million Czechs thus lost their freedom without a shot's being fired in their defense. Thirty-five highly trained and well-equipped friendly Czech divisions disappeared from the Order of Battle tentatively drawn up by British and French general staffs. Hitler had eliminated "that damned airdrome" (Czechoslovakia) with its arrowhead pointed at Germany's vitals, and now the output of the modernized Skoda arms factories would be pouring into Wehrmacht depots. Hitler's victims—and this included the English and the French—did not realize until years afterward that they had once again been frightened out of the forest by a paper tiger. While it is true that the Luftwaffe was able to alert 1,230 first-line aircraft, including 600 bombers and 400 fighters, during the Czech crisis, what only Luftwaffe High Command knew was that nearly half this number was earmarked for use in the east, leaving the rest of the Reich perimeter spread too thin to counter any serious air offensive by the RAF or the French.* Worse, only five fighting divisions and seven in reserve were available to hold ten times that many positioned by the French in the west. Nor could the uncertain Allies, who mistakenly believed the Luftwaffe had the power to "Guernica" London and Paris at a stroke, know that the Luftwaffe they so greatly feared was already developing serious cracks in its freshly poured foundations.

Changes in the smoothly running Luftwaffe command, later to be know as OKL, *Oberkommando der Luftwaffe,* began immediately upon General Wever's death. First, Wever was replaced by Kesselring, then Wilhelm Wimmer was removed from his post as Chief of the Technical Office and transferred to an operational command in Air District III. Wimmer was in no sense being fired from a job where he had performed so flawlessly for so long, but was elevated to accommodate one of the Führer's inspired decisions. The new technical chief, Hitler decided, must be Ernst Udet, who was as puzzled about the sudden move as anyone else. He protested to both Goering and Milch that he was happy as Inspector of Fighters and Dive-Bombers, a position he was probably better qualified to fill than anybody else, but that he was no administrator and had a deep loathing for the intricacies of office routine. A disaster was in the making, but Goering made no move to avert it. Explained Milch: "Hitler quite properly saw in Udet one of Germany's greatest pilots. Unfortunately, he also saw in him, quite erroneously, one of Germany's greatest technical experts in the field of aviation. Bowing to necessity, Goering appointed Udet to the post. This was surely not easy for him, for he and Udet had been on anything but good terms for the past decades. . . . It goes without saying that I voiced a number of objective reservations, but I do not believe Goering made any attempt to understand these. For him, the important thing was to enhance his own position with Hitler."

---

*The respected American magazine *Forum* reported in March 1939 that the Luftwaffe possessed twelve thousand aircraft at the time of the Munich crisis, and sixteen thousand to eighteen thousand a bare six months afterward.

Udet inherited a straightforward and simple command setup from Wimmer; the Technical Office was logically divided into four compartments: Research, Development, Procurement, and Internal Admistration and Budget. This manageable structure was shattered into thirteen different departments just when Udet was beginning to believe he could manage the four, and now he had to deal with three times as many department heads as previously. On top of this, a whole new office, Supply and Procurement, was created by OKL, and Udet was put in charge of this as well—adding yet another nine departments, plus the testing stations at Rechlin, Travemünde, Tarnewitz, Pennemünde, and Udetfeld, plus the Industrial Section. In effect, Udet became the Luftwaffe's quartermaster general, a post he would never had dreamed of acquiring on his own volition. Unfortunately for Udet, his top aides and personal associates in this sprawling office, Colonel Max Pendele and Generals August Ploch, Rulof Lucht, and Günther Tschersich, were primarily engineers and not administrators, and staff conferences dedicated to solving mammoth organizational problems usually degenerated into technical discussions about engines, guns, and new aircraft prototypes, occasionally enlivened with anecdotes from Ploch about his experiences at Lipetsk. (Ploch was one of the few Luftwaffe general officers who was fluent in Russian.)

Adrift in a sea of perplexing bureaucratic problems, Udet could not cope with the responsibility. Department heads—and there were so many of them—often waited months for Udet to make some crucial decision. Normally, Udet should have reported to Goering through Milch, but Goering created a situation whereby Udet could seek audience with the field marshal over Milch's head. This arrangement soured the once-agreeable relationship between Milch and Udet, adding acrimony to the general chaos. But the frequent meetings between Udet and Goering were fruitless. The Luftwaffe's top legal officer, General Freiherr von Hammerstein, recalled that these two middle-aged fighter pilots spent their time reminiscing about the days when they flew Fokkers over the Western Front. And Goering himself was to admit later that "mention of work was scrupulously avoided."

"Internally," observed Hammerstein, "everyone was working against everyone else."

Another ingredient to this stew of inefficiency and unhappiness was the appointment of Hans Jeschonnek as the Luftwaffe's new chief of staff, replacing Hans-Jürgen Stumpff, the interim successor to the ebullient Kesselring, transferred like Wimmer to an operational command. Jeschonnck took the reins of command as a brigadier general shortly before his fortieth birthday; Goering, like Hitler, believed in youth as a vital factor as far as the Luftwaffe was concerned. The Luftwaffe was seen as a creature of National Socialism, unlike the imperial-minded navy and the Prussian-minded army. Jeschonnek was himself a Prussian, but was thoroughly imbued with the Nazi spirit. Although Wever had seen in Jeschonnek his eventual replacement, he intended the grooming process to continue for several more years. Now, the rush of events place Jeschonnek in the critical spot long before he was ready.

Jeschonnek was a product of his times. He was not yet sixteen when he gained admittance to the Cadet School at Berlin-Lichterfelde, Germany's West Point, where his character and outlook were formed into the Prussian army mold. He ended the war as a nineteen-year-old fighter pilot, and remained in the Reichswehr first as an ordnance officer and later as one of the youngest Truppenamt staff officers in the secret air arm. A disciple of the stab-in-the-back theory of Germany's downfall, Jeschonnek early in his career was among those who envisioned Adolf Hitler as the demigod who alone was capable of erasing the shame of an undeserved defeat. Jeschonnek was the total soldier; he was lean, erect, and trimly uniformed, and associates noted that he never *walked* anywhere, he strode. His heavy features, accentuated by a narrow skull, were as immobile as granite, and he was generally as talkative. Despite his new rank and power, Jeschonnek remained an ascetic, his life austere. Co-workers often observed him in the great colonnaded headquarters dining hall, usually alone, breakfasting on cereal, coffee, army bread, and issue jam. He seldom drank, and then joylessly, his relaxations confined to long, silent marches through the woods and occasional games of skat shared with

Wolfram von Richthofen, who commented that the new chief of staff was a cheerful loser.

Jeschonnek's decisiveness and his youth were the very things that worked against him as a chief of staff. In his dealings with the older, tougher and more experienced division, corps and air fleet commanders, his youth was a distinct handicap. To his subordinates, Jeschonnek could never assume the father image radiating from Wever, or the stern Dutch-uncle figure presented by Kesselring. Possessed of a naturally caustic tongue, Jeschonnek frequently revealed an inner rage at his chronic inability to deal with others on a human level by cutting sarcasm. Exchanges of opinion concerning procedures, tactics or equipment were interpreted by Jeschonnek as contrariness and obstructionism, to be summarily rejected. Jeschonnek's inflexibility never wavered. His devotion to Hitler eventually got on Goering's nerves. Once, following a Führer conference, Goering shouted at Jeschonnek, "You always stand there like a lieutenant with your thumbs at your trouser seams when you talk to Hitler!" Jeschonnek was just as inflexible in his attitude toward the use of air power during war. His view—unlike Wever's —did not extend beyond the nearest horizon.

Hitler had delivered two knockout blows inside Europe using the overrated Luftwaffe as a club, and he was already planning the final demolition of the territorial provisions of the Versailles Treaty using the same instrument. However, he had not failed to take note that the RAF had finally badgered enough money from the Chancellor of the Exchequer to begin its own expansion. Hitler was continually reassuring the Wehrmacht and the Luftwaffe high commands that he wanted no war with Britain and would continue to exercise every political skill at his command to avoid it. Yet, on the remote chance that the British government would stiffen its spine and declare war on the Third Reich when Hitler made his next moves in Europe, he asked Goering what the Luftwaffe's chances were. Goering referred the question to the commander of the Second Air Fleet, Lieutenant General Hellmuth Felmy, whose job it would be to fight the greater share of the air battles against the West. Felmy, a realist who had been flying since 1912 and had helped create the Luftwaffe as it then stood, replied unequivocally in a long memorandum dated September 22, 1938: "With our present available resources, only a harassing effect can be counted upon. Whether this can lead to the attrition of the British will to fight depends in part upon imponderable and, in any case, unforeseeable factors. . . . A war of annihilation against England appears to be out of the question with the resources thus far available."

With this unpleasant news at hand, Hitler again summoned Goering and ordered that he get moving on a program to increase the Luftwaffe's strength by a factor of five. Goering turned the planning of this stupendous feat over to Jeschonnek and his staff late in October, and by November 7, Jeschonnek had the figures in hand. Needed would be: 58 bomber wings, 16 fighter wings, 8 dive-bomber wings, 1 ground-attack wing, and other special mission units to make up an additional 43 squadrons. In all, about 20,000 first-line aircraft. In addition, Germany's antiaircraft defenses—which Goering had taken away from the army—were to be fattened to a total of 2500 heavy 88-millimeter guns and 3000 light 37-millimeter and 20-millimeter rapid-firing cannon.

On December 6, Goering summoned the various department heads to Karinhall to disclose the details of the Führer's new program. Udet, who was then able to squeeze less than three hundred combat planes a month through the muddled and leisurely production program, was thrown into fresh despair. Others, aware of Germany's shortage of strategic materials of nearly every kind, declared frankly that the program was impossible. Goering shrugged off the protests and said that he expected that the Führer was to receive a fully developed presentation no later than the following month, January 1939.

On January 8 of the new year, Milch convened a staff conference at the Air Ministry, away from the dreamy atmosphere of Karinhall and away from Goering's bellowed rhetoric, and they got down to business. Milch pointed out that the Luftwaffe had been pinched by material shortages for the past two years. He reminded them that the plan for peacetime mobilization, drawn up in January 1937, was still far from realization, and that when it was inaugurated, one of the first moves forced on them was to cut the allotments of iron, steel and aluminum by 60 per cent. He reminded them also that nine months previously, on April 1, 1938, the schedule called for the completion of 9,800 aircraft of all kinds, but that only 4,800 had been delivered— and 2,000 of those belonged to the delivery goal left over from a previous schedule. Regarding the staggering number of flak guns the Führer wanted, Milch produced figures dating back to late 1937, when he had reported to Goering that the shortage of iron then existing meant that the production goal for these guns set for 1942 probably would not amount to more than 25 per cent of the planned total. With the importation from Spain during 1937 alone of 1.62 million tons of iron, 956,000 tons of pyrites, and 2,000 tons of other minerals, and with the exploita- tion of low-grade ore deposits inside Germany itself, the situa- tion had eased somewhat, but nowhere near enough to provide the necessary raw materials for Hitler's ambitious expansion program. As it was, the Luftwaffe had to fight for every ton of the scarce metal; the army required prodigious amounts for its own production schedules for tanks, armored vehicles, artillery and the myriad other tools of war; the navy had its own claims to the pile, irrationally realized in one instance in 1938 when Hitler agreed to the laying down of the keel of an aircraft carrier, the *Graf Zeppelin,* that might add prestige but which would be virtually useless by itself. Then there was the matter of cost to realize the new program, amounting to about fifteen billion dollars.

One by one, the Luftwaffe department chiefs were consulted as to feasibility, and one by one they declared it hopeless. How- ever, Colonel Josef Kammhuber, Chief of the Organization Staff, suggested a scaled-down plan calling for the expenditure of only five billion dollars, but only Stumpff believed the plan workable. The conference reached dead end, and Milch stood up and said, "Kammhuber, pack up your stuff! We're going to see the Field Marshal [Goering]. The Führer's program is the objective, but at least the Kammhuber program must be car- ried out. Have any of you gentlemen anything more to say?"

At this, Jeschonnek, who had been brooding throughout most of the conference, jumped up and said, "I object! In my opinion, it is not our duty to stab the Führer in the back. If the Führer has ordered this program, he knows by what means it can be carried out!"

Milch replied, "All right, Jeschonnek, *you* come along with me to the Field Marshal." They returned from Goering's huge office at the end of the hall a short time afterward, Milch glum, Jeschonnek triumphant. Milch reported that Goering believed that, somehow or another, the Führer program could be accomplished—or at least he had confidence that every department head would do his utmost to see that "as much as possible" of the program was carried out. Kammhuber, a pragmatist and an organization expert, demanded to know what that meant when translated to cash and hardware. No answer was forthcoming, and Kammhuber requested immediate relief from staff duty and a posting to an operational unit. Faced with the unyielding statistics concerning availability of raw material and plant production capacities on the one hand, and with an "as much as possible" dictate on the other, the Luftwaffe department heads simply let the program fade out of mind, leaving Udet to keep his production lines puttering along on a peacetime, business-as-usual basis. "Thereafter," remarked Kammhuber, "the Luftwaffe began to drift."

Despite its manifold problems, the Technical Office and Supply and Procurement Department headed by Udet could always count on a surplus of designs with which to equip the combat groups. Ingenuity, even brilliance, was never lacking. This was especially so in the case of ideas originating inside the design offices themselves, where designers were not fenced in too tightly by Air Ministry requirements spelled out in tortured detail. In 1937, for example, the ministry invited Arado and Focke-Wulf to submit designs for a new reconnaissance and ground-support plane to replace the ageing He.46. Aside from improved performance, what was wanted above all was outstanding visibility. Although Blohm und Voss, the shipbuilders with an aircraft plant in Hamburg, had not been invited to submit a design, their new technical director, Richard Vogt, decided to enter the competition anyway. What emerged from Vogt's board and out of the factory was a prototype unlike any other in the world. Vogt's B.V.141 struck those who gazed upon it for the first time as some kind of ghastly manufacturing mistake. The plane, if one could call it that, looked like two different aircraft that had been disassembled and then put back together with some of the major components missing. The pencil-like fuselage was little more than a boom acting as a carrier for the tail surfaces at one end and the nine-cylinder BMW radial engine at the other. The crew compartment, an angular greenhouse faceted like a cut diamond with innumerable flat panes of glass, was offset from the—a fuselage, was it? —some feet away from the engine, knifed through the bottom by the paddle-shaped wings. Udet came out to see for himself and, typically, shucked his peaked cap for a worn leather helmet and flew this asymmetrical bird around the outskirts of Hamburg. Why not? he said. Vogt produced other prototypes with changes, including a longer fuselage for improved stability, a slightly wider landing gear track, and, in a radical experiment to improve the field of fire for the gunner-radioman aft, cut off the starboard horizontal tail surface, making the creature seem odder than ever. However, every pilot who flew the improved B.V.141B-O praised its pleasant handling characteristics, and with a top speed of 272 miles per hour, armed with four machine guns, capable of carrying a 450-pound bomb load, and with a maximum range of nearly 1,200 miles, the unorthodox craft exceeded the ministry's specifications, and then some.

A second shock awaited the evaluation board when the Focke-Wulf entry arrived at Rechlin for testing. Designer Kurt Tank, a believer in twin-engine reliability for a craft whose duties would force it to operate within easy range of heavy ground fire, installed a pair of small, 430-horsepower Argus engines on extremely thin booms. The crew compartment, almost entirely glass, was centered on the narrow, knife-thin wing. The Technical Office had not expected a twin-engine design, but Tank pointed out that the total horsepower met the requirements at no great increase in weight, and besides, the configuration he had chosen provided for interchangeable crew compartments to meet special mission requirements—a heavily armored one for ground attack, one with dual controls for aircrew training, a standard nacelle for normal reconnaissance.

But the Air Ministry was in no mood for unorthodoxy, or for designs ahead of their time. Chosen instead was the conventional-looking Henschel 126, a high-wing monoplane with an uprated radial engine providing only 193 miles per hour top speed, but with good slow-speed characteristics. Not only did the Hs.126 look more normal, and therefore more comforting, but unit costs were one-third less than for the F.W.189. How long it could live in the air under combat conditions was another matter.

Inside the special projects shop at Heinkel's Marienehe plant, workers were getting used to the banshee whistling and whining sound of an aircraft engine unlike any ever heard before. They were hearing the sound of the future, prematurely arrived thanks to the skill of a twenty-seven-year-old dreamer named Pabst von Ohain, who had the backing of Ernst Heinkel, to whom no idea was ever radical. Ohain had developed plans for a pure turbojet engine while still an undergraduate at Göttingen University. By September 1937, Ohain was successfully test-running his engine, fueled first with hydrogen, then with petroleum. Thus encouraged, he designed and built a more powerful version developing 1,100 pounds of static thrust. By January 1, 1939, airframe designers were making detailed plans for the He.178 jet fighter, whose round Duralumin fuselage was only 24½ feet long. Heinkel had never been more excited by anything in his life, and hoped to successfully mate the engine to the airframe for test flights late that summer.

But the Luftwaffe High Command expressed little interest in Heinkel's jet, even after successful runs at Rechlin produced a top speed of 435 miles per hour with the turbojet burning cheap kerosene. OKL, pressured by Goering and Hitler for mass quantities of airplanes, assigned the lowest priority to research and development, and, with Jeschonnek's accession to the chief of staff's throne, allowed the theory of dive-bombing to go mad.

In mid-1936, Junkers began design work on a new bomber. Unlike the Do.17 and the He.111, the Junkers design had no connection with Lufthansa's civilian requirements, but was created purely as a warplane in line with the theory then prevailing that if bombers were built primarily for speed, then defensive armament could be dispensed with altogether. Using their own engines, Jumo 211Bs developing 1,200 horsepower, Junkers produced a twin-engine craft weighing only six tons and with the phenomenal speed of 340 miles per hour. Prototypes began flying in January 1937, but by the time initial bugs had been worked out and Junkers was ready for contracts and series production, experience in Spain revealed the fallacy of the unescorted bomber theory. The Condor Legion had learned that lesson with Do.17s around Bilbao, and German fighter pilots on other Spanish fronts had seen how easy it was for them to gun down Republican bombers, even late model Russian SB-2s, when they ventured out without adequate fighter protection.* OKL ordered that the Ju.88 be given guns. Work stopped while extensive alterations were made to the cabin enclosure to provide the necessary armament. Meanwhile, the Luftwaffe's training wing, the *Lehrgeschwader,* was conducting extensive high-altitude bombing exercises at Greifswald, and with distressing results. Although carried out by top crews and against no opposing ground fire, bombing from an altitude of 13,000 feet put only 2 per cent of the bombs inside a circle with a radius of 330 feet. When release altitude was cut in half, the average increased to between 12 and 25 per cent. Then the Ju.87 Stukas took over from the He.111 and Do.17 horizontal bombers, and put 25 per cent of their bombs in a circle with half the radius, i.e., 165 feet. Since the vaunted German optical and technical genius had still failed to come up with a decent bombsight, the conclusion reached by OKL was that horizontal bombing with accuracy was an unrealizable goal. Therefore, all future Luftwaffe bombers must be built to deliver their bombs in a dive.

Udet's Technical Office received the new dictate from

---

*Russia supplied 210 SB-2, twin-engine bombers to the Spanish government, but only 32 survived the war. Not all, of course, were destroyed by German air action, but Bf.109 pilots found them easy meat.

Jeschonnek, and it was duly passed on to the Junkers managing director, Dr. Heinrich Koppenburg. Once again the Ju.88 workshop was thrown into upheaval as engineers undid all that had gone before, tearing apart the wings to make them stronger, beefing up the fuselage, adding dive brakes, and strengthening the tail section to withstand the terrific G-forces that would be imposed during pullout. First test flights with the modified bomber proved that the wing loading was totally unacceptable, so back into the workshop went the Ju.88 to have four feet added to the wing. Month after month slipped by, and still the Ju.88 remained an unfinished product. Koppenburg was furious with OKL, complaining that he had catalogued 25,000 alterations demanded by Jeschonnek's younger engineering aides. The final result was not a superspeed, unarmed, six-ton wonder, but a laden craft grossing nearly thirteen tons, festooned with five machine guns and with its maximum speed cut by almost 100 miles per hour. Milch, disgusted with the entire project, described the Ju.88 as it then was as a "flying barn door which was capable of becoming a bird again only after it had dropped its bombs."

In order to impress on the rest of the world the fact that the Luftwaffe did indeed possess a wonder bomber, a stripped version of the Ju.88, the fifth prototype model, was readied for an attempt on the thousand-kilometer record for aircraft carrying a two-ton payload. On March 19, 1939, pilot Ernst Seibert and engineer Kurt Heintz climbed inside the Ju.88V5 and took off from Dessau. Fifty-six minutes later, they had set a new record for the course with a speed of 323 miles per hour—7 miles per hour faster than the RAF's Hawker Hurricane I fighter, then Britain's finest. No one outside the Luftwaffe knew that this particular Ju.88 bore little more than superficial resemblance to the production versions, or that the endless changes insisted upon by OKL so bogged down the pace of manufacture that only eighteen of these wonder bombers would be ready for operations by September 1.

There appeared on the plans for the Concentrated Aircraft Procurement Program issued by Jeschonnek in November 1938 an item calling for the creation of sixteen so-called Destroyer

Wings. The *Zerstörergeschwader* was an invention of Hermann Goering's, who gave a contract to Willy Messerschmitt to produce a long-range, twin-engine strategic fighter capable of escorting the deep penetration bombers then envisioned in 1934 wherever they might go. Messerschmitt produced the Bf.110, and armed as it was with two cannon and four machine guns firing forward and a single gun firing aft, it was certainly capable of destroying any bomber then flying. However, the Bf.110 was sluggish on the controls and had no dive-bombing capability whatever. To remedy this defect, OKL called for an altogether new design that would supplant the Bf.110 not only as a day fighter, but as a high-speed reconnaissance plane and a dive-bomber as well. Now that Messerschmitt had taken over the BFW company, his planes henceforth carried his personal prefix, and the new design was known as the Me.210. Jeschonnek's procurement program called for "as many Me.210s as possible, at least sufficient for seven or eight Geschwader." In addition, the chief of staff demanded Me.210s to equip eight dive-bomber wings. Of course, the Führer Program was fantasy to everybody except Jeschonnek, but even so, the Air Ministry placed a production order for a thousand Me.210s based on nothing more than plans, performance forecasts, and Willy Messerschmitt's hard-driving sales pitch. Messerschmitt got his lucrative contracts a full ten months before the first prototype Me.210 was even flown. To commit so many man-hours, so much raw material, and so many precious Daimler engines to an untested airplane was madness. The first Me.210 to be test-flown exhibited so much longitudinal instability that it was almost uncontrollable, and the second model, extensively reworked, came apart in the air during flutter tests. One Me.210 after another crashed, and pilots regarded them simply as death traps. Pilots ordered to perform tests instinctively flew with one hand on the stick and the other on the parachute rip cord. Finally, Milch called a halt, and demanded Messerschmitt's resignation, which was not forthcoming. Layoffs and wasted material, Milch estimated, had cost the Luftwaffe six hundred aircraft.

The confusion arising from Hitler's ever-shifting attitude toward England coupled with Jeschonnek's mania for dive-bombing led to another, and far more serious, fiasco. Ten months after General Wever's death, on April 29, 1937, Goering suddenly ordered the cancellation of Wever's cherished "Ural bomber" program. The order was not given because Goering had suddenly taken a deep interest in the deployment of air power—indeed, he was spending less and less time inside the Air Ministry and more and more time at Karinhall—but because Generals Kesselring and Milch prevailed upon Goering to take the step. The only strategic-minded staff officer left at OKL was General Deichmann, who argued his case with both Goering and Milch without avail. Deichmann pointed out that both the Do.19 and the Ju.89 could fulfill strategic and maritime missions that would certainly be required in time of war when equipped with more powerful engines, which were then beginning to be produced. Milch described Deichmann's statements as "pure fantasy," adding that "the Ju.88 program leaves no industrial capacity available for the production of four-engined bombers." Goering's own motives are easily understood; he wanted to remain in Hitler's good graces. In fact, he admitted to Milch that this was the case. "The Führer," said Goering, "does not ask me *what kind* of bombers I have. He simply wants to know *how many!*" Accordingly, the promising models of the Do.19 and the Ju.89 were broken up for scrap.

The months passed, and with them yet another shift in the thinking inside the Air Ministry. It was decided that the Luftwaffe might require a strategic bomber after all, and specifications were let to Heinkel, and Heinkel alone, calling for a new four-engine aircraft capable of carrying 4,400 pounds of bombs a distance of 1,000 miles, or a ton of bombs over a range of 4,140 miles; in other words, a bomber capable of blanketing the British Isles, reaching above the Arctic Circle, and making the journey to Moscow and beyond. This exciting design challenge was reduced to absurdity by the Air Ministry requirement that the He.177, as it was to be called, be built with the capability of delivering its bombs by diving. Heinkel's design study, worked up by Siegfried Günther, revealed that the bomber would gross approximately thirty tons. Of course, it is easy enough to put a thirty-, forty-, or even a hundred-ton bomber into a sixty-degree dive, as later specifications would require, but pulling it out again without the disintegration of wings, fuselage, tail and engines is something else again. Heinkel's technical director, the finicky-minded Heinrich Hertel, thought he might be able to get the monster to recover from thirty-degree angle dives if a way could be found to reduce drag to an absolute minimum. He hooked up a pair of new Daimler-Benz 606 twelve-cylinder engines combining 2,700 horsepower driving a single propeller through a complicated gearing system, and with one of these hybrids installed in each wing, produced, in effect, a twin-engine bomber with four-engine capability.

That was the theory, but the facts were otherwise. On the He.177's maiden flight, the pilot had to execute a panicked landing when the needles on the oil temperature gauges suddenly flicked over to the peg in the red areas, indicating the danger of imminent fire. Because the engines were inverted, fuel inevitably dropped from the carburetors to splash against the red-hot manifolds. Connecting rods were prone to breakage, punching holes in the crankcase and allowing the hot oil to spray everywhere. Even if fire was avoided, valves fouled after a maximum of six hours' running time, and major overhauls were required. Everything was so jammed together it was almost impossible to install fire walls. He.177s on routine, level test flights ignited like roman candles, exploding spectacularly in midair.

Heinkel told Udet that the sane solution would be to abandon the coupled-engine approach and revert to a straightforward four-engine design such as utilized on the now-defunct Do.19s and the Ju.89. Of course, this would rule out diving, but then at least the Luftwaffe would have a fast, extended range bomber that would not be forever incinerating crews. But Udet vetoed the idea, telling Heinkel that "the He.177 must be capable of diving at all costs, otherwise it won't have a chance."

At all costs.

The He.177, alternately given top priority, then canceled, then ordered into production again during the next eighteen months, killed crew after crew. In all, nearly fifty of the hugely expensive bombers were wiped out by fire or broke apart in the air when test pilots, bound by orders, forced them into dives from which the He.177 could never recover. An indication of just how much the Luftwaffe's commander in chief interested himself in the critical developments inside his own command is revealed in a statement he made during a conference at Karinhall four years after work on the He.177 began. Goering shouted at Heinkel, "Why didn't somebody ask *me?* I could have told them that to dive with a four-engined plane is lunacy."

Heinkel was summoned to an audience with Hitler after the He.177 program had reached the point of no return; the Führer demanded "absolutely honest replies" to his questions. Heinkel recalled that "in comparison with Goering, [Hitler] had an astonishing grasp of aeronautics, even in its details." Heinkel explained the obstinate insistence upon diving capability for the He.177 on the part of Udet, Jeschonnek, and others at OKL.

According to Heinkel, Hitler sprang to his feet and cried, "But that's madness! I've heard nothing of this until today. Is it possible that there can be so many idiots?"

Fortunately for the rest of the world, the answer was yes.

If strategic bombing was the Luftwaffe's crippled orphan, training was its stepchild, still being carried out largely under the schemes created during the Lipetsk period. Indeed, OKL did not get around to setting up the Office of Chief of Training until February 1, 1939. General Deichmann, its chief of staff, was distressed at the acute shortage of schools; only three for bomber pilots, one for naval flyers, and, incredibly, only one fighter school. Deichmann's request for money and men to create additional training centers was turned down by Jeschonnek, who replied that "all available technical resources are needed for the activation of [new] combat units." The aircraft industry, despite its problems with such designs as the Ju.88 and the He.177, was geared up and running with the production of the older He.111s, Stukas, Dornier bombers, and increasing numbers of Me.109s—more planes, Deichmann realized, than the Training Office could man with qualified crews. The crisis became even more acute after April 3, 1939, when Hitler issued a directive concerning war preparations, appended to which were details of *Fall Weiss*, Case White, spelling out what would be required of the various branches should Hitler decide to launch an attack on Poland. The Luftwaffe was assigned a major role in such an eventuality, offensively against the Poles and defensively against France and Britain should they intervene.

Desperately seeking a solution, the Luftwaffe Training Office was forced to enlist the help of the National Socialist Flying Corps to use its clublike schools and instructors for purposes of giving primary flight instruction. These schools were scattered all over Germany, each using its own methods, and anything like a uniform curriculum and centralized command was out of the question. In fact, the chief of training himself had no direct supervision over the pilot training program, if indeed it could be called a program. Jeschonnek left this important command function to the air fleet commanders, who were naturally more interested in immediate results for their own particular units than in creating any kind of systematized course of instruction throughout the Luftwaffe.

Besides having to farm out beginners to the Nazi Flying Corps, the Training Office was forced to the unprecedented measure of seeking help down to *Gruppe* level, feeding twenty-five students at a time to various groups that had limited numbers of trainers at their disposal. This meant that group commanders had to somehow work with almost as many student pilots as they had operational pilots, with whom they were already frantically busy trying to whip them into a combat-ready state. No more absurd situation can be imagined for an air force preparing for war than to give its chief of training responsibility while withholding the necessary authority. Jeschonnek's reasoning was that since Germany could only fight a lightning war, preparing for a protracted conflict by the accumulation of reserves was out of the question. Instrument training required to cope with night flying and with bad weather, advanced navigation, and other tools of the war pilot's trade had to be given short shrift. So great was the rush, and so short were technicians and materials, that the Training Office could not even provide an altitude chamber for crew testing or for aeromedical research.

Fighter pilots were assigned to operational squadrons with seldom more than 160 hours of flying time in their logbooks—less than half that acquired by British and American pilots at the same stage—and squadron leaders were supposed to make up the difference in an already busy tactical training schedule.

This chaotic system resulted in a high fatality rate throughout, worsening an already bad situation. In August, with Germany plunging toward Armageddon, the Training Office began drawing up a list of shortages. The Luftwaffe lacked 139 single-engine fighter pilots, 11 bomber crews, 54 twin-engine fighter crews, 36 dive-bomber crews, 61 tactical reconnaissance crews, and 11 strategic reconnaissance crews. This meant that when the shooting started, no fewer than 412 first-line warplanes would be missing from the Luftwaffe Order of Battle, idle for lack of crews to fill the cockpits.

No Luftwaffe units were worked harder during Europe's final weeks of peace than were the cherished groups of Ju.87 Stukas, which were being remorselessly groomed for the leading role in the war Hitler was determined to launch against Poland. One of the more experienced Stuka outfits, Group I of the 76th *Stürzkampfgeschwader*, commanded by Captain Walter Sigel, was sent up from its usual base in Austria to Cottbus, sixty miles southeast of Berlin, as part of the Luftwaffe's general deployment of its strike forces toward the east. It was Sigel's pride that his was one of the early units to be so deployed, especially since I/St.G.76 had been handpicked for a showpiece demonstration to be held for the benefit of senior Luftwaffe commanders, including Generals Hugo Sperrle, Bruno Loerzer, and Wolfram von Richthofen. Sigel's outfit was equipped with the latest Ju.87Bs, mounting new Jumo 211D engines rated at 1,200 horse-power, nearly twice as powerful as those used in Spain. Sigel hoped to stun the onlooking air commodores with a mass formation diving attack of the entire group, twenty-seven aircraft in all. He succeeded, but in a way nobody could have dreamed of.

The demonstration was scheduled for the morning of August

15. The hour chosen, six, was undoubtedly selected for the dramatic postsunrise effect it would offer. Just prior to the scheduled takeoff time, a weather reconnaissance plane landed at Cottbus with a report on conditions over the strike area, a wooded section of Silesia near Neuhammer-am-Queis, about thirty minutes' flight time away. Conditions were far from ideal. The weather pilot told Captain Sigel that it was clear above 6000 feet, but below that he would find seven-tenths cloud cover all the way down to 2500 feet. Below that, however, visibility was good. This meant that Sigel would have to trust finding a hole in the clouds over the strike area, lead his group down through the murk, and break into the clear with about five seconds left to line up on the target, release bombs, and pull out. As group commander, Sigel had three choices: to request postponement of the strike until the weather was clear all the way down, to ask that the exercise be scrubbed, or to carry on as planned. Since Sigal was a German officer, and since a galaxy of fearsome Luftwaffe generals were gathering to personally witness I/St.G.76's star turn, only the last option was thinkable, Shortly after 5:30 A.M., Sigel led his group off the field at Cottbus.

Once Sigel left the ground, he was in constant radio communication with the twenty-six other Stukas forming up in squadron strength behind him, but there was no radio link between his airborne group and the strike area at Neuhammer. Thus he could not know of the disaster in the making. Between the time the weather plane had surveyed the area and returned to Cottbus and the time Sigel's group neared the strike zone, early morning ground fog formed into an opaque white blanket covering almost the entire area, rising in places to merge with the fringes of cloud. No more dangerous weather conditions for a dive-bombing attack could have been created.

Sigel, with his Stukas arrayed behind him, approached Neuhammer at an altitude of 12,000 feet, estimating his position by dead reckoning and upon checkpoints which were in the clear on the flight out of Cottbus. Above, a pale blue windowpane sky; below, a sea of rolling clouds tinged with red. The generals were waiting. Sigel rolled the Stuka on its back and shoved the stick forward. The altimeter needle began unwinding in a futile race to keep up with the altitude that was being eaten away at the rate of 375 feet per second. Sigel's bomber plunged into the dirty gray wet muck at a dive angle of seventy degrees doing nearly 300 miles per hour. Closed in by the white world about him, his eyes straining to see past the mist being churned by the prop, Sigel felt time drag. By now, the entire group, echeloned out on his wings, were hurtling through the clouds with him. *Where was the clear air promised by the weather pilot? Any instant now* . . .

Then the horrified Sigel saw not two thousand feet of clear space, but a limitless canopy of trees rushing toward him. Already tensed to the breaking point, his reactions were instantaneous. He screamed a warning to the others and slammed the stick back. Through the blur of a grayout, Sigel saw that he missed death by a matter of feet; the Stuka was zipping through a firebreak below the treetops. His warning came too late for the two dive-bombers riding his tail. They plunged into the earth, sirens wailing, and exploded—as did all nine Stukas of the second wave. The high squadron's Ju.87s convulsively came out of their dives, but two of them stalled out and smashed into the trees to join the eleven others. Fragments of metal and flesh were scattered across a wide area, and fires started in the summer-dry secondary undergrowth. Plumes of smoke, pyres for twenty-six airmen who had died before breakfast, rose lazily into the air, blending with the fog that began to dissipate not long afterwards.

The tragedy at Neuhammer, worst of its kind in the recorded history of aviation, was kept secret for a long time afterward. OKL was notified immediately, of course, as was the Führer. One account has it that when Hitler was given the news, he "stared speechlessly out of the window for ten minutes." The reaction is believable; Hitler was a mystic, a believer in astrology, and the wiping out of thirteen of his vaunted Stukas at one stroke was surely an omen. His war against Poland, in which the Luftwaffe was counted on to play a decisive role, was scheduled to begin sixteen days later.

At noon on August 22, Adolf Hitler convened yet another Führer conference at the Eagle's Nest high above the quaint little village of Berchtesgaden in the Obersalzburg. Wehrmacht staff officers were in agreement that the use of the word *conference* was incorrect; these weekly gatherings were usually given over to harangues, pep talks and exhortations, leaving little or no time left for exchanges of opinion. This last meeting before the outbreak of hostilities was no exception. Hitler began with a paean of self-praise, stressing his authority and the confidence expressed in himself by "the whole of the German people." He pointed to the weakness of the other powers, and warned that "a showdown, which would not be safe to put off for four to five years, had better take place now." Poland, he said, had to be liquidated. He dismissed thoughts of strong reaction from France and England. A blockade would no longer be effective because Germany was far more self-sufficient than it was during the last war. An attack from the direction of France's underground Maginot Line was "impossible." The English did not want to wage a long war. Then, with heavy sarcasm, Hitler added: "Our enemies are little worms. I saw them at Munich." And as for their vain hope that Russia would leap to Poland's defense, his political genius had already taken care of that; friendly relations had been established with Josef Stalin, and within seventy-two hours Germany and Russia would sign a treaty of nonaggression. Any threat from the east was therefore nullified.

The campaign against Poland must proceed at a great pace; speed was essential if the Wehrmacht was not to get bogged down with the coming of autumn rains on Poland's notoriously bad roads. "A quick decision," he said, "in view of the season." The army generals present pointed out that it would be no small task; after all, Poland was nearly as large as Germany. The plans to reach speedy victory had been drawn months before. To annihilate the Polish forces would require almost every one of Germany's first-line divisions, fifty-six in all, including sixteen which were armored or motorized. All that would be left were twenty-five reserve, training and second-echelon divisions. General Siegfried Westphal, and all other Western Front commanders, knew that there was not a single German tank available to them should the French decide to strike for the Rhine. The prospect of having to stave off two million French troops, complete with armor and artillery, with the motley divisions at their disposal filled Westphal with dread. "Every expert serving at that time in the Western Army," he later wrote, "felt his hair stand on end when he considered the possibility of an immediate French attack."

The Luftwaffe's role in the forthcoming lightning war was paramount. First of all, the Polish air force must be eliminated at the outset, and the way further paved for the infantry by smashing every vestige of Polish communications. Everything depended on the German air arm. Hitler had been holding forth for most of the afternoon, but during a pause in the harangue, Erhard Milch managed to raise a small but vital point: because of the general confusion reigning in the arms industry, there was a critical shortage of 110- and 550-pound bombs in Luftwaffe depots. At the projected rate of expenditure, the Kampfgeschwaders and Stukageschwaders had only a thirty-day supply on hand. Suppose the war lasted longer than that? Suppose, God forbid, that the bomber fleets would have to be thrown against France and England? Bombers without bombs are useless. Milch asked for a crash program to be added to the other crash programs to produce more bombs. Hitler rejected Milch's plea, saying that such a program was "unnecessary and superfluous."

As to the Luftwaffe's numerical superiority over the Poles, however, there was no question. Available for employment in the attack were nearly 2,000 first-line planes. Quartermaster returns indicated an operational readiness for 648 horizontal bombers, 219 dive-bombers, 210 fighters (Me.109s and Me.110s), 30 ground-attack planes, and 474 reconnaissance and transport craft. Goering held in personal reserve another 133 small planes for communication work, and, in the unlikely event that any Polish bombers survived to get off the ground and approach Germany, another 216 day fighters were kept in reserve in eastern Germany for air defense. Against all this, so reported Luftwaffe intelligence, the Polish air force could field a maximum of 900 planes, half of which were assigned to training units. The Poles had no more than 160 fighters available, and none of them were in the same league with the new Me.109s.

Seeing doubt and hesitation on the faces of the assembled generals, Hitler closed his fists and exhorted them: "Close your hearts to pity! Be harsh and remorseless! Act brutally! Be steeled against all signs of compassion! The time has come to test the military machine." So saying, Hitler announced that the opening shot in the execution of Case White was being moved up from September 1 to Saturday, August 26.

Goering, who had ostensibly been angling for a peaceful settlement of the Polish question only days before, leapt up and began applauding the entire speech, dancing around the table in a heavy-footed frenzy of admiration and anticipation.

When the conference broke up, General Wilhelm Speidel, Chief of Staff for the First Air Fleet, by no means shared Goering's enthusiasm. Speidel recalled, "I left the Führer's meeting in unmistakable dismay."

The long summer of waiting was over, and the Luftwaffe, a creature of Versailles, of Seeckt, of Brandenburg, of Wimmer and those who followed after, a-building for nineteen years— secretly, slowly, erratically, then brazenly and quickly—was, ready or not, to be put into the cauldron.

III
ANVIL

In starting and waging a war it is not right that matters, but victory.
—Adolf Hitler

Above: Labeled as the Heinkel 113, this rejected design was pressed into service as propaganda tool. It posed as the production version, but few were actually built. *(Peter Bowers.)* □

Left: General Ernst Udet, casually dressed for his record-breaking flight in Heinkel's He.100D, poses with the proud designer. *(Lufthansa.)* □

The lean, rakish F.W.200 airliner was later pressed into service as a long-range reconnaissance plane and jury rigged as a tactical bomber. Adolf Hitler chose it as his personal carrier on diplomatic missions. *(Lufthansa.)* □

A Ju.87 Stuka, wearing Nationalist markings but flown by a German pilot, wheels through Spanish skies. *(Peter Bowers.)* ☐

Ageing He.46s performed workhorse reconnaissance service over Republican territory. *(Peter Bowers.)* ☐

The additional fuel tank mounted on their belly extended the range of the He.51s, which served as escorts to the Condor Legion. *(Peter Bowers.)* ☐

Guernica, near the sea, offered a sunlit and densely packed target to destroying waves of He.111s of the Condor Legion.
(Peter Bowers.) □

Those Polish P.6 fighters that survived the initial ground attacks rose to duel the Luftwaffe's finest in a hopeless contest.

(Peter Bowers.) ☐

The Henschel 123 saw heavy service as a tactical support plane in Poland. *(Peter Bowers.)* □

Warsaw in flames.
(Air University Archives.) □

Stukas plastered pin-point targets from Norway to France, beginning with Poland.   *(U.S.A.F.)* □

A Ju.88 on the attack.
(Air University Archives.) □

Hawker Hurricanes were flown from the carrier *Glorious* to make-shift Norwegian bases north of the Arctic Circle.
(Author's collection.) □

Goering's cherished "Destroyers," Me.110 fighters, one of Messerschmitt's least successful designs. *(Author's collection.)* ☐

A Fokker T.5 bomber escorted by D.XXI fighters. They were blooded in Finland but decimated by 109s in 1940.
(Royal Netherlands Air Force.) □

Me.109s, combat tested in Spain, swept the skies of French fighters and reconnaissance planes, making the job of Wehrmacht Panzers easier in the race for the sea. *(U.S.A.F.)* ☐

Left: The Dutch Fokker G.1, an eight-gun fighter, was as good as anything in its class, but only twenty-three were available when the blitzkrieg struck the Lowlands.
(Royal Netherlands Air Force.) ☐

Right: Much of French air power was wiped out in the early hours of the assault that left fighter fields cratered beyond use. This Luftwaffe reconnaissance photo shows the effects of carpet bombing.
(Air University Archives.) ☐

The Luftwaffe's under-gunned, short-range He.111 bombers made a shambles of Rotterdam and selected tactical targets in France. *(U.S.A.F.)* □

Originally passed off as an airliner, the Do.17 emerged in warpaint as the Flying Pencil that helped win the war in the West.

(Peter Bowers.) ☐

The giant He.177 could have been the Luftwaffe's major strategic weapon, but attempts to make it a dive-bomber ended in fiasco, perhaps saving England. *(Peter Bowers.)* ☐

13

TRIAL BY COMBAT

I must emphasize that operations by the German Air Force have been in
conformity with the rules of warfare.
—General André Armengaud,
French Air Attaché, Warsaw

It was Hell come to Earth.
—General Kutrzeba
Commander, Army of Poznan

By Friday, August 25, the Wehrmacht was fully deployed along
the Polish border in a line stretching from the Baltic Sea in the
north to the flanks of the Carpathian Mountains in the south.
The assaulting divisions were divided into Army Group North,
made up of the Third and Fourth German Armies, and Army
Group South, containing the Eighth, Tenth and Fourteenth
Armies. Only the Third Army was not in touch with its neighbors. Poised in East Prussia, it was separated from the bulk of
the army groups by the fifty-mile-wide Danzig Corridor. This
fact did not concern Army Group North's commander, Field
Marshal Fedor von Bock, because the Third Army was among
the best-trained and best-equipped in the Wehrmacht. Its star
commander, General Heinz Guderian, leader of the XIXth Motorized Corps, had helped forge the Panzer concept to its present reality. Guderian not only was equipped with German armor, but had supplied himself with 278 brand-new Czech tanks
confiscated the year before. At zero hour, the Third Army
would strike across the border and move straight for Warsaw,
only seventy-five miles away. While the Fourth Army smashed
across the Corridor to join forces with the Third, the main
thrust would be executed by Army Group South, lunging first
for Krakow, then leaving some divisions to reach westward

across the Vistula while the rest swung northward to form the second arm of the pincers designed to trap the Polish army in pockets before there was time to effect any kind of unified fighting withdrawal. Both army group commanders counted heavily upon being unmolested by Polish air units; they based their expectations on total disruption of Polish army communications in the interior, and they looked upon the Luftwaffe to provide dawn to dusk reconnaissance over Polish territory to provide up-to-the-minute tactical reports on dynamic changes in the tactical situations developing from Blitzkrieg warfare. To assure maximum effective liaison between German air and ground forces, the Luftwaffe placed 288 light planes under direct army control.

To practiced eyes in Berlin, it was obvious that the Wehrmacht was throwing everything it had into the coming battle in the east. With the crack assault units already moved forward, support and rear-echelon troops began pouring through the streets of the capital and out of the Brandenburg Gate. The Wehrmacht's regular motor transport units exhausted their inventory of four- and six-wheeled trucks; the American CBS radio correspondent William Shirer watched in amazement a motley parade of furniture vans, grocery trucks, and livestock lorries disappearing toward the frontier, all packed with soldiers. And for days the skies over Germany thundered with engines as the Luftwaffe moved toward its hour of destiny.

Paralleling the grouping of armies, the Luftwaffe was organized into paired operational commands: the First Air Fleet, under General Albert Kesselring, and the Fourth Air Fleet, commanded by General Alexander Löhr. One of the key figures in the drama that was about to unfold was Lieutenant General Wolfram von Richthofen, who now bore a rather exclusive title: *Fliegerführer zbV*, which meant Air Commander for Special Duties. With his experience in Spain as commander of the Condor Legion behind him, Richthofen had created a strike force within the strike force, whose duties would be close ground support for the attacking Panzers and infantry. So concerned was Richthofen with providing the army with what it needed from the air that he offered to share his quarters and command post inside Schönwald Castle, six miles from the frontier, with General Walther von Reichenau, commanding the Tenth Army. It was a happy arrangement, for Reichenau's armor was scheduled to punch holes in the Polish defenses while Richthofen's ground-attack formations blasted a clear path ahead. This was interservice cooperation at its closest, a thing Richthofen had learned to value while dealing with some of Franco's generals in Spain.

The Luftwaffe ground crews sweated mightily all that hot Friday afternoon and into the evening bombing up the He.111s, the Do.17s, and the Ju.87s. Armorers completed filling the belts with machine-gun ammunition, folding them neatly into the boxes and stowing them into wing and fuselage compartments. Engines, Jumo and Daimler and Bramo, were being run up all along the line, listened to and tuned by mechanics who feared the wrath of airplane commanders should fouled plugs or faulty fuel flow cause them to abort their first combat mission over enemy territory. Pilots continued to pore over their meticulously worked-up target maps and badgered unit meteorological officers, seeking assurance that tomorrow's weather would be fine. The pilots would certainly not be flying over unknown country; after all, the first hundred-odd miles had been German territory until the summer of 1919, and there were Silesians in the crews who had lived there as children. And, in a few cases, pilots wearing civilian clothes had crossed the frontier by train to examine firsthand the fixed targets carefully indicated on their maps.

These tense preparations continued among the two air fleets until just shortly after 8 P.M. Then a message was flashed from Berlin canceling the entire operation. Angrily, the Luftwaffe commanders ordered their adjutants to get on the telephone and pass the word down to the waiting squadrons, due to take off less than nine hours later. What was the Führer up to? What had happened was that the British had reaffirmed their guarantees to Poland in a new Anglo-Polish mutual assistance pact. Worse, Benito Mussolini had informed Hitler that Italy could not, after all, offer any military assistance should Poland's allies declare war on Germany. The Wehrmacht remained poised in its jump-off position for another six days, and the Luftwaffe commanders idled away their time at the forward bases, anxiously watching the sky. If the attack were postponed for any length of time, an early fall with its usual dismal northern European weather would nullify all their plans.

Then, on the morning of August 31, Hitler decided to execute Case White as planned. By 1 P.M. all the necessary field orders had been cut and passed along to the freshly alerted Luftwaffe units. Their war would begin at dawn on the following day.

The Luftwaffe's first day of air war began in confusion and fog. The thick white stuff blanketed almost the entire length of the thousand-mile front, thinner in some places but lying impenetrable in others. An early reconnaissance plane flew off to Warsaw, the intended victim of Goering's plans for Operation Seaside, a mass bombing attack by the combined He.111 groups of both air fleets, and reported a ceiling of only six hundred feet over the Polish capital. The mission was scrubbed and the bomber crews stood down. The reconnaissance pilot reported the skies strangely empty of enemy fighters.

An even more critical mission was canceled in the north, where the weather was worst. The huge steel bridges spanning the Vistula at Dirschau had been selected for quick seizure by the secretly trained paratroopers of General Kurt Student's elite Seventh Air Division. The spearhead of the Third Army needed the bridge at Dirschau in order to funnel its tanks, motorized infantry, and support elements across the river to link up with Fourth Army once the Corridor had been breached and the breakout from East Prussia accomplished. Capture of the bridge before the Poles could blow it was planned to coincide with the general advance at 4:45 A.M., but with the paratroopers already aboard the clammy interiors of the Ju.52s with engines ticking over, it was seen that an air drop was out of the question. The jump was called off, and the contingency plan substituted at the last minute. Fifteen minutes before H-hour, three Stukas were scrambled from Elbing and streaked for Dirschau, less than ten minutes away. Their mission was to bomb the approaches to the bridge on both sides of the river in an attempt to destroy the wires leading to the demolition charges placed beneath the spans. The Stukas were forced down to 150 feet, but even at this low altitude visibility was minimal. The bombs, a total of three 550-pounders and a dozen 110-pounders, would have to be delivered in a dip-and-run maneuver; there would be no repetition of the Neuhammer disaster. The Stukas reached the bridge area without being fired on and dropped their bombs. The attack was followed an hour later by a flight of Dorniers operating at higher altitude that made pinpoint accuracy impossible, and the best the pilots could report was that fires had been started in the town of Dirschau. Polish engineers stumbled through the craters fishing for the torn wires leading to the charges, and an hour after the Dorniers had droned away, the charges were reset and fired. The bridge rose into the air, then plunged into the river. This, the first Luftwaffe attack of the war, had gone for nothing.

As the morning wore on, visibility began to improve in the interior and the Fourth Air Fleet was able to launch its bombers against the major Polish air bases in the south. Reconnaissance pilots reported the fields in the clear, many of them packed with a variety of Polish aircraft. The bombers struck at a dozen fields that morning—Lvov, Katowice, Krosno and nine others. Hardest hit was the airdrome at Krakow, only fifty miles from the border. Sixty He.111s appeared over Krakow and carpet-bombed the field from twelve thousand feet. The Heinkel gunners stared into the sky, expecting an onslaught of fighters, but all they could see were the escorting Me.110s high overhead. The first strike was followed by a classic Stuka attack in group strength that saw thirty-odd Ju.87s plunging down to unload thirty tons of bombs on hangars, shops and parked aircraft. Now the slender Do.17s raced across the field, streaming 110-pounders that tore up runways and scattered wreckage left by the others. The field at Krakow was turned into a smoking shambles and the Luftwaffe had not sustained a single casualty. Other strike groups returned from sorties to report similar results. Here and there isolated Polish fighters were seen, but no real opposition was encountered. Was the enemy to allow its air force to be destroyed on the ground without a fight? To air crews and senior commanders alike, the behavior of the Poles was puzzling, and even ·a little disquieting.

To the Polish army, outnumbered in any case by almost two to one, the absence of fighter cover to keep away the German reconnaissance planes perpetually buzzing overhead, and to drive off what followed, spelled doom. To meet the left wing of the German Tenth Army's thrust toward the Warta River, the Polish commander in chief, Field Marshal Smigly-Rydz, ordered three thousand men of a cavalry brigade, plus supporting units, to drive westward toward the village of Wielun, twelve miles from the German frontier. A Luftwaffe reconnaissance plane, scouting the terrain for targets of opportunity, spotted the dust raised on Poland's dry roads and flew back to base with the position marked on his map. Thirty minutes later, shortly before one o'clock in the afternoon, the slaughter began.

The Stukas fell on the struggling, two-mile-long column of men, horses and wagons before it could disperse into the fields and nearby woods. The sky rained bombs and the earth heaved with their heavy detonations. Animals and men were dismembered and wagons blown to splinters. The terrified horses bolted from the road, and many were cut down by machine-gun fire delivered by Stukas strafing at treetop level after they had unloaded their bombs. Dead and dying horses and wrecked vehicles piled up on the narrow road and in the ditches, blocking the way for those who frantically sought escape from the howling Stukas. What had been a tightly disciplined military brigade became a struggling, disorganized mob. The Stukas, bothered only by light flak coming from the town, dive-bombed at leisure, howling down to 2500 feet before pulling out and climbing back up to execute second and third parabolas of destruction. A hundred and twenty bombs were hurled on the defenseless Poles; then the Ju.87s formed up and flew away. They were replaced by a fresh group, whose pilots hounded the survivors on the road and in the fields and in the town. When the Stukas had finished their work, thirty Do.17s of K.G.77 appeared over Wielun and unloaded on the fleeing cavalry squadrons. The Polish cavalry brigade had been wiped out, and not one Polish fighter had appeared during the hours of its destruction.

By late afternoon on the first day of war, the Luftwaffe had good reason to believe that the Polish air force had been destroyed on the ground. But this was not the case. The burning wreckage that littered the dozen airfields plastered by German bombers was not that of Poland's first-line aircraft, but were the remains of old trainers and aircraft that were not immediately serviceable. Forty-eight hours before Poland was invaded, all of the airworthy fighters, bombers and reconnaissance planes had been moved to emergency airstrips and were being saved largely for the defense of Warsaw. Explained Major F. Kalinowski, "It seems quite naive of the Germans to have believed that during the preceding days of high political tension, and with their own obviously aggressive intentions, we would leave our units sitting at their peacetime bases. . . . the Germans' opening air blast completely failed in its purpose. . . ."

Moreover, German Intelligence grossly overrated the strength of the Polish air force on the day war began; it numbered not 900 aircraft, but only 396, and of these but 160 were fighters. The Polish fighters, most of them PZL P.11s, were gull-winged monoplanes of a design dating back to 1931. Top speed at sea level was only 186 miles per hour, but at 18,000 feet, the P.11 could do 240 miles per hour, which was fast enough to catch German bombers flying at that altitude. The majority of P.11s were armed with only two light machine guns, but later versions carried four. It was not until late that afternoon that the P.11s were committed to battle in force.

A few minutes past 5:30 P.M. the first German bombers appeared over Warsaw—ninety He.111s of K.G.27, escorted by thirty-six Me.110s. Thirty P.11s climbed up to get at the Heinkels, but were bounced first by the Me.110s, and in the melee that followed, five of the P.11s were shot down. On the second day of battle, the light, maneuverable Polish fighters began to take the measure of the faster but clumsier Me.110s. In a duel over Lodz, sixty miles west of Warsaw, outnumbered P.11s shot down three Messerschmitts and lost only two of their own. Two days later, however, when the P.11s went for a bomber formation, they were bounced by Me.109s, which simply shot them to pieces; eleven Polish fighters were blown out of the sky. Polish survivors of these air battles would limp back home only to find that Stukas and Dorniers had been there first, leaving the runways cratered and the hangars and fuel dumps blazing. After the first forty-eight hours of war, the Luftwaffe hammering of communications rendered impossible any systematic defense. The telephone and teleprinter systems were gone, and interception became a matter of hazard. Spares were unobtainable, grounding one plane after another.

On September 3, with the German assault developing into a pincers movement deep inside the frontier, France and Great Britain declared war on Germany. Now, thought Field Marshal Smigly-Rydz, his allies would move quickly and overwhelmingly against the common enemy to relieve the irresistible pressure against his own beleaguered forces. Poland might yet be saved.

In the House of Commons, debate swayed back and forth over what form the initial strike by the Royal Air Force against Germany should take. It was suggested to Sir Kingsley Wood, the State Secretary for Air, that Bomber Command should be turned loose with masses of incendiary bombs to set ablaze the Black Forest. The suggestion was received with horror. "Are you aware," Sir Kingsley said archly, "that it is private property? Why, you will be asking me to bomb Essen next!" Instead, ten twin-engine Blenheim bombers of No.107 and No.110 Squadrons set off across the North Sea after lunch on September 4 in weather so bad they were flying in and out of clouds between fifty and a hundred feet over the water. The Blenheims reached Wilhelmshaven and attacked German warships lying in Schillig Roads. Three hits were scored on the pocket battleship *Admiral Scheer,* but all bounced off the armored deck without exploding. Five of the ten Blenheims were shot down by ship- and shore-based antiaircraft guns, one of them plunging in flames on top of the cruiser *Emden.* Fourteen Vickers Wellingtons from No.9 and No.149 Squadrons managed to reach the port of Brunsbüttel, but the flak was so hot and the visibility so poor that the *Scharnhorst* and the *Gneisenau* lying there were in little danger. Neither was hit, but one of the Wellingtons was brought down in flames by antiaircraft fire, and another was bagged by one of the Me.109s of J.G.77 sent out from Nordholz to deal with the British incursion. Aside from these abortive—

and costly—attempts to deal deathblows to the German fleet, the RAF dispatched bombers over Hamburg, Bremen, and the Ruhr. Not one plane carried bombs; they showered down leaflets instead. Such was the British government's contribution to Poland during its hour of agony.

Four months prior to the German assault on Poland, the supreme commander of all French ground forces, General Maurice Gamelin, sixty-eight, had assured the Polish government that the French army would launch an offensive against Germany immediately after the war started. It was not until September 7 that the French army moved out of its own country and entered the Saar, using only nine out of the eighty-five divisions that were available. On a narrow front only fifteen miles wide, the French advanced timidly, averaging less than two thousand yards per day against almost no opposition. By September 12, the "offensive" halted after gaining five miles of ground and the capture of twenty deserted villages. The French troops were ordered to dig in where they were, that is, at the approaches to the sketchily built Siegfried Line. A few shots were exchanged, and some French soldiers were killed by mines and booby traps set by the Wehrmacht for looters in the abandoned towns, but that was all. Two weeks later, the French invaders were headed back to the underground security of the Maginot Line, without having drawn off a single soldier, airplane or tank from the battleground that was Poland.

Field Marshal Smigly-Rydz never forgave Gamelin for the lies the French general presented as truth when the Polish General Staff requested information as to what, exactly, France was doing to alleviate their nation's plight. Wrote Gamelin on September 9: "More than half of our active divisions on the northeast front are engaged in combat. . . . the Germans are opposing us with a vigorous resistance. . . . the Germans are reinforcing their battlefront with large new formations. . . . We know we are holding down before us a considerable portion of the German Air Force. . . ." One wonders where Gamelin summoned the nerve to present all this, over his own signature, to the Polish commander in chief through the military attaché in Paris.

By the end of the first week of fighting, the Polish army no longer existed as an organized combat force. The swift-moving Panzers and motorized infantry sundered entire armies and corps again and again, until all that was left were pockets of stubborn resistance, one isolated from the other and all cut off from supplies or reinforcements. The Luftwaffe bombers had worked over Polish rail lines so thoroughly that no trains could run, and any transport that ventured onto the roads was quickly dealt with by Stukas and strafing fighters. Only once did the Wehrmacht find itself in serious trouble, and when it did, the Luftwaffe's quick reaction proved decisive.

In its headlong dash to reach the gates of Warsaw by September 8, Reichenau's Tenth Army Panzers outstripped the Eighth Army's infantry divisions, trying vainly to maintain contact with the Tenth Army's northern flank. Now it was a German force, four divisions plus supporting elements, that was in a pocket on the south side of the Bzura River, some sixty miles west of Warsaw.

Here was the opportunity the Polish commander of the Army of Poznan, General Kutrzeba, had been waiting for. When the Germans smashed across the frontier on September 1, Kutrzeba had deployed his infantry and cavalry in a defensive posture and waited to deal with the mechanized invaders as best he could. But the German spearheads bypassed his army on both flanks, leaving Kutrzeba poised to deliver a blow that had nowhere to land. With the heavy combat moving eastward, Kutrzeba began marching his men to the sound of the guns. Experience at such places as Wielun had shown that large formations could not survive under a sky dominated by German planes, so Kutrzeba wisely laid up by day, sheltering his men and horses deep in the woods, and moved only at night. Stragglers from regiments already shattered by the Germans appeared to add their numbers to the Army of Poznan, including a wary handful of cavalrymen whose brigade had been largely wiped out in a charge across the plains to take on a regiment of German tanks. By the time Kutrzeba's army reached the village of Kutno, sixty-five miles west of Warsaw, its numbers had increased to approximately 170,000 men. Kutrzeba concentrated only his assault forces, dispersing the others between the Vistula and the Bzura in an area covering something like six hundred square miles of plains, forests, and lakes. Kutrzeba sent out cavalry and armored patrols and discovered that the German rear guard, which he greatly outnumbered, was deployed just across the Bzura. On September 9, the Poles swarmed across the river and fell on the Germans. Hard fighting went on all during the night and into the next day. Polish cavalry and what few light tanks Kutrzeba had at his disposal cut deep wedges into the German line, and the Eighth Army's 30th Infantry Division was especially hard hit. The commander of Army Group South, General Gerd von Rundstedt, got on the phone to General Kesselring and demanded immediate and overwhelming air support for the mauled German troops at Kutno. Kesselring knew exactly which call to make first: straight on to Richthofen and his Special Duty Group.

No other general was more current with the situation on the ground than Richthofen. When duty did not absolutely require him to be inside his command post, he was either up near the front with his specially equipped signals units—or he was over enemy territory in the cockpit of a Fiesler Storch doing personal reconnaissance. He had already been shot down once, on the first day of the war, by flak that crippled his light plane but left him unharmed. Richthofen had at his beck and call a reconnaissance squadron, two Stuka groups, a group of Me.110s, and a group of ground-attack planes that looked like updated versions of World War I fighters. Thus, like a surgeon or a master carpenter, Richthofen could reach for the right tool to do the job at hand.

The biplanes assigned to the air operations around Kutno were Hs.123A-1s, built around a massive BMW 880-horsepower radial engine that provided a top speed of just over 210 miles per hour. But neither speed nor ceiling mattered with the Hs.123, which was meant to operate right down on the deck; five hundred feet was considered extreme altitude to the pilots who flew these ground-attack planes. The *"Ein-Zwei-Drei,"* as it was sometimes called, could carry a variety of armament: a pair of twin 7.9-millimeter machine guns firing through the propeller, or a pair of 20-millimeter cannon in pods under the wings, or underwing containers loaded with ninety-four small (4.4 pound) antipersonnel bombs, or four 110-pound high explosive bombs. Moreover, the Hs.123s carried a small auxiliary fuel tank underneath the fuselage fitted with a special igniter so that it could be jettisoned with a napalmlike effect, a tactic borrowed from He.51 units operating with the Condor Legion in Spain. Originally designed as a dive-bomber and built by Henschel, the locomotive-makers, the solid Hs.123 could absorb more flak than any other Luftwaffe plane in service and still keep flying. Protected by the big radial engine in front, and with an armored headrest at the rear, Hs.123 pilots' chances of survival when operating at zero altitude were better than most. The Henschels had proved themselves in Spain from 1937 onward, but in Poland they were a sensation.

The Hs.123 group, II/L.G.2, began the war with thirty-six operational planes, and after ten days of almost continuous action, thirty still remained. Richthofen threw them all against Kutrzeba's assault forces late in the morning of September 11. The Henschels roared down on the Polish concentrations in a corridor thirty to fifty feet high separating the Poles from the Germans.

To Kutrzeba's men, almost none of whom had been under air attack before, the next twenty minutes were like a nightmare in hell. The machine guns cut swaths in the ranks of men and horses; hundreds of the lightweight scatter bombs flamed and exploded; the heavier detonations of the 110-pounders tore gouts out of the earth, ripped through trees and flung jagged metal shards thudding into men and animals. Even when the last of the various missiles had been delivered, the 123s were not finished with their low-level attacks: the pilots discovered that when the BMW engine was pushed to 1,800 rpm, the resultant effect on the three-bladed, variable-pitch airscrew produced an ear-splitting and indescribable sound that was both inside and outside of the man subjected to it. Even hardened soldiers were unnerved, and ran in all directions to escape; horses simply went insane. The Henschels were followed by Stukas, which were followed by Dorniers and Heinkels pulled out of the battle for Warsaw, and they in turn were followed by cannon and machine-gun-firing Me.110s. The assault on the battered 30th Infantry Division was stopped cold, and the survivors of the day-long air attack began withdrawing across the river under the merciful cover of darkness. The wounded were, for the most part, brought back aboard whatever vehicles were left, and cavalrymen walked through the carnage left by Richthofen's pilots' putting pistol and rifle bullets into the heads of the wounded horses.

Dawn brought the return of the Henschels and a repetition of the horrors of the day before. The Army of Poznan was forced back into its twenty-by-thirty-mile enclave that became a Luftwaffe shooting gallery. The Poles replied with rifles, machine guns, and light flak, knocking down some of their tormentors, but the numbers thrown at the pocket from all around the compass were overwhelming. No square foot of that blasted area was safe. Recalled General Kutrzeba: "A furious air assault was made on the river crossings near Witkovice which, for the number of aircraft engaged, the violence of their attack and the acrobatic daring of their pilots, must have been unprecedented. Every movement, every troop concentration, every line of advance came under pulverizing bombardment from the air. . . . The bridges were destroyed, the fords blocked, the waiting columns of men decimated. . . . Three of us found some sort of cover in a grove of birch trees outside the village of Myszory. There we remained, unable to stir, until about noon when the air raids stopped. We knew it was only for a moment, but had we stayed there the chances of any of us surviving would have been slight."

Kutrzeba tried to fight his shaken forces out of the trap and the hell of air attack, but found himself fenced in on all sides by the German Fourth, Eighth, and Tenth Armies, part of the latter having been ordered back from the siege of Warsaw to complete the encirclement of the Army of Poznan. On the sixteenth and seventeenth, the Luftwaffe delivered all-day attacks on the shrinking perimeter, and after that resistance was futile. Fifty thousand haggard Polish soldiers surrendered on the next day, and 105,000 gave themselves up on the day afterward. A few thousand of Kutrzeba's men managed to escape through the German net before it was drawn too tightly, wading through marshes by night and hiding by day. But all the rest were either herded into captivity or lay mute in the fields and in the forests around Kutno.*

At first light on the morning of September 17, Russian tanks and infantry rolled into Poland. The advance was swift and orderly against practically no opposition; what was left of the Polish army was penned inside Warsaw, surrounded by German armor at Modlin and in the Kampinoska Forest thirty miles north of the capital, while a pitifully small number of troops were still fighting desperately with their backs against the sea trying to hold Gdynia and Danzig, which the Poles called Gdansk. As agreed in Moscow three weeks earlier, the Red Army ground through Poland until it reached the partition line halfway across the country, a line running south from East Prussia past Brest-Litovsk and to the Carpathians. There the Soviets halted, waiting for the Wehrmacht to finish the kill; the carcass had already been divided.

The Wehrmacht used all its arms to methodically reduce the pocket of resistance on the Baltic. The area here is flat and featureless, except for a low ridge stretching seven miles inland from the sea. Initial advances across the hard sand were stopped by vicious and accurate Polish machine-gunning and heavy rifle fire. With no wish to incur needless casualties, the assault elements of the Third Army moved in its heavy artillery and began bombarding the area with high explosive. The fire was regu-

---

*General von Reichenau was so impressed with the performance of the Special Duty Group that he sent a personal message to Richthofen on September 17 expressing his "sincere thanks and grateful appreciation to you and to the units under your command for the effective support rendered to the Tenth Army during the battle of [Kutno]." Reichenau praised the "extreme effectiveness and accuracy" of Richthofen's fliers, adding that it was his "personal conviction that our victory could not have been so complete without the support of the Luftwaffe." Not always do infantry generals so compliment air generals, but there is not doubt that the immediacy and ruthlessness of the Luftwaffe's reaction beginning on September 11 saved the three German armies concerned considerable embarrassment, not to mention heavy casualties.

lated by one of the German navy's Heinkel reconnaissance planes that buzzed overhead, wirelessing back corrections. The small island of Westerplatte, lying in the sea just off Danzig, stubbornly resisted the shelling and the tentative infantry advances. During the shelling, Polish defenders took shelter in one of the huge steel-and-concrete bunkers that proved impervious to the guns the German artillery had at hand. The battleship *Schleswig-Holstein* anchored in the bay and opened up with its eleven-inch guns. The concrete was seared and pitted, but still the great dome of the bunker remained intact. Then Stukas were called in, and in the ensuing half hour succeeded where the battleship had failed. The 550-pound bombs delivered with stunning accuracy smashed through ten feet of reinforced concrete to mangle everyone inside. Those who had sought cover in trenches because there was no more room inside the bunkers counted themselves lucky. The Westerplatte fell, and in a gesture reminiscent of the nineteenth century, the German commander allowed his Polish counterpart to retain his sword as a Wehrmacht tribute to Polish courage. There now remained Warsaw, whose ordeal had lasted longer than that of any other city in Poland.

Trapped inside the beautiful old city were nearly a hundred thousand Polish troops. They were joined in trench-digging and in converting buildings to strongpoints by civilian men, women, and even children determined to defend the city to the last. On the day after the Russians crossed the Polish frontier, the leaders of the government and even Field Marshal Smigly-Rydz made their way out of the doomed country and sought temporary sanctuary in Rumania. Leaderless, Warsaw fought on.

The skies over the city were never free of German planes. All that was left to defend Warsaw was a spontaneously formed unit calling itself the Deblin Group, composed of older P.7s, what was left of the P.11s, and one example of a PZL P.24, which looked much like the others except for a closed cockpit. One of the instructors at the Polish air force training center at Deblin, a lieutenant named Szczesny, commandeered one of two pre-production P.24s, and with the help of an armorer, installed a pair of machine guns. Thus equipped, he attached himself to the Deblin Fighter Group. Lieutenant Szczesny and the plane's designer had every reason to be proud of the P.24; he shot down one German bomber on September 14, and bagged another on the following day.

The almost continual air bombardment and shelling by German artillery—and some of the heavier pieces had been transferred *away* from the west to aid in the reduction of the capital —cloaked Warsaw in a perpetual cloud of smoke through which fires could be dimly seen. Richthofen complained of "chaos over the target," of "aircraft nearly colliding in the act of bombing." Only rarely were German pilots able to pinpoint their assigned military targets, and the city suffered indiscriminate bombing.

By mid-month, Goering considered that the situation in Poland was such that mass transfer of Luftwaffe units back to the west for rest and refitting was indicated. One group after another was pulled out and returned to home bases in Germany, leaving Richthofen, now in charge of winding up aerial operations over Warsaw, with less than half the bombers with which the Luftwaffe began the campaign. But, as events were to prove, it was all that he needed.

On the morning of September 25, a diluted version of Operation Seaside began. First over the city were swarms of Stukas, stacked up in groups several thousand feet apart, waiting their turn in line to scream down into the cauldron below. After two hundred-plus Ju.87s had flung themselves at the city, the first heavy bombers appeared. Richthofen was loath to send them in; they were not the He.111s designed for the job, but thirty Ju.52s fitted out for troop-carrying missions, and therefore were without bomb racks. The cargo doors were removed and crewmen used coal shovels to scoop up the loose thermite incendiary bombs, which were sown over the city by the ton. Sortie after sortie was flown until Warsaw floated in a sea of fire. Two of the lumbering Ju.52s. were shot down by Polish flak and fell into the inferno they had created. Attempts to battle the flames had to be abandoned; the rain of high explosive, totaling five hundred tons, had smashed water mains and choked the streets with rubble that had once been proud buildings. The pyre that was

Warsaw blazed brightly, the flames visible in the nighttime sky fully ten miles away.

Surrender negotiations began the following morning, and on August 27 the capitulation was made formal. With Warsaw, so fell Modlin and the diehards still holding out in the forest of Kampinoska. Thus a nation of thirty-five million was delivered into the hands of her enemies. The cost to the Wehrmacht was relatively cheap: 10,761 killed in action, including 189 pilots and air crew. The Luftwaffe lost 285 planes, mostly victims of intense ground fire during the low-level operations that had been so effective.

14

BLITZKRIEG NORTH

Today our wings are spread over the Arctic. They are sheathed in ice.
Tomorrow the sun of victory will touch them with its golden light.
—Sir Samuel J. G. Hoare,
Secretary of State for Air

To commit troops to a campaign in which they cannot be provided with
adequate air support is to court disaster.
—Lieutenant General Claude Auchinleck

The campaign in Poland proved the Luftwaffe to be the Wehrmacht's loudest trumpet. The rest of the world, heretofore familiar only with the three-year slugging match in Spain and,
before that, World War I struggles lasting months with gains
measured in yards, was stunned at the overrunning of sixty
thousand miles of courageously defended terrain in only
twenty-six days. Blitzkrieg, lightning war, was a reality and not
just another empty coinage of the German propaganda mill,
and to the Luftwaffe went the credit for making possible the
swift cleaving stroke that sundered Poland with such terrifying
speed. The Poles were among the first to admit that they were
virtually helpless in the face of overwhelmingly superior enemy
air power. At combat level, where it ultimately counts, a surviving Polish pilot of the Fighter Brigade, Witold Urbanowicz, has
recalled the frustration, the fatigue, the agony and the heart-
break of being thrown against the Luftwaffe when the Fighter
Brigade was committed to battle:

"The sky was full of German planes. Colonel Pamula shot
down two bombers, then his ammo ran out and he was attacked
by two Me.109s. He steered straight for one of the enemy
fighters, then bailed out only seconds before the fatal impact.
On the first day we of the Brigade lost ten aircraft destroyed

and another twenty-four so badly shot up they were out of action. Mechanics and pilots worked through the night to patch up the battle-damaged P.7s. . . . By September 8, there were only sixteen planes left to [the Brigade] and we were forced to move our operational base further and further back as the Panzers ground forward. We flew lacking sleep and often without food. The fuel situation was so tragic that air patrols were sent out to find tank cars on railway lines. Then, after checking whether or not they actually contained fuel, trucks were sent out to bring the precious gasoline back in barrels. But the trucks could not keep pace with the planes, held up by increasing chaos on the roads which were under constant attack from the air."

France, obviously due to receive the Wehrmacht's attentions next, had not neglected to send skilled observers to Poland to study at first hand the new methods of German warfare. General A. Armengaud, of the Armée de L'Air, returned to Paris and prepared a lengthy memorandum detailing the Wehrmacht's use of armor and aircraft to punch holes in Polish defenses before fanning out on both flanks to destroy the Polish forces in the field. Armengaud said that the Luftwaffe's role in the Polish defeat had been "the most decisive" because the defenders' maneuverability was frustrated, and because "the command is made blind and cannot get its orders through." Armengaud's stress on the effectiveness of the Luftwaffe was seconded by the French intelligence organization, the *Deuxième Bureau*, which pointed to the wide-ranging air strikes that "resulted in almost complete paralysis of the Polish High Command, which was incapable either of completing mobilization or concentration, or carrying out reinforcements of supplies, or of executing any kind of co-ordinated maneuver." Just how seriously the French High Command regarded these sober appraisals of the Luftwaffe's capability in influencing the outcome of great land battles and, indeed, the course of a war itself, will be seen.

Dr. Joseph Goebbels' Propaganda Ministry lost no opportunity in exploiting the brilliant successes of the Wehrmacht in the field, stressing especially the role played by the Luftwaffe.

Wehrmacht cameramen returned from Poland with thousands of feet of motion picture footage shot during the campaign. Cinematographers rode hunched inside the cramped confines of Heinkel, Dornier, and Fiesler crew compartments, recording with stark clarity the remorseless assault against Polish targets. Editors, sound technicians, and graphic artists went to work producing the first full-length documentary of its kind, an epic of destruction calculated to awe, if not terrify, selected audiences. The film revealed the Luftwaffe at work methodically reducing to rubble numbers of nameless villages, climaxed by the holocaust created in Warsaw. *Baptism of Fire* was readied for early spring showings in Berlin, Rome, Oslo, Bucharest, Belgrade, Ankara, and Sofia.

In England, the British people waited for the onslaught from the sky. The Committee of Imperial Defence estimated that the initial air bombardment of London would last for sixty days, killing six hundred thousand and wounding a million. With macabre efficiency, the government had ordered thousands of cheap, papier-mâché coffins distributed in convenient stacks throughout the city, ready to receive the Luftwaffe's victims. But no bombers came, and the Londoners' grumbling was turned away from Goering and directed against short rations and the nightly blackout with its dangers and inconveniences.

The British, still overestimating the Luftwaffe's operational strength and understandably impressed with its performance in Poland, could not fathom the reason for the continuing empty skies over the island. But the German air generals understood well enough: Adolf Hitler, as supreme commander, had forbidden air strikes against English cities and ports, just as the Kaiser had once done twenty-five years previously. On April 3, 1939, Hitler's Directive No. 1 for the Conduct of the War specified that the Luftwaffe's primary function was to halt action by the British and French air forces against the German army and against German territory should Allied bombing raids be attempted. "Attacks on the English homeland are to be prepared," ordered the Führer, but he added, "The decision regarding attacks on London is reserved to me."

Five months later, with the war in Poland forty-eight hours

old, Directive No. 2 instructed the Luftwaffe that attacks on British ships on the high seas, in the Channel, or in port "will only be made in the event of English air attacks on similar targets and where there are particularly good prospects of success." Again Hitler stressed that he held in his own hand "the decision about attacks on the English homeland. . . ." Regarding France, he warned that "offensive action will only be undertaken after French attacks on German territory. The guiding principle," Hitler explained, "must be not to provoke the initiation of aerial warfare by any action on the part of Germany."

On September 9, Hitler pointed to the "half-hearted opening of hostilities" by England in the air and by France on land, but Directive No. 3 reminded the Luftwaffe that the Führer's personal approval must be obtained for any flights beyond the western frontier of Germany. On the day that Warsaw, smothered in smoke and flames from end to end was forced to surrender, the British Air Ministry had the unwitting bad taste to issue a press release announcing that the RAF had dropped eighteen million leaflets over Germany since the war began. This shower of useless paper could hardly be considered provocative, and on September 30, the latest directive restrained the Luftwaffe as before, except that local reconnaissance flights just across the Reich's border with France were permitted. There was no question of strategic reconnaissance flights over the British Isles for the simple reason that they were not needed: from 1937 through the summer of 1939, a special Lufthansa unit under the command of Lieutenant Colonel Theodore Rowehl had been engaged in extensive photographing and mapping of the island, using specially (and secretly) equipped He.111C passenger planes while on ostensible route-proving flights that also included much of interior France and parts of Russia.

The matter of any sustained aerial offensive against either France or Great Britain was, in any case, academic. For one thing, the prodigious expenditure of 110- and 550-pound bombs in Poland had eaten away almost half of the Luftwaffe's inventory, and it was only late in the campaign that Milch had finally prevailed in his pleas to Hitler and Goering to give priority for replenishment and stockpiling. Added to the combat losses were another 279 aircraft variously damaged, amounting to a total of nearly 12 per cent of the Luftwaffe's first-line effectives. Turning to Udet's latest production figures, Jeschonnek could see that output was still limping along as though no war were in progress. Udet was squeezing from the German aircraft industry barely 600 planes a month, and of these only 185 were bombers, 125 were fighters, 40 were reconnaissance planes, and 30 were late-model ground-attack machines; all the rest were trainers, transports, seaplanes, or communications planes of no direct benefit for defense or serious assaults.

The lag in aircraft production was symptomatic of the roseate attitude prevailing at Hitler's headquarters. The optimism was generated by the heady success in Poland and by the pitifully weak reaction from both Great Britain and France. Moreover, the idea that the final battle against the Franco-British combine would be short and utterly decisive had taken firm root, allowing for no unpleasant long-range planning. Explains General Walter Warlimont, deputy chief of the Wehrmacht's Operations Staff: "In the face of the successful Polish campaign, Hitler refused to order mobilization in the full sense of the word; later on, partial mobilization was ordered, but the economy was specifically exempted. This business of the 'gradual establishment of increased military preparedness,' as it was called, in preparation for 'special commitment of the Wehrmacht' brought nothing but confusion, as I can testify from personal experience—the tragedy of which I shall never be able to forget.

"To put it briefly," continues Warlimont, "none of the carefully thought-out measures to protect the armament industry by keeping its skilled workers on the job was put into effect. Not until it was no longer possible to ignore the fact that the West meant business was any attempt made to undo the damage. By then, of course, it was no longer a matter of putting a certain paragraph of the mobilization plan into effect, but of ordering back every single skilled worker from the Front—provided, of course, he was still among the living."

If there was a bright spot for the harassed Udet, it was the fact that, after a year of frustrating delay, the Ju.88 "wonder bomber" was at last ready for operations. Moreover, Goering had lifted responsibility for mass production of the Ju.88 from Udet's unsteady shoulders by giving carte blanche to Dr. Heinrich Koppenberg, the ramrodding member of the Junkers board of directors, to requisition arbitrarily what he needed to assure quantity production. Koppenberg at once began raiding Heinkel, Messerschmitt, Dornier, Henschel, and Arado for key engineers, requisitioning scarce strategic materials and assigning subassembly jobs to the rival firms. The ill will thus generated by Koppenberg's high-handed methods can be imagined, but the Ju.88 had received a class I priority, and Koppenberg was backed all the way to the top.

On October 16, elements of Group I of K.G.30 went into action against the only targets permitted by the Führer directives, the British fleet. The Ju.88s were commanded by Captain Helmut Pohle, an experienced test pilot who had helped nurse the wonder bomber through its continuing trials at the Rechlin test center. Pohle's twelve Ju.88s took off from their base on the island of Sylt, just west of the Danish border, shortly after 11 A.M. and steered for the Firth of Forth, the narrow arm of the sea leading into Edinburgh, 460 miles distant and near the Ju.88's maximum limits of penetration. The loose formation reached the Firth only to discover that the chief prize, the heavy battle cruiser *Hood*, was already nosing inside the sluice gates leading to the city docks; she was therefore out of bounds. Pohle lost no time in leading the others across the Firth to the naval base at Rosyth on the far bank. Pohle picked the largest ship he could see and stood the Ju.88 on its nose. He dived the Ju.88 through a storm of flak thrown up at him by the ships through a full nine-thousand-foot plunge before yanking the lever that released the eleven-hundred-pound bomb he was carrying. The heavy projectile struck the cruiser *Southampton* almost amidships, crashed through the main deck and two others only to emerge through the starboard side without exploding; it did, however, smash to kindling the admiral's barge that lay alongside before plunging harmlessly to the bottom of the sea. Pohle was jumped by a trio of eight-gunned Supermarine Spitfires of No.602 Squadron, whose motto was "Beware the tormented lion." Pohle raced for safety, but the Spitfires were more than 100 miles per hour faster, and they shot the Ju.88 down into the sea. Pohle, the sole survivor, was fished unconscious from the water by British fishermen. The other Ju.88s managed to inflict damage on the cruiser *Edinburgh* and the destroyer *Mohawk*, but No.603 Squadron bagged a second Ju.88 and flak accounted for a third.

On the following morning, four Ju.88s of K.G.30 reached farther north, roaring over the huge base at Scapa Flow only to find the harbor empty of all except the aged depot ship the *Iron Duke*. Near misses tore out her sides, and when the Ju.88s flew back across the sea, she was towed away and beached. The bombers, holed by flak, landed back at Sylt to report the disappearance of the British fleet. Indeed, the big ships had sailed for the safety of western Scotland, out of reach of the Luftwaffe.

The RAF, restricted like the Germans to purely maritime targets, began daylight operations in force across the North Sea late in September. Eleven twin-engine Handley-Page Hampdens discovered a pair of German destroyers near the small island of Helgoland, thirty-five miles off the German coast, but hardly had the attack gotten underway when a swarm of Me.109s dropped out of the sun to jump the unescorted bombers. Five Hampdens were promptly shot down into the sea. On December 3, twenty-four Vickers twin-engine Wellingtons were over the Helgoland area and found themselves in five-tenths cumulus clouds at seven thousand feet. By dodging in and out of the muck, the Wellingtons managed to evade prowling Me.109s and return home unharmed, but the net result was only the sinking of a minesweeper by a dud bomb. On December 14, still operating on the theory that tight formations and good gunnery obviated the necessity for long-range escort fighters, a dozen Wellingtons of No.99 Squadron flew through uncertain weather to attack German shipping reported in the Shillig Roads. Forced down to eight hundred feet by cloud base, the Wellingtons flew through a torrent of steel thrown up by flak ships covering the area. They were then bounced by Me.109s, and in the confused melee that followed, five Wellingtons tumbled into the ocean, some of them in flames, and another went in before reaching England. Half of the raiding force had been wiped out at a cost to the Luftwaffe of only one fighter, shot down while flying into the fire of one of the bomber's twin-gunned tail turrets. Somehow, Bomber Command gained the impression that the heavy losses were all due to flak, that tight formations were proof against fighters. Only the pilots of J.G.1 and the missing British crews could have told them differently.

The battle over Helgoland Bight had revealed to the Luftwaffe fighter pilots the sure means of dealing with Wellingtons with little risk to themselves. The bomber was armed with a turret in the nose, one in the tail, and another in the belly, six light machine guns in all. But there was no turret on top, and the traverse of the other three stations was limited so that the guns could not be brought to bear on fighters attacking from the sides. All this was carefully diagrammed for the benefit of those Me.109 and Me.110 pilots who had yet to engage British bombers in combat. Thus, when the next large-scale Wellington assault was launched on December 18, the Messerschmitt pilots were primed and waiting.

Twenty-four Wellingtons set off from England, bound for Wilhelmshaven basking under cold but clear and sunny skies. Two of the bombers developed engine trouble shortly after takeoff and peeled away to return home. The remaining twenty-two closed ranks and flew on across the dappled gray sea. Visibility was brilliant, perhaps *too* brilliant, or so it seemed to the gunners, stiff with cold, who peered anxiously into the plate-glass sky on the lookout for enemy fighters. At ten minutes to two, the German naval radar station on Helgoland picked up the British formation. The plot was passed on to the commander of J.G.1, whose eighty-odd Me.109s and Me.110s were based on the Frisian Islands, that necklace of outcroppings in the sea guarding the approaches to Germany's western shore. The Wellingtons, flying at over 225 miles per hour, reached Wilhelmshaven before they could be intercepted, but discovered that all of the German ships were either in harbor or tied up at the docks and were therefore immune from bombs, which might fall astray and kill civilians. The bombers wheeled in the sky and flew for home.

What followed next can only be described as a massacre.

Packs of machine-gun and cannon-firing German fighters fell on the ranks of British bombers, which, having nowhere to hide, continued to bore through the crystalline air as though locked on rails. The Luftwaffe fighters almost got in each other's way in lining up for the turkey shoot. Diving at a shallow angle at speeds better than 330 miles per hour, the Messerschmitts delivered attack after attack on the bombers' port and starboard sides, unmolested by the British gunners, who could only traverse their turrets helplessly back and forth. The Wellingtons, lacking self-sealing fuel tanks, flamed easily, and one after another, they fell blazing into the sea. In a battle lasting less than thirty minutes, ten of the Blenheims were shot out of the sky, and two more, riddled and with smoking engines, ditched in the ocean. Of No.37 Squadron's six bombers that had set out so confidently from England, only one limped home. The German pilots discovered that when the British gunners were able to bring their .303-caliber guns to bear, they shot very well indeed: two Me.109s were knocked out of the sky and several Me.110s staggered back to base badly damaged.

Major Schumacher, commander of J.G.1's fighters, was full of praise for the courage of the Blenheim crews, but as a combat leader, he could not refrain from commenting on Bomber Command's employment of its forces. "It was criminal folly on the part of the enemy," wrote Schumacher, "to fly at 4000 to 5000 metres in a cloudless sky with perfect visibility. . . . After such losses it is assumed that the enemy will not give the Geschwader any more opportunities of practice-shooting at Wellingtons." Bomber Command could only agree, and even after the "Wimpeys" and the Hampdens were belatedly equipped with self-sealing fuel tanks—bought from the French—they were afterward confined to flight under the stars.

Only two weeks after the Wehrmacht's triumphant but exhausting efforts in the east, Adolf Hitler ordered his armed forces to prepare for the grand assault against the west. Neutral Belgium, Holland and Luxembourg would be invaded in order to "defeat as much as possible of the French Army. . . . and at the same time to win as much territory as possible in Holland,

Belgium and in Northern France to serve as a base for the successful prosecution of the air and sea war against England. . . ." Code-named *Fall Gelb* (Case Yellow), D-day was set by the Führer for November 25, barely six weeks hence. The heads of the army, navy, and air force—Field Marshal Walther von Brauchitsch, Grand Admiral Erich Raeder, and Hermann Goering—were aghast: the weather was rotten, even for a northern European autumn; the bulk of the Panzers were still in the shops for overhauls; there was a great shortage of small-arms ammunition; the fighting troops needed recuperation; there was the matter of the Luftwaffe's bombs; the French army, despite its lackluster showing in the Saar "offensive," could not be taken so lightly. Hitler turned stone ears to all these arguments, save that of the weather. On October 18, he authorized Luftwaffe's fighters to cross Reich frontiers into France to escort reconnaissance machines. On October 22, he advanced D-day to November 12. The new month began with leaden skies that hurled torrents of rain and sleet at the intended battlefields. The attack was postponed, and postponed again. And again, until the number of postponements would reach twenty-nine.

The Luftwaffe reconnaissance squadrons stayed on perpetual jittery alert, not against enemy intrusion, but waiting for the heavens to open wide to reveal the sun shining in a blue sky. With the ground assault apparently impending, the need for tactical reconnaissance of enemy airfields and troop dispositions was acute.

On the morning of November 24, dawn broke redly in a near-cloudless sky. From a base near Ramstein, a Do.17P lifted into the air bound on a photo mission in the Metz-Verdun area. The Dornier carried a crew of three, commanded by the pilot, Staff Sergeant Arno Frankenberger, an airman with considerable experience: Frankenberger had been a glider instructor during the Luftwaffe's formative years, and since then had logged more than a thousand hours of powered flight. Frankenberger, a lean, pleasant-faced man with dark hair and blue eyes set wide apart, had volunteered for these penetration jobs, despite the fact that the appearance of four RAF Hawker Hurricane squadrons in France made the missions far from milk runs.

Frankenberger's Dornier was still twenty miles north of Verdun when three Hurricanes of No.73 Squadron dropped out of the sun and fastened onto the Flying Pencil's tail. Frankenberger fire-walled the throttles and expertly skidded through the sky, but he felt the Dornier shudder from the impact of the slugs fired at him by twenty-four machine guns. The strikes sounded like gravel flung against a tin roof. The rear gunner returned the British fire with his single MG.15 gun and the flight deck filled with the acrid smell of burnt cordite. Frankenberger's port engine burst into flames, and Frankenberger ordered the other two men to bail out. Now alone in the flaming airplane, Frankenberger went to work. He steadied the Dornier for level flight, left the controls and scrambled forward to lock the single free-firing MG.15 into a fixed position with the barrel aiming along the axis of flight. Then Frankenberger regained his seat and waited. As he had hoped, one of the Hurricanes flew alongside the smoking plane to look inside. Frankenberger lolled his head against the perspex window, feigning death. He let the Dornier ease itself into a shallow dive. To the Hurricane pilot, inexplicably named Pussy Palmer, it seemed that the German and his plane were finished. He was wrong. Frankenberger suddenly jerked upright, chopped back on the throttle, and watched as the Hurricane slid forward directly in front of him. Frankenberger pressed down on the firing button and sent thirty-four 7.9-millimeter slugs ripping through Pussy Palmer's fighter. Palmer ducked and dived. Frankenberger's aim had been true; bullets shattered the Hurricane's windscreen, knocked out its cooling system and ruined the hydraulics. Palmer managed to land wheels up in a nearby field.

Palmer's two wingmates then expended the balance of their ammo into the Dornier, and Frankenberger wondered why he was not killed. The starboard engine now blazed up, but Frankenberger would not quit. He fought the crippled plane down to a landing he was able to walk away from, and when he was a safe distance from the wreck, he looked up to see the two Hurricanes circling overhead. Frankenberger waved at them.

"We all admired and respected this German's guts," said

Flying Officer Paul Richey, one of the Hurricane pilots. Frankenberger was captured and was given a World War I-era binge in the Hurricane squadroom's mess on the following night. He was amazed to find himself seated in front of a crackling fire holding one of the squadron's silver mugs, which was constantly being replenished. The RAF pilots politely admired his wallet-sized photographs of his wife and baby, openly admired his fine-quality flying suit and soft leather boots, and, later at dinner when it all got too much for him and he broke down and wept, his enemies maintained a discreet silence. The binge broke up at one the next morning, when Frankenberger had to be escorted back to the gloomy citadel at Verdun. He kissed the Hurricane pilots on both cheeks before leaving, but by then British reserve had been dissolved in alcohol, and there were no embarrassed giggles. Wearing one of the pilots' sweaters, and another's blue greatcoat forced on him by his hosts, Frankenberger walked outside escorted by a gendarme. It was snowing hard.

The Luftwaffe training organization knew something was afoot when, in the waning days of winter, air fleet commanders —with Jeschonnek's blessings—began requisitioning large numbers of the most experienced instructors. Wanted above all else were pilots of multiengined aircraft with proficiency in instrument procedures; that is, pilots capable of steering a course from one point to another under conditions of zero visibility. Such men could not be found in great quantity, and the hard-pressed flight schools were loath to see them go. With these irreplaceable instructors went large numbers of Ju.52s as well. Was the long-delayed assault against the west actually to begin, and in the coldest winter Europe could remember since 1895? The "Phony War," the *"Drôle de Guerre,* the *Sitzkrieg,* was obviously going to turn serious, but no one below the level of OKL knew where. Few dreamed that Hitler had determined to move not to the west, but to the north, toward Scandinavia.

From neutral Sweden, Germany purchased eleven million tons of high-grade iron ore yearly. The fields were located at Gällivare, more than a hundred miles above the Arctic Circle.

During the worst of the winter months, the Gulf of Bothnia is frozen solid, and the Swedish ore was sent by rail to the nearby Norwegian port of Narvik and from there loaded aboard ships destined for Germany. The route to Hamburg, more than twelve hundred miles away, lay among the sheltered Norwegian coastal waters, fed by the warm waters of the Gulf Stream and therefore open all the year round. As early as September 19, 1939, Britain's First Lord of the Admiralty, Winston Churchill, had wanted to sow heavy mine fields across Norwegian territorial waters. Churchill spelled it out in a memorandum on that date, followed ten days later by another in which he mentioned the care needed in handling Sweden. "Germany acts upon Sweden by threats," he noted. "Our sea power gives us also powerful weapons which, if need be, we must use to ration Sweden," he suggested. Thus, in one sweep, Churchill broached the idea of violating neutral waters and using the Royal Navy as some kind of Damoclean sword to hang over Swedish heads; the word *ration* was only a euphemism for blockade.

When, on November 30, Soviet Russia launched an unprovoked attack on its tiny neighbor, Finland, the world's imagination was stirred at the heroic—and effective—defense David put up against Goliath. In London, Kermit Roosevelt announced the formation of an International Brigade, patterned after those used in Spain, but lacking political commissars. In New York, playwright Robert Sherwood sat down to write *There Shall Be No Night*. In Washington, D.C., President Roosevelt spoke of the "rape of Finland." In Paris, Premier Édouard Daladier ordered the Soviet Trade Mission closed. In Rome, thousands rioted outside the Soviet Embassy, the Pope offered up prayers, and Benito Mussolini wrote a letter to Hitler cautioning him against further friendly relations with the Russians. Then Mussolini withdrew the Italian ambassador from Moscow and gave his blessings to thousands of Italians who wanted to form a volunteer corps to fight for the Finns. In Stockholm, Swedish air force pilots packed their bags and headed for Helsinki to form a volunteer fighter squadron. Norwegians made their way to Finland to offer to do what they could.

Here was an opportunity Churchill found too good to miss. He got permission from the cabinet to send British troops to Finland, a project that had the blessings of the French. Envisioned were two British divisions and some fifty thousand French volunteers. (Incredibly, the Allied War Council even made plans to bomb the Russian oil fields in the Middle East— despite the fact that no bombing at all was being conducted against the real enemy, Germany.) Churchill's projected use of this force followed the two birds with one stone concept: en route to the winter-dark and cruelly cold Karelian Isthmus where the Finns were locked in struggle with overwhelming numbers of the Red Army, the expeditionary force would conveniently seize and occupy the Norwegian port of Narvik, lay hold of the railroad that led into Sweden and seize the Swedish town of Gällivare and its ore mines. All this, of course, for the Scandinavians' own good. As to the morality of the operations on land and the mining of Norwegian territorial waters, the rationalization is to be found imbedded in Churchill's note of December 16: "No technical infringement of International Law, so long as it is unaccompanied by inhumanity of any kind, can deprive us of the good wishes of neutral countries," wrote the First Lord, who added that ". . . we have a right, and indeed are bound in duty, to abrogate for a space some of the conventions of the very laws we seek to consolidate and reaffirm. Small nations," he continued, "must not tie our hands when we are fighting for their rights and freedom. . . ." The penultimate sentence drove in the final, pious justification: "Humanity, rather than legality, must be our guide."

One wonders which small nations Churchill was referring to; both Czechoslovakia and Poland, whose rights and freedom Britain had sworn to guarantee, were writhing under the brutal heel of the SS and the Gestapo, and the British and French armies along the Western Front were idling their time away with no thought of an offensive to liberate the conquered millions, and in so doing retrieve the honor lost at Munich and later during the month of September when the deadliest countermeasures consisted only of war by leaflets.

The First Lord considered the possibility of neutral Norway's objecting to the mining of her waters. Might she not then refuse to export valuable aluminun and other war materials which the Air Ministry so badly needed? In that case, said the First Lord, Great Britain could stop sending the Norwegians bauxite and other goods, which "could bring the whole of Norway, centering upon Oslo and Bergen, to a complete standstill. In short, Norway, by retaliating against us, would be involved in economic and industrial ruin." There, that would fix those small nations.

Regiments were combed for officers and men with experience on skis, and eventually a few hundred were found and sent to the French Alps for refresher courses and formed into the 5th Scots Guards Battalion. Before the expedition against Norway and Sweden could be launched and the Finns rescued, the Helsinki government was forced to meet Russian terms. The war ended on March 13, 1940, after 103 days of the bitterest air and ground warfare. It was just as well that the lunatic invasion scheme was never executed; the mind boggles at the prospect of France and Britain becoming involved in a war with Russia in 1940; logistics alone would have doomed the impetuous Allies to swift defeat, not to mention the capital to be gained by the Wehrmacht on the Western Front.

In Germany, meanwhile, Admiral Raeder was drawing the Führer's attention to Scandinavia. In October, Raeder suggested to Hitler that the securing of naval bases along Norway's thousand-mile coastline would be a great advantage in countering Britain's superiority at sea. Hitler mulled this over, believing that a neutral Norway was to Germany's best interest. Then, when the Russo-Finnish war began and word got out concerning the Allies' plans to rush to Finland's aid across those precious ports, rail lines, and ore fields, Hitler reacted by ordering a study to be made of the problems involved. Germany certainly had no grudge against the Norwegians, who had freely sheltered, fed and educated thousands of German children during the hard years following Germany's defeat in 1918.* Even the *City of Flint* affair did not ruffle Hitler's feelings for long.

---

*Among them, West Germany's Nobel Prize-winning President, Willy Brandt, who keeps a summer home in Norway to this day.

This American-owned freighter, carrying cargo for England, had been captured on the high seas by the German navy and was being sailed for Kiel with a prize crew. The ship stopped in Haugesund on November 3, where the Norwegians dutifully seized her and interned officers and crew. After violent protests from Berlin, the Norwegians released the ship, and later the crew.

Then, on February 16, 1940, Hitler was spurred to action by an event occurring deep inside a Norwegian fjord. There lay the German supply ship *Altmark,* in whose holds were packed some three hundred British merchant sailors made captive after losing their ships in the South Atlantic. On the day in question, the destroyer HMS *Cossack* steamed into Jössingfjord over the protests of a Norwegian patrol boat and lay alongside the *Altmark,* whereupon the British boarded the German ship after the fashion of Barbary pirates and released the prisoners. Fourteen days later, on March 1, Hitler issued a directive for *Fall Weserübung,* Exercise Weser, calling for the simultaneous occupation of both Norway and Denmark. He called for the operation to assume the character of a peaceful occupation, using the minimum of forces. "Weakness in numbers," he stressed, "will be made good by skilful action and surprise in execution."

No better description could have been given of what was to follow.

At 6:15 A.M. on April 9, nine Ju.52 transports appeared over Masnedö, one of the many islands that go to make up the small nation of Denmark, and disgorged ninety-six German parachute troops, two platoons belonging to General Kurt Student's crack 7th Airborne Division. They thumped to earth and rushed for the mile-and-a-half-long bridge connecting the island with Sjaelland, upon which sits the capital city of Copenhagen. The bridge was seized without a shot's being fired. At about the same time, a battalion of infantry stepped off the regular Warnemünde-Gedser ferry, arriving like so many armed tourists, and started marching for Copenhagen, less than ninety miles away. They met no resistance. Forty-five minutes

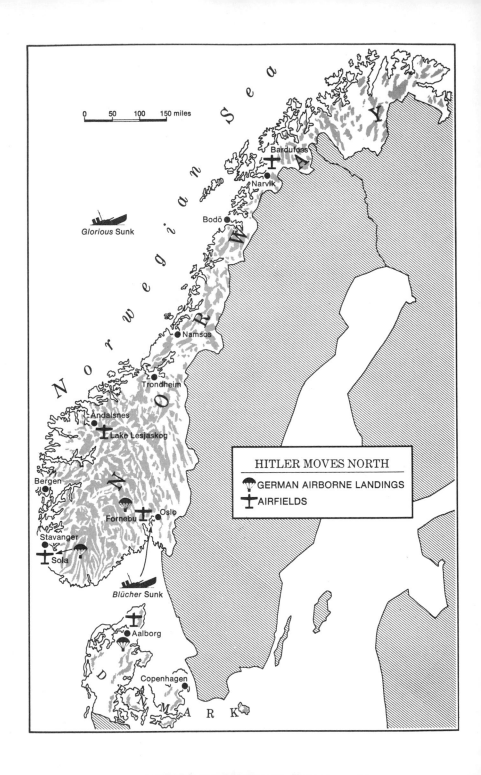

0   50   100   150 miles

Glorious Sunk

Blücher Sunk

HITLER MOVES NORTH

GERMAN AIRBORNE LANDINGS
AIRFIELDS

Bardufoss
Narvik
Bodö
Namsos
Trondheim
Åndalsnes
Lake Lesjaskog
Bergen
Fornebu
Oslo
Stavanger
Sola
Aalborg
Copenhagen

N o r w e g i a n   S e a

N o r w a y

D e n m a r k

after the first paratroopers were dropped, another platoon drifted down over Aalborg, near the western tip of the country, and seized the large airfields there. The drop was unopposed. In Copenhagen itself, a small German transport tied up along a quay in the heart of the city since dawn suddenly came to life. A battalion of German infantry, about 850 men, stepped off the gangways of the *Hansestadt Danzig,* formed up on the dock, and marched off in columns of threes for the nearby Amalienborg Palace. Seeing them enter the great square before the King's residence, the King's Guard, smartly uniformed in dark blue and bearskin shakos, unslung their rifles and opened fire. The German infantry quickly deployed and opened up with Mausers and Lugers. Six of the Guardsmen were killed and another dozen fell wounded on the smooth cobblestones before resistance was crushed. German bicyclists and motorized infantry moved across the frontier connecting Schleswig with Jutland, and were met with sporadic fire by the surprised Danes before ruthless machine-gunning cut short the action.

Formations of He.111s and Do.17s roared low over Copenhagen, convincing King Christian X, then seventy, that a call for further resistance would only mean turning beautiful Copenhagen into another Warsaw. The king hesitated briefly, then decided it was all over. At 8:34 A.M., Berlin received the word that Denmark was received under the protective wing of the Third Reich. More than sixteen thousand square miles of territory had been gained at a cost to the Wehrmacht of twenty killed and wounded.

The function of the Luftwaffe in the seizure of Norway, nearly eight times the size of Denmark, was primarily that of a transport service. For Exercise Weser, 1,008 aircraft were available, of which almost half were troop carriers. Besides the old, reliable Ju.52s, the Luftwaffe had at its disposal a number of four-engine Ju.90Bs, Lufthansa derivatives of the scrapped Ural bomber design. Lufthansa was also relieved of its small fleet of Focke-Wulf 200 Condors, clean and elegant-looking four-engine passenger liners with a range of over 2,500 miles. The F.W.200s had the unfortunate tendency of breaking their backs when landing with an overload, but they offered the longest legs in the Luftwaffe's inventory. The emphasis upon an air shuttle service instead of bombers and ground-attack planes was laid because the expedition's commander, General Niko-laus von Falkenhorst (who, to Goering's outrage, was put in charge of Luftwaffe operations), intended to execute the Führer directive ordering a bloodless, almost friendly invasion. Falkenhorst had on call sufficient numbers of bombers with which to overfly Norway for purposes of intimidation, as well as two Me.110 wings to deal with any unexpected opposition from the air, but he hoped that they would not be needed. Norway, then, would not face the murderous onslaught the Poles did seven months previously. Because of this, and because of the rigid demands of secrecy imposed by the plan for simultaneous landings at six different locations hundreds of miles apart, the Luftwaffe was forced to forgo a preventive air strike against a purely military target, an omission that would cost the German navy dear.

Of the six separate task groups dispatched from German ports —at staggered times to take into account the varying distances they had to cover to assure simultaneous arrival—Group 5 was considered by Falkenhorst to be the most important. Leading the parade was the flagship *Blücher*, a new twelve-thousand-ton heavy cruiser, accompanied by the pocket battleship *Lüt-zow* (formerly the *Deutschland*) and the cruiser *Emden*. Ac-companying this armada were a number of torpedo boats and lesser powered craft. Aboard the *Blücher* was the expedition's naval commander, Admiral Oskar Kunmetz, the field com-mander of the invading forces, General Erwin von Engle-brecht, a thousand infantrymen of the 163rd Division, a military band already tuned up for a triumphant march up Oslo's Karl Johansgate, the administrative staff destined to oversee the oc-cupation, elements of the Gestapo, the payroll for the invasion forces, plus, of course, the new cruiser's full complement of eight hundred officers and men.

At eleven thirty on the night of April 8, Group 5 entered the mouth of Oslofjord opposite the town of Fredrikstad. It was here that the first Norwegian resistance to the unannounced invasion began. Captain Leif Olsen, commanding the 214-ton whaler *Pol III*, used as a guard dog, challenged the nearest German ship, a torpedo boat, and received in answer a sudden burst of machine gun fire. Mortally wounded, Olsen ordered *Pol III* full ahead and the sturdy whaler rammed the enemy craft. The two boats went to the bottom of the fjord locked together in a tangle of wood. With fifty miles still to go, the Germans maintained speed in order to reach Oslo at the scheduled time of 4:15 A.M. A few miles farther on, the task force came under fire from the small islands of Rauöy and Bolaerne, but no hits were made. General Englebrecht ordered the group to pause while landing parties were disembarked to deal with the forts. The convoy proceeded up the fjord amidst wispy patches of accumulating fog through which the pale disc of the moon could barely be seen. The fjord narrows sharply to between five hundred and a thousand yards in places beginning twenty-five miles south of Oslo, and the formation tightened for the final dash for the capital.

Shortly after four, the *Blücher* neared the quaint little shoreside town of Dröbak, eighteen miles down the fjord from Oslo. From the bridge Englebrecht and Admiral Kunmetz could see outlines of the small dark mountains running into the sea, larger and more rounded on the left, smaller and more angular on the right. Located just left of center of the fjord was the outcropping of South Kaholmen, a rocky island not fifteen hundred feet in length. The island looked dark, brooding and deserted. Between Kaholmen's eastern edge and the mainland stretched only six hundred yards of open water, a stretch the *Blücher* and the others would have to pass before entering the broader stretches of the fjord curving into Oslo itself. It was now four twenty-one, and the flagship was already six minutes late. Members of the German Legation staff would be gathered at the quay behind Oslo's City Hall, stamping their feet against the cold and wondering what had delayed the *Blücher*'s impressive entry.

On South Kaholmen, Colonel Birger Eriksen, commanding Fort Oscarsborg, watched the approach of the huge cruiser and its handmaidens. Oscarsborg had been guarding the narrows since 1643, and in the summer of 1893 had received truly impressive armament: three monstrous guns, manufactured by Krupp in Essen, weighing forty-five tons each. These coastal defense rifles threw shells eleven inches in diameter weighing 760 pounds. The guns were capriciously named *Moses, Aaron* and *Joshua*. Eriksen's gunnery officer was Lieutenant August Bonsak, an artilleryman with ten years' experience. Of the total garrison on Oscarsborg of forty-five men, half were new recruits, but the veteran Bonsak had quickly drilled them into shape. The guns, which had not been fired in anger for forty-seven years, were lovingly maintained with the same fanatic care Norwegians give their homes, boats and cars, and were in flawless condition. When the *Blücher* was eighteen hundred yards south of Oscarsborg, Moses opened fire. The tremendous flash lit up the hills and the water with an eerie blue glow, and the peal of thunder reverberated back and forth across the narrow confines of the fjord. The massive projectile slammed into the *Blücher*'s lower superstructure where the small reconnaissance plane was hangared and exploded. Bonsak's new gunners then let Aaron speak, and the second shell tore into the *Blücher*'s portside amidships, just above the waterline. In flames and starting to list, the stricken cruiser drifted up the fjord with its light and heavy flak guns filling the air with red, blue, yellow and green tracers. Guns on the opposite side of the fjord opened up on the *Lützow,* scoring hits, but with shells of too small a caliber to damage the pocket battleship seriously. The *Blücher* plowed on, but the the others backed down the fjord, not wanting to risk the deadly shooting from those Krupp guns.

Now past the limit of traverse of Moses and his brothers, the *Blücher* was being tracked by the torpedo battery located on North Kaholmen, only a few yards distant from its sister rock. The gunner was a sixty-one-year-old retired commodore named Anders Andressen who had shown up at Oscarsborg the day before upon learning that the British had, after all, laid their minefields off north and central Norway. Through a stroke of luck, the torpedo tubes were loaded and ready: the weekly inspection had been held the day before and, contrary to regulations, the torpedoes had not been returned to storage. Andressen squeezed the electrical trigger and a large fish leapt from the tube and streaked for the burning cruiser, wallowing only three hundred yards away. The *Blücher* was holed forward below the waterline and tons of seawater began pouring in. At six twenty-two, the once-proud flagship rolled over on her back and plunged bow first to the bottom of the fjord, three hundred feet down. Something like a thousand men perished, leaving the survivors to swim for their lives through the freezing-cold oil-scummed water. Not wanting to risk dueling with Fort Oscarsborg, *Lützow* and *Emden* unloaded their troops on the eastern bank some distance away, leaving them to make their way on foot to Oslo. There would now be no band to serenade them ashore. This done, *Lützow* wirelessed news of the stunning event to Hamburg, calling for the Luftwaffe to obliterate North and South Kaholmen.

The first waves of Ju.88s appeared in the skies over Oscarsborg shortly before 8 A.M. after the long flight from northern Germany and began plastering the area. But Norwegian officers and men, plus the handful of German sailors and soldiers who had swum to the island and been made prisoner, were all sheltered fifty feet underground inside the caserne, protected by thick walls of reinforced concrete. The earth heaved and shook around them, with only brief pauses, until six that evening, but there were no casualties. Even the three big Krupp guns somehow escaped direct hits during the storm of high explosive, though under such bombardment manning any of the guns was out of the question. Oscarsborg fell early the following morning.

An hour after the *Blücher* went down (and before the first air strikes against Oscarsborg began) the first wave of German bombers appeared over southern Norway to execute low-level demonstration missions. These were thirty-six He.111s of K.G.26, whose pilots had been briefed to expect little, if any opposition. As the group roared over Sarpsborg, Greaker and Fredrikstad, word was telephoned through to the airfield at Fornebu, just west of Oslo. Captain Erling Munthe-Dahl, commanding the fighter force charged with the protection of the capital, scrambled together his entire command: five British-built four-gun

Gloster Gladiator biplanes. Two others, for lack of fresh spark plugs, had been dragged to cover under the trees. Lieutenant Rolf Thorbjorn Tradin led his section south down the fjord to 5,500 feet, underneath the rapidly dispersing clouds. Tradin spotted the Heinkels flying two thousand feet below and in his excitement estimated the number of enemy bombers at seventy-plus. Tradin radioed for the attack to begin.

In the melee that followed, Tradin shot down a Heinkel in flames, Sergeant Per Waaler bagged another, while Lieutenant Dag Krohn claimed two. Krohn, who was flying farther south down the fjord than the others, found himself surrounded not only by He.111s, but by Do.17s and the Ju.52s and Me.110s—the second wave making up the air-landing force and its escorts bound on seizure of Fornebu. "I believe there were about a hundred and fifty German planes," recalls Krohn. "I got two of them, an He.111 that crashed southwest of Fornebu, and a Do.17. Then I was attacked by Me.110s and had to climb into the clouds to save my life. My radio came alive with a call from Captain Munthe-Dahl, who advised that Fornebu was under attack and that we were to land anywhere but there. I came out of the cloud and headed north, where I landed on the frozen surface of the northeastern bay of the Tyrifjord. I found Lieutenant Tradin's Gladiator already there."

Sergeant Per Schye found himself alone in a sky filled with enemy bombers. He dived again and again, spraying bursts of .303 slugs at bombers that crossed his sights. He flew through cloud and emerged to find his guns trained on a solitary Do.17 flying leisurely in front of him. Schye shoved the throttle forward and opened fire, keeping the button depressed until the Dornier filled his windscreen. Schye's bullets knocked out both engines, and the Do.17 wobbled down to a crash-landing north of Oslo. Then the Norwegian Gladiator bucked and shuddered from the impact of cannon and machine-gun fire. Schye shot a glance into his rearview mirror and saw an Me.110 riding his tail, its nose ablaze. The pilot, Lieutenant Hellmut Lent, bloodied with four kills in Poland and against British bombers over Helgoland, was a dead shot; cannon shells exploded against the Gladiator's lower port wing, sending fragments inside Schye's cockpit. His left arm was riddled, and he spiraled down to attempt a landing. Faint with loss of blood, Schye did not notice the high-tension wire stretching across the rocky field he had chosen. The wheels caught up in the wire and the fighter pitched forward to the ground. Schye managed to climb out of the wreckage and into the arms of a farmer, who drove the dazed and bleeding pilot to a nearby hospital.

The Luftwaffe plan was for Fornebu to be seized by paratroops, followed by airborne infantry landed on the airfield once the opposition was beaten down. But the leading squadrons of Ju.52s, twenty-nine planes in all, had encountered dense fog that blanketed the southern approaches to Oslo, and pilots found themselves on instruments to keep oriented. With visibility at times cut to twenty yards in a tightly packed formation, the inevitable happened: two of the ungainly transports collided in the murk, plunging all aboard to unknown graves. A recall order was sent out from Hamburg, and the Ju.52s, loaded with parachutists, wheeled in the sky and turned for home. The leader of the second group, however, thought he saw clear holes in the fog and decided to press on. The first J.52s to drop down for a landing at Fornebu found the Norwegians waiting.

Lieutenant Gunnar Halle told the author how he watched the few airworthy Gladiators take off to duel with the German bombers, then saw two of them return to rearm and refuel, only to be burnt to ashes by strafing and bombing Heinkels and Messerschmitts. Halle, who only the week before had been called up for a refresher course on Tiger Moth trainers, found himself under air attack and with no fighter available for him to fly. He dashed across the field watching "little tufts of earth spurting up" all around him to man one of the machine-gun emplacements sited on the edge of the airfield. One of Halle's first bursts riddled a Ju.52 just flaring out for a touchdown. Slugs tore through the metal hull, killing and wounding a number of the troopers packed inside, and the pilot shot the throttles forward and managed to blast the Junkers loose from gravity and back into a climb attitude. Me.110s criss-crossed the field, firing at the Norwegian gunners, who stuck to their posts until, one by one, the guns overheated and seized. No longer capable of resisting, Halle and the others made their way out of Fornebu and into the countryside to begin a long trek on foot, by skis and by fishing boat to eventually reach England.

Fornebu was secured by a few platoons of infantry landed by the Ju.52s that had waited until the machine-gunning stopped, and a few hours later the first group of transports returned with the paratroops, who, instead of jumping, merely stepped off the planes as though they were arriving tourists. There followed an orderly march through Oslo witnessed by greatly surprised, but stonily silent, Norwegians, who were just beginning five years of dreary occupation.

Before noon on the day of invasion, every Norwegian port of any importance was in German hands; Oslo, Kristiansand, and Egersund in the south, Bergen and Trondheim farther up the west coast, and Narvik in the far north. The important airfield at Sola, eight miles from Stavanger, was taken by 120 of Kurt Student's paratroops, who jumped from ten Ju.52s after the Me.110s had destroyed the only two Norwegian fighters in strafing attacks on the field. Troop carriers began landing at Sola shortly afterward, and by early afternoon, 180 Ju.52s unloaded more than two thousand fully armed infantrymen without incident. Within twenty-four hours, the Luftwaffe secured all seven of Norway's operational airfields, and hundreds of bombers, fighters and Stukas poured in to await British countermoves.

In London it was decided that the only possible riposte lay in landing whatever forces could be assembled at three widely separated points with two entirely different objectives. Narvik, almost at the top of the world, with its precious port and rail lines leading to Sweden's ore fields, was the primary objective. The secondary prize was Trondheim, more than three hundred miles to the south. Trondheim, Norway's ancient capital, was where King Haakon VII hoped to reestablish the Norwegian government and so to carry on the fight against the Wehrmacht. Accordingly, a small invasion force was hastily assembled and sent plowing across the North Sea, aimed at Norway's rocky shore, over which towered soaring mountains blanketed with snow.

The staff work was appalling, reminiscent of the Crimea, when whole cases of boots for left feet only were despatched to Lord Cardigan's troops. The 148th Brigade, with just over two thousand men, was at first embarked in Scotland, bound for Trondheim, but an hour later was disembarked and told they were going to Namsos, farther north, instead. A week later, the brigade was hurriedly reembarked aboard two cruisers and a transport, but it was decided not to risk the transport ship in the face of overwhelming German air superiority, and half the troops were removed from the *Orion* in total darkness and transferred to two more cruisers. Lost in the shuffle was one battalion's entire quota of three-inch mortars. Field telephones were loaded aboard one ship, while all the necessary cables were sent off in another. One battalion managed to locate its mortars in the welter of equipment stowed aboard, but could not find the ammunition, the crates, in all probability, having been left behind on the blacked-out docks in Scotland. The troops were burdened with three enormous duffel bags that comprised the British quartermaster's pride, the famed "Arctic Kit," which included a smothering lambswool-lined coat weighing fully fifteen pounds, but which did not include either skis or snowshoes. No protective white camouflage suits were provided, nor was there any motor transport or antiaircraft guns. The French, who eagerly contributed a demibrigade of Alpine warriors, the noted *Chasseurs Alpins,* sent more than four thousand men ashore with skis, but without the necessary bindings that would allow them to be used. The ships were not combat loaded, so that when the hurried offloading began, equipment was dumped ashore in no sane order, company ledgers before rations, toilet paper before ammunition. Hours were wasted sorting out the jumble, hours in which the officers and men cringed against the fear of air attack that lay over the ports like a sickness.

Troops were put ashore at Namsos, 127 miles by road north of Trondheim, and at Aandalsnes, more than 160 miles to the south of the old capital, reached only through a narrow, winding road snaking east through the Roms Valley and then north again. Trondheim, then, would be taken with a pincers movement using men ignorant of warfare in the snow, incapable of moving through the country, and confined to the roads. Behind them they left their ports naked to the air. With both brigades ashore by April 18, nine days after the German invasion, the campaign for Trondheim properly began, only to end less than two weeks later in dismal, predictable failure.

The first Dorniers, Heinkels and Stukas appeared over Namsos just after the French troops disembarked on the heels of the British. The shuttle bombing, for that is what it amounted to, began on the morning of the twentieth and continued until dusk. When one formation of fifteen or twenty bombers had unloaded, it was followed soon afterward by another. The railway station was destroyed and the tracks uprooted. The abandoned school containing much of the expedition's reserve stores went up in flames, as did the hospital where an estimated two years' supply of drugs and medicines was housed. The French lost much of their equipment left on the quays. Most of the neat wooden houses were burned, and twenty-two Norwegian civilians were killed. A British naval officer described Namsos that night as a "mass of flames from end to end." Aandalsnes was similarly crushed by unopposed bombing, but with heavier loss of materiel: within a ninety-minute period of attack, He.111s, concentrating on the quayside, destroyed three hundred thousand rounds of rifle ammunition, three thousand rounds of scarce 40-millimeter Bofors ammunition for the promised antiaircraft guns, eight hundred rounds of the long-lost mortar ammunition, since turned up, and so many provisions that the British troops were put on half rations. Like Namsos, Aandalsnes was wrapped in flames and deprived of electricity and running water. After their first experiences on the road under fire from strafing Me.110s and dive-bombing Ju.87s, brigade officers forbade movement by day along the exposed roads, except when absolutely necessary. The British commander, Major General Carton de Wiart, V.C., who had arrived in Namsos on April 15 under a rain of German bombs, signaled the War Office in London, saying, "I see little chance of carrying out decisive, or indeed, any operations unless enemy air activity is considerably restricted." Two days later, with his forward elements seeking cover in the deep snow from the low-flying Luft-waffe, Carton de Wiart was more specific: unless he could be given air superiority, there "would be no alternative to evacuation."

On April 24, the aircraft carrier *Glorious*—the only one available to the British navy in northern waters—launched eighteen Gloster Gladiators of No. 263 Squadron into a snowstorm over the open sea 180 miles off the central Norwegian coast. The destination was the frozen lake at Lesjaskog, twenty miles down the valley from Aandalsnes and eighty miles southeast of Trondheim. Lake Lesjaskog, eight miles long and eight hundred yards wide, offered the only possible fighter strip for the short-ranged biplanes, whose mission was to protect the rear bases (already in rubble) and to offer fighter cover for the infantry. A less sanguine commander than Squadron Leader J. W. "Baldy" Donaldson would have wept at what he found waiting for him in the isolation of Lesjaskog. Some two hundred Norwegian civilians had managed to scrape two feet of snow from the lake's surface to create a makeshift runway eight hundred yards long, but Donaldson discovered that the vital stores were dumped along the lake edge in unmarked and unlabeled crates, that the starter trolleys had been sent out with dead batteries, that there was no refueling truck, that there were no spare oxygen bottles, that only one armorer was available to service the squadron's seventy-two guns, that there was a dire shortage of belted machine-gun ammunition and that, worst of all, the squadron's regular ground crews had been left behind, replaced by others who neither knew any of the pilots nor were familiar with the aircraft they were supposed to service.

The pilots were up at three the next morning, just after first light, to discover controls and carburetors frozen and the wheels of the fighters welded fast to the ice. It was not until two hours later, with German reconnaissance planes already come and gone, that the first patrol of two fighters could be launched. These managed to find and shoot down a slow-flying He.115 floatplane making its way up the valley. Two hours later, while the pilots and mechanics were still struggling to get more fighters airborne, the Luftwaffe arrived in force. "From then on," remembered one of the British pilots, "the attacks were incessant. The enemy, fresh out of nice cosy hangars, I suppose, with all expert assistance at hand, came in constant relays of three, splitting for individual attack at from five hundred to six thousand feet. One of these approaches in V formation dropped twelve bombs, destroying four Gladiators and wounding three pilots. . . . Baldy himself was rather concussed by a nearby blast, but stuck it out until he was steady on his pins again." With their bombs expended, the He.111s swept back and forth across the surface of the lake, all machine guns working. The ground personnel assigned to No. 263 Squadron dropped their tools and fled for their lives into the woods, leaving the pilots and a few others out in the open still trying to fire up the remaining Gladiators.

Donaldson and a few others managed to get airborne during the day, claiming five He.111s, but by noon ten of the squadron's fighters lay in cinders, and by nightfall only five Gladiators were left. These were flown off to a disused Norwegian army parade ground near Aandalsnes. As a fighter base, the frozen lake at Lesjaskog had lasted exactly twenty-nine hours. On the following morning, two Gladiators were sent up on patrol. Poor maintenance coupled with the brutal cold did for them both; one pilot had to bail out when his engine seized over the mountains, and the other made it back to the field with failing oil pressure and a big end seizure that could not be fixed. The three remaining fighters were sent up at 10 A.M. to intercept a group of He.111s on another of their frequent raids on Aandalsnes, but because there was no oxygen left, the British pilots could only buzz uselessly beneath, watching the Heinkels unload at leisure from an altitude of 25,000 feet. By early afternoon, only one Gladiator was considered flyable, but since by then there was no fuel left, it made little difference. After forty-eight hours of operational life in Norway, No. 263 Squadron was stricken from the order of battle. The surviving pilots and service troops loaded aboard the small freighter *Delius* and started back for Scapa Flow. The ship dodged bombs and machine-gun fire from eight that morning until two that afternoon before steaming out of range. To one of the pilots it seemed that "the Luftwaffe meant to pay us out thoroughly for what we did to them in the air."

The *Delius* returned to England on May 1, one day before the British evacuations from Namsos and Aandalsnes began. Norwegian ski troopers, who are as at home in deep powder snow as anywhere else, had helped guard the flanks during the retreat of the Allied brigades back to the sea, while other Norwegians—manning isolated machine guns and even four pieces of field artillery—put up rear-guard actions against the cautiously advancing Germans. The British troops were severely limited in what they could take aboard the waiting destroyers, and most of the Arctic Kit was left behind, as well as the entire stock of pack saddles for reindeer that had been provided. Although both bases were abandoned without interference from the Luftwaffe, the ships were set upon in earnest while at sea, and bombing lasted for two hundred miles out. The French destroyer *Bison* was sunk, many of her survivors taken aboard the HMS *Afridi*. Not long afterward, the Ju. 88s put two 550-pound bombs through the destroyer's hull, and she, too, rolled over and died in the gray waters of the North Sea.

The ejection of the Allied brigades from central Norway resolved a crisis of nerves inside Führer headquarters that had been mounting steadily since the campaign began. To Hitler, the entire operation loomed as a disaster. First there was the shocking news of the loss of the *Blücher*. There was the abortive paratroop mission against Oslo, and it seemed to Hitler that the airfield had been taken only by hazard. Norwegian resistance infuriated Hitler, who drafted an order for the arrest and execution of hostages. Ignorant of the true state of affairs, he envisioned the loss of Trondheim by the British pincers movement. Paratroopers dropped at Dombaas, south of Aandalsnes, to seize a rail junction were cut up by Norwegian infantry upon landing, and the survivors, some sixty in all, were driven to cover inside a farmhouse and there taken captive by ski troopers, with their mission failed. Worst of all was the depressing news that had flowed in from Narvik. The port had been seized early on the morning of April 9 (at about the time Copenhagen was invested) by General Eduard Dietl and two thousand experienced troops of the crack 3rd Mountain Division. But in two separate encounters inside the convoluted network of fjords around Narvik, all ten of the German destroyers that had put Dietl's men ashore were sunk, his ammunition stores exploded aboard a freighter, and the commanding admiral was killed. Under the fifteen-inch guns of HMS *Warspite,* and threatened by apparent landings, Dietl's men abandoned Narvik and tentatively started through the snow for Sweden, only twenty miles away.

General Alfred Jodl, observing Hitler's reaction to all this, made such comments in his diary as "excitement terrible . . . chaos in command . . . renewed crisis . . . Führer increasingly worried. . . ." Hitler wanted to cancel the entire operation, and on April 17 demanded that Dietl, a personal friend for many years, and all his men be evacuated by air, a logistical impossibility due to the fact that there were no fields near Narvik. But when the British did not come, Dietl led part of his men back into the town, dispersing others in small combat packets occupying the bleak heights guarding the periphery of the harbor. Dietl armed the sailors who had escaped death aboard the destroyers with rifles and machine guns captured from a Norwegian depot, clothed them in Norwegian army uniforms, disposed them around Narvik, and sat down to await the siege. With every German ship sunk or run aground, with the nearest friendly troops still fighting their way up the valleys hundreds of miles to the south, Dietl knew that all that stood between him and disaster was the Luftwaffe.

The first move to supply Dietl by air was a calculated gamble and a tribute to the air crews who undertook the risk. On April 14, the day following the destruction of the German fleet at Narvik, a dozen Ju.52s loaded to the gunwhales with men, shells, and all that goes to make up a mountain battery appeared over Lake Hartvig, ten miles north of the port. Was the frozen surface of the lake strong enough to hold a fully laden Ju.52? There was only one way to find out: the first transport made its slow approach and set down; the heavy plane skidded across the glassy surface, but the wheels did not break through.

One by one, the others put down and unloaded. By that same afternoon, the field pieces had been manhandled into place, adding to Dietl's defenses; but more importantly, the men of the 3rd Mountain Division were assured of a lifeline.

While Dietl's men fought off probing attacks by the British, French and Polish troops landed in the vicinity to back up Norwegian forces already there, the Luftwaffe geared up for an all-out effort. On May 1, General Hans-Jürgen Stumpff was appointed commander of the Fifth Air Fleet with headquarters in Oslo, and charged with the supply and reinforcement of Narvik. Stumpff tried every expedient: handfuls of men were flown into the bay aboard floatplanes and told to make their way inside the defensive perimeter; small detachments of paratroops and mountain infantrymen—who had never jumped before in their lives—were hustled out of transports and dropped on top of Bear Mountain, fifteen miles east of town. Stumpff was handicapped by sudden withdrawals of large numbers of Ju.52s for the impending Wehrmacht assault in the west, and by sudden lashings of blizzards as winter fought in giving way to spring, but unhampered as they were by any kind of fighter opposition, the remaining overworked Ju.52 crews managed to reinforce Dietl with eleven hundred men, several tons of food and all the ammunition required. Stumpff equipped KG.30's reconnaissance squadron with new Ju.88Ds that could range 750 miles and return. He demanded, and got, new Ju.87R Stukas with less bomb carrying capacity but with extra fuel tanks that made them almost as long-legged as the Ju.88s. Under Stumpff's direction, the large airfield at Vaernes, outside Trondheim, was packed with more than two hundred bombers, ready to deal further blows at the British fleet engaged in the Allied buildup before Narvik, four hundred miles to the north. Then during the last week of May, Stumpff's crews returned from missions to report that the Royal Air Force had somehow managed to get fighters back into Norwegian skies: on the twenty-third a Do.17 was shot down, an He.111 failed to return from a mission the following day, and on the twenty-fifth, three of the slow-moving Ju.90 four-engine bombers fell to the guns of British biplanes.

It was on May 21 that Baldy Donaldson led No. 263 Squadron

toward the improvised airfield at Bardufoss, twenty minutes to the north of Narvik. The flight from the decks of HMS *Furious* to the sod airstrip began with disaster: the Fairey Swordfish torpedo bomber chosen to escort the fighters to Bardufoss led one section through ragged cloud and straight into the side of a mountain shrouded in mist. The Swordfish and two Gladiators piled up, but the remaining fighter escaped destruction by inches when the pilot executed a violent loop. Three of the fighters were sent to Bodö a hundred miles south of Narvik, to offer protection to Allied troops who were moving there after being driven across the mountains by the Germans advancing toward the north. The Gladiators were engaged in combat at once, and within less than twenty-four hours all three were written off and two of the pilots were in the hospital. That same evening waves of bombers descended upon Bodö out of a clear sky and systematically reduced the little town to burning wreckage; low-flying Me.110s strafed those fleeing for safety in the hills nearby.

The remaining Gladiators at Bardufoss were joined a week later by seventeen Hurricanes of No.46 Squadron, which arrived in the middle of a German air raid. Despite the lack of ground-to-air communications, let alone radar, the scrappy little biplanes and their more elegant, heavier-gunned brothers managed to dull the Luftwaffe's cutting edge, knocking down thirty-seven bombers and transports; but they could not prevail against the overwhelming odds. The Royal Navy continued to serve as targets in the shooting gallery that the approaches to Narvik had become. The battleship *Resolution* took a bomb that ripped through three decks before exploding and had to limp home, robbing the fleet of its only fifteen-inch guns. The antiaircraft cruiser *Cairo*, Lord Cork's flagship, fought back at the Luftwaffe for fourteen days running, expending 5,700 rounds of four-inch ammunition and burning out half her guns before a lone Ju.88 struck home with a bomb that killed and wounded thirty of her crew. The cruiser *Curlew* was sunk outright, as was the Polish destroyer *Grom* and the large troopship *Chobry*, which went down in flames. Stumpff ordered a group of Stukas of St.G.1 moved forward to an improvised base two hundred miles south of Narvik; thus every first-line aircraft in the Luftwaffe's inventory except the Me.109 was committed to the battle. The Ju.87s made a shambles of the jetties and quays at Harstad, staging area and depot of the Allied Expeditionary Force, and damaged the cruiser *Aurora* so badly she had to turn home for repairs. It was in Norwegian waters that the Admiralty in London realized sickly that ruling the waves now meant ruling the sky as well, a belated discovery that would be driven home to the U.S. Pacific Fleet nearly two years later.

Narvik was taken on May 28 by French Foreign Legionnaires and Norwegian infantry moving down on the town from the north, and by the Polish brigade fighting their way over the hills from the south. Dietl's outnumbered men were forced back into the mountains beyond, where they faced capture by the Norwegians or flight into Sweden. The rejoicing in Narvik was short-lived, for no sooner was the port cleared than orders came for its evacuation. Indeed, orders to abandon the entire Norwegian enterprise reached General Claude Auchinleck three days before the attack began, but it was instructed to be carried out anyway so that demolition of the ore-handling facilities and the railway could be accomplished. This was largely a useless undertaking, since as the sappers went to work laying charges and blowing them, the ice was breaking up in the Gulf of Bothnia, and Germany would continue to receive ore direct from Sweden in the usual way.

Mercifully, a cloak of mist and fog shrouded the beginnings of the evacuation, but June 2 broke clear and cold, and the Luftwaffe arrived in force over the Narvik area. They found the place hotly defended by Hurricanes and Gladiators, and by the end of the day, the hard-working RAF pilots could claim another nine enemy bombers destroyed. Evacuation of the 24,500 men of the expeditionary force, scattered along the coast from just below Narvik to Tromsö, a hundred miles to the north, began on June 4 and lasted four days. Poor flying weather coupled with the German ignorance that Norway *was* being abandoned enabled the puzzled troopers to be gotten aboard ship and away without loss. Lying offshore was the carrier *Glorious*, waiting to receive the residue of No. 46 and No. 263 Squadrons.

Although none of the pilots had ever executed a tricky carrier landing before, and although none of the planes was equipped with arresting gear, the pilots gallantly agreed to try it. Skill and luck put all eight Gladiators and all ten Hurricanes down safely. Last to leave the airfield at Bardufoss were the RAF ground crews, who blew the place apart, leaving only a single narrow strip as a courtesy to the remaining half dozen or so Norwegian Fokker biplanes and Tiger Moth trainers.

Thus left in the lurch, and the last to learn about his allies' plans to leave, the Norwegian commander in chief, tough General Otto Ruge, had no choice except to surrender his worn-out, discouraged, and skimpily supplied forces to the Germans, who by now had poured a hundred thousand troops into the country. The King, Crown Prince Olav, and the nation's gold reserves left Tromsö aboard a British destroyer to sail for England, but General Ruge voluntarily stayed behind.

Removed at last from the frigid positions they had occupied for the past six weeks, the common troopers, now safe and warm aboard ship and headed for home, finally had the opportunity to learn why they were so precipitately removed from action at the moment of victory. Only vague rumors had reached them from in the hills above Narvik, but now they were told of the German Blitzkrieg against France and the Low Countries. At about the time the first man was putting foot aboard ship at Harstad, the last man was putting foot aboard ship at Dunkirk. While the futile battle for Norway was going on, the war had been lost on the continent. Surely England would be next.

One last act in the northern drama remained to be played out.

At three forty-five on the afternoon of June 8, *Glorious* was approximately three hundred miles out from the coast of Norway. The big carrier, one of only four in the British navy, was escorted by only two destroyers. No air scout was aloft. The unmistakable outlines of the carrier were spotted by lookouts on the pocket battleship *Scharnhorst*, which opened fire with her eleven-inch guns at a range of just under fourteen miles.

The first shell struck the hangar deck at four thirty-five, destroying the parked Hurricanes and igniting stores of high-octane aviation fuel. Another shell gutted the bridge, and a third exploded aft. The blazing carrier heeled over and sank at five forty, carrying with her more than fourteen hundred men to the bottom of the sea.*

The Norwegian fiasco cost the British a precious carrier, three cruisers, and seven destroyers sunk, with another dozen ships of the line badly damaged. It further claimed nearly two thousand casualties on land, and at least seventy aircraft were destroyed, some of them in futile attacks across the North Sea to reach well-defended German airfields. It cost Prime Minister Neville Chamberlain his job, taken on May 10 by Winston Churchill, whose obsession with iron ore had given impetus to the ill-conceived venture in the first place.

In assessing his enemy's conduct of the campaign, Adolf Hitler commented, "From the military point of view it can only be described as frivolous dilettantism."

Which is a verdict beyond dispute.

---

*Both destroyers, *Acasta* and *Ardent,* were blown apart in the course of the brief action, but not before *Acasta* scored a torpedo hit on *Scharnhorst* that sent her home for repairs. Only one able seaman aboard *Acasta* survived to tell the tale.

This war is sheer madness, we have gone to war with a 1918 army
against a German Army of 1939. It is sheer madness.
—General Maxime Weygand

Crew after crew was being offered up as a sacrifice. It was as if you
dashed glassfuls of water into a forest fire in the hopes of putting it out.
—Captain Antoine de Saint-Exupéry,
Group 2/23, Armée de l'Air

In the dark hours before dawn on May 10, 1940, Luftwaffe pilots
at bases all across Germany were roused from sleep and given
fifteen minutes to appear in briefing rooms. There, unshaven
and unfed, crews learned that the attack on France and the
Lowlands would begin at first light. The long winter of waiting
was over. The endless blackboard drills, navigation exercises
and intensive study of thousands of target photographs were at
an end; the crews felt confident of finding their preselected
airfields, rail heads and marshaling yards even blindfolded.
With one truly notable exception, this pervasive confidence
proved justified.

Numerically—and numerically only—the Wehrmacht was
matched on the ground by the combined Allied force of 136
divisions; 94 of these were French, and a good many were
uselessly buried underground inside the famous Maginot Line.
The French and the British actually outnumbered the Wehrmacht in tanks, some of which were heavier gunned than those
commanded by Generals Heinz Guderian and Erwin Rommel.
But it was in the air that the Allied struggle for France was lost
even before it began. Against 1,444 bombers of Air Fleets 2 and
4, the French and the RAF could send aloft only 830 fighters,
and these would have to cope with Kesselring's and Loerzer's

1,264 Messerschmitts, of which more than a thousand were Me.109s. Overall, the two German air fleets deployed in the west mustered just under 4,000 first-line planes (including some 400 Ju.52 troop carriers), while the Armée de l'Air and the RAF had in France less than half that number, i.e., 1,654 planes. Only 400 of these were bombers capable of interfering with the movement of German troops and armor. Since the French possessed so few fighter aircraft to defend their works, it might be assumed the deficiency would be made up in antiaircraft weapons. But here the story is equally dismal: where the Luftwaffe could field more than 9,000 20-millimeter rapid-fire and motorized 88-millimeter heavy flak guns, the French Army possessed roughly 1,500 pieces, of which only 17 were new 90-millimeter guns, and the reserve was largely composed of 75-millimeter weapons left over from World War I.

An almost endless series of strikes during the years just prior to the war further crippled aircraft production already suffering from chaotic changes in design requirements. Although eight months and a week had dragged by since the Blitz on Poland, May 10 found the nationalized French aircraft industry pottering around with the manufacture of sixty planes a month. None of the four fighters in French service (one of which was an American import, the Curtiss 75A Hawk) belonged in the same sky with the new Me.109E and its fuel-injection engine. The Bloch 152, the Moranc Saulnier 406 and the Curtiss were from fifty to seventy-five miles per hour slower than the 109E. The Dewoitine 520 was only twenty-five miles per hour slower, but less heavily armed, and there were few of them to go around. The Bloch 152, although a tough, sturdy design, suffered from incurable ills: it was sluggish at altitude, guns froze up because of faulty heating systems and the range was a meager 350 miles. So disorganized was the production of the fighter, of which unlimited numbers were ordered by a panicky government, that, of the first 120 delivered, only 25 came with propellers, and the rest were sent out lacking gunsights.

The Armée de l'Air had on inventory exactly 54 dive-bombers to use against the invading Wehrmacht and its 2,400 tanks. The plane in question was a Latécoère high-wing monoplane with a 640-horsepower Hispano-Suiza engine. The grotesque-looking machine flew at 80 miles per hour, was armed with but two guns and carried a pair of 500-pound bombs. Yet the French somehow believed the plane required a crew of five men. A British Hurricane pilot who examined one of these Latécoères was moved to comment, "The men who dared dive those ghastly contraptions with that load aboard were worthy of the name."

Thus equipped, the French combat pilots—torchbearers of the traditions set by Guynemer, Fonck, Nungesser, Madon and others—prepared to deal with Hitler's best.

The Luftwaffe air offensive in France followed the pattern established in Poland, but on a much larger scale. On the first day of operations, German bombers struck fifty airfields used by the Armée de l'Air, nine used by the RAF, and eleven others in Holland and Belgium. Inexplicably, three He.111s bound for the large airfield at Dijon, far south of Paris, instead unloaded their bombs on Freiburg, a German town 20 miles inside the Rhine, killing nearly sixty civilians. Freiburg lies 132 miles east and north of Dijon, and the gross navigational error was never accounted for, but the opportunity to accuse the British of inaugurating terror raids was not missed by Hitler, and the truth of the matter was kept secret for many years.

The attacks subsided at dusk, only to resume with greater fury at dawn. What happened at the Bomber Command base at Conde-Vraux near Rheims on the morning of May 11 is typical of the more successful of these Luftwaffe strikes. At about the time the commander of No. 114 Squadron received orders to launch his bomber squadron against the Panzers pouring through Luxembourg, nine Do.17s of K.G.2 were taking off from their base across the Rhine at Aschaffenburg, nearly two hundred miles away. The twin-engine Blenheims were lined up on the field and topped with fuel and loaded with bombs. While the crews waited to climb aboard and start the mission, the Do.17s were contour-chasing their way over hills and through valleys, unopposed by all but the lightest of ground fire. The Dorniers were over the field with their bomb-bay doors open

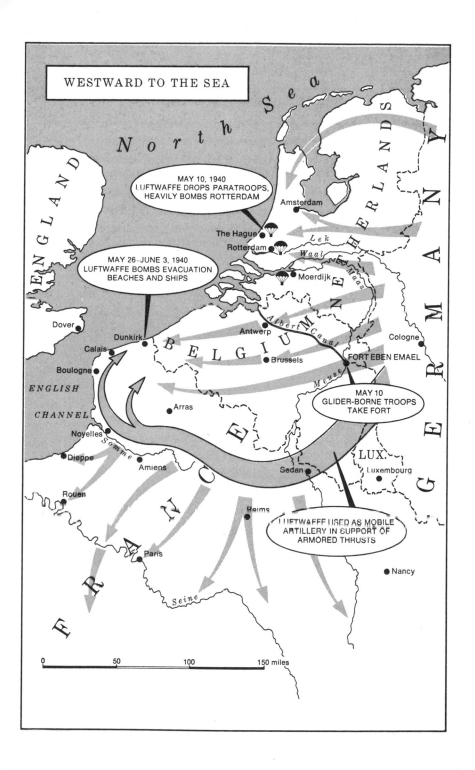

WESTWARD TO THE SEA

North Sea

ENGLAND

MAY 10, 1940
LUFTWAFFE DROPS PARATROOPS,
HEAVILY BOMBS ROTTERDAM

Amsterdam

The Hague
Rotterdam

Lek

Waal

NETHERLANDS

MAY 26–JUNE 3, 1940
LUFTWAFFE BOMBS EVACUATION
BEACHES AND SHIPS

Moerdijk

Maas

Dover

Dunkirk

Antwerp

Albert Canal

Cologne

Calais

BELGIUM

Brussels

FORT EBEN EMAEL

Boulogne

Meuse

ENGLISH

Arras

MAY 10
GLIDER-BORNE TROOPS
TAKE FORT

CHANNEL

Noyelles

Somme

FRANCE

GERMANY

Dieppe

Amiens

Sedan

LUX.

Rouen

Reims

Luxembourg

LUFTWAFFE USED AS MOBILE
ARTILLERY IN SUPPORT OF
ARMORED THRUSTS

Paris

Nancy

Seine

0   50   100   150 miles

before the British could react; one moment the sky was clear, and in the next it was raining 110-pound high-explosive bombs. The Dornier pilots simply walked their sticks across the unguarded runway once, and once again, then turned back into the sun to fly home for breakfast. They left behind them eight Blenheims on fire and the remaining dozen so badly damaged they were scrapped—the whole squadron wiped out in less than two minutes. On the following morning, nine Blenheims of No. 139 Squadron got off a bomb-damaged field elsewhere, but ran into a swarm of Me.110s and Me.109s en route to the target, and seven of the nine were quickly shot down.

The Luftwaffe operations in France provided shock, but no surprises; it was in Belgium and in Holland that innovations and controversy surfaced. Sited below Liège was mighty Fort Eben Emael, guarding the important city and the Albert Canal. This concrete bastion, only five years old, was nearly half a mile long and almost as wide. Festooned with three- and five-inch gun turrets, plus numerous machine-gun cupolas, Eben Emael was garrisoned with twelve hundred Belgian soldiers and was considered virtually impervious to ordinary ground attack. It may well have been, but the Wehrmacht planned nothing ordinary for this key defense position. At a few minutes past five on the morning of May 10, nine gliders swooped silently down on top of the fort and eighty-five highly trained sappers leaped out. They had been towed by Ju.52s from Cologne and released over Aachen, fifteen miles from the target. At the controls were some of the Luftwaffe's champion glider pilots, men who had earned their wings and awards in the Rhoen skies during the thirties. Using newly developed shaped charges, the sappers blasted the gun emplacements one by one, finishing off others with the simple expedient of shoving short-fused explosives down the barrels and ducking for cover when they blew. Belgian heads were kept down with accurately placed bursts of Schmeisser machine-pistol fire. The glider troops clung to the fort under fire from Belgian guns outside the area until relief appeared on the following morning. Eben Emael fell at the cost of just six German dead.

Other gliders put troops down at three vital bridges spanning the Meuse, and two were seized before the Dutch guards had time to ignite the demolition charges. In a trick to be emulated more than four years later by the American 82nd Airborne Division over Normandy, the Luftwaffe scattered dummy paratroopers across a wide area, drawing away enemy troops who felt foolish at discovering they were charging fields littered with uniformed bundles of straw with their pockets stuffed with exploding firecrackers.

Holland fell in five days, but its pilots and soldiers provided the world with an altogether new meaning of Dutch courage.

The 1st Air Regiment of the Dutch air force could deploy 132 aircraft on the morning the German invasion spilled across the frontier. Of these, 52 were modern fighters, 9 were modern bombers, and the rest were biplanes or old ground-attack machines and artillery observation craft of no use as interceptors. The single-seater Fokker D.XXI, a light, handy monoplane with four guns, had already proved itself in Finland, and the newer Fokker G.1 twin-engine fighter that mounted eight guns firing forward and one aft was as good as anything in its class, but there were only 23 of them. The Dutch air force had followed the events in Norway with understandable keenness and had prepared its defense; the airfields were reinforced with added flak batteries and machine-gun posts, the runways were carefully littered with iron stakes and other obstacles, leaving only narrow strips for their own fighters' use. Leave was canceled, and the 1st Air Regiment was alerted to expect an attack from the east anytime after May 2.

But the first attack came from the west: He.111s bound for softening-up strikes against Holland's airfields had swung out over the sea to make their runs from an unexpected direction. The ruse was not entirely successful; Dutch fighters jumped the Heinkels at the coast and shot down the group commander. German paratroops aboard Ju.52s bound for the capture of Ypenburg airfield just outside The Hague were killed and wounded before they had a chance to jump. Between determined attacks by Fokker D.XXIs and fierce antiaircraft fire, thirty-seven out of fifty-five Luftwaffe transport planes of Special Group 9 were shot out of the sky. Crippled Ju.52s, some of them on fire, tried to make emergency landings on Ypenburg field, but were torn to pieces when they slammed into the hidden obstacles. The stubborn courage of Dutch pilots is perhaps best typified by the actions of a young sergeant-pilot named J. Roos. Early on the morning of the second day of combat, Roos took off alone from the field at Buiksloot, north of Amsterdam; Sergeant Roos was flying one of eleven D.XXIs left over from the aerial carnage of the day before. Roos was jumped by a trio of Me.109s and he decided to fight. Before he could whip his fighter around, cannon shells thudded into his plane and the engine began to smoke. Reflected in his mirror was one of the Me.109s directly on his tail, guns firing. Roos jettisoned his canopy and watched it fly backward and smash into the 109's propeller. The Messerschmitt lurched in the air and fell away. Roos hauled his plane inside a cloud, wondering what to do next. He came out of the cloud and found one of the German fighters in front of his guns. Roos pressed Button A and the 109 went down in flames. The third enemy fighter appeared again and this time flamed Roos's Fokker. But with the canopy gone, Roos experienced little difficulty in bailing out.

Despite the sharp resistance encountered everywhere, the key airfields and bridges were taken by Kurt Student's four thousand paratroops, and their job was to hold on against the determined Dutch counterattacks until the 9th Panzer and 22nd Infantry Divisions could complete the investment of Fortress Holland. In yet another demonstration of military unorthodoxy that characterized Luftwaffe operations in Holland, the vital Willems Bridge spanning the Maas River running through the center of Rotterdam was seized by airborne troops flown directly to the spot and landed in the river aboard a dozen old Heinkel 59 floatplanes. The troops dug in on both sides of the river, almost in the heart of the city, and began fighting for their lives.

On May 13, the troops holding both ends of the Willems Bridge were down to sixty men, half the number that had been put there by the He.59s two days earlier. The bridge was under intense machine-gun and artillery fire, but so far had sustained only superficial damage. By now, tanks of the 9th Panzer Division had fought their way through to the outskirts of Rotterdam and were waiting to enter the city and crush the hard core of Dutch resistance there. General Rudolf Schmidt, commanding the forces besieging Rotterdam, sent a message to the Dutch commander, Colonel P. Scharroo, urging capitulation. Otherwise, warned Schmidt, he would be forced to use measures that "could result in the complete destruction of the city." Meanwhile, Kesselring's Second Air Fleet had been ordered to prepare for a precision attack against selected areas of the city, positions marked on a map under the guidance of General Student, who, as usual, was right up at the front.

Aware that the city might well be handed over without more fighting, Kesselring wanted to make sure that an air bombardment of Rotterdam was, in fact, necessary. He recalled: "Goering and I spent hours of heated argument over the telephone as to how the attacks demanded were to be carried out, if at all. As a result, I repeatedly warned the bomber wing commander to pay particular attention to the flares and signals displayed in the battle area and to keep in constant wireless contact with the Air-Landing Group. Our anxieties were increased because after Student's morning message our wireless communications were cut off so that Air Command was no longer informed of what was happening in and around Rotterdam; there was the additional danger of dropping bombs on our own troops."

Erratic communications between the combat zone, the group commander of K.G.54 and Kesselring's own headquarters invited confusion and disaster, and that is precisely what happened. Colonel Scharroo, stalling for time, presented Schmidt with one evasive answer after another, and in exasperation Schmidt told him to surrender by 6 P.M. that day, the fourteenth, or else. Ignorant of this final ultimatum, an even one hundred He.111s took off from bases inside Germany in time to arrive at the approaches to the city by 3 P.M. It was then that they would, in theory, receive the go/no go signal either by wireless or by spotting flares fired up in their general direction from the bridgehead.

A recall order went out, but was not received by any of the Heinkel radio operators. The attacking bombers split in two groups, one approaching Rotterdam on a course paralleling the river, the other flying at right angles. Smoke and haze filled the air, forcing the squadrons down to just above two thousand feet. A veritable barrage of red flares streaked upward, unseen by any of the pilots of one wave, but spotted at the last moment by the leader of the second group. These turned away to bomb a British troop concentration near Antwerp, but fifty-seven He.111s flew steadily on to unload ninety-seven tons of high explosive on a triangular section of the city measuring roughly a mile and a half on each side. Ironically and tragically enough, it was some of the most accurate bombing of the war; not one paratrooper was killed by German bombs, but the target area was gutted and flames leaped across the city. Tanks rolled forward across the bridge and into the inferno. Infantry following behind came under rifle fire from the Dutch, determined to resist to the last. Student was struck in the head by a well-aimed round fired by a Dutch reservist, a delicatessen keeper in civilian life. The wound kept Student out of action for weeks. Rotterdam capitulated, and with it, all of Holland.

In the confusion and terror of the moment, a member of the Netherlands government released a figure of 30,000 killed, although a later body count turned up only 814 corpses. The inflated toll of the dead did nothing to lessen the belief in France that the Luftwaffe was invincible, a feeling beginning to seep through the wrongly equipped, undersupplied and chaotically led Allied airmen futilely trying to brake the German tide.

The Wehrmacht's shove into Holland and Belgium was largely a feint, a snare for the Allied High Command, who believed that the Germans intended to sweep through Liège and curve behind Paris in a knockout drive to the east, a repetition of Schlieffen Plan that had been tried in 1914. Accordingly, the best French divisions and all ten British divisions and two-thirds of the available French bombers and fighters were sent pell-mell across Picardy and into Flanders. Generals and privates alike were perplexed at the timid resistance encountered. Well they might have been; they were rushing into a carefully laid trap of the German General Staff's making. Two German army groups were gathering in the dark forests of the Ardennes, preparing their massed Panzer divisions for a swift left-hook movement that would carry them westward to the sea, not behind Paris, but behind the pocketed Allied armies still delivering punches in the air. The next two whirlwind weeks would bring the Luftwaffe to the pinnacle of triumph, and to the edge of Waterloo.

An unwitting ally of General Heinz Guderian's XIX Panzer Corps was the Intelligence section of the French Ninth Army Headquarters, whose denseness about German intentions in the face of clear evidence passes all belief. Among the few French reconnaissance groups whose planes were not destroyed on the ground before they could fly a single mission was Group II/33, equipped with twin-engine Potez 63s which were not only 100 miles per hour slower than the German fighters, but were lightly armed and so designed that the pilot's vision was restricted to straight ahead and a little above and to the sides; what was to be seen depended upon the eyes of the gunner and the observer and the automatic camera. On an average, one out of three Potez crews returned from their low-level missions, and those that did return wondered why they bothered to risk their lives. On the night of May 11, a pilot named René Gavoille flew over the Ardennes and returned to II/33's field near Laon reporting with pardonable excitement that the place was alive with motorized convoys; he could see the dim blue slivers of lights winding for miles through the woods. The French High Command dismissed the report as "nocturnal illusions." A second mission was laid on in broad daylight the next day, and the Potez limped home streaming oil and perforated with flak holes. This time the observer clearly saw not only endless trucks and tracked vehicles, but a frightening number of tanks. A call put through direct to the Ninth Army's Intelligence chief elicited only disbelief; everybody knew it was out of the question to move armor and motorized infantry through the Ardennes! Sharp prints were pulled from the negatives brought back from the mission, but even this evidence was rejected. Captain Gavoille was ordered out again early on the thirteenth, but the mission came to grief when the Potez was set upon by Me.109s and shot down in flames. The crew survived a crash landing in a French field, but they never forgave the uncompromising blockheadedness of their own higher command. Two precious days had been thrown away, and when Allied air power was called into action too late, the felony was compounded.

The experience of the RAF in operations against Luftwaffe fighters and flak in the north, i.e., in Holland and Belgium, was a harbinger of things to come in the Ardennes sector. On May 10, thirty-two single-engine Fairey Battles, unarmored and carrying only two guns, were sent against German columns; thirteen were promptly shot down, and the rest returned home damaged. Six Blenheims were sent against Waalhaven airfield; five were shot down by Me.110s. On May 11, eight Battles were sent against German infantry on the move through Luxembourg; Luftwaffe flak shot down seven. On May 12, nine Blenheims set off to bomb gray columns near Maastricht; Me.109s got all but two. French ground-attack Group I/54 lost eight out of eighteen planes shortly afterwards. Five Battles, manned by volunteers, took off to bomb a bridge near Vroenhoven, taken intact and planted with flak by the Germans two days earlier. All five planes, fifteen men, were shot to pieces. Forty-eight hours after the war began, the bomber strength of the Advanced Air Striking Force was whittled from 135 to 72 planes.

At 7 A.M. on Monday, May 13, the "Phony War" ended for the second-line French troops holding the historically revered and tactically important town of Sedan, fifty miles upriver from Verdun on the banks of the Meuse. The hot summer sky throbbed with the uneven beat of Daimler engines. Dozens of Do.17s flashed over the rooftops of Sedan and loosed long strings of bombs on the other side of the river. Troops crouched in shallow holes and artillerymen lying on the earth near to their guns felt the explosions rumbling up from the rear and felt compassion for those who were catching it in the nether echelons. Seemingly endless waves of Dorniers and He.111s roared overhead all that morning. At eleven, there was a pause, when it became clear that there was hardly a telephone line left intact from Sedan to Second Army HQ; the lines had been blasted to shreds, and the narrow roads were cratered and useless. The sky emptied of medium bombers only to be replaced by whole groups of Stukas, attacking in squadrons, stacked up in layers. Now the bombing began in earnest. Added to the howl of the propellers, the tortured roar of the engines, the unearthly whine of Udet's "trumpets of Jericho" were the cracking explosions of five-hundred-pounders ripping into bunkers, gouging the earth, up-ending French artillery pieces. No sooner had the low squadrons unloaded than those circling higher up, like vultures, flipped over and hurled almost vertically down to strike through the smoke and dust before pulling away in a long, buzzing sigh. These were Stukas of Richthofen's VIII Air Corps, a self-contained tactical strike command formed for just such missions and put together with the cement of experience gained in Poland. The bombers were watched over by Me.109s and Me.110s at altitude. French pilots, no doubt deeply aware that they were flying in the same skies so staunchly defended by their spiritual (and actual) fathers more than twenty years earlier, threw their fighters against the swarms of German planes, claiming twenty-one kills while losing many of their own—but what were three or six Curtiss Hawks or Moranes against formations of forty and fifty bombers escorted by sixty, seventy, or eighty Messerschmitts? The dive-bombing of French positions on the south bank of the Meuse continued without let-up until three that afternoon. Unlike the doomed British bomber pilots and the hapless French Potez crews, the Luftwaffe airmen did not have to endure storms of flak; there was little fire from the ground after the first few waves of Stukas had come and gone. Explained General Édouard Ruby, whose inexperienced troops had suffered the most: "Their only concern was to keep their heads well down. Five hours of this nightmare was enough to shatter their nerves, and they became incapable of reacting. . . ."

The Meuse was crossed that same afternoon at Sedan and at Dinant, forty miles to the north. The dazed French defenders at Sedan could offer little resistance, but at Dinant, spared the remorseless air bombardment featured at the other end of the line, they gave General Rommel's troops paddling across to the other bank in rubber rafts relatively severe casualties from rifle, machine-gun and artillery fire. By nightfall, however, both bridgeheads were secure, and engineers threw up pontoon bridges so reinforcements could begin pouring across.

At daybreak on the following morning began what the Luftwaffe would later acclaim as the "day of the fighter." Ten of the vulnerable Fairey Battles managed to sneak past the German flak guns to attack the narrow pontoon bridges before the Messerschmitts were up and all returned safely to base. But the bridges were undamaged. Me.109s of J.G.53 and J.G.2 were quickly ordered up over Sedan, and they arrived in time to disrupt a French bomber squadron escorted by fighters. In the melee that followed, nearly half of the bombers were shot down and the remnants scattered after pressing home attacks with what the Germans described as suicidal courage. With their own bomber force expended, the French High Command begged for help from the sorely tired survivors of the RAF's Advanced Air Strike Force, already ravaged by the operations of two days before. Gathering up what little strength remained and what few bombers still able to fly, Air Marshal Sir Arthur Barratt assembled a mixed force of 71 Battles and Blenheims, summoned his Hurricane squadrons, was provided with French pilots flying Moranes, Curtisses, and Dewoitines—250 fighters in all—and launched a last desperate effort to destroy the German bridgeheads from the air. What followed can be likened to the charge of the Light Brigade, or Pickett's efforts at Gettysburg.

The bombers rushed across the lush valleys of the Meuse at altitudes low enough to achieve some hope of success in hitting the ridiculously narrow pontoon bridges, but high enough to avoid 20-millimeter flak; not high enough, however, to escape the continual cracking of 37-millimeter and the dreaded 88-millimeter shells. Hit squarely, Battles and Blenheims simply exploded in the air. The British and French fighters tore into superior numbers of Me.109s, trying to keep them away from the bombers, but Me.110s operating at the same level as the Blenheims bored in and began killing. The valleys rang with the scream of engines, the canvas-ripping sound of machine guns and the whine of smoking airplanes plunging down to crash into the green hills. Parachutes, Allied and German, blossomed in the clear blue sky. Bombs rained down on both sides of the river and beyond the town of Sedan, temporarily halting the movement of German reinforcements, killing some and knocking out trucks. But there were not enough planes or enough bombs or enough brave men. The Me.109s broke through the Allied fighter screen and got to the Battles and Blenheims. Barratt's charge lasted little more than an hour. The wreckage of forty bombers and fifty fighters littered the countryside. Of the four Battle squadrons committed, twenty-four out of thirty-one planes failed to return. As the RAF Official History points out, "No higher rate of loss in an operation of comparable size has ever been experienced by the Royal Air Force."

Resistance along the Meuse evaporated. French divisions retreated from the relentless grinding of German tanks backed by select infantry and always preceded by dive-bombing Stukas and fighters flashing overhead at seven hundred feet per second, spraying the roads with cannon shells and machine-gun fire. The roads leading back to the interior were turned into a chaos of fleeing civilians inextricably mixed with diehard French units frustrated at being able neither to use the roads to reach better defensive ground nor to offer tactically sound resistance to the onrushing Germans. A French artillery officer (recalled Alexander Werth) managed to set up his seventy-five by the side of a road jammed with refugees, a road partially blocked with blazing automobiles set on fire by strafing Me.109s. The Wehrmacht was advancing through a field on the other side of the road, but before the seventy-five could be put into action, German guns opened up, killing and wounding refugees milling around in the crossfire. Trucks loaded with troops weaving their way north were caught up in the solid flow of terrified civilians headed south. Bombs and machine-gun bullets aimed at these futile convoys riddled military and civilian alike, and French refugees spat abuse at their own men for not stopping the *Boches* miles away and for getting them killed on their own roads; the appearance of military vehicles anywhere behind the dissolving line was the signal for merciless strafing attacks. Coming on top of the horror of Rotterdam, news that the Germans were indiscriminately gunning helpless French refugees presented the world with an image of the Luftwaffe as a terror weapon capable of any atrocity.

There was another side of the coin, however. Squadron Leader "Bull" Halahan, commanding No. 1 Hurricane Squadron, which had been in France since September, was forced down in Belgium following a combat in which he destroyed an Me.109 and an Arado observation plane. One of Halahan's pilots, Paul Richey, recalled: "He had witnessed some rough scenes in Belgium, among which he described four regiments of French Senegalese troops proceeding to the front at a trot, looking neither to the right nor to the left, with implacable expressions on their faces. A Heinkel force-landed in a field beside the road, and a selection of Senegalese doubled across to it, dragged the German crew of four out and promptly decapitated them on the spot. Then they resumed their progress, without a word or change of expression."

The Panzers in their hooking movement south and west rolled over one Allied airfield after another, often only thirty minutes behind the departing squadrons. Off. balance and thinned by attrition, neither the AASF nor its sister group operating in France, the Component Force, could hope to slow the fast-moving German columns now rolling effortlessly across the gentle terrain of northern France. Bomber Command in England was thrown into the land battle on the hot, cloudless day of May 17 when Blenheims of No. 82 Squadron were dispatched to bomb troops on the move near Gembloux. Hurricanes were assigned, in the Churchillian phrase, "to cleanse the skies of the enemy," by appearing over the target area in advance of the bombers. The unescorted Blenheims were bounced by Me.109s long before they could reach the protective umbrella of fighters, uselessly orbiting Gembloux, and eleven out of the twelve Blenheims were shot down in familiar beam attacks delivered by cannon-firing Messerschmitts.

On May 19, it was decided that the remaining aircraft and crews of the Component organization, being pushed steadily westward, could operate more effectively and more safely from southern England. The order to pull out came so suddenly that the resultant evacuation was more of a rout than a move: 120 Hurricanes—damaged but repairable—were abandoned to the Germans, along with great quantities of stores and equipment. Only 66 out of the Component's original 261 fighters reached England; the remaining 75 had been lost in only ten days' combat. Thus sixteen squadrons disappeared from the RAF's Order of Battle.

On the evening of May 20, at about the time the last Hurricanes flew off to England, Heinz Guderian's 2nd Panzer Division completed its sprint across France and reached the sea thirty miles above Dieppe. The Allied armies were now cut in two, and with the fall of Boulogne and Calais a few days later, the only port remaining in Allied hands was Dunkirk. With German armies above and below them, the British Expeditionary Force was poised between the jaws of a nutcracker; only some kind of miracle could prevent the greatest disaster at arms in the history of the Empire.

The miracle arrived in the form of a Führer directive ordering the Panzer divisions to halt in their tracks. The order was given on May 24, and when it reached Guderian he was "utterly speechless." His tanks were arrayed along the river Aa, less than twenty-five miles from Dunkirk. The genesis of this incomprehensible order lay in Goering's desire for the Luftwaffe to deliver the coup de grace to the encircled enemy. His chief of Intelligence, General Josef "Beppo" Schmid, recalled: "I happened to be present when Goering learned that the German tanks approaching from both east and west had reached the outskirts of Dunkirk. Thereupon, without even stopping to think, he decided that the British Expeditionary Force had to be conquered from the air. I heard the telephone conversation which he subsequently had with Hitler. Goering described the situation at Dunkirk in such a way as to suggest that there was no alternative but to destroy by air attack those elements of the B.E.F. trapped there. He described this mission as being a specialty of the Luftwaffe, and pointed out that the advance elements of the German Army, already battle weary, could hardly expect to succeed in preventing the British withdrawal. He even requested that the German tanks be withdrawn a few miles in order to leave the field free for the Luftwaffe."

Kesselring's Second Air Fleet was assigned the task of obliterating Dunkirk harbor and annihilating the BEF. Kesselring was against the idea and got on the phone with his objections to Goering, who "must have been sufficiently aware of the effect of almost three weeks of ceaseless operations on my airmen not to order an operation which could hardly be carried out successfully even with fresh forces." Kesselring brought to Goering's attention the fact that Fighter Command was committing their new Spitfires to action from bases in southeastern England and that Luftwaffe casualties were bound to be heavy, especially since the Ju.88s operating from bases in Holland would have to fly the gauntlet down the Channel to reach Dunkirk. Kesselring added that "it could not be done even with the support of [Richthofen's] VIII Air Corps," whose short-range Stukas would have a long way to fly from their bases in France. Jeschonnek concurred with Kesselring's appreciation of the problems involved, but shied away from putting the case to the Führer; Goering had pledged his word to Hitler that his Luftwaffe would not fail in this its greatest challenge and bid for glory.

Code-named Dynamo, the British evacuation of the Dunkirk pocket began on May 27 under a hail of high explosive and incendiary bombs falling on the town and the harbor. Huge oil storage tanks on the outskirts of the town mushroomed into flame and the black smoke roiling up three miles in the sky served as marker beacons for the Luftwaffe and the RAF alike. Fighter Command could spare only two hundred Spitfires and Hurricanes for the Dunkirk operation, and these were parceled out a few squadrons at a time in an attempt to provide air cover throughout the daylight hours. Luftwaffe fighter and bomber pilots discovered that odds of three and four to one in their favor were no deterrent. Major Werner Kreipe of K.G.2 returned from Dunkirk with his shot-up bomber group describing how the enemy fighter pilots attacked "with the fury of maniacs." A dozen Spitfires of No. 610 Squadron, based at Biggin Hill south of London, waded into forty Me.109s and shot three down in flames while losing two of their own. Twelve Do.17s were bounced by a handful of the sleek Supermarine fighters, and only half of the Dornier squadron returned to base. The II Air Corps alone suffered the loss of twenty-three aircraft and sixty-four pilots and crew; casualties on this one day alone exceeded the total of the ten previous days of combat.

Yet Dunkirk was bombed throughout the day by incoming fresh waves of He.111s, Ju.88s, and Ju.87s from bases in Germany, Holland and France, and there was hardly a half hour when gaggles of high-flying Me.109s and Me.110s were not constantly overhead. The harbor was a scene of ships milling about, some trying to reach the slender wooden mole projecting a mile into the sea where groups of hungry, unshaven troops waited to be picked up, some weaving erratic courses through the water churned up by bombs, drifting aimlessly after taking direct hits from Stukas. The French freighter *Aden* was sunk during the morning, and the troop transport *Côte d'Azur* went down that afternoon. Troops huddled on the exposed beach stretching from Dunkirk twenty miles north were machine-gunned and bombed all day long by seemingly endless waves of German planes flying in from every direction. Unaware of the bitter air battles being fought on their behalf miles away and out of sight, the pummeled troops turned their wrath on their own pilots. "Where the bloody hell're our fighters?" was a common enough phrase during the next days of waiting to be picked up. A Hurricane pilot of No. 213 Squadron crash-landed on the beach north of Dunkirk after losing a duel with German fighters, and when he tried to join the others in getting aboard a ship headed back for England, he was rudely shoved aside by a British infantry officer bitter at not having seen a single RAF fighter during the hours of hell he and his men had spent on the beach dodging bombs. Another Hurricane pilot shot down over the sea was taken aboard a destroyer only to be greeted with insults and abuse by troops who had embarked from the broken port thirty minutes earlier. By nightfall, only 7,669 troops had been gotten out of Dunkirk.

The next day brought gray skies, but enough visibility for the

Luftwaffe to make a morning appearance with formations a hundred and fifty strong. Six ships of various kinds were sunk before the weather turned foul, grounding Kesselring's bombers. More than seventeen thousand troops were evacuated. The heavy rains continued throughout the morning of the twenty-ninth, then at noon the skies cleared, and once again Dunkirk was swamped with bombers. There were now so many destroyers, freighters, tugs, fishing boats, private yachts, Cunard lifeboats borrowed for the occasion, sloops, trawlers, and minesweepers dashing back and forth that collisions posed nearly as many dangers as did falling bombs. On May 31, a day brilliant with sun, six destroyers were damaged when they rammed each other and other ships while frantically dodging bombs. Nonetheless, nearly seventy thousand men were taken from the beaches and from the town by that evening. The Luftwaffe discovered that bombing the beaches was having almost no effect; dropping 110- and 550-pound bombs in the soft sand was like stuffing firecrackers deep into sawdust. With the perimeter shrinking by the hour, the bombers were concentrated solely on shipping, and losses were so grievous that after ten ships—including three destroyers—were sunk by dive-bombing Stukas on June 1, the evacuation of the remainder of the BEF was carried out at night.

Although 243 out of the 861 ships involved in the withdrawal from Dunkirk were sunk, prodigies of labor and valor enabled 338,226 British and French troops to be taken safely across the Channel to fight another day. When Dynamo was ended on the afternoon of June 4, the Panzers at last rolled into the rubble of the town to make captive the French soldiers who were left behind. Dunkirk was a shell, and the beaches nearby were refuse heaps of abandoned war materiel.

Hitler's generals never forgot their anger over the infamous stop order that robbed the Wehrmacht of a crushing triumph, and Goering had failed in his bid for glory. But the Führer saw in Dunkirk a great victory, and ordered church bells rung for three days throughout Germany to celebrate the battle's end. Luftwaffe commanders, counting more than three hundred dead airmen, did not need to ask for whom the bells tolled.

The Panzer armies began rolling south on the morning after Dunkirk fell, their paths cleared by tactical units of two air fleets reaching deep inside France to sow destruction on airdromes in the interior crowded with recent factory outputs and warplanes not long arrived from America. Paris was declared an open city and fell on June 14. Aged Marshal Philippe Pétain, custodian of French honor with the sudden flight of the government to Bordeaux, asked the Germans for an armistice seventy-two hours later. When Hitler was given the news at his field headquarters, he stepped outside and danced a jig for Wehrmacht photographers. Leaving Paris in the hands of the 87th Infantry Division, German armor raced for the sea to seize the remaining Atlantic ports.

Reinforcements had swelled the number of British troops still operating in central France to more than nine divisions, about 136,000 men, and when Pétain ordered Frenchmen to lay down arms, General Alan Brooke broke off contact with the German vanguard and began loading them aboard large ships sent out from England to ports as far north as Cherbourg and as far south as Nantes on the River Loire. Only sixty British fighters were available to cover this final evacuation—but enough to harry the incoming Luftwaffe bombers sufficiently to spoil their aim and allow the heavily laden liners to slip away during the night. All the liners but one. On June 17, the twenty-thousand-ton *Lancastria* eased out of Saint-Nazaire with six thousand British troops aboard. Hurricanes buzzed overhead, but from the cloud cover that partially blanketed the port, Ju.88s descended in steep dives and struck the big ship with heavy bombs. She blazed up and leaked flaming oil across the sea. Three thousand men perished in this, one of the last Luftwaffe bombing attacks of the campaign.

News of the disaster reached Winston Churchill in the quiet of the cabinet room that same afternoon. He ordered the story suppressed, saying, "The newspapers have got quite enough disaster for today at least."

No better picture of the French air force in defeat has been given than the one painted by Sergeant Romain Gary, who flew his last mission of the campaign in a Bloch 210 bomber before moving on to the sprawling field at Bordeaux-Mérignac. He remembered: "From every corner of the sky innumerable aircraft of every size and shape were coming in to land in a continual stream, piling up on the ground. Bizarre machines of which I neither knew the type nor the purpose, some of them dating from the First World War and others barely emerged from blueprint, were disgorging onto the grass passengers who were even more bizarre. . . . The landing ground was thus becoming a sort of retrospective of all the prototypes which the *Armée de l'Air* had evolved in the course of the past twenty years: before dying, the French Air Force was remembering its past. . . .

"I saw a young pilot of the Fleet Air Arm, with one of the most impressive displays of medals you could ever hope to see on a warrior's chest, step down from the cockpit of his fighter plane with a little girl asleep in his arms whom he must have held on his knees during the flight. I saw another pilot disembark from his Goeland plane with what could only have been a party of agreeable inmates of a third-rate provincial brothel. I saw, in a Simoun aircraft, a white-haired sergeant and a woman in slacks with two dogs, a cat, a canary, a parrot, two rolled carpets and a picture by Hubert Robert propped against the side of the cockpit. . . . I saw, and shall never forget, the faces of my comrades, pilots of Dewoitines 520 and Moranes 406 fighter planes, just back from their last combats with their wings riddled with bullets, and their young commander tearing off his Croix de Guerre and stamping it into the ground. I saw a good thirty or so generals standing around the control tower, waiting for nothing and looking like nothing. . . . And always the weird, the incredible aerial fauna fleeing the shipwreck of the sky. . . ."

On the afternoon of June 21, the 1940 Armistice terms were handed to the French inside the same railway car parked on the same spot in Compiègne Forest that had witnessed Germany's humiliation nearly twenty-two years before. Hermann Goering, dressed in a sky-blue uniform and carrying his new field marshal's baton, was among those present. When the document humbling France had been delivered, he walked outside with Adolf Hitler and the others. As he stood for a moment in the warm summer sunshine, he was filled with the knowledge that his Luftwaffe was triumphant from the Arctic Circle to the Bay of Biscay.

But he also knew that across the Channel lay England.

EPILOGUE

The fall of France marked the end of the Luftwaffe as Germany's major cutting edge in power politics and as a decisive military weapon. This was not realized at the time. In Berlin, the Luftwaffe's Judge Advocate General, Dr. A. Kraell, listened as Ernst Udet exclaimed, "The war is over. Our [aircraft production] plans aren't worth a damn! We don't need them any more!" But more than seventeen hundred days of combat lay ahead for Germany, and Udet's euphoria evaporated during the Battle of Britain, when the Luftwaffe was summoned to wage strategic warfare with a tactical air force.

The medium bombers available for use against England—and there were only 818 combat-ready machines out of an authorized strength of 1,638—had neither the bomb-load capacity nor the range necessary to deliver crippling blows to British industry, and they were so lightly armed that fighter escort was needed every mile of the way. On hand were 240 twin-engine Me.110s to help with the job, but these awkward "Ironsides," as Goering liked to call them, needed fighter protection themselves and were virtually useless in their intended role. How wide was the gap between plans and reality concerning the strength of the vital Me.109s is revealed in the returns of the Luftwaffe quartermaster general. On August 3, 1940, the air fleets assigned to the west were authorized a strength of 1,171 single-engine fighters, but only 1,065 were actually available, and 187 of these were unserviceable. A total of 118 were assigned for the defense of the Reich, leaving only 760 fully operational

Me. 109s available for the assault on England. The British could deploy 714 Spitfires and Hurricanes, backed by a string of radar stations and positive ground control; thus the single-engine fighter strengths were about equal. More importantly, an energetic spurt of British production of fighters exceeded Udet's lagging program by three to one; during August, a month of intense air combat with heavy losses on both sides, only 160 Me. 109s rolled out of the Messerschmitt plant at Augsburg, while the RAF received 476 new interceptors for use against the dwindling number of German bombers.

The battle began in mid-July with attacks on Channel shipping, continued with efforts to knock out Fighter Command on the ground and in the air, and ended during the winter after unrelenting day and night raids on ports and industrial areas that lay within reach. The Blitz subsided during the atrocious winter weather, picked up again in the spring, then was abandoned as the time approached for the invasion of Russia. Although grievous damage had been inflicted on London and other cities, the campaign ended with the RAF and England's industrial capacity still intact. That the Luftwaffe had failed for the first time to execute a major assignment came as no surprise to the operational commanders responsible for carrying it out. Remarked Field Marshal Kesselring, whose Second Air Fleet had lost nearly a thousand planes during the battle, "Just as in 1939 we had entered the war against Poland in a state of unreadiness, so [in 1940] we were not equipped for an extensive economic war. To be sure, we made life more difficult for the English on their island, but we could not sever Great Britain's vital arteries."

Goering, the commander in chief, contributed bombast to Hitler before the battle began, withdrew to the dreamworld of his Prussian hunting lodge during the crucial months of the fight and emerged at the end to castigate the surviving German crews for causing him embarrassment in front of the Führer. Even more incredible was the action taken by Erhard Milch. Major Werner Baumbach, a Ju.88 squadron commander wounded over London, has recalled how "the German reports of victories, designed for propaganda purposes to conceal the

failure of the Luftwaffe against England, were a very sore subject with our formations employed on the operations. When
Field Marshal Milch visited certain bomber groups which were
based in Holland, K.G. 30 made no secret of its indignation. The
squadron leaders who had actually flown in these operations
bluntly told the Field Marshal that it was impossible to produce
the results required of them with the aircraft, bomb sights and
armament at their disposal, that the English fighters were just
as superior to German bombers as German fighters were to
British bombers and that night bombing could have no decisive
effect, as we had neither bomb sights for night operations nor
enough bombers.

"Milch seemed grateful for our frank statements," Baumbach
continued, "and said he would immediately seek a remedy. He
did produce a remedy: one group of the Wing which had borne
the heat and the burden of the attacks on British warships and
merchant vessels was broken up 'as punishment for mutiny and
defeatism.' The officers were transferred and reduced in
rank. . . ."

Milch's action against K.G. 30, inspired by Goering, was
symptomatic of the malaise permeating the Luftwaffe High
Command. Hitler called Goering on the carpet and berated
him for the air arm's failure to live up to Goering's boasts.
Goering then turned on Udet, and in one memorable interview
shouted, "If I weren't in trouble, I wouldn't need you!" Milch
also added dagger thrusts at the hapless Udet, who was described by an old comrade, Fritz Siebel, as "gravely ill, apathetic, plagued once again by serious hemorrhages, headaches
and an intolerable buzzing in the ears for which no doctor
seemed able to find a cure." At a meeting on August 18, 1941,
with the Russian war two months underway, Milch openly criti-
cized Udet before the members of the Reich's Industrial Council, pointing out that Udet had inaugurated no fewer than sixteen aircraft production programs since the war began late in
1939. "They were never followed," Milch declared, "and no one
even took them seriously any more. They were nothing but a
basis for invoices to the Luftwaffe."

Udet could point to the fact that a year earlier, immediately after the fall of France, the Luftwaffe had been dropped suddenly to fifth priority in the armament program by a decision coming right from the top. The British were sending over bombers in increasing numbers, and although the Wellingtons, Whitleys, and Blenheims were no better than the Luftwaffe's own medium bombers, the writing was in the wind; moreover, American aircraft production was being stepped up, and already more than three thousand American-built planes had been delivered to the British. Udet warned, "If we cannot considerably increase the fighter forces and go off the defensive by 1942, the war is lost." But by now, nobody was listening to Udet, and Goering and Milch schemed to neutralize him. The sensible move would have been to assign Udet to an operational fighter headquarters, where he would have been usefully employed; but instead Goering gave Milch unprecedented powers over German industry, undercutting Udet's primary function. Udet retained his title, but the power had slipped away.

Goering summoned Udet to his hunting lodge on the Romintern Heath and, again recalling their days of comradeship shared on the Western Front in 1918, affably suggested that Udet needed a long leave. Udet accepted only grudgingly and took a month off. He returned late in September to find that Milch had indulged in wholesale firings and sweeping administrative changes; almost all of Udet's friends had been kicked out, replaced by efficient strangers.

On the cold, gray morning of November 17, Udet awoke alone in his apartment on Pilkallen Allee in Berlin and put on a red silk dressing gown. He picked up the telephone and called his mistress, Frau Inge Bleyle. "Inge," he said, "I can't stand it any longer. I'm going to shoot myself. I wanted to say good-bye. They're after me." Frau Bleyle was still begging Udet to wait, that she would be right over, when the explosively loud crack of a pistol shot rang in her ear. She rushed over to Udet's flat, scene of so many gay parties, and found him dead. Scribbled on the wall over the bed was Udet's farewell message to Goering: *Iron Man, you deserted me.*

Udet was given a state funeral, his death explained as "a result of testing a new weapon." Not long afterward, Goering instigated court-martial proceedings against all of Udet's top subordinates, but wisely decided to quash them when the findings only too clearly revealed his own negligence and lackadaisical attitude toward command responsibilities.

Milch moved quickly and ruthlessly to jack up the Luftwaffe's aircraft inventory. He told General Jeschonnek that he could boost the output of fighters, including the new radial-engine Focke-Wulf 190, from 360 to 1,000 a month. Jeschonnek declined, saying that bombers were more important, and besides, only 170 fighter pilots were being graduated every month and so the additional fighters would be useless. In ferreting out strategic materials, Milch discovered that many airframe manufacturers had been stockpiling huge amounts of aluminum and other scarce goods, but were still invoicing for more. He learned that the navy had secretly prevailed upon the Messerschmitt works to develop and build tropical barracks of Duralumin, which was Luftwaffe property, so that the navy would have "termite proof billets available when the time came to occupy the recovered German colonies." Under Milch's energetic guidance, factory output jumped from a total of 12,401 aircraft of all types in 1941 to 24,807 by the end of 1943, and continued to rise sharply after that.

But no amount of effort could negate the planning and design doctrines laid down in the years before. Germany went to war against the Soviet Union still lacking the strategic bomber that General Wever had seen as a prerequisite to victory over the Russians. The He.177 was ordered back into production, but was still cursed with the highly flammable dual-engine arrangement, and more test crews were killed in vain attempts to prove an unworkable design; neither Milch nor Jeschonnek could find it in them to authorize a straightforward four-engine conversion that would have given the Luftwaffe strategic capability even at a late date. The one major strategic air strike laid on by the Luftwaffe against Russian industry showed just how effective such missions could be. In June 1943, Groups II and III of K.G. 55 attacked the Gorky Tank Factory near Novgorod with outstanding results. Agents reported that eight hundred new

T-34s were destroyed inside the works or in parks nearby awaiting shipment to the front. But as the Wehrmacht was pushed
farther and farther back, these targets lay beyond reach; no
Ural bombers were available to fill the gaps.

The greatest debacle inside Russia, the siege of Stalingrad,
was not suffered by the German Sixth Army alone, but was
shared by Luftwaffe crews ordered to supply the surrounded
city by air. The haste with which the Luftwaffe was thrown
together had left no time for an organized air transport command, despite the manifest need for one. Trapped inside the
battered city were a quarter of a million German and Rumanian
troops; Hitler wondered if they could be provisioned sufficiently with whatever aircraft the Luftwaffe had on hand.
Jeschonnek was not at all sure it was possible, but his Prussian
soldier's attitude and his mesmerization by the Führer would
not allow him to express his doubts. Goering heatedly disagreed
with the Wehrmacht chief of staff, General Kurt Zeitzler, that
the Luftwaffe was incapable of delivering the minimum of four
hundred tons of supplies required daily by the Sixth Army, and
told Hitler that it could indeed be done.

Again the schools were raided for instructor pilots and Ju.52s
to add to the mélange of planes scraped together for the airlift
that began in November 1942, in temperatures thirty degrees
below zero. In such appalling weather, the doomed crews could
average only ninety-four tons daily before the battle ended
nearly three months later. When it was all over, the frozen
survivors of Sixth Army were marched away to captivity along
with their commander, Field Marshal Friedrich von Paulus,
and 488 planes and 1,000 air crew were added to the Stalingrad
graveyard. The figure includes 165 He.111 bombers, never intended as cargo carriers. All 5 of the He.177s, hurriedly rushed
to the front loaded with supplies, exploded in flames on their
first wartime mission.

Goering's reaction in the midst of the airlift disaster is revealing. General Paul Deichmann recalls: "On the evening of 21
December 1942, during an official visit to the Führer Headquarters at the Wolfsschanze near Rastenburg in East Prussia, I
stopped by to see Goering in the Führer's bunker. I knocked at

the door of the room reserved for Goering. General Boden-schatz opened the door and asked what I wanted. Behind him I could see Goering sitting at his desk. He was weeping loudly and kept bending forward over the desk. . . . Goering asked me to come in, and without paying any attention to me he continued for several minutes to abandon himself to his grief. Then, interrupted repeatedly by fits of weeping, he asked me a few questions and dismissed me again, only to immerse himself once more in his sorrow."

Goering could cry like a woman over men lost forever in hopeless operations, then reverse his field and turn on those who threatened to tarnish his own reputation. When the Afrika Korps was finally driven out of Tunisia in the summer of 1943, the remnants of the Luftwaffe fighter wings were down to about 130 operational Me.109s and were transferred to Sicily to meet the overwhelming onslaught of Allied bombers and fighters softening the island for invasion. The 109s had to deal with not only the heavily armed American B-17 Flying Fortresses, but with Spitfires, Beaufighters, Lockheed P-38 Lightnings, and Curtiss P-40 Kittyhawks. The German fighter pilots simply could not cope with these massed, shining armadas. On June 25, 1943, following an abortive attempt by J.G. 77 to stop a concerted attack by B-17s, the general of the fighter arm, Adolf Galland, telephoned J.G. 77's commander, Colonel Johannes Steinhoff, who recalled a conversation that even twenty-five years afterward seemed "unreal."

"Steinhoff," Galland said, "I've just had a teleprint from the Reichsmarshall. Don't, please, get agitated when I read it out to you. Take no action for the moment. But I've got to inform you. Listen:

" 'During the defensive action against the bombing attack on the Straits of Messina the fighter element failed in its task. One pilot from each of the fighter wings taking part will be tried by courts martial for cowardice in the face of the enemy.

(signed) Goering, Reichsmarshall' "

After discussing this incredible order among themselves, Steinhoff's group commanders volunteered to submit themselves for the court-martial proceedings; none were willing to draw straws or cast dice to choose the "cowards" in the wing. But Galland prevailed on Goering to cancel the monstrous order and the trials were never held. The effect of Goering's teletype on the pilots' morale can be imagined.

The Luftwaffe's chief of staff fell victim to his own inflexibility. In July 1942, just prior to the first appearance over Europe of the U.S. Eighth Air Force's B-17 fleets, Hans Jeschonnek attended a briefing in the captured Russian town of Kalinovka. His Intelligence chief, Beppo Schmid, warned that they soon must expect to feel the weight of America's tremendous production capability, especially regarding the Flying Fortresses, whose planning and testing stages dated back to 1935. Jeschonnek interrupted Schmid with an astounding remark. "Every four-engine bomber the Western Allies build makes me happy," he said, "for we will bring these four-engine bombers down just like we brought down the two-engine ones, and the destruction of a four-engine bomber constitutes a much greater loss for the enemy." Schmid may well have asked, *Bring them down with what?* Jeschonnek stubbornly insisted on bomber priority at the expense of fighter production.

Jeschonnek's resolve, indeed his entire moral fiber, began to weaken as the RAF stepped up its nighttime area bombing of German cities, indiscriminately dumping thousands of tons of high explosive and incendiaries on urban centers and industry alike. Jeschonnek's comment was made, incredibly enough, in the middle of Bomber Command's campaign designed to obliterate the major German cities. Sir Arthur "Bomber" Harris explained the grand design: "In no instance, except in Essen, were we aiming specifically at any one factory. . . . The destruction of factories, which was nevertheless on an enormous scale, could be regarded as a bonus. The aiming points were usually right in the center of town."

On May 30, 1942, one thousand four-engine Stirling and Halifaxes—the kind Jeschonnek said made him happy to see built —struck at Cologne and left the city in flames; less than 4 per cent of the raiding force was shot down. These dark armadas ranged across the Reich to Berlin and beyond, facing makeshift Luftwaffe night-fighter defenses that were never able to turn them back. Some kind of plateau of horror was reached during Operation Gomorrah, when the great port city of Hamburg was raided nightly between July 25 and August 3, 1943, creating fire storms with hurricane winds that left some 40,000 German civilians dead in the ashes. Coventry's own 380 dead had been avenged a hundred times over.

Jeschonnek was now in a deep depression, and was pushed over the edge two weeks after Hamburg's destruction. Reprisal raids ordered by Hitler were carried out by small numbers of German bombers but were half-hearted measures at best: greater hopes lay in the V-1 powered glider bombs then under construction at Peenemünde on the Baltic coast. On the afternoon of August 17, Fortresses of the U.S. 1st Air Division bombed the Messerschmitt factory at Regensburg, followed by a 229-plane strike against the vital ball-bearing plants at Schweinfurt. That same night, Bomber Command dispatched 597 heavies to Pennemünde and they rained down hundreds of tons of bombs on the "miracle weapon" plant. Luftwaffe night fighters, drawn to Berlin by a feint staged by only twenty De Havilland Mosquitoes, were late in attacking the British raiding force and managed to down only forty of the big bombers.

Jeschonnek learned of the raid at eight the following morning. The damage reports were black indeed. Coming on top of the continuing hammer blows delivered elsewhere in the Reich on an around-the-clock schedule, this apparent disaster to his cherished V-1 works was more than Jeschonnek could bear; nor had he fully recovered from the mental crippling inflicted by the fiasco of the Stalingrad airlift. While his staff waited breakfast for him, and while his secretary, Frau Kersten, was on the telephone summoning the chief for a situation conference, Jeschonnek reached a decision. He put down the telephone receiver, scribbled two notes, then withdrew his Walther automatic pistol from its holster. Nobody heard the shot that ended his life at the age of forty-four. One of the notes specified that two of his enemies were not to attend the funeral; the other was more to the point: "I can no longer work together with the Reichsmarshall. Long live the Führer!"

Too late were the proper priorities established that would have enabled the Luftwaffe to stave off, if not altogether halt, the disaster that was visited upon Germany during the final year of the war. Through dispersion of factories, some of which were moved underground, and through herculean efforts by all concerned, Milch managed to turn out more than forty thousand aircraft during 1944, the year during which Allied air raids were reaching crescendo. That is to say, the German aircraft industry reached its potential four years too late. More than 60 per cent of the 1944 production output were fighters—but too few of them were the jets that, had they been produced in sufficient numbers early enough, might well have been able to halt the American daylight bombing raids until countermeasures could have been brought into play. Willy Messerschmitt's twin turbojet fighter, the Me.262, had been awarded a contract for prototypes as early as March 1, 1940. Flight tests of this advanced new fighter elicited wild enthusiasm among the fortunate few Luftwaffe fighter pilots who flew it. In production form, the Me.262 developed speeds of just under 540 miles per hour and boasted a service ceiling of 37,500 feet. When, finally, authorization was given early in 1944 for full-scale production, Hitler stepped in and ordered that the plane, desperately needed as an interceptor, be converted into a bomber. This despite the fact that the Arado 234 jet bomber, a plane designed as such and with a speed of 461 miles per hour and a range of one thousand miles, only awaited sufficient engines in order for whole groups to be equipped.

Hitler's nonsensical tactical interference was finally voided, but like so much else concerning the Luftwaffe's disheartening command failures that nullified technical superiority, the utilization of these aircraft in the right roles came too late to alter the outcome of the war. American bomber crews who faced the Me.262 during the final months of combat, and who were startled, sometimes fatally, at the appearance of Me.163 rocket-powered interceptors with 600 mile-per-hour speeds and an initial climb rate of 16,500 feet per minute, realized how lucky they were that the Reich was crumbling before more of the dangerous interceptors could be sent into German skies.*

The Luftwaffe's offensive death spasm occurred on New Year's Day 1945 with air strikes on American and British airfields throughout Belgium and Holland. Eight hundred carefully husbanded Me.109 and F.W.190 fighter-bombers—plus a weird assortment of night fighters—were launched at 9 A.M. and caught their opponents by surprise. At Eindhoven, two Canadian squadrons of Typhoons were caught while still taxiing on the runway and shot to pieces. Similar results were reported elsewhere, but in some cases the Luftwaffe squadrons failed to find the target, and those who did ran into unbelievable concentrations of antiaircraft fire from batteries sited especially to knock down the streams of V-1 "Doodlebugs" trundling through the sky bound for London. When Operation Ground Plate, as the combined attacks were called, ended less than two hours later, 206 Allied planes lay smashed or burning, but that many German fighters failed to return from the strike, and another hundred limped back so badly damaged they had to be written off. Worse, about 200 experienced German fighter pilots had either been killed or were on their way to prisoner of war camps.

Unreality prevailed to the end.

Karinhall was emptied of whole train loads of Goering's fabulous art treasures bought, borrowed and looted from Europe's finest museums, and then was dynamited to rubble in the face of the advancing Red Army. Goering hastened to Berlin, now a gaunt and shattered city, and paused briefly to help Hitler celebrate his fifty-sixth birthday on April 20. Deep in the underground bunker, where the lights blazed day and night, the festivities were brief. There was talk of the cosmic meaning for Germany in the death of the American President eight days earlier; Hitler's astrologers, never far away, indicated that

---

*Americans, especially New Yorkers, remained in blissful ignorance of the fact that Messerschmitt had developed a four-engine bomber, the Me.264—known as the *Amerika-Bomber*—based on designs laid down in 1941 and first flown in December 1942. The Me.264 had a range of more than nine thousand miles and could have unloaded more than two tons of bombs on Manhattan. But only one of these strategic bombers was built.

Roosevelt's death portended well for the fortunes of the Reich. Outside, bombs continued to fall on Berlin; Mustangs, Thunderbolts, P-38s, Typhoons, and Tempests ranged freely across the Reich, strafing everything that moved. Most of the Luftwaffe was grounded for lack of fuel.

Goering left the bunker on the following morning, only to be driven to an air-raid shelter at the appearance of B-17s, now a familiar sight in Berlin skies. When the all-clear sounded, he resumed the car journey to the Obersalzberg above Berchtesgaden to join his family. Two days later, on the twenty-third, the latest Luftwaffe chief of staff, General Karl Koller, flew in with an alarming message: the Leader had suffered a collapse; admitting the situation was "hopeless," he nevertheless vowed to remain in Berlin and, said Koller, "intends to accept the consequences and shoot himself." General Koller urged Goering, as Hitler's deputy, to assume full leadership because Hitler "had made himself the commander of Berlin and thus automatically has excluded himself from the conduct of affairs of state as well as from the leadership of the Wehrmacht."

At first Goering protested, saying, "[Martin] Bormann is my deadly enemy. He's just waiting for a chance to get me out of the way. If I act now, I'll be branded as a traitor. If I don't act, I'll be accused of letting Germany down in her most difficult hour." So saying, Goering refreshed himself on the law of September 29, 1941, that made provision for the Führer's deputy to take over in case the Leader himself became incapacitated. Goering fired off a radiogram to Hitler (miraculously, communications were still working) referring to the law and asking if Hitler agreed to relinquish his powers. The message, which was sent at 3 P.M., gave Hitler until seven that same evening to reply. The text ended, "May God protect you. I hope you will decide to leave Berlin after all and come down here as soon as possible. Your most loyal, Hermann Goering."

With the fatal message sent, Koller recalled how Goering seemed "energetic and ready for action, as if some heavy weight had been lifted from his shoulders. He looked forward to contacting [Eisenhower] and kept reiterating his confidence that he could work out a satisfactory agreement with the Americans and the British. . . . he seemed to be a different person somehow. During dinner he beamed, and was clearly looking forward to the new task that confronted him."

When Hitler received Goering's wire he flew into a rage and ordered the Reichsmarshall stripped of offices and rank, naming as his replacement the veteran General Ritter von Greim. Hitler fired back a telegram to the Obersalzberg informing Goering that the Führer was still in action and that "what you have done warrants the death penalty." At 7 P.M., the time Goering had anticipated assuming the leadership of the Reich, the front door was thrown open to admit armed, black-uniformed men of the SD, who promptly placed Goering and his entire staff under house arrest. Two days later, while Goering and the others wondered when they would be marched outside and shot, they were all forced into underground shelters to sweat out a cascade of American bombs that obliterated the greater part of the mountain homes owned by the Nazi hierarchy. Goering and his family were moved to the relative safety of Mauterndorf Castle, where Goering had spent so many happy childhood hours, and the sinister SD guards were replaced by combat troops of the Waffen SS. On the afternoon of April 30, when news of Hitler's suicide reached the SS commander, he rang through to Kesselring and asked if Martin Bormann's orders to liquidate Goering and his family should be carried out. This was all news to Kesselring, who ordered the SS to withdraw from the castle grounds immediately.

When General Alfred Jodl signed the instrument of surrender inside the little red schoolhouse at Rheims on May 7, Goering was still at Mauterndorf trying to make contact with the Americans and obtain an audience with Dwight Eisenhower. On the following day, Goering was taken into gentle captivity by a detachment of Americans from the 36th "Texas" Infantry Division, which had set out to find the Reichsmarshall in jeeps. Brought before the divisional commander, General Robert J. Stack, at his headquarters at Zell am See, Goering was his old, affable self and willingly accepted champagne pressed upon him, cracked jokes with officers and troopers who had come to gape, and posed agreeably in front of a large unfurled

Lone Star flag. A furious Eisenhower cut short these amenities, and Goering was hustled to more spartan accommodations to await the opening of the International Military Tribunal at Nuremberg.

Under the supervision of an American medical officer, Goering was put on a strict diet and began withdrawal from the habit of popping enormous amounts of paracodeine tablets in his mouth throughout the day. By the time the trials began, Goering had shed sixty pounds and was entirely free of the drug habit for the first time in more than twenty years. One of the judges, Sir Norman Birkett, observed carefully the chief defendant during the 218 days the tribunal was in session. He found Goering "suave, shrewd, adroit, capable, resourceful; he quickly saw the elements of the situation, and as his self-confidence grew his mastery became more apparent. His self-control, too, was remarkable, and to all the other qualities manifested in his evidence he added the resonant tones of his speaking voice, and the eloquent but restrained use of gesture."

Indeed, the qualities mentioned by Sir Norman—which were so woefully lacking during the Luftwaffe's continuing series of command crises—so nettled the American prosecutor, Justice Robert Jackson, that he blew up in court. In trying to elicit a straightforward answer from Goering concerning the military preparations for the occupation of the Rhineland in 1936, Jackson was visibly losing his temper at Goering's measured, sometimes convoluted, sometimes logical, responses.

"You mean," Jackson said, "the preparations were not military preparations?"

No, Goering answered, they were "general preparations for mobilization, such as every country makes, and not for the purpose of the occupation of the Rhineland."

Jackson shot back, "But were of a character which had to be kept entirely secret from foreign Powers?"

Goering replied calmly, "I do not think I can recall reading beforehand the publication of the mobilization preparations of the United States." At this, Jackson pulled the earphones from his head and slammed them on the desk. There was an embarrassed silence, then the president called for an adjournment to allow the prosecution to recover its equilibrium, not to mention its dignity.

Despite Goering's skillful maneuverings, the judgment at the loser's court at Nuremberg was a foregone conclusion. On October 1, 1946, Goering and many other of the chief defendants were sentenced to death by hanging. There was to be no appeal; the hanging was to commence on the night of October 15. Two hours before he was to mount the scaffold, Goering asked to receive the last rites of the Lutheran Church. But Christianity was still earthbound and not yet ready to transcend mortal judgments: the sacraments were refused. Goering crunched down on a capsule containing cyankali, somehow obtained against all the vigilance and security precautions that prevailed, and five minutes later lay dead on his bunk.

Unlike Udet and Jeschonnek, Goering left no scribbled messages of reproach behind.

There was no one left to blame.

APPENDIX:
The Men, the Machines

From modest—and sub rosa—beginnings in 1920, the German air weapon grew to maximum personnel strength during the winter of 1943–1944. Returns from the Luftwaffe quartermaster general show that on November 1, 1943, there were 2,089,000 enlisted men, officers, engineers, and uniformed officials in the German air force. The figure dropped only slightly toward the end of the war, to a total of 1,501,700. To these figures must be added another 800,000 or 900,000 civilians and auxiliaries, including foreign workers, who were on Luftwaffe payrolls. The Luftwaffe reached peak strength in flying personnel in January 1945 with 26,411 officers and 632,486 NCOs qualified as trained air crew. This last figure is misleading in that, by this stage of the war, the pilot-training standards had deteriorated alarmingly, and with few exceptions the Luftwaffe airmen encountered by Allied fighter and bomber pilots were far from the caliber encountered two years earlier, although there was never any lack of desperate courage, even at the last.

The quartermaster general's casualty table demonstrates the very high losses sustained during the training phase of a Luftwaffe airman's career:

The above figures include both commissioned officers and noncoms, and it should be borne in mind that the Luftwaffe, unlike the USAAF, employed a healthy percentage of corporals and sergeants as bomber and fighter pilots.

From September 1, 1939, through to the end of the war in May 1945, the German air armament industry turned out a total of 113,514 aircraft of all types. The ten most numerous were:

The figure concerning the ill-fated He.177, which looks impressive at first sight, loses all its appeal when certain facts are understood. As we have seen, at least fifty He.177s, and most of their crews, were lost during the initial testing phase. Further, the production was spread over a three-year period and significant numbers could not be grouped together at any one time. It was not until January 21, 1944, that thirty-five He.177s could be made operational for a strike against London. Operation *Steinbock*, designed as a reprisal for Allied air raids on large German cities, witnessed the employment (at night) of these leviathan bombers, beginning their shallow diving attacks at 23,000 feet while still over Germany to unload their bombs at speeds of 430 miles per hour, too fast for British night fighters to follow. But the bombs dumped in this manner were scattered far and wide. Three weeks later, thirteen He.177s set off for London, but eight turned back immediately with overheating or flaming engines. The same dismal serviceability problems remained to the end of the war, by which time there was neither fuel nor crews available for a strategic bombing effort.

The table below shows clearly how emphasis shifted away from offensive considerations when the Allied Bomber Commands began to make their weight felt over Germany during 1943. It also reveals that the production potential of the air armament industry was not realized until too late in the war, as far as the Luftwaffe was concerned. The table lists total output, by category, from the beginning to the end of the war.

SELECTED BIBLIOGRAPHY

PUBLISHED DOCUMENTARY MATERIAL

Documents Concerning German-Polish Relations and the Outbreak of Hostilities Between Great Britain and Germany. London, 1939

Documents on British Foreign Policy. London, 1947.

Documents on German Foreign Policy, 1918–1945. 10 vols. Washington, 1957.

Nazi Conspiracy and Aggression. 10 vols. Washington, 1946.

Official Documents Concerning Polish-German and Polish-Soviet Relations, 1933–1939. London, 1939.

Rise and Fall of the German Air Force. London: The Air Ministry, 1948.

The Spanish Government and the Axis. Washington, 1946. (From the German Foreign Office Papers.)

Trial of the Major War Criminals. 42 vols. Nuremberg, 1948.

Trials of War Criminals before the Nuremberg Military Tribunals. 15 vols. Washington, 1951–1952.

GENERAL WORKS

Acier, Marcel, ed. *From Spanish Trenches.* London, 1939.

Angress, Werner T. *Stillborn Revolution.* Princeton, N.J., 1963.

Ascart, J. M. *Chasseurs du Ciel.* Paris, 1952.

Astier de la Vigerie, Francois d'. *Le Ciel n'etait pas vide.* Paris, 1952.

Barclay, C. N. *Armistice, 1918.* London, 1968.

Bartz, Karl. *Swastika in the Air.* London, 1956.

Baumbach, Werner. *Broken Swastika.* London, 1960.

Baynes, Norman H., ed. *The Speeches of Adolf Hitler, April 1922–August 1939.* 2 vols. New York, 1942.

Bekker, Cajus. *The Luftwaffe War Diaries.* London, 1967.

Benoist-Méchin. *Histoire de l'Armée Allemande.* 10 vols. Paris, 1938, 1964.

Beumelberg, Werner. *Kampf um Spanien: Die Geschichte der Condor Legion.* Berlin, 1939.

Bewley, Charles. *Herman Goering and the Third Reich.* Toronto, 1962.

Bloch, Marc. *Strange Defeat.* Oxford, 1949.

Blood-Ryan, D. H. W. *Goering, the Iron Man of Germany.* London, 1938.

Blum, Leon. *De Munich à la Guerre.* Paris, 1965.

Blumentritt, Günther von. *Von Rundstedt: The Soldier and the Man.* London, 1952.

Bodenschatz, Karl. *Jagd in Flanderns Himmel.* Munich, 1935.

Bongartz, Heinz. *Luftmacht Deutschland.* Essen, 1939.

Borchert, Hubert W. *Panzerkampf im Westen.* Berlin, 1940.

Broch, Thedor. *The Mountains Wait.* London, 1943.

Buckley, Christopher. *Norway—The Commandos—Dieppe.* London, 1952.

Bullock, Alan. *Hitler—A Study in Tyranny.* New York, 1952.

Butler, Ewan, and Young, Gordon. *Marshal Without Glory.* London, 1951.

Caidin, Martin. *Me.109.* New York, 1968.

Carr, Edward Hallett. *German-Soviet Relations Between the Two World Wars*. Baltimore, 1951.

Carsten, F. L. *The Reichswehr and Politics, 1918–1933*. London, 1966.

Carton de Wiart, Sir A. *Happy Odyssey*. London, 1950.

Churchill, Winston S. *The Second World War*. 6 vols. New York, 1948–1953.

Ciano, Count Galeazzo. *The Ciano Diaries*. New York, 1946.

Clemenceau, Georges. *Grandeur and Misery of Victory*. New York, 1930.

Cole, Christopher, ed. *Royal Air Force: 1918*. London, 1968.

Craig, Gordon A. *The Politics of the Prussian Army*. London, 1955.

D'Abernon, Viscount. *An Ambassador of Peace*. London, n.d.

Daniels, H. G. *The Rise of the German Republic*. New York, 1928.

De Gaulle, Charles. *The Call to Honor, 1940–1942*. London, 1955.

Derry, T. K. *The Campaign in Norway*. London 1952.

Douglas, Sholto. *Years of Combat*. London, 1963.

———. *Years of Command*. London, 1966.

Edmonds, Sir James E. *The Occupation of the Rhineland*. London, 1944.

Ellis, L. F. *The War in France and Flanders*. London, 1953.

Everard, C. *Luftkampf über Spanien*. Berlin, 1937.

Eyck, Erich. *A History of the Weimar Republic*. 2 vols. Cambridge, Mass., 1962.

Fokker, Anthony, and Gould, Bruce. *Flying Dutchman*. New York, 1931.

Frischauer, Willy. *The Rise and Fall of Hermann Goering*. Boston, 1952.

Galland, Adolf. *The First and the Last*. New York, 1954.

Garnett, David. *War in the Air, September 1939–May 1941*. New York, 1941.

Getz, O. B. *Fra Krigen i Nord-Trondelag, 1940*. Oslo, 1940.

Gibbons, Floyd. *The Red Knight of Germany*. New York, 1927.

Goering, Hermann. *Aufbau einer Nation*. Berlin, 1934.

Görlitz, Walter. *The German General Staff*. New York, 1953.

———. *The Memoirs of Field Marshal Keitel*. London, 1965.

Goutard, A. *The Battle of France, 1940*. London, 1958.

Green, William. *Warplanes of the Second World War*. 10 vols. London, 1960–1968.

Gritzbach, Erich. *Hermann Goering, Werk und Mensch*. Munich, 1938.

Guderian, Heinz. *Panzer Leader*. New York, 1952.

Hambro, Carl J. *I Saw It Happen in Norway*. London, 1940.

Hébrard, J. *25 Années d'Aviation Militaire*. Paris, 1947.

Hegner, Henri. *Fokker, The Man and the Aircraft*. Letchworth, 1961.

Heinkel, Ernst. *Stormy Life*. New York, 1956.

Hermann, Hauptmann. *The Rise and Fall of the Luftwaffe*. London, 1943.

Hewins, Ralph. *Quisling*. London, 1965.

Hindenburg, Paul von. *Out of My Life*. 2 vols. New York, 1919.

Hitler, Adolf. *Mein Kampf*. Boston, 1943.

Hoeppner, Ernst von. *Deutschlands Krieg in der Luft*. Leipzig, 1921.

Holborn, Hajo. *A History of Modern Germany*. London, 1969.

Horne, Alistair. *To Lose a Battle*. London, 1969.

House, Edward M., and Seymour, Charles, eds. *What Really Happened at Paris*. New York, 1921.

Ironside, Sir Edmund. *The Ironside Diaries*. London, 1962.

Jones, H. A. *Over the Balkans and South Russia*. London, 1923.

Kemp, P. K. *Victory at Sea.* London, 1957.

Kesselring, Albert. *A Soldier's Record.* New York, 1952.

Keynes, John Maynard. *The Economic Consequences of the Peace.* New York, 1920.

Klein, Burton H. *Germany's Economic Preparation for War.* Cambridge, Mass., 1959.

Koht, Halvdan. *Fra Skanse Til Skanse.* Oslo, 1947.

Koller, General Karl. *Der Letze Monat.* Mannheim, 1949.

Lee, Asher. *The German Air Force.* London, 1946.

Liddell Hart, B. H. *The German Generals Talk.* New York, 1948.

————. *The Other Side of the Hill.* London, 1948.

Lloyd George, David. *Memoirs of the Peace Conference.* 2 vols. New Haven, 1939.

Ludendorff, Erich. *Ludendorff's Own Story.* 2 vols. New York, 1919.

Lutz, Ralph. H. *The German Revolution: 1918–1919.* Stanford, Calif., 1922

Macintyre, Captain Donald. *Narvik.* New York, 1959

Manstein, Eric von. *Lost Victories.* Chicago, 1958.

Manvell, Roger, and Fraenkel, Heinrich. *Goering.* London, 1962.

Martienssen, Anthony. *Hitler and His Admirals.* London, 1948.

Mason, Francis K. *Battle Over Britain.* London, 1969.

Melzer, Walther. *Albert Kanal unde Eben Emael.* Heidelberg. 1957.

Morgan, John H. *Assize of Arms.* 2 vols. London, 1945.

Munthe-Kaas, O. *The Campaign in Northern Norway.* Washington, 1944.

Neumann, Georg P. *Die Deutschen Luftstreitkräfte in Weltkriege.* Berlin, 1921

Nicholson, Harold. *Peacemaking: 1919.* New York, 1933.

Nowarra, Heinz, and Brown, Kimbrough. *Von Richthofen and the Flying Circus*. Letchworth, 1956.

O'Neill, Robert J. *The German Army and the Nazi Party*. London, 1966.

Osterkamp, Theo. *Durch Höhen und Tiefen Jagt ein Herz*. Stuttgart, 1952.

Paquier, Pierre. *L'Aviation Bombardement Française en 1939–1940*. Paris, 1948.

_____.*Combats de Chasse*. Paris, 1946.

Payne, L. G. S. *Air Dates*. New York, 1957.

Rabenau, Friedrich von. *Seeckt: Aus Seinem Leben*. 2 vols. Leipzig, 1940.

Rawlings, John. *Fighter Squadrons of the R.A.F.* London, 1969.

Richards, D. J., and Saunders, Hilary St. G. *The Royal Air Force, 1939–1945*. 3 vols. London, 1953.

Richey, Paul. *Fighter Pilot*. London, 1941, 1969.

Rickman, A. F. *Swedish Iron Ore*. London, 1939.

Rieckhoff, Heinz J. *Trumpf oder Bluff? 12 Jahre Deutsche Luftwaffe*. Geneva, 1945.

Robertson, Bruce, ed. *Air Aces of the 1914–1918 War*. Letchworth, 1959.

Roques, Paul. *Le Contrôle Militaire Interallié en Allemagne, Septembre 1919–Janvier 1927*. Paris, n.d.

Rosinski, Herbert. *The German Army*. London, 1966.

Roskill, S. W. *The War at Sea*. 3 vols. London, 1961.

Ruge, General Otto. *Krigens Dagbok*. Oslo, 1946.

Saint-Exupéry, Antoine de. *Flight to Arras*. New York, 1942.

Salesse, Charles. *L'Aviation Chasse Français en 1939–1940*. Paris, 1955.

Schacht, Hjalmar. *Account Settled*. London, 1949.

Schliephake, Hanfried. *The Birth of the Luftwaffe*. Shepperton, Surrey, 1971.

Schmidt-Pauli, Edgar von. *Geschichte der Freikorps, 1919–1924.* Stuttgart, 1936.

Seive, Fleury. *L'Aviation d'Assaut dans la Bataille de 1940.* Paris, 1948.

Sheean, Vincent. *Not Peace but a Sword.* New York, 1939.

Shirer, William L. *The Rise and Fall of the Third Reich.* New York, 1960.

———. *The Fall of the Third Republic.* New York, 1969.

Slessor, Sir John. *The Central Blue.* New York, 1957.

Stackelberg, K. G. von. *Legion Condor: Deutsche Freiwillige in Spanien.* Berlin, 1939.

Steer, G. L. *The Tree of Gernika.* London, 1938.

Stehlin, Paul. *Temoinage pour l'Histoire.* Paris, 1964.

Steinhoff, Johannes. *The Straits of Messina.* London, 1971.

Taylor, A. J. P. *The Origins of the Second World War.* New York, 1946.

Taylor, Telford. *The March of Conquest.* New York, 1959.

Tedder, Arthur. *Air Power in War.* London, 1948.

Thomas, Hugh. *The Spanish Civil War.* New York, 1961.

Thompson, Laurence. *1940.* London, 1966.

Thorwald, Jurgen. *Ernst Udet: ein Fliegerleben.* Berlin, 1954.

Thyssen, Fritz. *I Paid Hitler.* New York, 1941.

Townsend, Peter. *Duel of Eagles.* London, 1970.

Trevor-Roper, H. R., ed. *Hitler's War Directives, 1939–1945.* New York, 1964.

Tuohy, Ferdinand. *Occupied, 1918–1920.* London, n.d.

Udet, Ernst. *Ace of the Black Cross.* London, 1937.

Wallace, Graham. *R.A.F. Biggin Hill.* London, 1957.

Warlimont, Walter D. *Inside Hitler's Headquarters, 1939–1945.* London, 1945.

Watt, Richard M. *The Kings Depart.* New York, 1968.

Webster, Sir Charles, and Frankland, Nobel. *The Strategic Air Offensive Against Germany, 1939–1945.* London, 1961.

Westphal Siegfried. *The German Army in the West.* London, 1951.

Wheeler-Bennett, Sir John W. *The Nemesis of Power.* London, 1964.

_____.*Hindenburg: The Wooden Titan.* London, 1936, 1967.

PERIODICALS

Bingham, Sir Francis. "Work with the Allied Control Commission in Germany, 1919–1924." *Royal United Services Institute Journal,* Vol. 69, 1924.

Bowers, Peter. "Professor Junkers' Tin Donkeys." *Air Progress,* Spring 1961.

Brindley, John T. "Luftwaffe at Zurich, 1937." *Air Pictorial,* February 1971.

Casari, Robert. "The Rise and Fall of the Austro-Hungarian Air Forces." *Air Progress,* Summer 1961.

Haight, J. McVickar, Jr. "Les achats d'avions Americains par la France." *Revue d'Histoire de la Deuxieme Guerre Mondiale,* No. 58.

Hubatsch, W. "Problems of the Norwegian Campaign, 1940." *Royal United Services Institute Journal,* 1958.

Martin, Harold G. "Germany's Zeppelins in World War I." *Air Progress,* 1956–1957.

McClure, Victor A. "Gladiators in Norway." *Blackwood's Magazine,* Vol. 249, February-March 1942.

Morgan, J. H. "The Disarmament of Germany and After." *The Quarterly Review,* 1924.

_____. "Le Problème de la Sécurité." *Revue des Deux Mondes,* 1925.

_____. "The Problem of the Rhineland." *Journal of the Royal Institute of International Affairs,* May 1945.

Platz, Reinhold. "I Designed for Fokker." *R.A.F. Flying Review,* Volume 14, No. 9.

Tallman, Frank. "Fokker E.III: A Pilot Report." *Flying,* May 1964.

OTHER SOURCES

Invaluable to the historian is the series of lengthy and detailed monographs, forty in all, produced for the U.S. Air Force Historical Division, Aerospace Studies Institute, The Air University, Maxwell AFB, Alabama. Authors and consultants include men who helped create the Luftwaffe, then rose to command through its years of triumph and decline. Among them: Field Marshal Albert Kesselring, Generals Paul Deichmann, Josef Kammhuber, Hermann Plocher, and others. Numbered among the contributors are such familiar names as Field Marshal Erhard Milch, Generals Karl Bodenschatz, Hellmuth Felmy, Bruno Loerzer, Josef "Beppo" Schmid, Wilhelm Speidel, and Hans-Jürgen Stumpff.

The project began in 1952, while memories were still fresh and with access to the massive collection of Luftwaffe documents gathered at Karlsruhe, today housed at the Archives Branch of the USAF Historical Division. The Karlsruhe Collection consists of directives, situation reports, minutes of meetings, aerial photographs, war diaries, personal diaries, strength reports, and other materials. Those monographs, some of which are more than 100,000 words long, cover every significant phase of the Luftwaffe's history. Often highly critical of Luftwaffe command decisions and sometimes intensely personal, they make rewarding reading. Those especially pertinent to the scope of this present volume include the following.

Command and Leadership in the German Air Force. Study No. 174.

Development of the German Air Force, 1919–1939. Study No. 160.

Effects of Allied Air Attacks on German Bases and Installations. Study No. 185.

Historical Turning Points in the German Air Force War Effort. Study No. 189.

German Air Force Operations in Support of the Army. Study No. 163.

German Air Force Airlift Operations. Study No. 167.

The German Air Force General Staff. Study No. 173.

The German Air Force in the Spanish War. Study No. 150.

The German Air Force in Poland. Study No. 151.

The German Air Force in France and the Low Countries. Study No. 152.

The Organization of the German Air Force High Command and Higher Echelon Headquarters Within the German Air Force. Study No. 190.

Training in the German Air Force. Study No. 169.

INDEX

(Numbers in italics indicate pages on which illustrations appear.)

The author is grateful to the following individuals for unstinted assistance in providing material, written, verbal and graphic, that help make up the substance of the Luftwaffe's early struggles and initial triumphs.

Mr. Edward Thompson, Secretary of the Royal United Services Institute in London, and his willing librarians, Mr. Norman Kemp and Miss Stephanie Glover. The R.U.S.I staff, along with those experts in the Imperial War Museum, prove invaluable every time.

Colonel Irving Breslauer, of the Air University at Maxwell A.F.B. in Alabama, and Mrs. Gloria Atkinson of the Albert F. Simpson Research Center at Maxwell. The air researcher who cannot be in London is fortunate to have available the extensive archives at Maxwell's Research Studies Institute.

General Adolf Galland, wartime Chief of the German Fighter Arm, now a consultant in Bonn. Captain Erwin Grossman, a flak officer under Kesselring's command, with whom the author shared many conversations about the Luftwaffe during a skiing trip near Lillehammer, Norway. Wing Commander Robert Stanford Tuck, one of the R.A.F.'s great Spitfire pilots who dueled with the Luftwaffe until shot down in 1941 in a sweep over France. Bob Tuck now raises bull calves near Sandwich, in Kent.

Colonel Gunnar Halle, Royal Norwegian Air Force. Commander Hansen, of the Oscarborg Fortress down the Oslofjord, who explained in detail how the *Blücher* was sunk, and showed the author where the defenders took cover when the Luftwaffe plastered the tiny island with bombs. Major Nils Borchgrevink and Major Fredrik Meyer, of the Forvarets Krigshistoriske Avdeling, in Oslo. Herr Hans-Joachim Kroschinski, of the Gemeinschaft der Jagdflieger, the Luftwaffe's fighter-pilots' association, in Malente-Gremsmühlen, West Germany.

Major K. Carstens, of the German Air Attaché's Office in London. Colonel Y. J. Beek, of the Royal Netherlands Air Force. Major Richard Milburn, of the Air Attaché's Office in the U.S. Embassy in London.

Mr. Walter J. Palham, of London's Lufthansa office, dug deeply into the airline archives in Germany for rare photographs. Peter Bowers and Martin Caidin, in California and

Florida respectively, always generous with their own collection of aviation photographs.

George Bailey, of Vienna and Berlin.

A number of Basques in Fuenterrabia and Guernica, who wish to remain nameless.

And to my editor, Bill Decker, who is no stranger to the sky.

> Herbert Molloy Mason, Jr.
>
> Little Mystole
> nr. Canterbury
>
> England
> 1972

ABOUT THE AUTHOR

Herbert Molloy Mason, Jr., was born in Texas in 1927, but has lived much of his life in New York and abroad. He attended the American University of Beirut in Lebanon, L'Alliance Française in Paris, and graduated from Trinity University. During and after the Second World War, he was a U.S. Marine serving aboard battleships and aircraft carriers. A former magazine editor, Mr. Mason has been writing professionally since 1962. His most recent book, *Death from the Sea*, is a study of the Galveston hurricane of 1900.